ALSO BY JOHN GUY

A Daughter's Love: Thomas More and His Dearest Meg

Queen of Scots: The True Life of Mary Stuart

The Tudors: A Very Short Introduction

The Reign of Elizabeth I: Court and Culture in the Last Decade

The Tudor Monarchy

Tudor England

Contributor to *The Oxford History of Britain, The Oxford Illustrated History of Britain, The Short Oxford History of the British Isles: The Sixteenth Century, The Oxford Illustrated History of Tudor and Stuart Britain*

THOMAS BECKET

THOMAS BECKET

Warrior, Priest, Rebel

A Nine-Hundred-Year-Old Story Retold

JOHN GUY

Random House | New York

Published in the United States by Random House,
an imprint of The Random House Publishing Group,
a division of Random House, Inc., New York.

Random House and colophon are registered trademarks
of Random House, Inc.

This work was originally published in the United Kingdom by Viking,
a division of Penguin Books Ltd.

LIBRARY OF CONGRESS CATALOGING-IN-PUBLICATION DATA

Guy, John
Thomas Becket: warrior, priest, rebel / John Guy.
p. cm.
Includes bibliographical references and index.
ISBN 978-1-4000-6907-1
eISBN 978-0-679-60341-2
1. Thomas, ? Becket, Saint, 1118?–1170. 2. Great Britain—History—Henry II, 1154–1189—Biography. 3. Christian martyrs—England—Biography. 4. Christian saints—England—Biography. 5. Statesmen—Great Britain—Biography. I. Title.
DA209.T4G89 2011 942.03'1092—dc23 2011042794

[B]

Printed in the United States of America on acid-free paper

www.atrandom.com

9 8 7 6 5 4 3 2 1

First U.S. Edition

Book design by Virginia Norey

CONTENTS

NOTE ON UNITS OF CURRENCY

IN CITING UNITS OF CURRENCY, THE OLD STERLING DENOMinations of pounds, shillings, and pence have been retained. There are 12 pence (12d.) in a shilling (1s.), twenty shillings in a pound (£1), and so on. A mark is roughly 13s. 4d., although the precise correlation would depend entirely on the silver content of the coins tendered in payment, so conversions are not feasible. The sum of £100, the equivalent of around £60,000 (US $96,000) today, is the amount needed to pay the household expenses of an average baron for a year. One thousand silver marks would be worth around £400,000 (US $640,000) today. Some rough estimates of the contemporary purchasing equivalents for Anglo-Norman and Angevin units of currency, where applicable, are given in the text.

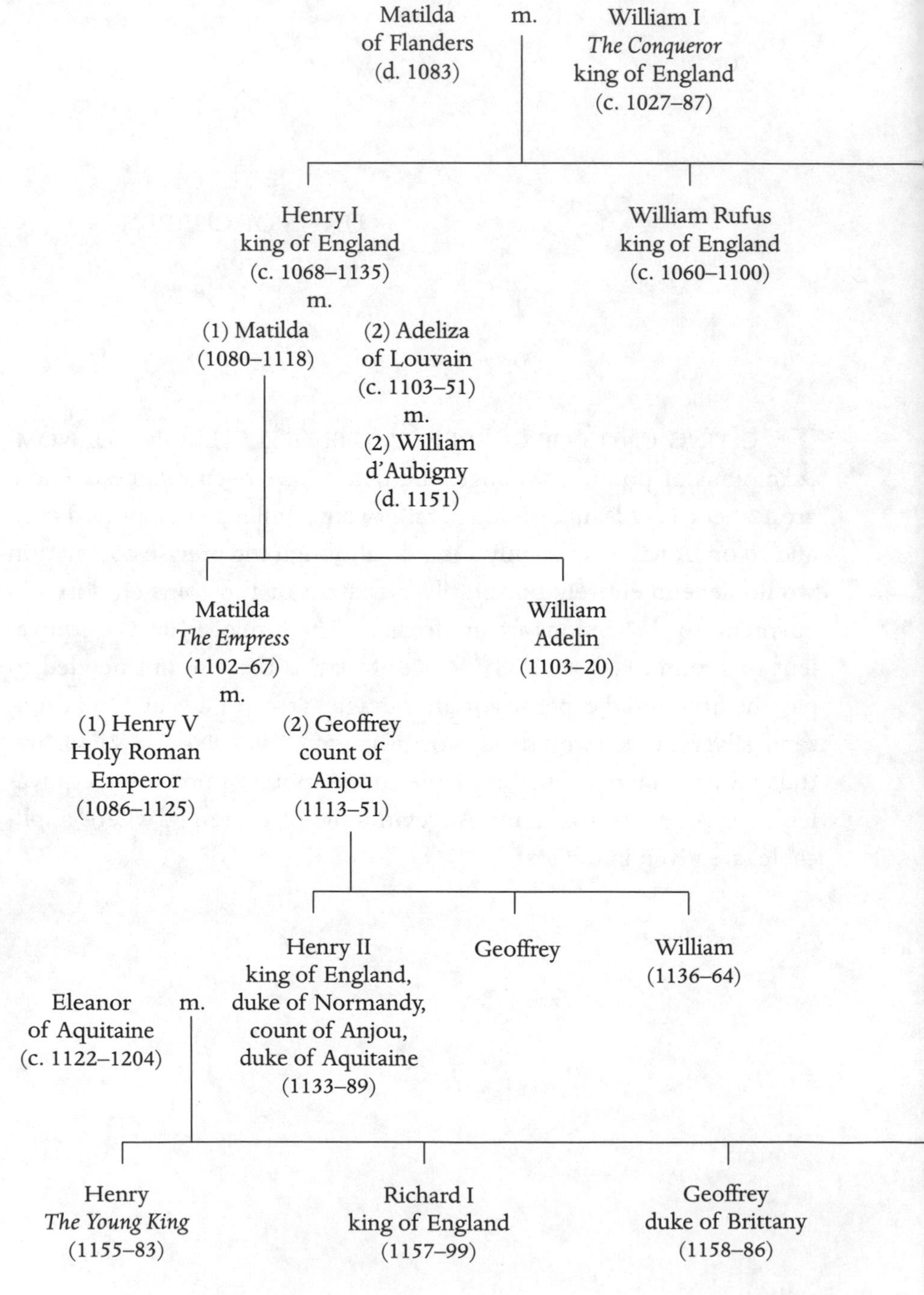

Matilda
of Flanders
(d. 1083)
m.
William I
The Conqueror
king of England
(c. 1027–87)
Henry I
king of England
(c. 1068–1135)
m.
(1) Matilda
(1080–1118)
(2) Adeliza
of Louvain
(c. 1103–51)
m.
(2) William
d'Aubigny
(d. 1151)
William Rufus
king of England
(c. 1060–1100)
Matilda
The Empress
(1102–67)
m.
(1) Henry V
Holy Roman
Emperor
(1086–1125)
(2) Geoffrey
count of
Anjou
(1113–51)
William
Adelin
(1103–20)
Eleanor
of Aquitaine
(c. 1122–1204)
m.
Henry II
king of England,
duke of Normandy,
count of Anjou,
duke of Aquitaine
(1133–89)
Geoffrey
William
(1136–64)
Henry
The Young King
(1155–83)
Richard I
king of England
(1157–99)
Geoffrey
duke of Brittany
(1158–86)

THE NORMANS AND ANGEVINS

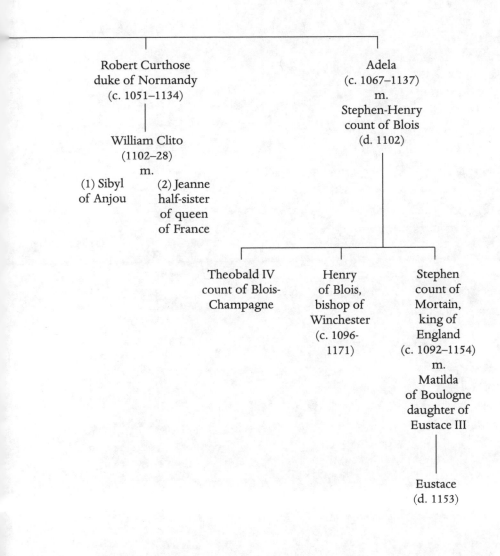

Robert Curthose
duke of Normandy
(c. 1051–1134)

William Clito
(1102–28)
m.
(1) Sibyl of Anjou
(2) Jeanne half-sister of queen of France

Adela
(c. 1067–1137)
m.
Stephen-Henry
count of Blois
(d. 1102)

Theobald IV
count of Blois-Champagne

Henry
of Blois,
bishop of
Winchester
(c. 1096-1171)

Stephen
count of
Mortain,
king of
England
(c. 1092–1154)
m.
Matilda
of Boulogne
daughter of
Eustace III

Eustace
(d. 1153)

John
king of England
(1167–1216)

3 daughters

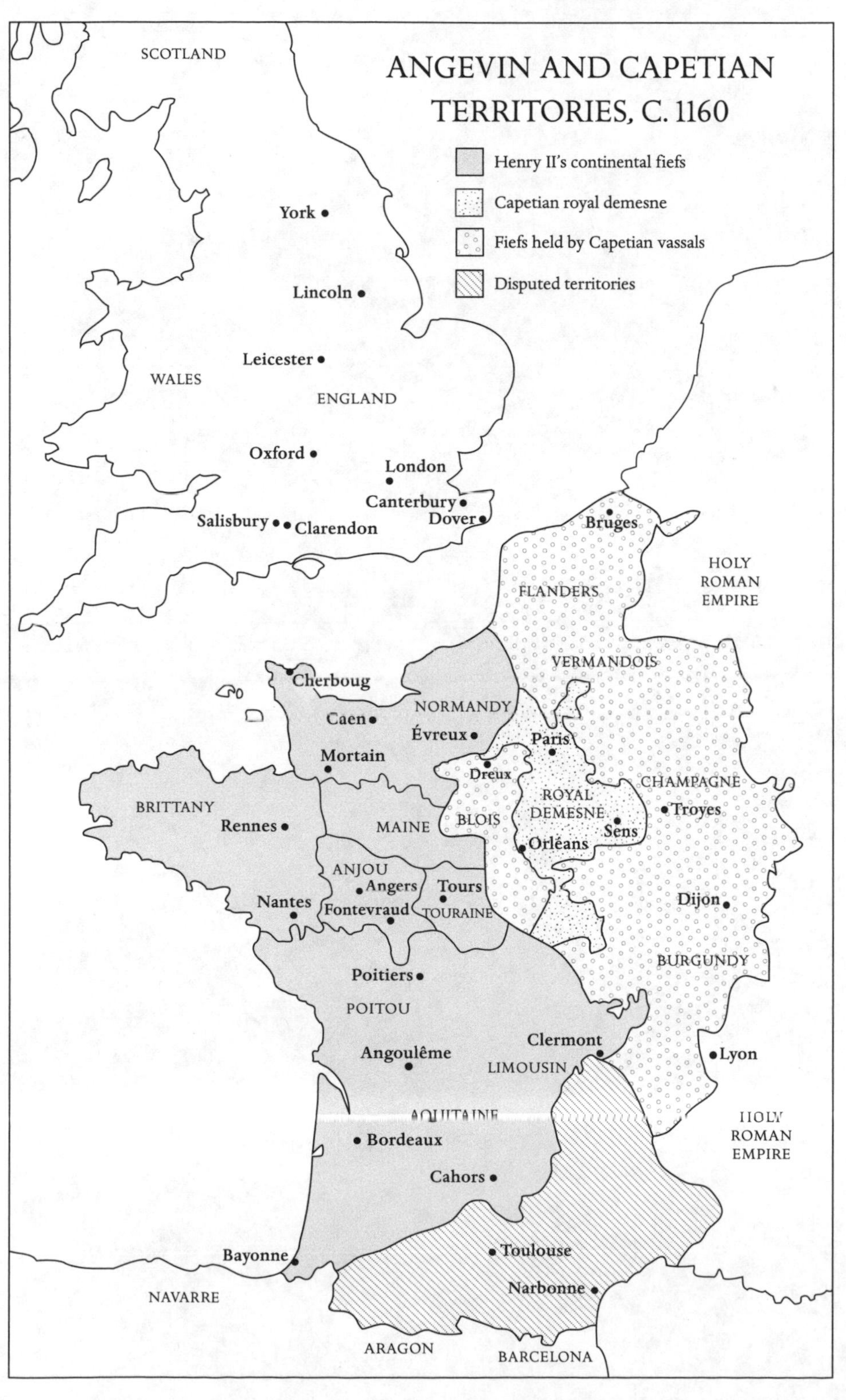
ANGEVIN AND CAPETIAN TERRITORIES, C. 1160
Henry II's continental fiefs
Capetian royal demesne
Fiefs held by Capetian vassals
Disputed territories
SCOTLAND
York
Lincoln
Leicester
WALES
ENGLAND
Oxford
London
Canterbury
Dover
Salisbury
Clarendon
Bruges
FLANDERS
HOLY
ROMAN
EMPIRE
VERMANDOIS
Cherboug
NORMANDY
Caen
Évreux
Paris
Mortain
Dreux
CHAMPAGNE
ROYAL
DEMESNE
Troyes
BRITTANY
Rennes
MAINE
BLOIS
Sens
Orléans
ANJOU
Angers
Tours
Nantes
Fontevraud
TOURAINE
Dijon
BURGUNDY
Poitiers
POITOU
Clermont
Lyon
Angoulême
LIMOUSIN
AQUITAINE
HOLY
ROMAN
EMPIRE
Bordeaux
Cahors
Toulouse
Bayonne
Narbonne
NAVARRE
ARAGON
BARCELONA

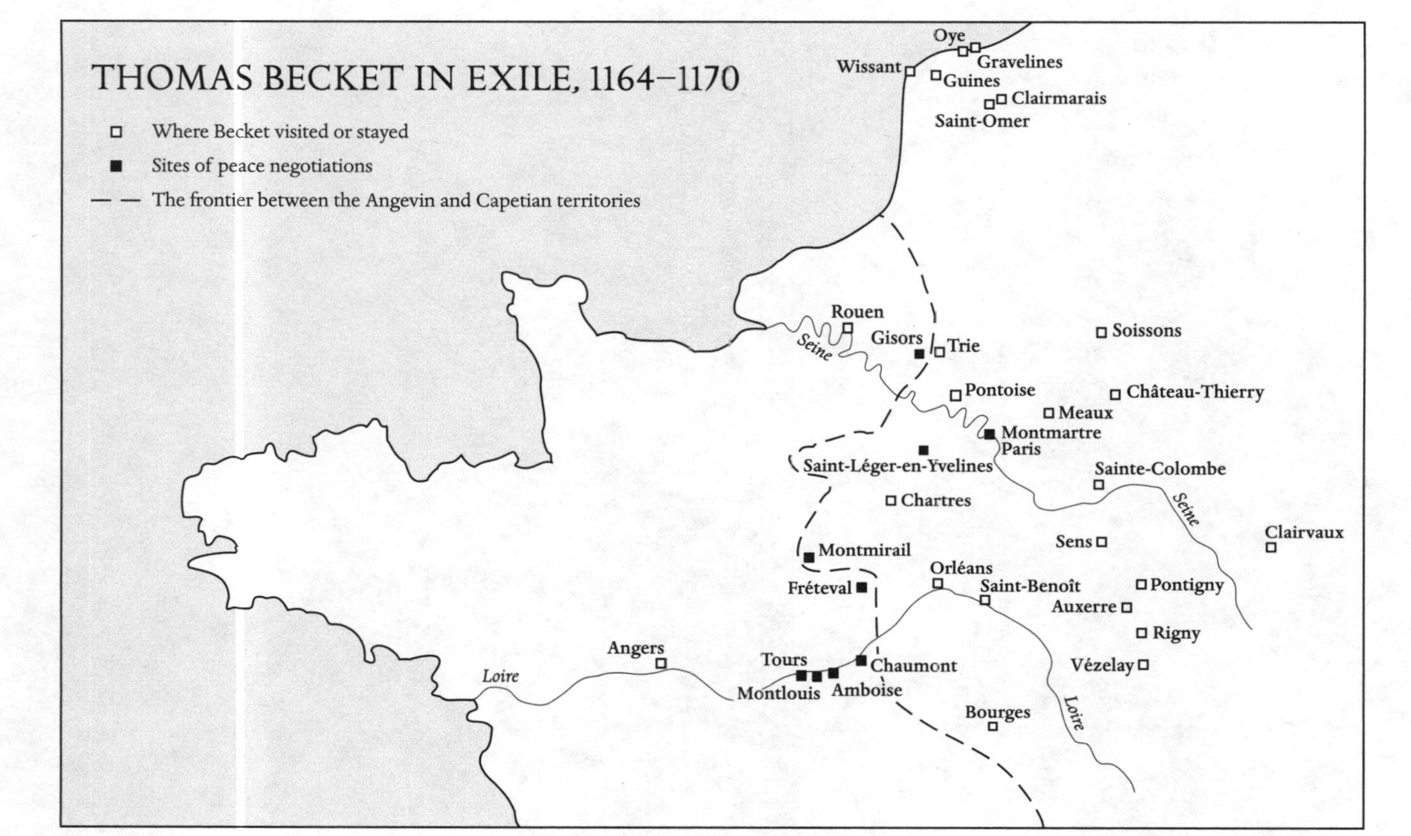
THOMAS BECKET IN EXILE, 1164–1170
Where Becket visited or stayed
Sites of peace negotiations
The frontier between the Angevin and Capetian territories
Oye
Wissant
Gravelines
Guines
Clairmarais
Saint-Omer
Rouen
Seine
Gisors
Trie
Soissons
Pontoise
Château-Thierry
Meaux
Montmartre
Paris
Saint-Léger-en-Yvelines
Sainte-Colombe
Chartres
Seine
Clairvaux
Sens
Montmirail
Orléans
Fréteval
Saint-Benoît
Pontigny
Auxerre
Rigny
Angers
Tours
Chaumont
Vézelay
Loire
Montlouis
Amboise
Bourges
Loire

PROLOGUE

SHORTLY BEFORE MIDNIGHT ON NOVEMBER 25, 1120, LESS THAN a month before Thomas Becket was born, a swift, sleek, newly refitted longship slipped out of the port of Barfleur in Normandy and entered the English Channel with fifty or so crew members and up to three hundred passengers on board. The vessel's high pointed ends, its single central mast and rectangular sail, and most of all its distinctive side rudder echoed Normandy's debt to the Vikings, who in the ninth and tenth centuries had overrun large areas of the British Isles and Flanders and, after sailing up the Seine, occupied much of northwestern France.

In or about the year 911, the weak King Charles the Simple, king of the West Franks, had made terms with Hrólf, a Viking lord said to be so huge that no horse could carry him. Charles salvaged the rest of his dominions by ceding to Hrólf the lands about the lower Seine and the city of Rouen that the Norsemen had already settled, turning poachers into gamekeepers and allowing them to carve out a fief that would evolve into the duchy of Normandy. Hrólf, in return, was baptized a Christian and did homage and fealty to Charles, placing his hands on the Gospels or the relics of a saint and swearing to be Charles's man and to preserve his life, limbs, and earthly honor. Better known to his successors as Count Rollo, Hrólf founded a powerful dynasty through intermarriage with the local inhabitants, shaping a people as famous for their courage, ingenuity, sociability, and piety as they were notorious for their wanderlust, violence, ambition, and greed. From the legacy of the Carolingians,

Count Rollo's successors gleaned lingering concepts of ducal sovereignty, and from their Viking inheritance expertise in seafaring and trading. Perhaps the greatest irony of the Norman Conquest of England in 1066 is that within three weeks of annihilating the Viking invaders of Northumbria, King Harold II, the last of the Old English kings, lost his throne to William the Conqueror, great-great-great-grandson of Hrólf.

The night of November 25 was bitterly cold. A hard frost covered the ground, but visibility was good. The sky was cloudless, and no mist or fog obscured the exit to the harbor and the open sea. Orderic Vitalis, a monk from the abbey of Saint-Evroult in Normandy, one of several contemporary chroniclers who did their best to uncover the true facts, erroneously reports that there were nine hours of moonlight. In reality it was closer to the new moon, so relatively dark. The stars, however, shone brightly, and since mariners set their course by the polestar, which they called *stella maris* (star of the sea), there were no good grounds on which the skipper could delay sailing. A modern expert has calculated that high water was at 10:43 P.M. that night. By midnight (continues Orderic) the surface of the sea was relatively calm, lapping against the shore, and there was a southerly breeze.

But this was to be no ordinary Channel crossing. In fact another chronicler, William of Malmesbury, scarcely exaggerates when he says, "No ship ever brought so much misery to England." Thomas fitz Stephen, whose father had been William the Conqueror's master steersman in 1066, was the skipper. Hearing that King Henry I, the ablest and youngest of the late conqueror's sons, planned a voyage from Normandy to England with his whole court, this seasoned mariner had obtained an audience with the king and begged to have his father's old job. He offered Henry his finest vessel, the *White Ship,* and the king decided that his sons William and Richard and his daughter Countess Matilda of La Perche should travel on it. Prince William, an ebullient, spoiled, fun-loving teenager, just seventeen and recently married, was the king's only legitimate son, on whom he doted. His elder siblings were bastards, for Henry was one of the most promiscuous kings of England, fathering at least twenty illegitimate offspring by a parade of mistresses (effortlessly beating Charles II, who sired a mere fourteen). "He gave way too easily to the sin of lust," says Orderic drily. "From boyhood to old age he was sinfully enslaved by this vice."

With his ship detailed to carry only passengers, without horses or heavy cargo apart from the royal treasure and some casks of wine, fitz Stephen's task looked easy. The king's children were to be accompanied by many leading courtiers and their retinues, and the crew members were elated at the prospect. When Prince William arrived at the quay, the sailors greeted him with cheers and shouts of glee. They asked for drink to toast him and were granted three "muids" of wine from the casks on board, amounting to roughly two hundred liters—far too much for fifty men—but fitz Stephen was unable or unwilling to interfere.

No sooner were the casks broken open than the men filled their cups and a great drinking bout commenced. Soon the sailors were swaying on their feet or rolling about on the deck. The worst behaved were a cohort of armed marine bodyguards "who were very disorderly, and as soon as they got on board insolently took possession of the benches of the rowers." As the party atmosphere took over, most of the passengers also joined in the fun.

When, finally, the sail was hoisted and the anchor weighed, some of the drunken passengers dared fitz Stephen to order his men to overtake the king's main fleet, which had departed at high tide. Henry's great warship, or *snecca,* a poetic word deriving from the Old Norse for "snake" or "serpent" (*snekkja*), was commanded by a highly paid master and a more professional crew. Fast and maneuverable, it was already disappearing over the horizon.

Confident of his seamanship and the skill of his crew, the skipper accepted the challenge. On hearing the order, the oarsmen did their work, and the *White Ship* cleaved the water like an arrow, the white foam flying off the blades. The safe passage out of Barfleur harbor was directly to the northeast, which should have been straightforward had the helmsman steered correctly. But in his haste to cut the corner, he steered too far north, where some dangerous rocks were submerged at high tide. Just at the point that the crewmen were trimming the sail to the wind, the ship, almost a mile from Barfleur and half a mile from the shore, struck a huge rock, probably the one in the current known as the Raz de

Barfleur, which even at high tide was still visible from the lighthouse on the cliff as an ugly brown shadow beneath the water.

Two of the oak planks on the starboard bow were smashed, and the water poured in. The sailors tried to free the vessel with their boat hooks, but the prow was stuck fast. The rowers fled in panic from their benches, leaving their oars to splinter against the rock. Some men drowned inside the ship; others were washed overboard. When the ship suddenly capsized, passengers and crew members were thrown into the freezing sea, where a brave few attempted to swim against the strong underwater current, while others thrashed about helplessly until they drowned.

Soon after the collision, a dinghy was launched carrying Prince William. He might have escaped, but on hearing his sister shrieking from the deck, he turned back to try to save her. He paid a high price for his rash gallantry, since as the dinghy nudged its way back through the foaming current toward the stricken longship, it was swamped by those who jumped down or clambered into it, plunging everyone into the sea. Two men, swimming nearby, grabbed hold of the spar, from which its sail had been set, and clung to it. One was a butcher from Rouen called Berold, the other a youth of noble birth: Geoffrey, a younger son of Gilbert de l'Aigle. Thomas fitz Stephen, already in the water but an exceptionally strong swimmer, inched his way toward them, calling out, "What has become of the king's son?"

"He and all who were with him have perished," they replied.

"Then it is misery for me to live any longer." Rather than face the king's wrath, the skipper decided that he would prefer to drown, for Henry had a reputation for exacting harsh reprisals when he felt he had been crossed or his trust had been betrayed. Applauded as "the Lion of Justice" by smooth-talking courtiers or poets eager for a fee, he summarily blinded or executed rebels and castrated thieves, even encouraging the governor of a castle whom his illegitimate daughter Juliana had wronged to slit the noses and put out the eyes of two of his own granddaughters. He was rarely a man to be trifled with or who allowed failure to go unpunished.

The *White Ship* claimed its final victim when Geoffrey de l'Aigle, suffering from hypothermia, could no longer hold on to the spar. Commending his soul to God and making the sign of the cross with his fingers, he disappeared beneath the water. Shortly after dawn, three fishermen arrived in a skiff to rescue Berold, the poorest of the travelers, who is said to have survived the cold because he alone was clad in sheepskin. Once carried to safety and revived with soup and wine before a roaring fire, he told his story to a large crowd and afterward lived in good health for twenty years. Doubtless the chroniclers obtained their information about the wreck from him or one of his audience.

The king and his companions, though several miles away when the ship went down, were said to have been able to hear the cries of those who were drowning but did not understand their cause and so continued on their voyage. They may have been afraid to return, for it was commonly believed that at night the dead rose out of their graves to frighten or harm the living, and that demons compelled the souls of the damned in hell to reenact the sins for which they were condemned. There were tales of mermaids with wings and claws and of wild men of the sea—maybe fish in human form or spirits lurking in the bodies of drowned men—and of great serpents or sea monsters that gobbled up distressed mariners and would regurgitate them on Judgment Day.

Henry landed around midday on the south coast of England, probably in Hampshire. When toward evening he asked for news of his children, those around him were struck dumb with fear and claimed ignorance. They wept privately for their own kinsfolk, but none dared to admit their loss or whisper the truth in case the king overheard. They continued their deception until the following day, when on the initiative of Henry's nephew Count Theobald IV of Blois-Champagne, a young boy threw himself at the king's feet, sobbing inconsolably, and, on being questioned as to the cause, broke the news. "So sudden was the shock," says Orderic, "and so severe the king's anguish, that he instantly fainted." He was carried by his attendants to his bedchamber, where he remained in seclusion for several days, grieving for his lost children, his knights and barons, and so many of his household officials. Besides dozens of the flower of Anglo-Norman society, they included eighteen highborn women, the daughters, sisters, nieces, or wives of counts and earls.

The Norman villagers, meanwhile, scoured the beaches around the bay of Barfleur until they located the wreck, which they dragged ashore with ropes at low tide. All the royal treasure was salvaged, as was almost everything else except the bodies. After a search lasting more than a week and in spite of generous rewards offered to experienced divers by the victims' relatives, very few bodies were recovered for burial, and those that were found were heavily disfigured, having been found far away from where the ship was lost after being swept along by the currents. The bodies of Richard, Earl of Chester, and several more could be identified only from their clothing. Prince William's body would never be found, his death triggering a royal and ducal succession crisis that would rock the stability of the Anglo-Norman state and dominate the minds of the chroniclers for almost thirty years.

THOMAS BECKET

1
ANCESTRY

ARCHBISHOP THOMAS BECKET, WHO FOR FOUR CENTURIES after his gruesome murder in Canterbury Cathedral would be nicknamed "lux Londoniarum" (the light of the Londoners), was the only surviving son of Gilbert and Matilda Becket, born very probably when the wreck of the *White Ship* was still the hottest news in town. The time was the afternoon of St. Thomas the Apostle's Day (December 21); the place a large house in Cheapside standing on the fief of the Marmion family, to whom a substantial annual quitrent was due.

Lying on the north side of Cheapside between Ironmonger Lane and Old Jewry, the Beckets' house was within earshot of the busiest street market in London. Most likely it was built of wood and limestone with narrow, unglazed windows. Its main living areas were the open hall, or main reception area, warmed by a central stone hearth, with a private chamber to the side where the family lived, slept, and entertained their closest friends and relatives. The open hall was lit by wax tapers, was furnished with trestle tables and stools, and had washing bowls and basins suitably positioned by the door or in an alcove. Servants, who waited on the family and prepared their meals, slept in the hall. Beneath the house was an undercroft, or cellar, perhaps serving as a warehouse to store goods. Possibly the kitchen was at one end of the hall behind a wooden screen, maybe outside in an annex to minimize the risk of fire. Water for cooking and washing was drawn from a private well or purchased from one of the city's many water carriers, who scooped river water from the Thames into leather pouches, selling them door-to-door. Soap was generally made from ashes, and the Beckets cleaned their teeth using green hazel shoots before polishing them with woolen cloths.

While Gilbert and Matilda's open hall was apparently larger than average, their living chamber may have been fairly cramped. Working back from documents compiled in 1227–28, it can be estimated that the property had a street frontage of 40 feet, a rear width of 110 feet, and a depth of 165 feet, but the greater portion of this area was taken up by a garden. The same documents show that the adjacent houses were approached via gatehouses and provided with outdoor latrines flowing into cesspits, so perhaps the Beckets' house had such amenities too.

Baptized in the nearby parish church of St. Mary Colechurch, Thomas was named after the apostle whose festival it was. His godparents promised to protect him from "fire and water and other perils" until he was seven and teach him the Lord's Prayer, the Ave Maria (Hail Mary), and the Apostles' Creed. Following time-hallowed rituals, the priest dipped Thomas in the font, then placed his thumb in holy oil, making the sign of the cross on the baby's forehead, shoulders, and chest, before wrapping him in a "chrism cloth," a white linen christening robe, as a symbol of purity and to keep him warm.

Whereas baptism usually took place when a newborn child was a few days old, Thomas was brought to the church by a midwife or nurse within hours of his birth, suggesting he may have appeared weak or sickly, or perhaps his parents had lost an earlier child and were determined to make sure their son was christened at once. His father was present at the church but not his mother, since canon (or church) law forbade a newly delivered woman to enter a consecrated space until she had been ritually purified in a special ceremony some forty days after her lying-in.

Around the year 1110, Gilbert and Matilda Becket had joined settlers from Rouen, the chief city of the Norman dukes, who had flocked to London, enticed by the city's expanding trade. Most likely Gilbert was a draper's merchant, since Cheapside and its environs were inhabited mainly by goldsmiths and those dealing wholesale in textiles, and Gilbert is known not to have been a goldsmith. Although they came from Rouen, their exact birthplaces are disputed. William fitz Stephen (no relation to the skipper of the *White Ship*), also born to Norman parents in London and one of Thomas Becket's early biographers, says that Gilbert came from a fairly humble family living close to Thierville in the valley of the Risle, not far from Bec Abbey, some twenty-five miles from Rouen. An anonymous Canterbury monk says that Gilbert's family was from Rouen itself and that Matilda (who is sometimes called Rose) was most likely born and raised in Caen. Married at around the age of twenty, the couple immigrated to England soon after their wedding.

The surname Becket usually means "little beak" or "beak-face," and young Thomas is known to have had an aquiline nose, probably inherited from his father. But it is far more likely that Becket derives from Bec, as in Bec Abbey. Surnames were optional in medieval society, and few people regularly used them. Gilbert and Matilda's eldest daughter, Agnes, was among them, calling herself Becket even after her marriage, but her brother never used the name, and when he is so addressed by others, it is usually derogatory. Before entering royal service, he preferred to call himself "Thomas of London" and afterward "Thomas the chancellor" or "Thomas the archbishop." Just one chronicler, Roger of Howden, refers to him in the modern way, as Thomas Becket, and then only once.

One of the most enduring and tantalizingly romantic myths about Thomas is that his mother was a Saracen princess. Still often repeated as true, the story first became part of the Becket legend as the result of an interpolation in a corrupt medieval manuscript first printed at Paris in 1495. The same story appears in a chronicle attributed to John of Brompton, abbot of Jervaulx. Gilbert, it is said, had traveled on a pilgrimage to Jerusalem as a young man, attended only by a servant. While praying one day in a church, he was surprised by a party of Saracens, who abducted him and led him into slavery. Held for a year and a half, he suffered great hardships but slowly ingratiated himself with his captors, who allowed him to come to their table, where he explained to them the customs and manners of the Europeans. The Saracen lord's daughter took a fancy to him and secretly visited him in prison, offering to become a Christian if he would make her his bride. When a few months later he broke free from his chains and managed to escape in the company of some merchants, she followed him. Arriving in London alone and knowing no words in French or English besides "London" and "Becket," she walked the streets desperately, mocked by bemused children, until by pure chance she was recognized by Gilbert's servant. Reluctant at first to marry her, but eager to see her baptized, Gilbert sought advice from the bishop of London, who, "perceiving the hand of God visibly concerned in the affair," decided to baptize her the next day. After the ceremony at St. Paul's—conducted by six bishops—she and Gilbert were married, and Thomas was conceived overnight.

Edward Grim, once the rector of the parish of Saltwood in Kent, who went on to write one of Becket's early biographies, claims that Matilda Becket experienced a series of mystical visions around the time her son was born. Since he did not even know the family then, he was almost certainly using a hagiographer's trick to signal his subject's future greatness. In her first vision, Matilda is said to have felt the whole of the river Thames flowing within her. Seeking an explanation from soothsayers, she learned that "the one who is born to you will rule over many people." Next she dreamed of going on a pilgrimage to Canterbury, but when she attempted to enter the cathedral, her womb swelled so large that she could not pass through the door. Her final vision concerned a blanket that magically and continually expanded. Seeing her baby lying uncovered in his cot, mother and nurse attempted to unravel the blanket, "but they found the chamber too cramped for this purpose and the larger hall too, and even the street." Finally a voice from heaven thundered, "All your efforts are useless. The whole of England is smaller than this purple cloth and cannot contain it."

When he was forty-six, Thomas would describe his parents as "citizens of London, not by any means the lowest, living without dispute in the midst of their fellow citizens." Slights against his ancestry—of which he would receive many over the course of his eventful life—always stung him. "I prefer," he would say, "to be a man in whom nobility of mind creates nobility, rather than one in whom nobility of birth degenerates. Perhaps I was born in a humble cottage, but through the aid of divine mercy . . . I lived very well indeed in my poverty." And he would fearlessly defend his family's honor when he felt it unfairly impugned. "What do family trees produce?" he would ask. "Which is more praiseworthy, to be born of middle-class or even more lowly stock, or to be born from the great and honored of the world, when St. Paul would say, 'Those parts of the body which we think less honorable we invest with the greater honor'?"

The description "middle-class" fits his parents perfectly. A prosperous London citizen, Gilbert was at best the son of a lesser knight or of a free agricultural tenant, but was at least a freeman's son at a time when the overwhelming majority of the Norman and English populations were tied laborers or peasants. Around thirty years old when Thomas was born, Gilbert would afterward rise to become one of the four sheriffs, or chief officers, of London. (The post of mayor did not yet exist.) The relationship between the Crown and city was close, and the sheriffs were its linchpins. William the Conqueror had relied on them to collect the city's annual "farm," or tax, and to keep order. His son William Rufus had expected them to pay for knights, for repairs to London Bridge after it had been severely damaged by a flood, and for the costs of building his magnificent "new hall" at Westminster beside the abbey. Half a century would elapse before the Normans would feel wholly secure within the city, but King Henry I would regularly stay there. Most likely Gilbert ranked among the fifty or so leaders of London's civic elite.

THOMAS BECKET, who spent most of the first twenty-five years of his life in or around the city, was in many of his habits and values a Londoner even after he had left to make a career elsewhere. Proud of their adopted home, the Norman immigrant families of his parents' generation had swiftly assimilated into civic society. With their underlying values of meritocracy and a self-governing community, Londoners believed passionately that they should be governed by themselves, remaining free to arrange things in their own interests and not in those of the lord who happened to own the land on which their houses were built. A rudimentary civic government and a representative assembly had existed since before the Conquest, when the citizens had gathered three times a year in the "folkmoot" to regulate their own affairs. So Londoners had a long-established tradition of self-government.

Early in his reign, William the Conqueror had confirmed these freedoms, which included the right to punish offenses committed on market days and to enforce the bargains made. The citizens then purchased a much amplified charter from Henry I, allowing them to elect their own sheriffs and hear lawsuits in their own civic courts. To improve their trade, they secured exemption from the tolls and customs duties imposed on them by other English cities or seaports. And to encourage their cooperation with the Crown, the king agreed to reduce their annual tax, while the royal family showed its generosity in other ways. Shortly before Thomas was born, Henry's first wife, Queen Matilda, had founded a new public bathhouse and latrine complex in the city, together with a leper hospital outside the walls.

Thriving chiefly on its commerce, London was a trading city and a major seaport. Ships could navigate the Thames as far as London Bridge, where cargoes traveling farther upstream had to be unloaded and transferred to smaller vessels on the other side of the bridge. Wharves and landings (or stairs) were scattered along the banks of the river, since each "lord" and district had their own. Wherries and ferryboats shuttled people, horses, fish, grain, and every type of merchandise from one bank to the other. Regulating trade themselves, the citizens had made sure, since 984–85 in the reign of King Æthelred, that ships landing fish at London Bridge would be expected to pay a toll. Within a century, merchants from Normandy and France, Flanders, Italy and Germany, Gascony, and the Mediterranean would be flocking to London, where they were required to display their wares to the customs officials on arrival and pay tolls on the wharf or on board their ships.

Increasingly the hub of a national network supplying food and commodities, London took advantage of a transport system based on ancient river routes and the old Roman roads. These roads, though full of potholes and poorly maintained, were adequate for sledges, carts, or wagons drawn by oxen or packhorses. Heavier loads were more suited to the river routes, which chiefly ran north along the Lea deep into leafy Hertfordshire; upstream along the Thames into Berkshire and Oxfordshire; or downstream along the coasts of Essex and Kent, and then onward by sea to the ports of East Anglia and Lincolnshire, and north toward Newcastle and Scotland.

Occupying an area slightly more than three hundred acres, the city looked very much like an irregular half ellipse nestled on the Thames, enclosed on the northern, or land, side by the old Roman walls but occasionally spilling outside, mainly to the south and west, into Middlesex and Surrey to create the suburbs of Southwark and Westminster. Although the old Roman walls had become dilapidated, with many gaps and holes, the core remained largely intact except along the riverbank, where everything had collapsed into the mud. Accordingly, access by road was through one of seven gateways, which were surmounted by lofty towers, or keeps, regularly used as prisons. Locked and barred at night to keep out thieves, four of the gates had a central opening for carts, with a passage for those on foot on either side, leaving three for pedestrians only.

The original Roman bridge had crossed the Thames near Fish Street Hill, the lowest point at which such a wide and fast-flowing tidal stream could be spanned. Its pre-Conquest replacement, built of timber and broad enough for two wagons to pass each other, was still standing in Thomas Becket's lifetime, though in constant need of repairs. Always the key point of entry to the city from Southwark and the south bank, this bridge played a crucial role in London's economy and defenses, for it would take another fifty years to get a project for a new stone bridge off the ground.

When Thomas was born, London had roughly 40,000 inhabitants and 120 churches, making it one of Europe's largest, wealthiest, most cosmopolitan cities. Among other recent immigrants were a close-knit community of Jews living a stone's throw from the Beckets, who established a significant presence in the city until 1290, when they would be expelled. Although usury was forbidden on religious grounds to Jews, Christians, and Muslims alike, some Jewish theologians made an exception for loans to Christians. Integrating themselves skillfully, the Jews evaded the prohibitions, counting royal officials and merchants among their most valuable clients. Flemish and Italian financiers could provide additional credit, circumventing the restrictions on usury by agreeing with the borrower to pretend that the original loan was ten or fifteen percent greater than it actually was. Close links existed between the Jews, the king's moneymen, and the goldsmiths of Cheapside and Lombard Street, some of whom also worked in the royal mint.

By the time Gilbert Becket served as sheriff, London was already divided into neighborhoods, or administrative units known as wards, each covering a block of streets and containing at least one and usually two or three parish churches. Associated with these wards was a new breed of officials, the aldermen, many of them recruited from the officeholders of the local trading guilds. Playing a vital role in policing the city, the aldermen regulated such basic elements of life as dumping rubbish and the location of stables and dung heaps; identifying the owners of stray pigs that fouled the streets; and removing structures intruding into public space or signs that hung too low. Probably Gilbert had first become one of these aldermen, making his name as a spokesman for the Cheapside community before putting his name forward for election as sheriff. It seems that Thomas came from a family that in its own very practical way believed in playing its part for the benefit of society.

The chief landmarks dominating the city were castles, churches, and monasteries. A mighty fortress begun on William the Conqueror's orders, the Tower of London guarded the eastern side of the city. At the western end, two lesser strongholds, Baynard's Castle and Mountfichet's Castle, protected Ludgate, one of the chief approaches to the city. Nearby was the cathedral of St. Paul's, still being rebuilt in a Norman style, on a much enlarged site after a disastrous fire, when the Beckets arrived. Strolling through the churchyard with his mother as a boy, Thomas sometimes found his path blocked by a huge pile of stones that were arriving almost daily by barge along the river Fleet, a tributary of the Thames. Situated just off the western edge of Cheapside, the cathedral was only a short walk from Gilbert and Matilda's house, and shortly before he died, Gilbert would found a chapel on the north side of the churchyard to house his tomb.

The nucleus of city life, St. Paul's Churchyard buzzed, for it was where the citizens tended to congregate for the most important religious festivals and where many of the larger civic assemblies convened by the sheriffs were held. Some two miles upstream at Westminster was its counterpart, the Benedictine abbey church refounded by King Edward the Confessor in honor of St. Peter. Larger than any other church building in England or Normandy, this was where William the Conqueror was famously crowned on Christmas Day 1066. Beside it stood the royal palace of Westminster; when Thomas Becket was a boy it had not yet supplanted Winchester, the oldest and most favored Anglo-Norman royal residence. The permanent home of the treasury, Winchester still had the obvious attraction of being nearer to the Channel ports on the king's usual route for crossing to and from Normandy, but Henry I often preferred to celebrate Christmas and Whitsuntide at Westminster. There, he sat "in majesty" wearing his crown and purple robes, close to the shops of the London merchants and their luxury goods, not to mention a thriving community of minstrels and entertainers. While Thomas was growing up, some of the most lavish and impressive ceremonial events of Henry's reign took place in either the palace's great hall or the nearby abbey church, but there is no way of knowing whether the future archbishop ever saw the king and his retinue of barons and knights pass by in procession on their way there.

The truly remarkable sequence of events that would allow a middle-class Londoner to rise to a position where he would become the equal of barons and knights, converse regularly with kings and popes, and one day come to defy a king was yet to begin.

2
UPBRINGING

SAID BY HIS EARLY BIOGRAPHERS TO HAVE BEEN DEEPLY ATtached to his mother from a young age, Thomas spent his early childhood among women. Up until the age of six or seven, he had his three sisters—Agnes, Rose, and Mary—for playmates. Almost nothing is known about them other than that the elder pair would one day marry and have sons, at least three of whom became priests. The youngest sister, Mary, became a nun, ending her days as the abbess of Barking in Essex, a position to which she would be called three years after her brother's shocking murder. One of Agnes's married children, a son called Theobald, became her heir and would inherit the family house in Cheapside, which a century later his descendants bequeathed to the crusading knights of the Order of St. Thomas of Acre as their London headquarters. Thomas would stay in contact with his sisters throughout his life and would sometimes help them financially, but his relationship with them was never especially close.

The Beckets, like all Norman immigrants, would have spoken French among themselves, but their servants would have been English, and Thomas would have been familiar with their conversations at an early age. After half a century or so, the initial culture shock of the Conquest had subsided. Normans and English were growing closer together through intermarriage, continuing the process begun before 1066, when large influxes of Danish and Norse settlers had been assimilated. Iconic of this intermingling would be King Henry I's marriage to his first wife,

Matilda. A daughter of the king of Scots, she was descended on her mother's side from the Old English kings of Wessex and named Edith at birth. On marrying Henry, she changed her name to Matilda, one of the most popular Norman girl's names, for which the chroniclers, notably William of Malmesbury, acclaimed her as a living exemplar of the union between the old and new royal families.

Becket's mother was the driving force in his education and most likely first taught him to read. As a merchant's wife, she can be expected to have been semiliterate, teaching him his ABCs and how to use the abacus, or counting frame, at home. When reciting the alphabet, Thomas would have begun by making the sign of the cross and then saying "Christ's cross me speed," as all children were taught to do. Around the age of seven, he may have attended a parish school, or song school, where choristers were taught basic literacy by the local priest. He was also taken regularly to church. More than conventionally pious, his mother was a devotee of the cult of the Blessed Virgin Mary, to whom she taught her son to pray. Frequently and generously giving alms to the poor, she is said to have habitually weighed her young son on the scales using bread, meat, clothes, and anything else useful for the poor instead of metal weights, after which she would distribute these goods as alms, hoping in this way to commend her son to God and the Blessed Virgin.

Around the age of ten, Thomas was sent to school at the Augustinian priory of Merton in Surrey. Founded as recently as 1115 by Gilbert Norman, sheriff of Surrey, whom Gilbert Becket may have known personally, the priory had recently moved from its original site to a picturesque new location beside the river Wandle. Henry I had given this well-regarded foundation a charter and granted it the manor of Merton to enable a church dedicated to the Blessed Virgin Mary to be built. Some fifteen miles from London, about half a day's riding distance away, the priory was too far for Thomas to commute daily, so he boarded during termtime. His early biographers assumed that a priory school was chosen because of some miraculous and holy qualities that his father saw in him, but this is overly romantic. Far more likely is that Gilbert Becket had run across its founder in connection with his role as a civic or guild official in London and had the place recommended to him. Maybe a deciding factor for Thomas's mother was the intense devotion of these monks to the cult of the Blessed Virgin Mary.

After settling in, Thomas joined the other pupils who were learning Latin from a textbook by the fourth-century grammarian Aelius Donatus. A classic work used by schoolmasters throughout western Europe until the beginning of the sixteenth century and in central Europe until the middle of the eighteenth, the *Ars Minor* was intended for the youngest students and conveys, in the manner of a catechism, information on the eight parts of speech. Thomas and his teacher repeated their lines again and again, until Thomas knew his by heart.

> MASTER: How many parts of speech are there?
> THOMAS: Eight.
> MASTER: Which eight?
> THOMAS: Noun, pronoun, verb, adverb, participle, conjunction, preposition, interjection.
> MASTER: How many are declined, and how many are not declined?
> THOMAS: Four are declined, and four are not declined.

The boys practiced their exercises daily and on becoming proficient tried their hand at simple translation, first working from Latin into English and then translating their English versions back into Latin and comparing them with the original author's text to improve their style. The older pupils were given carefully selected passages from Latin verse to learn and translate before moving on to "disputations" in grammar.

Afterward said to have a highly retentive memory, Thomas would sometimes have spoken a little hesitantly, because he suffered from a youthful tendency to stammer. His physical appearance may have helped to compensate, boosting his self-confidence. Unusually tall, growing eventually to over six feet in full age, he was good-looking, with a broad brow and thin face, large lustrous eyes, a fair complexion, and dark hair. But if clever and quick-witted, he lacked intellectual ambition and did not want to be stretched. His approach at school tended to be casual. Nobody placed him in the top rank of pupils or reckoned him a natural scholar. Since, however, nothing is said about punishments, he could not have been completely idle and must have done at least the minimum amount of work, well aware that schoolmasters instilled knowledge as much through beating as through teaching. Probably he coasted in class, but for all that he must have had some refreshingly happy memories of his teachers at Merton, as he would send for one of them, Brother Robert—an "honest man"—to become his chaplain and confessor soon after his appointment as the king's chancellor.

Returning to London after a year or two, Thomas was sent to one of the city's three grammar schools. Attached to important churches and usually providing a subsidized education apart from the costs of books and writing materials, which parents had to finance, these schools were run by the clergy, and most of the boys were likely to be destined for careers in the church. Students, who had to provide their own candles in winter, had to be able to read Latin and English before they arrived. William fitz Stephen, who also attended one of these city schools, names the ones from which Gilbert and Matilda Becket would have made their choice: St. Paul's, St. Mary-le-Grand, and St. Mary-le-Bow. All were within less than half a mile of their home, and St. Mary-le-Bow was the nearest.

Once there, at whichever school they chose, Thomas would have worked to improve his Latin style and composition and studied rudimentary logic and rhetoric. Depending on his level of attainment, he may have dabbled in astronomy, arithmetic, geometry, and music, although the level to which these were taken depended entirely on the pupils and the school. For middle-class students like Thomas, who would sooner or later need to begin a career, rhetoric, next to grammar and logic, was the most important subject and the cornerstone of the liberal arts, teaching them how to read letters or official documents critically and structure their responses; how to master the relevant arguments; and how to speak clearly and persuasively in public.

When Thomas learned to write is harder to judge. Writing with a quill pen on parchment, or with a stylus or sharp dry point on wooden writing tablets overlaid with colored wax, is unlikely to have been taught to pupils at Merton priory, but it may have been taught to abler pupils at a grammar school. That said, the usual way of putting words into writing while Thomas was alive was by dictating them to a professional scribe. Composition, even for a majority of the most brilliant scholars, was the "art of dictation" and taught as a branch of rhetoric. The physical act of setting words onto parchment was regarded as a separate skill. "Reading and dictating" were coupled together, not "reading and writing." It is possible that writing was hardly taught outside the emerging universities and that Thomas would learn to write only later while studying in Paris. Practical considerations also came into play, for penmanship was a seasonal occupation, almost impossible in winter, when the ink took too long to dry. Orderic Vitalis, one of the very few chroniclers to pen his own manuscripts, points this out, saying that his fingers were once so numbed by frost, he was abandoning his narrative until the spring. When scribes and copyists sent for hot coals, it was often to warm their handiwork rather than themselves.

But somewhere, Thomas was taught how to write. He needed tools for ruling the lines: a stylus, a pencil or charcoal stick, a ruler, a plumb line, and an awl for pricking the tiny holes that a scribe made in his parchment to mark the beginning of every line. Also required was a knife or razor for scraping the parchment, pumice for cleaning and smoothing it, and a boar's or goat's tooth for polishing the surface to stop the ink from splattering. As for writing equipment, quill pens, a penknife, ink, and an inkhorn were standard. Made from the feathers of geese or ravens cut away at the tip with a penknife to make a nib, quills had to be held gingerly so as not to let them blot or scratch the parchment, which was made from sheepskin.

Once the surface of the skin had been made ready and lines ruled in pencil, beginners would be taught how to grip the pen gently while letting their hands glide easily across the page, how to keep the letters on the line, how to size the letters in proportion to one another, and how to space letters and words evenly using a cursive script. Ordinary parchment (though not the finest vellum made of calfskin, which was used by monastic scribes) was relatively cheap, but students tended not to work on it. Instead, they took notes with a stylus on wax tablets, which was faster and easier and could be done in the rain, or even on horseback. It was even possible for students to buy ready-made tablets that folded into a diptych and were worn on a belt. When a note was required, the diptych was opened, exposing the waxed writing surfaces.

* * *

YOUNG ADOLESCENTS in London were especially privileged, enjoying unusual freedoms regardless of their position in society. Despite living in a densely packed city with its narrow streets, roaming animals (including hens and pigs), and open sewers, Londoners had access to green spaces of often Arcadian beauty, filled with trees and shrubs and belonging to religious houses or churches, while citizens of middling status like the Beckets had their own private gardens. Boys played games of bowls and quayles (*quilles* in French), in which a number of pins were set up in a line and the players had to knock them down with a stick. Blood sports involving dogs, hawks, and crossbows were strictly forbidden in the built-up area, but the city was surrounded by open fields, where the citizens enjoyed customary rights to hunt. Boys would trap rabbits, hares, and fowl in gins, snares, and nets while their fathers hunted for wild boars.

Just outside the city walls to the north lay Smithfield, where a thriving market for livestock was held on weekdays and horses were sold on Fridays. Martial exercises were integral to Anglo-Norman male bonding, and mock tournaments would be held at Smithfield every Sunday in Lent. Young riders, armed with shields and lances and divided into teams, would engage in sham combat during those tournaments. On Midsummer Day, teenage boys would wrestle, fence, and shoot with bows and arrows, while their sisters would dance to music until long after midnight, rattling their tambourines. Common throughout the year were horse races for boys, in which two or three galloped around an improvised course. Later in life, Thomas Becket would be regarded as an accomplished horseman, and it was at Smithfield that he first learned to ride.

Nearby lay Moorfields, a marshy area liable to flooding, used in summer for archery and field sports and in winter for skating. Boys would fasten rough skates made from the leg bones of animals to their feet, then using poles shod with iron propel themselves forward at high speed across the ice, tilting at one another until arms or legs were broken. To the northwest lay the fields and springs of Holywell, Clerkenwell, and Finsbury, where elms and reeds and willows grew in abundance. The ground began to rise gently at Clerkenwell, and on a warm summer evening the citizens and their families would go for country walks there and enjoy the panoramic view across the city.

On Easter Day, water sports took place on the Thames. Adolescent males in boats attempted to strike with their lances at targets fixed to a mast set up in the middle of the river without toppling overboard. Then there was a water tournament in which the combatants, playing at knights armed with shields and staves, tilted at each other in boats. On the mornings of saints' days and other religious festivals, miracle plays based on Bible stories or the legends of saints were performed in the city's parish churches. Acted by schoolboys or choristers, who took both male and female parts, the plays generally lasted until noon, after which everyone flocked outdoors to enjoy games of football, the favorite sport of schoolboys. Not yet an orderly game with rules or a fixed number of players, it involved a violent struggle between opposing teams regardless of who had possession of the ball. Played mainly in the summer months, it gave way in winter to bloody bull- and bearbaiting, both of which regularly drew large, excited crowds. Other cruel sports included pitting wild boars and fighting dogs against each other while bets were taken. Children tied cocks by their legs to a post and threw sticks at them, while on Shrove Tuesday, grammar school boys like Thomas were allowed to bring their own fighting cocks to school.

The school day began shortly after dawn and could last for up to twelve hours, depending on the season. Midday meals were not provided, but just downstream of London Bridge was a row of cookshops, the precursors of modern takeaways, where every kind of food—fish, meat, game, or fowl—could be roasted, baked, fried, or boiled to order. Customers, regardless of age or social status, could eat and mingle freely there, finding dishes to suit every taste and pocket. "Gourmets," says William fitz Stephen, who had obviously eaten there many times himself, "who have a mind to indulge, need not hanker after a sturgeon, a guinea fowl, or a woodcock." There were, however, the usual health hazards. Customers ordering meat pies, in particular, were vulnerable to random attacks of food poisoning.

From a relatively early age, Thomas Becket had a digestive ailment. This first came to light when he was forced to take care with what he drank. The wrong drink could trigger a bad reaction, and a groom named Jordan would later remember an incident at Croydon in which he had been forced to scour the district to find supplies of whey for Thomas to drink. Whey, the watery part of milk left behind after the separation of the curd in cheese making, was considered to be a woman's drink. So was mead, a low-alcohol drink made from fermenting water and honey, said to have medicinal and therapeutic value. Londoners of all ages preferred alcoholic drinks to river water for health reasons, not least because the city's public latrines, even in Roman times, drained directly into the Thames. Men's drinks were traditionally beer and wine. Claret, popular with courtiers and the richer merchants, was made by mixing wine with a little honey and spices that had been ground to a fine powder and sealed in a linen bag, which was removed before the drink was served. As an adult, Thomas Becket drank cider rarely and wine only in moderation. More usually, it seems, he drank beer or wine diluted with a little water. But even these could upset his stomach if he was under pressure.

ABOUT THE TIME that he reached the age of puberty, Thomas was introduced to someone leading a very different lifestyle than a London merchant's son. Richer de l'Aigle, a Norman aristocrat, made several visits to the city to see to his business affairs, lodging at Gilbert Becket's house. Already in his mid- to late thirties, Richer was the older brother of Geoffrey de l'Aigle, who had clung for his life to a spar when the *White Ship* capsized before succumbing to hypothermia and drowning. Since his ancestral estates had long included lands to the north and south of Thierville, near Bec Abbey, his father may have known Thomas's grandfather. A fascinating character, he turns up regularly in the sources as an adventurer—brave, bold, and unpredictably dangerous.

That Richer played for high stakes had been proved two years before the *White Ship* had sailed, when he inherited the honor of Pevensey in Sussex from his father. The site where William the Conqueror had landed with his army in 1066, it included the ruins of an old Roman fort, within which a fine Norman castle with a great square keep and a nearly impregnable gatehouse had been built. When King Henry had announced that he wanted Richer's two younger brothers to share their father's English lands because they served in the royal guard, Richer defied him and made overtures to Henry's dynastic archrival, the Capetian ruler Louis VI of France. Always eager to woo Henry's malcontents, Louis provided Richer with a crack force of sixty knights to garrison his ancestral castle in Normandy, a gesture pitched exactly right to bring Henry to the negotiating table without turning him so violently against Richer that he would seek to destroy him. After a parley, the knights returned to France, but the following year Richer went on the rampage, terrorizing his neighbors and laying waste their lands. Finally, a settlement was brokered by Count Rotrou of La Perche, Richer's uncle on his mother's side and husband to one of the king's biological daughters who afterward lost her life on the *White Ship*. By its terms, Richer's inheritance would be upheld. Thereafter, he would be the living proof that revolt or resistance to the king could sometimes pay dividends in the Anglo-Norman world, but only if you were enough of a gambler and kept your nerve.

Thomas was dazzled by Richer, whose father had been a prominent courtier and who clearly conversed with kings and princes as easily as with his own Norman friends. They went out hawking and hunting together during his school holidays, staying for one whole summer at Richer's castle at Pevensey, where they rode daily to the chase with hounds and hawks. At ease in the streets of London, Thomas was suddenly brought face-to-face with the reality of power and might—this really was another world for the young Londoner. Even now, nine hundred years later, the ruins of Pevensey Castle dominate the gentle Sussex countryside and the small town that has grown up close by. The stone circuit wall around the castle's inner bailey, with its three majestic round towers, had not yet been built, but the Norman keep where Thomas would have lodged, now the home of birds that peer down inquisitively on the visitors below, would have been buzzing with life, with horses being led in and out of the stables, the fires of blacksmiths and armorers blazing beside an old Roman bastion, and the sun flashing on the weapons of Richer's retainers, all amid the chatter of the falconers and servants.

Soon falconry would become one of Thomas's chief pleasures; later in his career he would be renowned for his mews, where the birds were kept. So expensive was falconry that nothing signaled a person's high status more than the sight of a hawk, with its leather hood on, perching on the owner's glove, and Thomas was seduced by the sense of power that the sport gave him. While in Richer's company, he would sample for the first time the recreations of the aristocracy and learn to enjoy and appreciate them. Fit and athletic, he had already found his aptitude for riding and martial exercises on the fields at Smithfield. Said as late as his mid-thirties to be slim and lithe, supple as a willow, he would also one day acquire a reputation as a champion wrestler and fencer, sports that Richer may have taught him too.

In exile after his sudden flight from England in 1164, Thomas would tell his followers of an accident he had suffered while riding out one day through the Sussex countryside with Richer. One version of the anecdote is that his horse lost its footing while taking a shortcut across a narrow footbridge above a millstream that his companion had passed in safety. Both horse and rider toppled into the roaring current and were swept toward the mill, where they could have been crushed. A slightly different version has Thomas carrying a prize hawk on his wrist when his horse stumbled. Falling into the water, the bird somehow became trapped, and it was through diving in to save its life that he was carried away. In each retelling, the mill wheel stops just in time. But whereas in the second version it stops spontaneously, in the first the miller intervenes. Either way, Becket had the narrowest of escapes, and the tale provides a graphic illustration of his adolescent recklessness.

What the sources fail to encompass is the nature of Richer's affection for this impressionable teenager. Did their friendship become too intense? A tantalizing question also arises about just how and when it began. Robert of Cricklade, prior of St. Frideswide's Oxford, whose biography of Thomas was completed in 1173–74—two or three years after the bad leg he had acquired on a pilgrimage to Sicily was providentially cured following a visit to the murdered archbishop's tomb—says that Becket formally entered Richer's household as the elder man's secretary after leaving his grammar school, rather than meeting him during his school holidays. Gilbert Becket and Richer, says Robert, had been "fast friends and fellows" for years and one day agreed that "Thomas should betake himself away and become Richer's secretary." It was thus as Richer's protégé that Thomas "cometh for the first time into the king's court and amid courtly manners."

But if this is correct, and Thomas was indeed introduced into Richer's more glamorous adult circle, mingling with the great and the good at this early point in his life, things did not work out. Someone, most likely his mother, intervened and sent her son off to Paris to continue his education in the "schools" there, even though there is no evidence that he had any ambition or desire of his own to pursue his studies at a higher level. Clearly troubled by Thomas's vulnerability to an older man's subversive influence, Prior Robert chooses his words with studied ambiguity, saying that in Richer's company, "the world offered him her sweetness somewhat more freely than before," but that he remained "of pure conversation in all things on which there lieth most."

As significant a hint as one can expect from a man writing the biography of a canonized saint, this observation is highly suggestive. We will never know for sure what happened in Becket's adolescent relationship with Richer, but it is entirely possible that his mother, worried that their friendship was becoming too intimate, stepped in to separate them. By the time she did so, however, dramatic events were taking place in London and England that were fast spiraling the city and the country into chaos. It may have been as much to escape danger as to escape Richer that Matilda Becket sent her son to Paris, since at least he would be safe there.

3
POLITICS

UNTIL HE LOST HIS ONLY LEGITIMATE SON AND HEIR IN THE wreck of the *White Ship,* King Henry I seemed to be a born leader. Physically resembling his father, William the Conqueror, he was of medium height with bright eyes, receding black hair, a stocky physique, and a tendency to put on weight. He was intelligent and high-spirited, and while his acts of cruelty are alien to modern ethical standards, they were generally praised in his own lifetime as evidence of his determination to inflict just and summary penalties on evildoers. Unusually for a medieval king, he was abstemious except where women were concerned, avoiding excess and reducing the number of large, formal meals at court each day from two to one. Said to be eloquent and witty, he was a barely competent reader, but that still made him the first English king since Alfred the Great to be literate. Possessed of a didactic turn of mind that could provoke his younger courtiers to mock him behind his back, he was fully aware of the growing importance of charters and written documents as tools of government, once remarking in his father's hearing that "an illiterate king is a crowned ass."

Aiming to safeguard his father's inheritance on both sides of the Channel by whatever steps were necessary, Henry would for much of his reign achieve more raw, centralized power in his kingdom of England than anything seen since 1066, building on his father's achievements and making the greatest strides in the fields of royal justice and finance. But the inescapable fact is that he had come to power as a usurper, and that would return to haunt him.

William the Conqueror's principal legacy had been a transfer of landownership from the English to the Normans and a system of military feudalism in which every great lord was equipped with his own power and jurisdiction. The essence of feudalism was lordship. Lords and tenants bound themselves to each other in a hierarchy culminating in the king as overlord. Some two hundred Norman barons had displaced four thousand English thegns as the king's tenants in chief. According to Domesday Book, the comprehensive census of landholding compiled on William's orders in 1086, some thirty of these barons held more than a third of the land in terms of value, whereas less than one percent of the Old English population retained their pre-Conquest estates. Methods of agriculture would continue almost unchanged after the Conquest. The difference was that power was monopolized by the chosen few. King William's ability to inspire his followers and lead them to a glorious victory had enabled him to stamp his authority on them, but in the longer term his short temper, avarice, and intolerance would prove counterproductive. As his own reign progressed, Henry I would discover that he could rule England more effectively by surrounding himself with capable and well-educated advisers whom he trusted and by handling the leading barons tactfully.

One of his Achilles' heels would be his difficulties with the church, to which his father had made generous concessions. About 1072, William had issued a writ prohibiting "any matter which concerns the rule of souls" from being heard in the secular courts, reserving it for adjudication by churchmen in church courts in accordance with up-to-date church law and procedure. Keen to win a reputation for piety and as a patron and protector of the church, William had judged the two ancient provinces of the English church, Canterbury and York, to be backward and immoral. A high proportion of the parochial clergy, and even some bishops and archdeacons, were married or lived openly with their mistresses; almost as many were said to have purchased their livings and then treated them as sinecures or appointed their relatives to them, an offense known as "simony." Advised by his Norman bishops, William took as his benchmark the standards of the continental reformers, who had the moral regeneration of the whole church firmly in their sights.

These reformers, such as the great Cluniac abbot St. Hugh and St. Peter Damian, were motivated by ascetic ideals and had won over Pope Leo IX and several of his successors to their cause. Denouncing clerical marriage and simony as crimes against God, they demanded that the clergy be celibate and free from sin. William the Conqueror had at first cooperated with the pope, who in return for Norman support against his enemies in Italy had wholeheartedly backed William's invasion of England and enabled him to market himself as the agent of enlightened church reforms against the barbarians. He had also worked closely with Lanfranc, prior of Bec Abbey near Gilbert Becket's family home in Normandy, a moderate reformer whom he trusted and made archbishop of Canterbury. But growing fat and more dictatorial in his declining years, William had drawn a line in the sand, refusing to do fealty to the papacy when it was demanded and clamping down on contacts between England and the papal curia.

His change of attitude had followed hard on the election at Rome in 1073 of Gregory VII, a zealously reforming pope who sought to redefine his relations with the Christian community and so centralize his power. The key question was how far kings and princes would cooperate with the ascetic reformers. In an uncompromising effort to stamp his own authority on the secular kingdoms, Pope Gregory had pronounced a decree against "lay investiture"—the old custom whereby a king handed to a newly appointed bishop his ring and pastoral staff to signify that the king had appointed the bishop to the post. In response to the papal decree, William had attacked what he saw as blatant interference in his realms, but it would be only after his death, when the amenable Lanfranc was succeeded as primate by the saintly, steely Anselm, a reformer who had also made his reputation as a monk and later abbot of Bec, that a rift between the Anglo-Norman monarchy and the church reformers became inevitable.

ON HIS DEATHBED, William partitioned his territories, bequeathing Normandy to Robert Curthose, his eldest son, and England to William

Rufus, his second and favorite son. For his youngest son, Henry, there had been only a large sum of money, sowing the seeds of all that was to come. Little love had existed among the three brothers since an incident in late 1077 or early 1078, when Robert was in his late twenties and Henry only eight or nine. On that occasion, Henry and Rufus, "deeming their strength equal to that of their elder brother Robert," had urinated on him from the upper gallery of a manor house in Normandy, humiliating him in the presence of his followers. After his father's death, Rufus had swiftly laid claim to Normandy as well as England, while Henry—like an experienced cardsharp—had played his siblings off against each other, determined to carve out an inheritance for himself in either of their dominions and conquer the rest if he could.

Thoroughly incompetent as Duke of Normandy, where he was idle and overgenerous to his supporters until their insolence knew no bounds, Robert Curthose had ignored the danger signals, allowing Rufus to incite his barons to revolt. So ineffective was Robert, he sometimes found he could not even dress in the mornings, because his servants had run away with his clothes. Soon his garrisons had been expelled from his castles, and plunder became the order of the day. Using a mixture of English silver and diplomacy, Rufus had overrun the Norman strongholds one by one until he was the master of the lion's share of the duchy. When in 1091 he had invaded Normandy, his brother rallied his forces, but it was too late to turn the tide. Five years later, Robert had opted out, answering Pope Urban II's call to join the First Crusade against the Muslims and pawning Normandy to Rufus in exchange for 10,000 silver marks, the equivalent of almost £4 million today, before leaving for the East.

With England and Normandy reunited, Rufus had set about governing his empire in the way he knew best. A coarse, boorish man, effeminate and licentious, probably bisexual and much criticized by monks for his lax morals and long hair, he had ruthlessly milked what he believed to be his royal prerogatives over the church using his trusted agent, Ranulf Flambard, a lowborn clerk whom he made his chaplain and the keeper of his seal, eventually giving him the bishopric of Durham. Astute, arrogant, ambitious, and greedy, Flambard had taxed and robbed the church, keeping bishoprics and abbeys vacant so he could seize their revenues, until Anselm, who had arrived at Canterbury in 1093, rose up in protest, calling him "not just a bandit, but the most infamous prince of bandits."

At the Council of Rockingham in 1095, Anselm had asked the question that, under William the Conqueror, Lanfranc had never dared to ask. Addressing the assembled bishops and barons, he had demanded whether the duty he owed to the pope was compatible with the obedience he owed to the king. The issue was explosive, since a Norman bishop gave homage and an oath of fealty to the king. An eager convert to the higher principles of moral regeneration in the church as preached by the ascetic reformers, the new archbishop had also fiercely defended his obligation to visit Rome and the church's right to manage its own affairs without royal interference.

Unable to endure Flambard's plundering of his beloved church any longer, Anselm had set sail from Dover in 1097 and gone into exile at Rome. Lodging at the main papal residence at the Lateran, the seat of papal government throughout the Middle Ages, he was given a place of honor at church councils in which strict reforming decrees were enacted against simony, clerical marriage, and lay investiture. Inspired by his example, Thomas Becket would one day seek Anselm's canonization before he himself chose exile as a platform for his own aims. But whereas his predecessor had interpreted his role as fundamentally pastoral and had merely sought to dissociate himself morally from the king's evil deeds, Becket would seek to rectify them.

On Thursday, August 2, 1100, while out hunting in the New Forest, Rufus had been struck in the chest by an arrow intended for a stag. Falling forward to the ground, he drove the arrow through his body and died instantly. His highborn companions galloped off to safeguard their own interests, leaving his body unattended until some of his humbler servants threw a rough cloth over it and loaded it, "like a wild boar stuck with spears," onto a farm cart for burial.

Among those racing off was the king's younger brother, Henry, who dashed to Winchester to seize the castle and the royal treasury and proclaim himself king before Robert Curthose, now on his way home from his triumphs in the East, where his forces had played a leading part in the capture of Jerusalem, could do the same. Neither his prompt actions nor those of his associates suggest foreknowledge of the event, but the cloud of suspicion has never been entirely dispelled. To help win baronial consent to his accession as king of England, Henry sent Flambard to be imprisoned in the Tower of London and recalled Anselm, but he immediately quarreled with Anselm over whether the archbishop should give the king fealty.

The end result was a compromise, supported by the pope, whereby Henry agreed to recognize a clear demarcation between the functions of the bishops and abbots as feudal barons and as spiritual leaders. He could continue to receive their homage and oath of fealty for their temporal lands, but he must no longer appoint them or invest them with the symbols of their spiritual office. It was a major victory for Anselm, creating what was intended to become a Chinese wall separating the bishops' roles as feudal magnates from their duties as pastors. Naturally, this left a king as strong willed as Henry free to continue to browbeat the cathedral or monastic chapters into electing his nominees, since he could sequester their property and enjoy the profits for as long as they resisted his suggestions. But the ascetic reformers had vindicated the principle that lay investiture was illegal.

ROBERT CURTHOSE, meanwhile, had returned home to his duchy of Normandy, basking in the glory he had earned in the siege of Jerusalem and accompanied by a rich widow he had married while wintering on his journey home. Henry had to prepare to meet the inevitable invasion, since his brother had no intention of allowing his own claim to the throne to lapse. Secretly aided by Flambard, who had escaped from the Tower of London to Normandy by climbing down a rope after throwing a drunken party for his jailers, Robert had assembled a fleet and landed at Portsmouth in July 1101, wrong-footing Henry, who lay encamped between Hastings and Pevensey.

After hopelessly botching his campaign, Robert had agreed to a truce, enabling Henry to begin his preparations to conquer Normandy, first suborning his brother's barons with English silver as Rufus had done, then stirring up revolt throughout the duchy. After landing unopposed at Barfleur in April 1105, he had turned Bayeux into a blazing inferno and captured Caen. Returning the following year, he had destroyed the fortified abbey of Saint-Pierre-sur-Dives, near Falaise, before marching his army southward to Tinchebrai, where in a final, desperate throw of the dice, Robert had hurled everything he had left against Henry and was resoundingly defeated.

Captured alive on the battlefield, Robert had been sent to England, where he was imprisoned for twenty-eight years until his death. Henry had then begun a long, grueling slog, lasting some ten years, to recover the ducal castles, wresting them from their lawful occupants by fair means or foul. During these years, Robert's young son, William Clito, assumed his father's mantle, appealing for aid to King Louis VI of France and his chief ally, Count Fulk V of Anjou, and dragging Henry into a long guerrilla war. Clito's tactics were especially threatening, since Normandy's feudal subordination to the French monarchy went back to the days of Count Rollo and was a complex, long-standing bone of contention. The French king was the duke's feudal overlord, even if, after 1066, successive dukes other than Robert Curthose had avoided giving homage to him on the grounds that they were also anointed kings of England.

With King Louis posturing as Clito's protector, the battle for Normandy had come to center on the Vexin, the gateway from France into the eastern side of the duchy. Pointing like a dagger toward Paris itself, the Vexin was divided into a French zone (lying between the rivers Epte and Oise) and a Norman zone (between the Andelle and the Epte). Beyond this, no clear frontier existed, and in his final war William the Conqueror had been fatally wounded at Mantes while riding through the burning streets of the town in an effort to annex the French zone. Fighting between 1111 and 1116 would prove inconclusive, but in 1118 Louis led an army into Normandy from the east, while in a classic pincer movement Count Fulk besieged Alençon in the south. Driven to fight on two fronts, Henry was made more vulnerable by the death of his wife, Queen Matilda, who had been regent in England while he was campaigning.

These were the circumstances in which Henry had pulled off his greatest masterstroke, negotiating a dynastic marriage between his son Prince William and Count Fulk's daughter, for which the bride's dowry would be the disputed county of Maine, the gateway into Normandy from the south. Fulk made peace with Henry, after which Louis and Henry wreaked fire and slaughter on each other, destroying castles, towns, and churches and pillaging the goods of their enemies. Henry triumphed in a pitched battle but barely escaped with his life, when a sword pierced his helmet and drew blood. After a failed assassination plot in which he blinded and castrated the ringleader, a treacherous royal chamberlain, he began wearing his weapons indoors, sleeping with a sword and a shield beside his bed.

Prince William would marry Count Fulk's daughter just eighteen months before the *White Ship* began its fateful voyage. Immediately after the knot was tied, he would be acclaimed as Henry's successor by all the barons of England and Normandy, ending the war and leaving only King Louis to satisfy. This last piece of diplomacy would be overseen by Pope Calixtus II, who had arrived in France for a church council. After lengthy discussions and an interview at which Henry would humbly prostrate himself while carefully avoiding any recognition of the pope's claims to dictate the affairs of the English church, a peace was concluded. Louis and Henry settled their quarrel concerning the French king's right to feudal overlordship of Normandy by granting the duchy to William, who did homage to Louis, so binding him to Henry's succession plan without binding Henry to him.

The treaty, ratified by papal nominees in May 1120, enabled England and Normandy to be officially reunited and the issue of the feudal superiority of France over Normandy to be resolved—so long as William stayed alive. The sinking of the *White Ship* would shatter these hopes. Far more than just a family tragedy, it was a political catastrophe, a devastating blow, because William's drowning meant it would be only a matter of time before Louis and Count Fulk resumed their old alliance and Normandy was convulsed by rebellion again.

STILL IN HIS early fifties when he lost his son, Henry was young enough to have many more children. After consulting his advisers, he quickly announced his betrothal to Adeliza, the young and beautiful daughter of Duke Godfrey of Lorraine. Celebrated with pomp and pageantry on January 29, 1121, at Windsor Castle, the nuptials were followed by Adeliza's coronation the next day. But the couple were destined to be childless. Over the next three years, with his hopes that Adeliza would give birth to a son gradually diminishing, Henry spent heavily on mercenaries, castle building, and diplomacy in Normandy, aiming to wear down Clito and his supporters by a mixture of carrot and stick and to keep the French at arm's length.

Then, at his Christmas court at Windsor in 1126, he announced a new dynastic alliance between his only legitimate daughter, Matilda, the widow of the German emperor Henry V, who had died the previous year, and Geoffrey of Anjou, Count Fulk's son and heir. So desperate was Henry in his efforts to repeat his earlier tactics of isolating King Louis from his old ally that he crafted his new succession policy entirely around this alliance. On January 1, 1127, after moving his whole court to Westminster in readiness, he designated Matilda as his lawful heir and successor in England and Normandy and forced all the bishops and barons to swear oaths of fealty to her. She married the fourteen-year-old Geoffrey at Le Mans eighteen months later, leaving Count Fulk to honor his side of the bargain by granting Anjou and its dependencies to his son and taking himself off to the Holy Land to marry the heiress of the Latin kingdom of Jerusalem, never to return.

Matilda was a decidedly reluctant bride, and her nomination as Henry's successor would prove to be bitterly divisive. It had the effect of forcing even the most obedient magnates to doubt his wisdom, since in a deeply patriarchal society few could accept that a woman might rule unless her husband also became king. And Henry would allow his son-in-law's position to remain dangerously ambiguous. No oaths were taken to him or financial provision made. Eleven years younger than his bride, the teenage Count of Anjou was an arrogant schemer, a chancer who antagonized his superiors and despised his inferiors, making no secret of his belief that it was his birthright to rule over them.

Soon the ill-matched couple were quarreling violently, and when at last they were reconciled, Geoffrey's clumsy attempts to seize control of the castles of southern Normandy would create a rift and lead eventually to outright war with his father-in-law. As his reign drew to its close, Henry himself would come to wonder whether the marriage had been a mistake and would increasingly place all his hopes on the birth of grandchildren. The omens were bad, and during his final months, which he spent mainly hunting in Normandy, the chroniclers would record an eclipse of the sun, an earthquake, and violent winds, all occurring within a few weeks, which they would interpret as a stark warning of evil times to come.

WHEN HENRY DIED on December 1, 1135, on the eve of a hunting expedition in the forest of Lyons near Rouen, Thomas Becket was just three weeks short of his fifteenth birthday. The world as he knew it was about to be turned upside down by the fallout from the dead king's long struggle to secure the succession for his own bloodline. Much of this turmoil would be caused by the ambition of someone who had narrowly escaped the disaster of the *White Ship*. A few minutes before the doomed vessel had set sail, a dozen or so passengers had disembarked, among them two monks of Tiron Abbey and Henry's nephew Stephen, son of Adela, William the Conqueror's daughter. Stephen, as Orderic Vitalis laconically records, "was suffering from diarrhea." A stickler for politeness, he had urgently needed privacy, unobtainable amid the drunken revelry on board. He had decided to leave, perhaps also scandalized by the sacrilege of a group of "riotous and headstrong youths," who mocked and jeered at the priests bringing holy water to bless the vessel as the final preparations for departure were made.

Stephen's diarrhea was to change the course of history. A principal beneficiary of Henry's policy of generosity to nobles and kinsmen he felt he could trust, Stephen came to enjoy a princely inheritance in England and Normandy. At the ceremony at which Henry had attempted to resolve the succession crisis by naming his daughter Matilda as his heir, Stephen had vied with Robert, Earl of Gloucester, the king's eldest and favorite illegitimate son, for the honor of being the first of the lay magnates to take his oath to her, a contest that he won.

An oath took Matilda's claim to the succession to a much higher, spiritual plane. Regarded as sacred promises to God, oaths bound those who took them unconditionally. To break one was to commit perjury, for which the penalty was eternal damnation. By invoking God as his witness and by swearing upon the Gospels or the relics of a saint, Stephen made a holy promise to acknowledge Matilda as Henry's successor. If he reneged on his commitment, he could be excommunicated by the pope, or an interdict could be placed on his lands until he saw the error of his ways and made the appropriate spiritual and material reparations. The consequences of this oath, and of Stephen's eventual perjury, would be momentous. They did not simply jinx Henry's succession plan during his lifetime; they precipitated a long, vicious civil war after his death.

4
PARIS

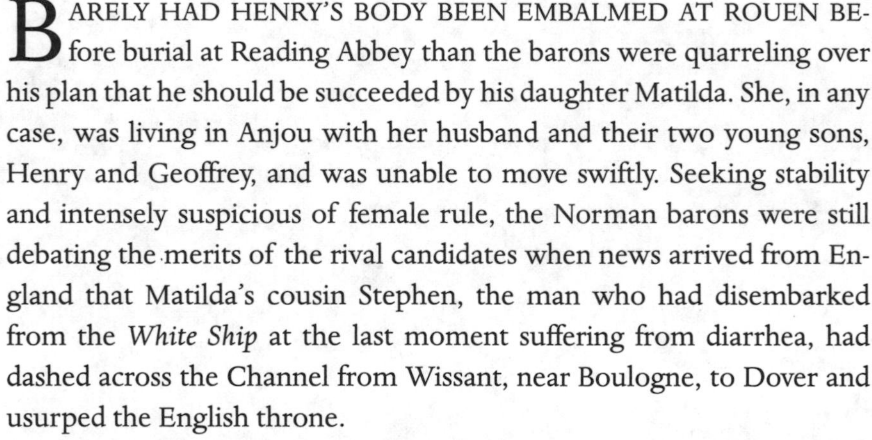

BARELY HAD HENRY'S BODY BEEN EMBALMED AT ROUEN BEfore burial at Reading Abbey than the barons were quarreling over his plan that he should be succeeded by his daughter Matilda. She, in any case, was living in Anjou with her husband and their two young sons, Henry and Geoffrey, and was unable to move swiftly. Seeking stability and intensely suspicious of female rule, the Norman barons were still debating the merits of the rival candidates when news arrived from England that Matilda's cousin Stephen, the man who had disembarked from the *White Ship* at the last moment suffering from diarrhea, had dashed across the Channel from Wissant, near Boulogne, to Dover and usurped the English throne.

Landing in Kent, Stephen had ridden at high speed to London, where his supporters convened a mass meeting of the citizens to "elect" him as king, saying that the kingdom was in danger "when a representative of the whole government and a fount of justice were lacking." "Peace" and "justice" were the slogans used by Stephen's faction, and if the author of the eyewitness chronicle known as the *Gesta Stephani* can be believed, the Londoners were "persuaded" by a mixture of bribes and threats to choose a king who would "make it worth their while."

Crowned in a great hurry at Westminster Abbey, Stephen shrewdly courted popularity by issuing a charter of liberties promising to respect all the laws and customs of the realm in force since the time of King Edward the Confessor. He had broken his oath to Matilda after Hugh

Bigod, the old king's steward and the most powerful baron in East Anglia, swore that her father had disinherited her on his deathbed. Armed with this highly spurious testimony, Stephen's brother Bishop Henry of Winchester had played the kingmaker, tricking the magnates into believing that their own oaths to Matilda could be safely ignored too, and brokering a deal with his fellow bishops by which his brother, once he had been crowned, would grant a second charter at Oxford in the church's favor as a reward for their support.

But for all his energy and skill in capturing the crown, Stephen lacked the vision and the leadership skills to succeed. A period of risk, passion, argument, and hope, his disputed reign quickly descended into failure. Many of his limitations were personal. Outwardly seeming to be generous and brave, smooth and ingratiating, and capable of intense activity, inwardly he was cunning, mistrustful, and of weak judgment. A stickler for protocol, valuing appearances over substance, he was a man too easily seduced by the trappings of power to recognize in time that England was only one part of the Anglo-Norman state.

The church alone profited from Stephen's usurpation, and then only at first. His Oxford charter, granted in 1136, conceded that "justice and power over all ecclesiastical persons and all clerics and their possessions, and over all ecclesiastical appointments, shall be in the hands of the bishops." That, taken at face value, was a step change, for it seemed to guarantee that the church would be free to manage its own affairs as never before. New prelates could be chosen without royal interference and would perform no act of fealty even for their lands. Restrictions on appeals to Rome were to be lifted, church councils could be summoned without royal consent, and restrictions on journeys to Rome were to be suspended so that the English bishops could travel freely to meet the pope. Or so it seemed at the time.

Stephen's honeymoon as king was brief. With Matilda and her scheming husband, Count Geoffrey of Anjou, resettling in Normandy, the rival claimants would pit the leading baronial families against one another. And by allowing the Norman insurgency to run free for fifteen months, Stephen found that when he finally returned across the Channel with an army of Flemish mercenaries, he had lost too much ground. Holding the balance of power was Robert, Earl of Gloucester, Matilda's half brother, with whom Stephen had vied for the honor of being first to take his oath to the future queen. Robert was still wavering in his support, deciding whose claim to recognize, but when Stephen clumsily attempted to assassinate him, he made his choice and backed his sister.

By the summer of 1138, when Thomas Becket was staying with Richer de l'Aigle at his castle at Pevensey and out hunting and hawking with him every day, the struggle came to focus on Stephen's perjury in reneging on his oath to Matilda. While Stephen did not deny he had taken the oath, he claimed it had been exacted by force and was, in any case, conditional. He had promised only (as he maintained) to uphold Matilda's right "to the best of his ability unless his father changed his mind and named another heir," which Hugh Bigod swore he had. To deflect attention from his perjury, Stephen spread lies that Matilda was illegitimate by canon law, saying that her mother had been dragged from the nunneries of Romsey and Wilton and forced to break a vow of chastity, whereas in reality she had merely been educated there, wearing a veil only to protect herself "from the lust of the Normans," covering her head appropriately "with a little black hood."

With her half brother Robert's support, Matilda appealed to the pope to intervene and enforce the oath. Stephen's utterly disastrous response, beginning in June 1139, was a series of dramatic maneuvers designed to sweep away most of Henry I's old officials in favor of his own friends and supporters. To this end, he purged from his court and government all those bishops and bureaucrats who he felt might oppose him—notably Bishop Roger of Salisbury, who for almost thirty years had served as a chief minister and royal troubleshooter—looting their treasure and confiscating their castles. In so doing, he unleashed a civil war.

BY THEN, just a few months before his nineteenth birthday, Thomas Becket had been sent to Paris by his worried mother, joining his fellow students from all over western Christendom in one of the most glamorous and cosmopolitan cities in Europe. Not yet a university in the accepted sense of the word, the loose collection of individual masters and students clustering around "schools," or centers of learning, within the city and its suburbs had lately established itself at the top of the ivy league. The nearby schools of Chartres, Laon, and Rheims were less fashionable; only those of Bologna and Salerno were equally distinguished, and at Bologna the main subject of study was law, which was not what Thomas had chosen to read. While he was in Paris, around twenty-five hundred students were living in the city or its environs, slightly over one-tenth of the urban population. But whatever his mother had originally planned for him, the main reason he wanted to be there was to enjoy himself, for Paris boasted an idyllic setting on the banks of the Seine and had a vibrant social scene. Restored once more to its former glory by the Capetian kings after centuries of relative neglect, the city was able to offer its students the luxuries and amenities that few others besides Florence or Venice could rival.

The ancient core of the metropolis was the Île de la Cité, an island in the middle of the Seine connected to the farther banks by two stone bridges and dominated by two quarters: that of the archbishop of Paris at the eastern end, including the old basilica of Notre-Dame, where the most respected of the schools was located; and that of the king at the western end, near the modern Palais de Justice. Both king and archbishop had their sprawling palaces, courtyards, and walled gardens. In between were crammed the houses of wealthy citizens, taverns and lodgings for students, and churches large and small—several with cloisters, most with towers, their bells vying with one another to be heard amid the constant bustle and rattling of carts. Not all was an earthly paradise on the Île de la Cité, since the citizens complained of excessive tolls for carrying goods across the bridges and of noxious smells from household waste and from roving goats and pigs. The old Roman paving stones were pitted with potholes in which water and refuse collected, and most of the city walls had either collapsed or been cut away to create new wharfs and quays. But amid the squalor was also great wealth and luxury. Slow, flat-bottomed barges pulled by horses or mules delivered merchandise to the city along the Seine from Mantes and Rouen, including textiles, spices, livestock, grain, salt, wax, and wine. Otherwise the river traffic included fish wherries, ferryboats, and occasionally pleasure boats.

In the evenings, students could gather together to discuss their lectures or to drink in the taverns (colloquially known as the "devil's monasteries"), where wine was served by the pot. If contemporary satirists are to be believed, sex was often on their minds and might readily be found in the taverns or outside the city walls, where women called *fillettes* loitered at night. One of Becket's sternest critics in later life, Peter of Celle, abbot of Saint-Rémi at Rheims, who was a student in Paris at more or less the same time, alludes to the dangers and temptations: "O Paris, how fit you are for seizing and ensnaring souls! In you there are nets of vices, in you the snares of evils, in you the arrow of hell transfixes the hearts of the foolish." The city, Peter warned, was a "place of delights," where "pleasures abound in excess, where there is a wealth of bread and wine." Quite so, but when he spoke of "pleasures" and "nets of vices," the chances are he was thinking of something other than food and drink.

Situated on the more rustic left bank of the Seine, the newest of the schools had recently overflowed into a building adjacent to the Augustinian abbey of Saint-Victor, just to the east of the city walls, before spilling out into the hilly suburb surrounding the abbey of Sainte-Geneviève. With the advantage that they were exempt from the archbishop's jurisdiction, inspirational teachers such as Peter Abelard could debate challenging new ideas here. In Abelard's case, this also meant that his career as a master could briefly survive the scandal of his forbidden love for one of his private women pupils, the beautiful and learned Héloïse, a love for which he paid a high price when she became pregnant with his child. After her baby was born, her uncle, who had already caught the couple in bed together, took a terrible revenge on him by having his servants enter Abelard's room at night and castrate him.

HARDLY ANY OF Thomas's friends while he was a student can be positively identified, perhaps because he tended to be on the defensive with strangers and was known as a bit of a loner. Everlin, later abbot of the monastery of St. Laurence at Liège, would dedicate an altar to him after his murder in memory of their old comradeship in Paris. A minor German chronicler says that Ludolf, later archbishop of Magdeburg, was his pupil, but since Thomas never rose to become a master or tutor, the chronicler may have meant to say they were fellow students. The most intellectually gifted Englishman whose student years coincided with Becket's was John of Salisbury, a man of extraordinary talents who would later become one of his most trusted and influential friends and advisers and be an eyewitness to his death.

Unlike Thomas, who was now as svelte as he was tall, John was physically small and fragile, but gregarious and warmhearted. A brilliant classical scholar and vivid raconteur, he was never happier than when making light of his own learning and gossiping to his friends over a bottle of good wine. Proficient equally in the liberal arts and theology, he would later go on to write a book called the *Policraticus* (*The Statesman*)—the most famous treatise on statecraft and politics in the Middle Ages—which he dedicated in verse to Becket, sending a presentation copy as fast as he could to his friend. Blessed with a perfect memory, John was so confident of his mastery of the classical sources that, for sheer bravado's sake, he once manufactured a supposedly long lost literary text, *The Instruction of Trajan,* which he attributed to the Greek historian Plutarch and mischievously cited in books 5 and 6 of the *Policraticus,* just to see if any of his friends would catch him out.

But although John's sojourn in Paris, which lasted up to twelve years, overlapped with Thomas's much briefer stay, the two almost certainly never met there. Despite this, they shared a deep nostalgia for Paris. Returning there in 1164, disguised as a student while making preparations for Thomas's possible flight from England, John would pen a wistful description of the city for his friend that he knew would strike a chord: "I saw such quantity of food; a people so happy; such respect for the clergy; the splendor and dignity of the whole church; the tasks so varied of the students of philosophy. I saw and marveled at it, just as Jacob marveled at the ladder whose summit reached to heaven, which was the path of angels going up and down." And ever the master of the apposite quotation, John cited Ovid: "A happy thing is exile in such a place as this."

Only by first dispelling the smoke screen created by the hagiographers can we hope to discover what Thomas may have studied in Paris and whose lectures he attended. A writer who generally sticks to the bare facts, Guernes of Pont-Sainte-Maxence, whose "life" of Thomas in Old French verse would appear some four years after Thomas's murder and who had sought out everyone he could find who had known Becket personally, reports that he studied chiefly in the arts course and not in theology. One of his masters is likely to have been Robert of Melun, an Englishman aged about forty who had studied under Hugh of Saint-Victor and briefly Abelard and had begun lecturing in 1137, when he taught dialectic to John of Salisbury. Dialectic, the art of reasoning or "disputation" by question and answer, was taught alongside rhetoric as the prelude to moral and political philosophy.

Robert was regarded as a stimulating teacher and a probing mind, even if his knowledge of Cicero—John's favorite classical author—was sparse. Since none of Robert's manuscripts survive, what he taught must be worked out from his students' notes, and if he followed the example of his own master, Hugh of Saint-Victor, he would have made sure that his ideas were recorded accurately. Only after Thomas had become thoroughly conversant with the topics is it likely that Robert allowed him to begin taking notes, and even then Robert insisted on checking his wax tablets every week. Like many teachers, he believed that his work came alive chiefly through the minds of his students and that rather than break fresh ground himself in any one branch of knowledge, his duty was to master and communicate all the various strands—theoretical, practical, logical, and philosophical—one by one in the hope of achieving a balanced and compatible knowledge of each, from which a valid worldview would emerge.

Despite his scholarly caution, Robert had an ace up his sleeve, being a rare example of a master who allowed his politics to enter the classroom. One of the earliest theorists to justify active resistance to a tyrant by the ministers of the church, he criticized the prevailing superstition of the divine-right ruler, challenging the idea that since kings and emperors ruled in the image of God, they could do no wrong and their subjects had an unwavering duty to obey them. Said to be accountable only to God, such rulers—anointed by bishops at their coronations with holy oil on their upper bodies and with chrism on the crown of their heads—claimed mystical, otherworldly powers like those of the Old Testament or Visigothic kings.

During the bitter contest over lay investiture, Pope Gregory VII had claimed that the pope alone could absolve a ruler's subjects from their allegiance, an argument Robert set out to expand on and critique. Following St. Ambrose, one of the early church fathers, he was prepared to defend active resistance to tyrants by the ministers of the church on moral grounds, claiming that a bad ruler's power comes from the devil. He offered no opinion as to the right of laymen (as opposed to priests) to resist tyrants—and Thomas had no intention yet of becoming a priest or monk. But Robert's questioning of received wisdom and his insistence that evil should not go unpunished, however powerful its perpetrators, must have made a deep impression on his young and susceptible audiences.

Other masters whose teaching may have struck a chord could not have included Abelard, who had left the schools to become a monk at the abbey of Saint-Denis immediately after the attack on him. Plausible candidates might include Master Alberic, Gilbert de La Porrée, and Robert Pullen, another Englishman. By far the likeliest, Pullen was able to weave together the most recondite passages from scripture in ingenious ways to support his arguments, a trick Becket would himself learn to master one day. Afterward rising to become a cardinal and head of the papal chancery, Pullen—an ordinary man from a humble Dorset family—must have been singularly astute, and Thomas could not have failed to marvel at how such a commoner had been able to elide seamlessly from a cathedral school in Exeter to the schools in Paris and onward to a political career. Might this perhaps explain why, later and in the very same year that Pullen gained his spectacular promotion, Thomas would himself choose to enter the household of an archbishop as a trainee clerk?

TWO YEARS AFTER Thomas had arrived in Paris, and when he was about twenty-one, a messenger came with the distressing news that his mother had died. Despite returning home at once, it is unlikely that he would have been back in time for the funeral. The best he could have hoped for was to pay his respects at her tomb and pray for her soul to the Blessed Virgin Mary as she would have wished. Rather than resuming his studies in Paris, he stayed in London and loafed about at home. Perhaps he had never intended to finish the whole arts curriculum, but only to sample as many lectures as took his fancy. Perhaps without his mother at his elbow pushing him to study, he felt he had already heard enough and decided to drop out. Or quite possibly he found it hard to concentrate in his bereavement, since his bond with his mother had been so close.

The second of these alternatives seems the likeliest. William of Canterbury says that Thomas decided to take what today would be called a gap year, while Herbert of Bosham, a genuine scholar reputed to be the finest Hebraist of the age, depicts him as foolish and vain. "He was intent," he says, "on the kinds of things that are sweet and fashionable . . . and so that he would stand out from the others, he cultivated clothes and an appearance more refined than those of others." Given the pressure to say otherwise at the time both were writing, such opinions should carry some weight.

But even had Thomas wished to continue his studies, it may have been impossible. Gilbert Becket, by now retired from his trade and living on the income from the rental properties he had accumulated over the years, had seen his wealth slowly dissipate after a series of disastrous fires. One of the worst had begun in the house of a man called Ailward near St. Swithin's Lane when Thomas was fifteen. Spreading east toward Aldgate and the Tower of London and west toward St. Paul's, it had wreaked havoc in Cheapside. Gilbert may just have been recovering from it when other, smaller fires broke out. He was forced to economize—he may even have had to withdraw his son's allowance. It cost £3–4 a year to support a student in Paris, a sum similar to the amount that could be secured in annual rent from several London properties, and that assumes Thomas was in France only to study. But Thomas loved the good things in life and was determined to enjoy himself. With Richer de l'Aigle, he had acquired tastes that his father could perhaps no longer afford, notably hunting and falconry.

And there may have been more. John of Salisbury, Becket's lifelong friend but also one of his most candid critics, says that as a younger man his character was far from blameless. He "indulged in the rakish pursuits of youth and was unduly eager to be noticed. . . . He was proud and vain, and silly enough to show the face and utter the words of lovers." All too aware of his readers' expectations after his friend's canonization by the pope, John hastily adds that "for chastity of body, on the other hand, he was admirable, indeed a model"—but unfortunately John does not specify which period in Thomas's life he is referring to. Thomas would be nearly thirty before John met him. John could not possibly have known how chaste his friend had been before then, and if, as seems likely, his "rakish pursuits" had taken place in his student days or shortly afterward, when Thomas first began to learn "worldly prudence," then a lot may have been left unsaid.

Truth and hagiography do not mix well, and Becket's student years would give his contemporary biographers considerable difficulty. Many of the less able students regarded lectures as drudgery fit only for swots. A student wag explains:

> *Learning that flowered in days of yore*
> *In these our times is thought a bore.*
> *Once knowledge was a well to drink of;*
> *Now having fun is all men think of.*

Did this sum up Thomas's outlook too? By the time he left Paris, he should have been able to debate fluently in extempore Latin, but he was embarrassed by his inability to do so. Stephen of Rouen, a monk of Bec, would gleefully mock him for such failings—except as Stephen despised Becket and all his works, the remark may have been a smear.

When it suited him to make an effort—whether in a crisis or because his career depended on it—Thomas later in life would prove that he could digest huge amounts of difficult material with remarkable speed and precision. His fellow Londoner William fitz Stephen describes him as a weak scholar in his youth, but "one of the most learned afterward." Having watched him develop intellectually after quarreling with the king, Roger of Pontigny, to whom Thomas would tell his life story in exile, concurs: "He could easily grasp anything as soon as he heard it, and once he had learned it, he could recall it without difficulty whenever and as often as he wished. In figuring out difficult ideas and disentangling perplexing questions he seemed to surpass many important and learned men with the sharpness of his fertile mind."

If we picture someone likely to become a late developer, the evidence falls into place. Becket had potential as an adolescent, but his quick ear and keen eye could not compensate for his laziness. At that stage he appears to be no more than a dilettante. Good-looking, smooth, and ingratiating, he could also be headstrong and a show-off. A Londoner born and bred, who saw the freedoms that he associated with civic life as a passport to get him from where he was to where he wanted to be, he had ambitions to put himself among the ruling class, most likely after encountering Richer de l'Aigle. In his twenties and early thirties, he would still be little more than a charmer: verging on the gauche, lacking ideals, mingling with the great and the good, imagining himself to be a young aristocrat, whereas in reality he was a newcomer and an outsider aspiring to be an insider. But somewhere along the way, he would find within himself the capacity for rigorous hard work he had always lacked. Many years would elapse between his studies in Paris and the moment when he would unlock his hidden talents, but that time was coming.

5

A FRESH START

AFTER A YEAR IN WHICH THOMAS DID RELATIVELY LITTLE, he took a job as a clerk with one of the citizens of London, a relative named Osbert Huitdeniers (Eightpence). A banker rather than a merchant, Osbert had succeeded Gilbert Becket some years before as one of the sheriffs of the city. William fitz Stephen believed that rather than working for Osbert personally, Thomas entered the municipal government of London as a clerk and accountant to the sheriffs, but since Osbert's term of office as a sheriff had only just expired when Thomas joined his staff, this discrepancy is easily explained. Osbert's background is shadowy and the nature of his banking operations unknown, but along the way he had built connections to the royal court. Thomas worked for him for two or possibly three years, acting as his secretary and keeping his accounts.

These were tumultuous years in London's history, and the citizens would play a crucial role in the story. The civil war had escalated dramatically while Thomas had been in Paris, as his mother had feared it would. On September 30, 1139, Matilda had landed in Sussex with her half brother Earl Robert of Gloucester. She went into hiding at Arundel Castle under the protection of her stepmother, Queen Adeliza, while he slipped away to Bristol to muster an army. On February 2, 1141, after more than a year of extensive if inconclusive fighting, they defeated and captured Stephen at the battle of Lincoln, imprisoning him in Earl

Robert's fortress at Bristol, where at first he was allowed the freedom to walk within the walls but afterward was kept in chains.

Seeing Stephen delivered into the hands of his rival by the god of battles, Henry of Winchester promptly changed sides. At a church council at Winchester specially convened on April 7, he proclaimed Matilda to be "Lady of England and Normandy" and began preparations for her coronation. Meanwhile, her husband, Geoffrey of Anjou, took his opportunity across the Channel, beginning a guerrilla war that would end three years later when the Norman barons capitulated and invested him as their duke. Seeking to win official recognition of his ducal title from the new French king, Louis VII, as speedily as possible, Geoffrey was to adopt the drastic but totally effective expedient of ceding to him a large tranche of the old Norman Vexin, including the stronghold of Gisors.

But Matilda's plans suffered a setback, for which the Londoners claimed the credit. When she arrived at Westminster at midsummer 1141, on the eve of her planned coronation, the citizens rallied. Just as she was sitting down to a banquet in the belief that she had triumphed, the bells rang in the city, and the Londoners came out of their houses armed to the teeth "as swarms of wasps issue from their hives." The whole city flew to arms, forcing Matilda and her supporters to flee. Like everyone else, the citizens had been wavering in their allegiance to Stephen, but he had bought back their loyalty, recognizing the city as a "commune" and granting it a whole raft of privileges equivalent to those of a northern Italian free city. Soon a Norman bishop could be found saluting "the glorious senators, honored citizens, and all of the Communal Concord of London." Since these "senators" included all the current and former sheriffs, Gilbert Becket and Osbert Huitdeniers would have ranked among them. Both are very likely to have been among the civic dignitaries sent to demand such generous concessions from Stephen.

Much of this had happened about the time that Thomas's mother died, so he would have learned the inside story on his return. The citizens had accepted Stephen's offer because Matilda had insisted that they pay a large arbitrary tax, or benevolence. When the sheriffs had begged her to abandon or reduce it, she had flown into a rage, "refusing to spare them in any respect or relax her extortion by the smallest amount." Her "mask of reasonableness" had come off, and "with piercing eyes, her forehead wrinkled into a scowl, every trace of a woman's gentleness obliterated from her face, [she] erupted into an unbearable fury." Ignoring the advice of her counselors, she had berated the Londoners, accusing them of opening their purses wide to succor her enemies.

That was just the citizens' side of the story. Is it equally possible that Matilda had merely tried to counter Londoners' opposition to fair taxation with the masculine firmness they had previously accepted from her late father? If so, she miscalculated, creating the impression that she was arrogant and unwomanly. Her apparent unwillingness to take advice, her excessive and unconstitutional demands, and her emotive use of language had convinced the citizens that she was a tyrant and that their allegiance should be returned to Stephen. When Henry of Winchester made the same choice, switching his loyalty back to Stephen as easily as he had swung round earlier to Matilda, she had no alternative but to abandon her efforts to be crowned, returning with Earl Robert to Oxford to rally her forces again.

Riding to Winchester in late July at the head of her troops, she planned to repay the turncoat prelate for his treachery. But within six weeks, she was encircled and defeated, with her half brother among the prisoners, canceling out the advantage she had gained at the battle of Lincoln. Without the aid of superior forces, she could never hope to win another victory, so the two sides agreed to exchange prisoners. Stephen was swapped for Earl Robert, but the result was a stalemate.

Then in December 1142, after more than a year of inaction and at more or less the same time as Thomas Becket went to work for Osbert Huitdeniers, Stephen's army laid siege to Oxford, and Matilda, trapped in a high tower, was let down with ropes one night and forced to flee on foot across the snow. One thing she would never lack was courage. Accompanied by a small escort and wearing white cloaks as camouflage, her party crossed the frozen Thames and walked eight miles through enemy lines to Abingdon before riding to Devizes in Wiltshire. Still, neither side had sufficient forces to inflict a lasting defeat on the other.

Over the next three years, the fighting would be concentrated south of the Thames and in the corridor between Winchester and Bristol. Stephen and his Flemish mercenaries pursued a scorched-earth policy in the districts controlled by Matilda, and with both sides resorting to acts of terror, the Londoners' trade was badly affected. If the Peterborough chronicler is to be believed, "Christ and his angels slept."

> Every powerful man built him castles and . . . filled them with devils and wicked men. Then both by night and day they took those people that they thought had any goods—men and women—and put them in prison and tortured them with indescribable torture to extort gold and silver—for no martyrs were ever so tortured as they were. They were hung by the thumbs or by the head, and corselets were hung on their feet. Knotted ropes were put round their heads and twisted till they penetrated to the brains. They put them in prisons where there were adders and snakes and toads, and killed them like that. Some they put in a "torture-chamber"—that is in a chest that was short, narrow, and shallow, and they put sharp stones in it and pressed the man in it so that he had all his limbs broken.

Thousands died of starvation, while the survivors ate grass or roots or killed their horses or dogs for meat. And neither Stephen nor the barons stepped back from sacrilege. When unable to pay their troops, they allowed the men to loot churches and monasteries and evict the clergy from their lands.

The young and impressionable Thomas Becket must have been following these harrowing events closely, since in later life he would reflect on them in a letter to Earl Robert's son Roger. Describing Roger's father as "loyal, prudent, magnanimous, and constant," he praised the earl's bravery at the battle of Lincoln, when he defeated Stephen and "threw him into prison in chains." What impressed him most was Robert's determination to honor his sacred oath to his half sister. "So much did he disdain the caprices of fortune, through his faith and virtue," he says, "that he did not fear to risk any peril in order to make good his religious oath, and finally, after capture, preferred to be imprisoned than allow his sister and his lady to suffer loss of her right."

A cautionary note should be sounded, since Roger—by the time Becket wrote this account in May 1170—had risen to become bishop of Worcester and was one of Thomas's key sympathizers in his own struggle with the king. Becket's sentiments appear to be genuine but came at a moment when he particularly relied on Roger's support. When Becket wrote his letter, he would himself be railing against a tyrannical king, and his benchmark would not be Matilda for all her wrangling with the Londoners, but Stephen, whom he depicted as a tyrant whose early affability and concessions to the church and the Londoners would be wiped out in a trail of blood and destruction. And yet, irrespective of how far he crafted his story to make it seem more palatable to its recipient, his letter proves that he knew the events of the civil war inside out.

SOMETIME IN 1145, Becket would make one of the most critical choices of his entire life. Clearly finding his duties as Osbert's secretary too humdrum, he opted for a fresh start by joining the household of Archbishop Theobald of Canterbury. Typically, he got this second chance through influence rather than his own merits. His new employer had been born close to Gilbert Becket's family home in Thierville, near Bec Abbey, and the two men may have been distantly related. Two brothers from Boulogne, Archdeacon Baldwin and Master Eustace, both friends of Theobald, lodged with the Beckets whenever they visited London. Seeing Thomas obviously underemployed, they suggested he seek out the archbishop's preferment. Visiting Theobald at his manor of Harrow, a few miles north of London, Thomas was quickly offered a post as one of Theobald's ten or so clerks—to Becket's evident surprise, since the archbishop's staff included some of the ablest scholars in the country. A variant of the story is that one of Theobald's officials, who also used to stay in London with Gilbert, had marked Thomas out and urged him to speak to the archbishop. After a brief conversation, Theobald was so impressed by Thomas's charm and intelligence that he offered Becket a job on the spot. Edward Grim identifies this intermediary, calling him "the clerk with the hatchet" or "hatchet man." And among Theobald's staff, there was indeed a marshal, a commoner called "Baillehache," who appears as a witness to one of the archbishop's charters.

Elected as archbishop in 1139, when he was approaching the age of fifty and at a time when Stephen's authority was already crumbling, Theobald, like his two most distinguished predecessors, Lanfranc and

Anselm, had built his career at Bec Abbey, where he had been prior and later abbot. Matilda, taking after her grandfather William the Conqueror, was a generous benefactress of the abbey and in her will asked to be buried there before the high altar. Stephen, by contrast, had little or no connection with the place and does not seem to have known anything of Theobald before he was recommended to the king by a visiting papal envoy.

When in 1141 the civil war had first become deadlocked, Theobald had declared himself neutral, winning adherents on both sides. Honest and devout, practical and sure-footed, his long experience in the ways of the world had taught him to measure carefully his responses to the bullying tactics of his superiors. With his inferiors, he could be far less benign. Impatient, even brutal, with his Christ Church monks when they formed cabals to undermine his authority, he happily likened them to dogs. Never much of a scholar himself but a generous patron of learning, he spared no expense in equipping his circle of highflyers with a library regarded as one of the finest in the whole of Christendom. Becket was fortunate to be admitted to Theobald's inner circle, and once there he must have found it a struggle to keep up. William fitz Stephen makes no attempt to hide the fact that in comparison to those around him, "Thomas was not so well learned." The gold standard would be set by John of Salisbury, who joined the archbishop's household in 1147, two years after Thomas, arriving with a letter of recommendation from no less a luminary than St. Bernard, abbot of Clairvaux.

Theobald's one significant vice was that he was prone to nepotism. Not content with appointing his brother Walter to the lucrative senior post of archdeacon of Canterbury, he would also employ his nephews in a variety of junior positions. Such influence was typical of the age and clearly suited Thomas. Scarcely could he have survived for very long without it in such an intellectual hothouse—this not least because the archbishop's clerks were expected to work as a team. Suppressing ambition as far as they could, they were meant to be collegial and mutually supportive, whereas Thomas was naturally competitive, flamboyant, and hungry to succeed. Under normal circumstances, his character and temperament might have ruled him out, but the stalemate in the civil war gave him a unique opportunity, obliging Theobald to become as much a politician as a pastor. Though lynx-eyed and farsighted, the archbishop lacked confidence as a negotiator and was a weak public speaker, whereas Thomas—already conquering his stammer—was a natural communicator, making up in silver-tongued oratory and deft footwork for what he lacked in learning.

Soon Becket's quick reactions and easy, winning manner had become as invaluable to his new employer as John of Salisbury's genius for drafting letters. "The archbishop," says Prior Robert of Cricklade, who knew him well, "was a simple man, somewhat quick of temper, and not as wary of word, if his mind was stirred, as the rule of meekness utmost demandeth." Sometimes he could be either too blunt or too rash, at other times too easily cowed by the powerful into understating his case. "Against either failing Thomas setteth his good will and wisdom in such a manner that, if in any matter the [arch]bishop happened to wax wrath, Thomas giveth forth answers all the meeker . . . On the other hand, if the speech of the archbishop happened to fail him . . . [he] hastened to succor him, and clothed it in clerkdom in such a way that at once the discourse appeared like a text with a fair commentary to it."

If it seems surprising that an archbishop would select Thomas as his spokesman, it is worth remembering that a religious vocation was unnecessary for the role. Theobald's clerks were not priests, even if the upper parts of their heads were shaved, or tonsured, to create a circular patch on the crown like those of the clergy and monks. When Becket returned to London to visit his father or sisters and walked along Cheapside, he might momentarily have been confused with a priest. But to take up his new post, he was ordained at most as a subdeacon and far more likely as a reader or acolyte, the lowest degrees of orders, which meant he was not bound to celibacy or any other religious vow and could not assist at the altar or in the sanctuary beyond reading the Epistle, lighting or bearing candles, and carrying the offertory at mass. As far as the clergy were concerned, he was little more than a glorified altar boy and would not be ordained even as a deacon until he was granted a church living or archdeaconry.

That he moved away from London on entering Theobald's service is certain, for just like the king's, the archbishop's household perambulated between his palace at Canterbury, his nearby castles at Saltwood and Rochester, and his many manor houses in Kent, Sussex, Surrey, and Middlesex. The archiepiscopal estates were huge, mostly concentrated in east Kent but scattered widely across southern England, and it was possible for Thomas to ride from London to Canterbury without straying from them more than a mile or two. Shortly before 1100, Anselm had acquired the use of a comfortable manor house at Lambeth on the south bank of the Thames, convenient to the royal palace of Westminster and the abbey on the opposite bank. But Lambeth was not yet the archbishop's habitual place of residence; more often he would lodge at Harrow or Croydon when he needed to be within riding distance of London.

No longer was Thomas's world that of his fellow Londoners, citizens, and merchants, but one of bishops, clergy, and church courts. Besides his fellow clerks, his immediate colleagues included the archbishop's crossbearer, a chancellor, two monk chaplains, a butler, a dispenser, a chamberlain, and a steward. Belowstairs were a master cook, an usher, a porter, a marshal, and numerous minor functionaries, such as grooms, purveyors, janitors, bakers, carters, washerwomen, and carriers—the last moving the archbishop's coffers from place to place and at Christmas and Easter delivering his traditional gifts of hens and eggs. Since Theobald was an important feudal landowner, he also needed a treasurer, an auditor, and several receivers to collect his rents, as most of his estates were not cultivated directly but leased out to farmers.

Elements of Becket's character would gradually emerge from the way he dealt with his fellow clerks. Two of them, Roger of Pont l'Évêque and John of Canterbury, had been recruited to Theobald's staff at roughly the same time as he had. Both, like him, were clever and ambitious, and both would come to play important parts in his story, though along profoundly different lines. No sooner had the three newcomers found their feet than they made a mutual pact to advance one another's interests. And since one of them was normally on duty, little or nothing escaped their gaze. After a few years, however, realizing that Thomas was becoming Theobald's favorite and the man he relied on most, the other two became jealous. Roger would soon turn into a dangerous rival, telling tales and twice orchestrating Thomas's suspension from his duties. But on each occasion Becket came back fighting. An instinctive politician, he spotted—and ruthlessly manipulated—Theobald's partiality for his own relatives, persuading his brother Walter, the archdeacon, who like Thomas himself adored hunting with hawks and dogs, to intervene with Theobald to reinstate him.

Over the next nine or so years, Thomas Becket would come to witness—and in part help to shape—a fundamental change in the relationship between king and archbishop that would influence him for the rest of his life. Exploiting his political talents to the full, he was about to become a mover and shaker; a man who could exude disruptive energy and had a clear vision of change shaped by the stalemate in the civil war; a man privy to the quarrels of kings, barons, and popes; a courtier and diplomat navigating his way around Rome, Paris, and elsewhere.

But before his new career could fully take off, he had to learn the craft of an archbishop's right-hand man, which meant serving an apprenticeship in the usual way.

6
APPRENTICE

INEVITABLY, THOMAS BEGAN HIS NEW CAREER AT THE BOTtom, assisting his fellow clerks with the legal and administrative work in which they all shared. How the archiepiscopal courts worked in the 1140s is still shrouded in mystery, but a generation later some cases were decided by the archbishop in person; others were delegated to the senior, more experienced clerks from his household, who either heard the entire case and gave judgment, or else listened to the evidence before reporting their findings to the archbishop, who delivered the final verdict.

As a novice in legal affairs, Thomas was most likely assigned tasks in the clerks' office that included filing documents and taking witness statements. Perhaps as he grew more confident, he offered advice on points of law or procedure to Theobald's brother Walter, who regularly stood in for the archbishop in the consistory court, where the less important cases were decided. William fitz Stephen describes Becket as "raw and modest" when he began his apprenticeship. He certainly had a lot to learn, since at Paris he had studied the liberal arts, not Roman or canon law, the subjects he mainly needed now.

To rectify this, Theobald assigned him a tutor, most likely the same master he had employed to teach his nephews. Soon Thomas was reading Gratian's *Decretum*, the finest and most up-to-date encyclopedia of canon law, first issued at Bologna, the preeminent center of legal learning, in about 1140. He may even have met the Italian jurist Master

Vacarius, whom Theobald had invited to Canterbury. One of the stars of the law school at Bologna, Vacarius would live and work in England for more than fifty years, going on to teach briefly at Oxford before moving permanently to York. It may well have been at Canterbury that he began writing his celebrated *Liber Pauperum* (*Book for Poor Students*), which contained selections from Justinian's *Digest* and *Code* interspersed with commentaries, and which would be used as a cheap student textbook on Roman law until the Reformation.

Whether or not Thomas knew Vacarius, this was when he first encountered the rudiments of a system of values that stayed with him for the rest of his life. Roman and church law prided themselves on being rooted in "equity and reason"; such principles, their advocates passionately believed, should underpin every aspect of a civilized nation's life. Their importance can scarcely be exaggerated, because these were years in which, under the influence of charismatic leaders such as St. Bernard and Peter the Venerable, the ascetic reform movement in the church gave a fresh impetus to canon law, which came to focus on a vast range of topics, including church property, sex and marriage, inheritance, the validity of oaths and contracts, and heresy. And as the flow of appeals to Rome increased, the pope began to appoint special legates and "judges delegate" (personal representatives) to handle tricky lawsuits. Papal power increased even more swiftly than it had during the disputes over lay investiture, and soon the character of the papal curia itself began to change as lawyers replaced cardinals trained in theology. The result was a model centered on the idea of a sovereign pope deciding lawsuits at Rome and hearing appeals from the church courts all over Europe—the prelude to the rise of a papal monarchy in the church.

When Thomas had acquired the basic skills he needed, Theobald sent him to sit at the feet of the masters of the law schools at Bologna and Auxerre. William fitz Stephen says that he spent a full year at Bologna—his teacher is likely to have been the distinguished civil and canon lawyer Master Albert de Morra, a future cardinal and papal chancellor—before continuing his studies at Auxerre, near Sens in northern Burgundy. There, for the first time in his life, he studied assiduously, throwing all his energy into the task. Of course, he was on a series of crash courses and very probably took shortcuts, studying *Summae* (cribs) of classic textbooks such as Justinian's *Institutes* rather than reading the real thing—although, if anything, by stripping the nuances from the originals, such cribs would have heightened his grasp of the fundamental principles.

As Theobald's clerk, Thomas also gained admission to the higher social circles that appealed to him. Since bishops and archdeacons often enjoyed hunting and hawking, it is a fair assumption that he began keeping his own falcons while living in the archbishop's palaces. Appalled by his friend's love of blood sports, John of Salisbury condemned both these and games of chance, especially dice, but his views were the exception not the rule. After his initial awkwardness among his fellow clerks caused by the gaps in his education, Thomas was settling down, ingratiating himself where he could and genuinely trying to succeed. Theobald, who despite his nepotistic tendencies was still not easily impressed by his underlings, said that he had never seen greater zeal and fidelity than those shown by his new clerk, a remark that stung Roger of Pont l'Évêque into giving his rival the nickname "Baillehache," insulting him by deliberately confusing him with the lowborn marshal who Edward Grim says first introduced him to the archbishop.

BY 1145, the atrocities of the civil war had sparked a fresh upsurge of rumor and superstition throughout the land. In Norwich, it was said that a boy had been crucified by Jews and that a miraculous light in the sky had revealed his corpse. In Hertfordshire, a pious recluse called Christina of Markyate became famous for her mystical visions and was said to have seen Christ returning to earth, disguised as a pilgrim. In Somerset, a hermit called Wulfric of Haselbury was the talk of his village, reciting the Psalter nightly in a tub of cold water and converting a sacrilegious knight to religion, so that in due course he became an abbot. Dabbling in prophecy and speaking in French despite his Saxon background, Wulfric established close connections with Henry of Winchester, Stephen's brother. When the king himself came to visit him, the hermit did not flinch from urging him to lead a better life. He even went on to prophesy, menacingly, that the throne of England would descend not to Stephen's eldest son, Eustace, but to Henry of Anjou, the eldest son of Matilda and Count Geoffrey.

Such prophecies reflected the deepening anxiety caused by the political deadlock after Matilda's perilous flight from Oxford through the snow. The tide briefly shifted in Stephen's favor as several of Matilda's supporters either changed sides or left to go on pilgrimages to Jerusalem, but when his new allies saw that Stephen did not really trust anyone and was liable at any time to use his familiar technique of a contrived quarrel at court as the prelude to seizing their lands, they returned their fealty to Matilda. Peace talks had failed, allowing little prospect of a settlement. If Matilda and her brother still dominated Bristol and the West Country, Stephen was ascendant elsewhere, despite some isolated pockets of resistance. As long as neither side was prepared to offer concessions, the war of attrition would continue, but with one key change. Before long Matilda, desperately short of money and finding it almost impossible to win over the doubters to the idea of female rule, lost confidence in her ability to reclaim the throne unaided and came to believe that she was fighting to recover her lost inheritance on behalf of her son Henry, for whose cause she became the champion.

IN THE SPRING of 1147, two years after the earnest Cistercian monk Bernard of Pisa had been elected pope as Eugenius III, Theobald traveled to Paris, where he settled a dispute between the monks of Bec and the canons of St. Frideswide's in the presence of the pope, then in France to preach the Second Crusade. Since his habit was to take two of his favorite clerks with him on such journeys, it is likely that Becket accompanied him or else interrupted his studies at Auxerre to come to Paris. Not yet strong enough to intervene himself in the English civil war, Pope Eugenius would reach a secret understanding with Theobald, offering to work with him in the future in ways that would greatly increase the archbishop's ability to influence political events.

Theobald had returned to Canterbury shortly before October 1147, when Earl Robert of Gloucester died of typhoid fever and Matilda's support collapsed. With her forces fast melting away, she found it necessary to retreat from her nearly impregnable headquarters at Devizes Castle, which she had requisitioned from Bishop Jocelin of Salisbury, to whom Pope Eugenius had ordered her to return it. Threatened with excommunication if she failed to comply, she delayed for as long as she could but finally left the stronghold in the hands of a small garrison with enough provisions to last for several years. She then set sail for Normandy to rejoin her husband and sons, never to return.

Now her strategy was to urge her followers to hold out until her eldest son, Henry, just turned fifteen and beginning to play a significant part in Angevin and Norman politics, came of age. Her plan was that her husband, Geoffrey, should one day abdicate as Duke of Normandy in favor of their son, who would become free to launch the ultimate campaign to reunite the duchy with England as his grandfather Henry I had done on the death of William Rufus. Young Henry had already shown his mettle on a clandestine visit to his mother when, landing at Wareham in Dorset at the age of fourteen with a few mercenaries hired on credit, he had marched to Wiltshire to assist her but had become trapped. Unable to advance or to retreat, he had cheekily parleyed with Stephen, whom he had persuaded to pay off his mercenaries and give him a safe-conduct and enough money to return home. Astonishingly, rather than taking him prisoner to get him out of the way, Stephen decided to whisk him safely out of the country before he created a more serious threat. Quixotic an act of chivalry though it was, it was also a fatal mistake.

Henry would live to fight another day. A hint of the sort of man he was likely to become can be gleaned from the fact that when he next returned briefly to England in 1149 to rebuild his support in the West Country, far from obeying Pope Eugenius's decree to make restitution to Jocelin of Salisbury, he confidently defied the pope, excluding Devizes Castle from his reparations and saying that he would "of necessity" retain it in his own hands "until God should show him that he could give it back."

WITH MATILDA SAFELY out of the way, Stephen might have triumphed but for the understanding between Theobald and the pope, for under the archbishop's influence, Eugenius, despite his earlier reservations, swung round to Matilda's side. The result was that Thomas Becket would emerge from his position as a lowly clerk over the next few years and come to play a crucial role in settling the succession in England and Normandy. This followed a church council at Rheims, summoned by Eugenius, who was still in France, in the same month as Matilda left England. Suspecting political moves against him and advised by his brother, Stephen expelled the diplomats delivering the papal summonses and sent three handpicked bishops to France as his official delegates, prohibiting the rest from attending. Having been forced to buy the church's support at the beginning of his reign with his Oxford charter, he now—with Matilda gone—intended to return to the policy of William the Conqueror's last years and severely restrict freedom of movement between England and the papal curia.

He had reckoned without the resourceful Theobald, who now transformed the old relationship between king and archbishop as it had existed in Lanfranc's and Anselm's time by politicizing it to a degree hitherto unknown. Skillfully evading Stephen's spies, he fled from Canterbury, hiring a fishing smack in a remote bay, taking with him Becket, Roger of Pont l'Évêque, and John of Salisbury. Their boat, says John wistfully, as he suffered badly from seasickness, "could carry no more than a dozen men and lacked even the most essential equipment; and so [Theobald] crossed the Channel rather as a survivor from a shipwreck than in a ship." When the archbishop eventually reached Rheims, he was given a hero's welcome, and Stephen's chosen delegates, who had disingenuously presented the archbishop's apologies to the council without his knowledge, were humiliated. Eugenius joked that Theobald had made his journey "by swimming rather than sailing," retaliating against Stephen by suspending those bishops who had obeyed the king's instructions to absent themselves from the council and especially Henry of Winchester, whose absolution the pope reserved to himself.

But what most enraged Stephen about this council was its decision, on Eugenius's advice, to deprive William fitz Herbert, the king's nephew, of the archbishopric of York and replace him with Henry Murdac, the Cistercian abbot of Fountains, on the grounds that Stephen had rigged the election. The furious king refused to accept Murdac and attempted to block his passage into Yorkshire—unsuccessfully, since he slipped through the net, reaching Beverley and then Ripon, from which he laid an interdict on the city of York.

In Rheims itself, the precincts of the basilica buzzed with activity. Becket found himself mingling with the great and the good, meeting the famous Abbot Suger of Saint-Denis, one of the chief architects of the reconstruction of the Capetian monarchy, who had risen through the church from peasant origins to become a leading royal counselor. He saw the celebrated theologian Peter Lombard in action. He even saw his own old Paris master Robert of Melun and perhaps the great St. Bernard himself.

The climax came on the final day when Eugenius decided to excommunicate Stephen. The supreme form of ecclesiastical censure imposed on an individual, excommunication is the process by which a ban is placed on the offender and the sacraments or other spiritual benefits are denied him until he confesses his sins and is absolved by the church, meaning that should he die before the ban is lifted, he will go to hell. The candles had already been lit for the ceremony when Theobald, to everyone's astonishment, knelt before the pope and begged for mercy for the errant king. So thunderstruck was Eugenius at the sight of so spontaneous a display of Christian charity, he "at first meditated in silence and then, sighing, spoke as follows: 'My brethren, behold this man who enacts the Gospel in our own time by loving his enemies and never ceasing to pray for his persecutors. For although the king has by his effrontery deserved our wrath and the wrath of God's church, nevertheless we cannot but commend such love or refuse to hear his prayers.'"

Theobald was playing a long game. He knew that no matter how obstinate and unpopular Stephen was as an individual, the king rightly thought himself strong enough to defy the pope. Had Eugenius imposed so terrible a sanction as excommunication on him without adequate explanation in advance or without giving him a sufficient opportunity to repent and mend his ways, public opinion would have veered back in his favor against the pope. Theobald intervened because he knew that a censure that appeared to be premature in the eyes of the world and that could not adequately be enforced would fail, because everyone in England yearned for peace and a return to normal life.

In April 1148, Theobald slipped back into Canterbury and was given a hero's welcome by the townsfolk and the Christ Church monks. But Stephen did not feel himself in any way beholden to him for his support against the pope. Instead, hearing a report of Theobald's return, he sent one of his loyal henchmen, Richard de Lucy—a committed royalist whom Thomas Becket would one day find himself excommunicating—to demand the archbishop's submission. When Theobald refused, his property was seized and he was frog-marched to Dover and deported to Flanders, where he took refuge at the Benedictine abbey of Saint-Bertin at Saint-Omer. His friends were free to come and go as they pleased, bringing him gifts of food and clothing and carrying messages to and from Stephen's court, but nothing could disguise the fact that the king had driven the primate into exile. It was only in July, when fresh peace negotiations failed and news of Theobald's expulsion reached Eugenius at Brescia in northern Italy, that the pope intervened, ordering Stephen to recall his archbishop and restore his goods. If he refused, England was to be laid under a general interdict suspending the spiritual benefits of church membership to the entire population, and if nothing changed, the king was to be excommunicated after all.

Eugenius had dramatically raised the stakes. When Stephen continued to defy him, Theobald put the papal interdict into effect, but his original instinct had been sound. John of Salisbury says that many of the clergy refused to comply with the interdict for fear of rekindling the civil war. Among the first to disobey were the Londoners, who lodged an appeal with Rome. Only in Theobald's own diocese of Canterbury did the clergy conform, and there too compliance must have been patchy, since John says that the monastery of St. Augustine's resisted the pope's decree for as long as 180 days.

When by the following spring the scale of the failure was fully known, Theobald believed he had no choice but to ratchet up the pressure, well aware of the rapacity of Stephen's henchmen, who he feared would ravage his estates and ransack his manor houses while the king turned a blind eye. Hiring another boat, he sailed from Gravelines in Flanders to Gosford in Suffolk, then galloped in disguise to Framlingham, where he took refuge in the castle under the protection of Hugh Bigod, who had defected to Matilda. From behind the high curtain walls of this mighty fortress, he resumed his authority over the English church, receiving bishops and hearing lawsuits with the help of his clerks, including Thomas. Knowing he had gone too far and was in danger of driving the archbishop straight into the arms of his enemies, Stephen settled the dispute and restored him to his lands, even paying compensation for the damage to his property. Theobald had shown that he could win even against the odds.

Whether Becket had been with Theobald at Saint-Omer and Framlingham is unknown, but in 1167 he would send a vivid account of the episode to Cardinal Boso at the papal curia. Reminding him that no one had better exemplified the church of Canterbury's obedience to the pope than Theobald, Thomas proceeded to recount how the archbishop had been forced into exile for obeying Eugenius's summons to the council. "Which other bishops have you ever seen or read about," he says, "who set themselves against princes to defend the Church's liberty and to preserve the institutions of the fathers, out of respect and obedience for the Apostolic See, except the archbishops of Canterbury? Indeed there is not even one who has done so in our own time, and you will find none if you read the ancient histories." Stephen, he continues, faced with Theobald's opposition, "did not stop attacking [him] until Lord Eugenius, of pious memory, ordered all the bishops to observe without leave of appeal the sentence issued against him and the interdict imposed on his lands. For the wolf is not easily kept away from the sheepfold, unless he is frightened by the stick and barking dogs."

Thomas would come to see Theobald's resistance as a shining example of an honest churchman's refusal to be bullied by a tyrant. Such resolute action, he claims, provided the precedent for his own sudden flight into exile. Here he spins his story to suit his own ends, because it was not Theobald who had chosen exile, but Stephen who had deported him, and the pope's interdict would signally fail. And yet the spin would be as important as the substance, for what Becket's letter also makes clear is that by the time his own career had arrived at its great crisis, he would be more of a politician even than Theobald, to whom it would never have occurred to search for precedents of churchmen standing up to tyrants.

* * *

AS THOMAS STEADILY gained knowledge and experience, he was sent alone on diplomatic missions to Rome. The first, in late 1149 or early 1150, concerned Theobald's bid to secure appointment as resident papal legate, able to represent the pope in England and armed with his authority. That it ended in success was a considerable triumph, since Stephen's brother Bishop Henry had previously held this role, giving him precedence over the archbishop and seriously undermining his authority. According to the monk Gervase of Canterbury, it was only Becket's powerful advocacy before Pope Eugenius that had swung the case for Theobald. Bishop Henry dashed to Rome himself in a last-ditch attempt to revive his candidacy, but he failed to outwit Thomas. The way was now open for the archbishop to intervene decisively in the civil war should he so choose.

When Stephen's sullen reaction was to threaten and ostracize Theobald, the archbishop came ever closer to declaring his outright support for Matilda and the Angevins. No longer could the king rely on his brother to crown and anoint his eldest son, Eustace, as his designated heir as he had planned to do, since Theobald—whose right it now was as both archbishop and papal legate to preside at the coronation ceremony—had objected. So with his eye fixed firmly on a dynastic settlement, Theobald sent Becket on a second, even more impressive embassy to Rome, where he secured a papal decree forbidding Eustace's coronation.

No sooner was the decree issued than Stephen sent Roger of Pont l'Évêque, Thomas's rival, to Rome to get it withdrawn. Now archdeacon of Canterbury following Walter's promotion to the bishopric of Rochester, Roger was as ambitious as ever and keeping his options open. How this played with Thomas we do not know. Maybe they respected each other's positions and politely agreed to differ, but given their competitive instincts, Roger's mission is more likely to have further sharpened their enmity.

Roger's petition for Eustace's coronation to be allowed was denied. Pope Eugenius ruled decisively in Theobald's favor, because Stephen had broken his oath to Matilda in assuming the throne. At long last she was vindicated in the eyes of the church, and Stephen was condemned by his perjury. Her difficulty was to translate that moral advantage into a political and military victory for herself or her son.

Whether Theobald's success in gaining the decree was due more to Becket's diplomacy or Eugenius's impatience with the delinquent Stephen is impossible to judge. Gervase claims that it was a crucial step in Becket's rise to greatness. But this is probably hyperbole, since Thomas says very little about his own role in the negotiations.

And once more caution is needed, because in his later references to the affair, Thomas again spins his story. In another letter, written in 1168, he would recall how one of the cardinals had spoken in Roger of Pont l'Évêque's defense, "saying that it was easier to hold a ram by the horn than a lion by the tail." By then, Thomas would place a radically different value on this argument, suspecting that it might have been preferable if Roger's petition had been successful after all and the papal prohibition had been overturned. For if Eustace had been crowned, then it would have been him (the ram), and not Matilda's son Henry of Anjou (by then Becket's nemesis), who would have succeeded Stephen.

Despite Thomas's subsequent U-turn, there is no hint that he recanted his part in the diplomacy or believed that Eugenius had been wrong at the time. Rather, his main purpose in referring back to the incident was to show that nobody could ever have foreseen how Stephen would be succeeded by an even greater tyrant—the ruler against whom Thomas would later make his stand.

IN THE SPRING of 1152, Stephen convened a great council of magnates and bishops at London to decide whether he could muster enough votes to proceed with crowning Eustace regardless of the papal ban. Determined to press for a decision, he presided at the meeting, with Eustace sitting at his right hand. Opening the discussion, he turned to the bishops, demanding their assent, but none was willing to usurp the primate's right of coronation, and when Theobald stood firm and told Stephen to his face that the pope had forbidden it, his support was solid.

At so public a rebuff, Stephen and Eustace flew into a rage. A chronicler relates how "both father and son, greatly disappointed and incensed, ordered the bishops to be shut up in one house together, and by threats and hardship endeavored to compel them to comply with their demand." When a putsch appeared imminent, a few bishops, declaring that Stephen "had never loved priests," yielded, but most refused to budge. Making his escape, Theobald boarded a ship and set off along the Thames as fast as he could in fear of his life.

As an anonymous "Life of Theobald" copied into the chronicle of Bec Abbey explains, the archbishop knew that he had reached a crossroads. Having watched the king degenerate from a protector of the church into a tyrant before his eyes, he was ready to support an invasion of England by Henry of Anjou. Already invested as Duke of Normandy in succession to his father, who had succumbed to a fatal bout of malaria, young Henry was mustering his troops. Informed by spies of Theobald's clandestine contacts with the Angevins, Stephen, says the Bec chronicler, let it be known that he no longer cared if anyone physically attacked his renegade archbishop, even though Stephen himself "was not prepared to touch a hair of his head." Hearing this, a dozen knights drew their swords and rushed from the court intent on assassinating Theobald, chasing him along the Thames, but he got away. Was Thomas at the archbishop's side as he escaped with this murderous band of knights hard on his heels? If so, he could hardly have forgotten such a harrowing experience—one that would have made him fully aware of what kings might attempt if they are crossed.

Theobald was not long in this, his final exile. Safely reaching Dover and embarking once more for Flanders, where he landed on April 6, 1152, he had been recalled to his own cathedral by the end of August, when his lands were restored to him. King Stephen finally backed down, accepting that the church had defeated him. His son Eustace would never be crowned, and in Gervase of Canterbury's view, "The whole of this was done by the subtle foresight of a certain Thomas, a clerk, of London," who had gained the papal legacy for his archbishop.

True or not, a milestone had been passed, for by his missions to Rome and proximity to Theobald during the archbishop's long tussle with the king, Thomas Becket had completed his apprenticeship in more ways than one.

7
INTO THE LIMELIGHT

BY THE TIME THEOBALD THWARTED KING STEPHEN IN HIS plans to crown Eustace, Thomas Becket held an uncontested position as the archbishop's right-hand man. Not yet in holy orders, tonsured as a clerk but not subject to a religious vow, he was still a layman—which did not prevent Theobald from giving him a generous share of church patronage or encouraging others to do so. As a reward for his work at the Council of Rheims in 1148 and for obtaining the papal legacy for Theobald, he received the revenues of the parish church of Otford in Kent, followed by those of St. Mary-le-Strand in London and Bramfield in Hertfordshire. Next, Thomas became a prebendary of St. Paul's and Lincoln cathedrals, receiving a share (*praebenda*) of the income from the cathedral lands. Intended originally to supplement the salaries of working priests with pastoral obligations, such posts were rarely more than sinecures. In a few instances, a prebendary had some formal duties laid down by the cathedral's statutes, and Thomas did have contact with Lincoln. He got to know Philip de Broi, a fellow prebendary of noble birth, quite well and about ten years later would be put on the spot when de Broi was charged with the murder of a knight.

The civil war, meanwhile, was ebbing to its close. When King Louis VII of France recognized Henry of Anjou as Duke of Normandy in 1151, which he did in exchange for a final tranche of what still remained of the old Norman Vexin, he removed the threat to the young duke's position on the Continent. Then just as Henry was poised to launch his invasion of England in the spring of 1152, there was sensational news. A church council at Beaugency had annulled the marriage of Louis and his wife, Eleanor of Aquitaine, on the grounds of consanguinity, even though they had cohabited for almost sixteen years and she had given him two healthy daughters. Since the couple were fourth cousins and related in a whole other tangle of ways within the prohibited degrees, the church should have either barred them from marrying in the first place or granted them a special dispensation. That it had done neither was a mistake that would cost the Capetian monarchy dearly.

Eleanor had been barely fifteen in 1137 when her father, William X, Duke of Aquitaine and Count of Poitou, died on a pilgrimage to the shrine of St. James at Santiago de Compostela, leaving her as his sole heiress. The same year, she had married the sixteen-year-old Louis shortly before he became king. A woman of truly exceptional intelligence and personality, she was famous for her sparkling black eyes and love of the sophisticated, courtly values of her ancestors, the counts of Poitou. Louis, as a second son destined for a career in the church until his elder brother's horse had stumbled over a pig in the streets of Paris, throwing him fatally to the ground, had been bred in the cloister. At first enchanted with Eleanor, he became more devout and ascetic as he grew older, and his passion for her had waned. For four years, rumors about the marriage had been rife. She, feisty and formidable, now turned thirty, had not borne him a son, raising doubts in his mind about her fecundity. This is more likely to have been his fault than hers, since she was overheard complaining that her husband was a monk, not a king. In 1147–48, when the ill-matched couple traveled to Antioch on the Second Crusade, the marriage was already on the rocks. Rumor linked Eleanor's name romantically to that of her uncle Prince Raymond of Antioch, although it is far from clear that the time they spent together had to do with anything other than her concern for the fate of her relatives and fellow countrymen in a dangerously vulnerable crusader territory. Quick to pick up on the gossip, John of Salisbury reported that they had been seen in each other's company day and night, arousing Louis's darkest suspicions.

Determined not to get sidetracked at Antioch and to fulfill his vow to go first to Jerusalem before campaigning elsewhere, Louis announced his immediate departure. Instead of meekly accompanying him, which is what a medieval ruler expected of his wife, the furious Eleanor quarreled with him in public, threatening to stay in Antioch without him. It was when he forcibly dragged her away from her uncle's palace that she is said to have asked for a separation.

At first Pope Eugenius personally intervened in an effort to reconcile the couple, meeting them on their return from the East and making them sleep in the same bed. But Eleanor demanded an annulment, and when it was granted, the dashing young Count of Anjou lost no time in making his suit. Salaciously hinting at a sexual motive, the chroniclers claim that Eleanor had first cast lascivious eyes on Henry when he had come to Paris to do homage for Normandy. But this is very much a monkish perspective. Their mutual love of power seems chiefly to have drawn the two together, for there is little solid evidence, at least at the beginning of their relationship, that it was a love match on either side.

For the nineteen-year-old Henry, Eleanor's attraction lay in the fact that she claimed descent from Charlemagne and was the sole heiress to an empire in southwest France composed of the fragments into which the old Carolingian provinces of Aquitaine and Gascony had disintegrated. The prospect of gaining Aquitaine had a massive impact on the young Henry's mind at a time when he had not yet been recognized as Stephen's successor and other members of Stephen's family in Blois-Champagne could block his expansionist aims. Admittedly with ill-defined frontiers that were difficult to defend, Aquitaine's vast territories extended south from the Loire Valley to the foothills of the Pyrenees and west from the central heights of the Auvergne to the Atlantic Ocean. Larger and richer even than the lands of the French royal demesne, they were a magnet for Henry. Combined with his existing fiefs in Normandy, Maine, Anjou, and Touraine, they had the potential to give him a continental empire that dwarfed the inheritance of the Capetian dynasty, a domain greater than had been held by any ruler since the disintegration of the Carolingian empire and with huge reserves of natural resources. With Aquitaine united to Anjou, much of the trade and traffic in western and southern France, and especially between Nantes, Poitiers, Bordeaux, and the Mediterranean, would fall into his hands. Only Duke

William X's failure to recover possession of the city and county of Toulouse stood in the way of a near monopoly of the trade along the river Garonne, connecting the Mediterranean and the Atlantic, and along the old Roman road linking Narbonne and Bordeaux.

For Eleanor, the attraction of marrying Henry seems to have lain in her unwavering, if perhaps naïve, belief that he would fill the power vacuum caused by her father's death and so restore Aquitaine to the glory it had enjoyed under her grandfather Duke William IX. A daring and intrepid ruler, educated and hardworking, William IX had led a large, loyal retinue of knights fearlessly into battle against the Spanish Muslims while building a reputation as a lyric poet and (on the downside) a lecher. It was said of him that he "wallowed in every kind of vice," founding a "convent of prostitutes" near the castle of Niort and painting the image of a viscountess on his shield, saying he wanted to bear her into battle in the same way as she used to bear him in bed. Deeply etched into Eleanor's consciousness was a determination to persuade her new husband to preserve Aquitaine's historical and cultural independence. She saw herself as an advocate for what was nothing less than a pro-Poitevin policy leading, one day, to a full-scale military campaign to recover Toulouse. Perhaps she felt she would be able to dominate Henry or sway his judgment, as she had clearly often dominated the far weaker and impressionable Louis. If so, she fundamentally miscalculated.

THE COUPLE were married on Whitsunday 1152 at Poitiers after exchanging messages by fast riders barely eight weeks after Eleanor was single again. The speed of their marriage caused another monkish flurry but may be explicable as the dilemma of a woman whose other prospective suitors had made no secret of their intentions to ambush and rape her on her way back to Poitou in order to stake their claim. Less than a month later, Henry was in Normandy again and ready to invade England. His sheer verve and audacity enraged King Louis, who considered himself doubly insulted, for not only had Henry married his ex-wife, and in unseemly haste, but he had also slighted Louis by failing to ask the king's permission as his feudal superior. "The marriage," said the chroniclers, "caused great dissensions, fomented into hatred, between the king of France and the duke," a hatred soon compounded by jealousy when Eleanor became pregnant with a son, named William after her father and grandfather.

Louis still had a winning card to play. Some ten years before, his sister Constance had married Stephen's son Eustace, whose cause he now decided to aid. The marriage had been loveless and childless, and far from his bride bringing him a princely dowry, Eustace had been forced to spend the treasure his father had looted from Roger of Salisbury to buy her hand. But when invited by his brother-in-law to preempt Henry's invasion by joining him in a two-pronged counterattack on Normandy, he quickly seized the chance. The more his thoughts dwelt on Henry, the more Eustace saw his own future as bleak, making the Capetian king's siren call irresistible. Moving at impressive speed, the allies invaded the duchy in the summer of 1152, laying siege to Arques, near Dieppe, and digging in at Neufmarché on the river Epte. Henry's troops retaliated in the French zone of the Vexin, reinforced by a crack unit of Breton mercenaries. So successful was he that Louis retreated to the safety of Paris. After little more than six weeks, Eustace was isolated and forced to return home.

By the second week of January 1153, Henry felt he could delay no longer and embarked for England from Barfleur. Braving a winter gale, his fleet of 36 ships carrying a force of 140 knights and 3,000 infantry landed safely at Wareham, where he had arrived five years before on his abortive raid to help his mother. After first relieving the garrison at her old headquarters at Devizes Castle, he launched a surprise attack on Malmesbury, where his troops entered the town and the outer bailey of the castle but failed to storm the keep. There followed a siege and an uneasy truce lasting for six months while Henry traveled from Bristol to Gloucester, where on April 19 he held his Easter court and loudly proclaimed his new title of Duke of Aquitaine. Afterward he marched around the Midlands, capturing castles or forcing their occupants to surrender them.

Returning south at the end of July, Henry planned to base himself at

Wallingford in Oxfordshire and open up the bridge across the Thames. First, however, he had to lay siege to Stephen's fortress at nearby Crowmarsh, which he had so far failed to take. Then he was forced to prepare himself for battle, as Stephen and Eustace arrived on the opposite side of the river to besiege Wallingford. For all his human failings and evil deeds, Stephen was a fine warrior and did not lack courage. A headstrong man who moved in fits and starts and was driven by the heart rather than the head, he was eager to fight a pitched battle for his son's sake as well as his own, but neither side's barons would fight. Most of these barons held multiple estates on both sides of the Channel. If a battle should turn against them, or if they should lose their feudal overlord's favor, their lands could be confiscated either in whole or in part. Voting with their feet, they chose to avert the losses to themselves that they knew would follow if their leaders stayed at loggerheads.

Neither Henry nor Stephen wanted this outcome, and both bitterly attacked the selfish motives of their leading men. Eustace, who saw clearly that any accord with Henry would spell the end of his hopes to succeed his father on the English throne, violently upbraided his men for their cowardice but was powerless to act.

In a last-ditch effort to settle things between themselves, Stephen and Henry held a "private conference," shouting at each other, man to man, across a narrow reach of the Thames at Wallingford. They tried to agree on terms that would leave them free to fight another day but failed. They then withdrew while delegations from both sides met to negotiate a final accord. Henry went off to attack Stamford and Nottingham, while Stephen marched to Ipswich, where Hugh Bigod had captured the castle. As to Eustace, Gervase of Canterbury says that after ranting against his father for being prepared to allow the barons to sacrifice him "to a vain shadow of peace," he rode away in disgust toward Cambridge, where he mustered a fresh force and set out for Ipswich himself. Halting along the way at the abbey of Bury St. Edmunds, he demanded food and money for his troops. When the monks refused, he gave the order to pillage the abbey and its lands; despoiling the church ran in his family and held no terrors for him.

In the opinion of the author of the *Gesta Stephani,* Eustace got his just reward when God struck him down for his sacrilege. On about August 17, at the age of twenty-four, he died of a heart attack, described by the chroniclers as "a burning frenzy." His death removed the final obstacle to an accord, and the chroniclers joined the monks of Bury in rejoicing over the death of a man whom they regarded as a chief persecutor of the church and a greater, crueler tyrant than his father.

THE PEACE was brokered by Theobald, who emerges as the towering figure in politics and effectively the kingmaker. Throughout these delicate discussions, Becket was constantly by his side, rapidly emerging as an adept and determined fixer whom Theobald afterward described as "my first and only counselor." Both had arrived at Wallingford shortly before Eustace and Stephen had left for Ipswich; it was an open secret that they had been in communication with the principals on both sides for several months. Theobald had begun by visiting Stephen. He and Thomas had then met with Henry during the siege of Crowmarsh. Loosely attached to the Angevin court since April 9, when he had mediated in Henry's ongoing quarrel with Bishop Jocelin of Salisbury over which of them should have Devizes Castle, Theobald had decided to push for a political settlement in which Henry ended up as king. It was, as Becket remembered afterward, a highly fraught few months. Theobald, he recalled, had endured "hardships beyond number," for had he dealt his cards in the wrong order, Stephen might easily have accused him of treason.

The affair of Devizes Castle and its surrounding lands played a crucial part in persuading the archbishop to switch his allegiance from Stephen to the Angevins. When Henry offered to swear an oath to restore such a valuable and strategically placed property to the church within three years as the pope had commanded, he created the impression that he would be willing to restore to the church the lands that Stephen and the barons had so shamelessly pillaged. By now an older and wiser man, Bishop Henry of Winchester had come to regret his part in his brother's usurpation and was ably assisting Theobald, coaxing Stephen into reaching an agreement and leaving the archbishop free to concentrate on Henry.

Becket knew every intricate detail of the Devizes Castle business and in later years would come to rue it as a portent of what was to come. In 1157, by which time the castle should have been restored, Henry defaulted and forced Bishop Jocelin to abandon his claim to it and the adjacent parkland in exchange for a pittance. Writing to the pope in 1168 when his quarrel with the king was approaching its climax, Thomas cited this as just one of innumerable examples of Henry's perfidy. "If I wished to run through the similar encroachments which he has made," he complained, "when properties were taken away from others in the same way, and liberty was taken from all in common, so that not even the hope of freedom is left to anybody, a whole day would not be long enough."

None of this could have been foreseen. After six months of meticulous diplomacy, Theobald and Becket would broker a reconciliation between Henry and Stephen that was a source of wonder to the chroniclers. On November 6, 1153, the two rivals met at Winchester and announced that they had settled their differences. It was little short of a miracle, "withdrawing the scourge which had long tormented England." Stephen led Henry through the streets in a grand procession of bishops and nobles, culminating at the king's palace within the castle walls, where in a great council Stephen declared Henry to be his "son and heir" and the lawful successor to the crown. In return, Henry conceded that Stephen should rule England for the rest of his life provided he and each of the magnates took a solemn oath excluding Eustace's younger brother William from the throne. In addition, all those lands and castles that had changed hands by force during the civil war should be returned to their legitimate occupiers in the reign of Henry I—the first indication that the future king was determined to restore the status quo as it existed in his grandfather's lifetime.

When Stephen and Henry rode together to London, the bells rang and the citizens cheered as they and their followers processed into the city in triumph. Six weeks later, after most of the smaller details had been sorted out by Theobald, the magnates came to Westminster for the king's Christmas court, and the treaty was sealed. Proclaimed in the form of a charter addressed by Stephen to "all his liegemen of England," the document fully described the agreements that had been made and the oaths that had secured them. Stephen formally adopted Henry and took an oath to maintain him as his "son and heir." Henry and his men did homage to Stephen, and Stephen's men did homage to Henry, "saving only the fealty that they owed to the king for as long as he lived." William too did homage to Henry, who confirmed to him all the castles and manors that he had inherited, that his father had conferred on him, or that were due to him by marriage in England and Normandy. Neutral third parties took possession of the Tower of London and the castles of Windsor, Oxford, Lincoln, and Winchester, swearing to return them to Henry on Stephen's death. Finally, Theobald, Henry of Winchester, and all the bishops and abbots took an oath to Henry at Stephen's command and promised to punish all infringements of the treaty on pain of excommunication or interdict.

NOT ONLY did the Treaty of Westminster end the civil war, but it also laid the foundation for everything that was to come. While Thomas Becket is not included in the list of witnesses to the document, nobody below the rank of bishop or prior is mentioned in it by name. But the new Angevin king owed his throne at least in part to Becket, given his role as Theobald's fixer and right-hand man from the siege of Crowmarsh onward. And Thomas was certainly well rewarded, replacing Roger of Pont l'Évêque as archdeacon of Canterbury when Roger was sent north to be archbishop of York. With an income of at least £100 a year, more even than Roger would receive in his new post and roughly the same as the annual expenditure of an average baron, the archdeaconry was a far more significant position than its name suggests, fast-tracking Thomas and putting him alongside the bishops and abbots in wealth and status.

His new position required Becket to take holy orders as a deacon. No longer was he allowed to marry or (strictly) to bear arms, even if the second of these rules was acknowledged throughout Europe more in the breach than the observance. A deacon was unable to celebrate mass but could baptize children, assist the priests at the altar, and administer the last rites to the mortally sick. The final pieces of the puzzle fell into place for Thomas when Theobald appointed him dean of Hastings and recommended him for the provostship of Beverley. With these rich livings under his belt on top of the archdeaconry, his position as the man whom Theobald had marked out for a glittering future career could not be questioned.

What nobody could have predicted was how short a time he would have to wait. Among those marveling at the turn of events was the chronicler Gervase of Canterbury, who describes how on October 25, 1154, ten months after the Treaty of Westminster, Stephen suffered a violent pain in his lower abdomen at Dover Priory. Taking to his bed, he died within hours of a bloody flux. Henry, who had been briefly in Aquitaine and was now back at Rouen with Eleanor, raced to Barfleur to await a favorable wind. While everyone held their breath, Theobald assumed the regency until December 7, when Henry and Eleanor landed near Southampton; they were jointly crowned by the archbishop at Westminster Abbey on the nineteenth. Thomas Becket was there too. For nine years, he had been Theobald's clerk and right-hand man, involved in the most delicate and thrilling of poker games involving church and state. During that time, the influence of the church and the papacy had dramatically increased, and the archbishop of Canterbury, for the first time since 1066, had entered the political arena, attending the Council of Rheims in defiance of the king, imposing a papal interdict on England, narrowly escaping assassination at the hands of a dozen of the king's knights, and refusing to crown Eustace.

Henry was now twenty-one, Becket just two days short of his thirty-fourth birthday. But what would clearly most amaze all the chroniclers was that less than six weeks after Henry's triumphal return, Thomas would be catapulted into the limelight as the new king's chancellor, one of the highest offices in the realm and a meteoric promotion for a middle-class Londoner. At a stroke he became Henry's confidant, with the right to attend all meetings of the king's council whether invited or not. He had important financial and judicial responsibilities and was chief custodian of the king's seal, besides being in charge of the royal scriptorium, or writing office.

Gervase especially marvels that Henry's decision to make Thomas chancellor was taken "at the very beginning of the reign," as if it had already been settled in advance. Just how Henry came to make his choice has always been thought mysterious or inexplicable, but it is one of the most intriguing and important aspects of Becket's story. As the king's chancellor, he would be constantly by Henry's side, but within a few years the different values and character flaws of the pair would begin to surface, culminating in a clash of titans that only one of them could survive.

8
ARRIVAL AT COURT

THOMAS BECKET WAS NOMINATED AS HENRY II'S CHANCELlor during the king's Christmas celebrations held at Bermondsey Abbey immediately after the coronation and was appointed to the post within a month. Theobald wished to plant his own right-hand man at the heart of the king's inner circle in the church's interests, recruiting two of Henry's most experienced Norman counselors, Bishop Arnulf of Lisieux and Bishop Philip of Bayeux, to lobby on his protégé's behalf.

Roger of Pontigny, to whom Becket would later pour out his heart in exile, explains how Theobald feared for the future:

> There was no little trepidation in the church . . . on the one hand because of the worrying youth of the king, and on the other because of the well-known antipathy of his courtiers toward the church's right to liberty. . . . The archbishop of Canterbury, then, as troubled by the present as he was fearful for the future, planned to raise some defense against the evil which was thought imminent. And it seemed to him that if he could introduce Thomas to the king's councils, he could therefore provide calm and peace.

The "evil" against the church that Theobald is said to have foreseen is often assumed to be Henry's own, in which case he would swiftly have come to repent of his role as kingmaker. But Robert of Cricklade, who knew and understood the archbishop, declares that at this early stage it was the barons, not the king, whose designs he wished to prevent. As Theobald himself explained in a letter to Henry, "The sons of this world counsel you to lessen the authority of the church so that your royal power may be increased."

The church had been heavily pillaged in Stephen's reign, and the barons were largely responsible. Theobald, now in his mid-sixties, would never lose sight of the fact that the young king's grandfather had successfully stamped his authority on the barons. The new king, he believed, was the only credible guarantor of public order, and if order was lacking, the church was at a greater risk than if it went its own way. The restoration of a strong king who was also a lover of law and order could only be a blessing for the church. That blessing, Theobald knew, must come at a price, but he was at heart a pragmatist, a staunch advocate of cooperation between church and state in the mold of his distinguished predecessor Lanfranc. Most likely he considered his own politicization of the primacy in Stephen's reign to be an aberration—a necessary evil driven by the exceptional circumstances of the civil war; one that could be reversed by placing his own man at the heart of the royal court to steer the king into pathways sympathetic to the church. Clearly, by restoring the power of the monarchy, Theobald imagined that he would also be able to restore the king's traditional role as a patron and protector of the church. Then he would be free to devote himself fully to his pastoral work before he died.

Age thirty-four when he arrived at court, Thomas was still as slim and fit as when he had ridden out from Pevensey Castle with Richer de l'Aigle as a teenager. The hair around his tonsure was as yet untouched by flecks of gray; his face, once thin, had filled out, although his broad brow, aquiline nose, and large, bright eyes were just the same. His slender, tapering, white fingers contrasted sharply with the rough hands of the men-at-arms who surrounded him. Now mainly occupied with his official duties, he had not yet lost his passion for outdoor sports. He still pursued them eagerly, riding out with his favorite hawks, falcons, and hounds almost as often as before. And in the long winter evenings, he liked to relax over a leisurely game of chess. He was a brilliant player. The same memory skills that helped him to recall the winning moves enabled him to quote charters and official documents at will, remembering the smallest, most intricate details of his dealings with the king.

William fitz Stephen, who entered the new chancellor's household as a lawyer and clerk soon after his appointment, vividly describes Thomas's intimacy with Henry, claiming that the two men worked closely together from the outset, forming an extraordinary bond of friendship. When they finished their day's business, they would play together like boys of the same age—in hall, in church, or wherever else they happened to be. Henry would often call at the chancellor's house at dinnertime, even arriving bow in hand from the chase, when he would ride his horse directly into the chancellor's hall. Sometimes he would merely take a drink, then leave after chatting with Thomas; at other times he would stay to eat, vaulting over the tables to sit down beside Becket while those around him made space. Such was their mutual rapport that Becket could one day apparently boast, "I know my lord king inside out." "Never," concludes fitz Stephen, "in the whole epoch of Christian history were two men more of one mind or better friends."

This verdict has dominated writings on Thomas Becket for nine hundred years, but niggling doubts arise from fitz Stephen's deep reluctance to illustrate his case in any specific detail. Bland assertions are all that he can muster. Despite painting a glowing picture of a relationship of near equals, as if Henry and Thomas were blood brothers, he is unable to conjure up a single credible anecdote describing the happy times the king and his chancellor spent together. Spinning his tale after Becket's murder to justify his canonization by the pope, fitz Stephen seeks to cast all the blame for the two men's estrangement onto Henry's shoulders, milking their earlier familiarity for all it is worth to castigate better the king's subsequent behavior.

For as long as Henry's favor lasted, Thomas would enjoy a life of luxury and conspicuous consumption. Always ready to flaunt his success, he maintained a household said by his friends to be second only in size to the king's and by his enemies to be larger and more sumptuous. The exact size of his retinue is unknown, but since he kept six ships on regular standby for crossing the Channel, in comparison to Henry's twenty-five, it is likely to have contained a core of around 150 knights plus their servants. To entertain his guests, he assembled a traveling zoo, purchasing troupes of monkeys together with parrots and other exotic birds from Africa. He even kept a pair of wolves for use as hunting dogs. Unsurprisingly, his lifestyle attracted charges of hypocrisy from those affronted by his excess. Heavily criticized were his expensive furnishings and fashionable clothes, including silks and furs; so were his armies of servants and throngs of guests, among them several who brought their mistresses to dinner.

For a newcomer to the chancellor's role, a magnificent household would be essential to the job, since apart from being one of the principal ways in which he could establish his position as a power broker, it was also his duty to keep open house for the king and his friends. Generous hospitality was a social obligation. It is, however, equally true that a chancellor who was a born aristocrat would not have felt the need to entertain so lavishly. As a middle-class Londoner and an upstart in the eyes of genuine aristocrats, Thomas was determined to have the very best of everything and to impress, so no expense was spared. He also meant to keep the company of aristocrats, inviting earls and barons regularly to dine in his hall. When they arrived, he would be the most courteous and considerate of hosts, greeting each of his guests individually as they arrived and correcting in an instant the slightest oversight in the seating arrangements. His table glittered with gold and silver plate. He served the most expensive delicacies and the rarest wines—no price was too dear to deter his purveyors or his cooks. A single dish of eels, which rumour said he had purchased at a market near Paris for the fabulous sum of £100—enough to keep whole families of laborers in comfort for a lifetime—was long remembered as an example of his prodigality.

Henry might have taken exception to his chancellor's displays of grandeur and ostentation, calling them presumption, but if fitz Stephen's version of the story is to be believed, no such petty thoughts yet crossed his mind. Given control over a significant proportion of the royal revenues, Becket was free to spend money in ways he felt were consistent with the king's greater glory, which is how he could afford to live as he did. With Henry's confidence in him seemingly unbounded, he chose to position himself as close to the king as possible, representing himself to the world as the nearest thing to Henry's alter ego and exercising powers that placed him above all others save the members of the royal family.

THOUGH FOUR or more inches shorter than Becket, Henry too was well above average height. With broader shoulders and a stockier frame than the chancellor, he also had a larger, rounder head. His reddish brown hair was close-cropped, his complexion ruddy, and his skin freckled from constant traveling in the wind and rain. His arms were as strong as a wrestler's, his legs sturdy but bowed in later life from riding for days and weeks on end. Said to be perfect for the stirrup, his feet were highly arched, even if an ingrown toenail could make him walk with a limp. A hearty eater, prone to put on weight like his grandfather if he was not careful, he feared that he would one day grow too fat to mount his horse. His most distinctive features were his blue-gray eyes, "dove-like and guileless" when he was calm but "shimmering with fire and like lightning" when he was angry. It was said that they "grew fiery and bloodshot when he was in a frenzy."

Always outgoing and gregarious, Henry was utterly self-assured, hence careless of his personal appearance or reputation as a host. In his hall, says Peter of Blois, the secretary on whom he would chiefly rely at the height of his later quarrel with Becket, many of the lesser courtiers had to eat inferior meat or fish that was four days old, endure gritty bread, and drink sour wine or muddy beer, which might explain why people flocked to dine with the chancellor. He took little interest in his clothing; often it was impossible to distinguish him from his servants. Dressed for much of the time in riding gear, his legs were bruised constantly from the kicks of his horses. How casual about his appearance he could be is shown by his hands, unlike Becket's coarse and rough. According to Peter, he wore gloves only for hawking.

Impatient of royal etiquette, Henry did what he wanted when he wanted, night or day, rather than pleasing others for the sake of it or working to a plan. Burning prodigious quantities of candle wax while consuming equally phenomenal amounts of wine, he would often sleep until noon. Walter Map, a chaplain entering his service shortly after Becket's murder, compares his uncouth habits unfavorably with his grandfather's. Whereas, he says, Henry I maintained discipline in his court, which he ran like clockwork—reserving mornings for work and afternoons for pleasure, announcing in advance his travel plans and the dates and places of the various stops along the route—his grandson did everything almost literally on the hoof, imposing his authority by his constant movement from place to place. And whereas the older Henry made himself accessible at fixed times before dinner, his younger namesake shunned regular hours. One messenger granted admission after waiting three days and nights found him lying propped up on one elbow, dozing as a servant massaged his feet. Another visitor found him sitting on the ground surrounded by his courtiers, sewing up a bandage after a minor hunting accident.

Famous for its shouted instructions and disruptive horn calls announcing hunting expeditions, Henry's court was likened by eyewitnesses to a variety of earthly hell. As Peter explains:

> If the king has promised to spend the day in a place—and particularly if he has announced his intention publicly by the mouth of a herald—you may be sure he will upset everyone's plans by starting off early in the morning. Then you may see men rushing about like madmen, beating packhorses, running carts into one another—in brief, giving a perfect imitation of hell. If, on the other hand, the king announces that he will depart early in the morning, he will be sure to change his mind and you may take it for granted that he will sleep until midday. Then you will see the packhorses loaded and waiting, the carts standing idle, the drivers dozing, the purveyors worrying, and all grumbling to one another. People run to the prostitutes and the doorkeepers of the court to ask of them what the king really intends to do, for a royal court is always followed most assiduously by minstrels, harlots, dicers, flatterers, confidence-tricksters, pickpockets, actors, barbers, or clowns, and those sorts of people often know its secrets.

A restless spirit always looking for a fresh challenge, Henry was never idle, working as need required or his mood dictated, sometimes late into the night. Described as a "human chariot dragging all after him," he would mount his horse at daybreak, come back in the evening after a hard day's riding, and then exhaust his companions by keeping them on their feet until midnight. His favorite recreation was hunting. "He has," says Peter, "forever in his hands bows, arrows, hunting nets, and swords." A man of boundless energy, he traveled more widely than any of his contemporaries, rarely sitting down except at meals or when in the saddle. In public or in private, in chapel or in council, he stood or paced to and fro. "He was intolerant of quiet," says Walter Map, "and did not hesitate to disturb almost half of Christendom."

But Henry's punishing schedule cannot by itself explain how he could govern at a pace and with an intensity never seen before in his dominions. He could do so partly because, like Becket, he had a highly retentive memory. It was said that he never forgot a face and could recall anything that he had heard that was worth remembering. An excellent linguist, fluent in Latin as well as French, he had a basic working knowledge of most of the dialects spoken in France, including Occitan, the vernacular of Aquitaine. Surprisingly unable or unwilling to converse in English, he spoke to his English subjects in French. Said to be a proficient reader, not merely a competent one, he knew more than enough to check what his advisers or secretaries had written, ensuring that his more important writs or charters met his requirements.

His sexual life, if tainted by bouts of debauchery, looks to have been more restrained while Becket was alive than it afterward became, even if he would talk openly to his courtiers of his erotic dreams. Although the royal doorkeepers in England and Normandy doubled as Henry's whoremasters, evidence in the early years of his reign as to how often he called upon their services is hard to find. Rumor had it that his first son, William, a sickly child who died at the age of three, was a prostitute's offspring, but since Eleanor always accepted the baby as her own, it seems an unlikely tale. An irregular succession of casual affairs, especially when Eleanor stayed as regent in England and Henry was on the Continent, is the most likely scenario. One of these flings was with a noblewoman in Staffordshire named "Avice." Another was with the sister of Roger of Clare, Earl of Hertford. And a biological daughter called Matilda by an unknown woman would be made abbess of Barking on his instructions after the death of Becket's youngest sister, Mary.

Henry's chief weakness was his temper, which could flare up in seconds like a whirlwind. His favorite expletive—the one to which Becket would become accustomed—was *par les olz Dieu,* "by God's eyes," or, when he was especially roused, "by God's eyes and throat" or "by God's eyes and testicles." Says Peter of Blois, quoting the Bible, "The king's wrath is the harbinger of death." Entering the royal bedchamber every morning, Peter reports, he would first look at the king's face before daring to speak to him, afraid that anything he said might further inflame Henry if he was in a difficult mood. "To speak to an angry prince," he confides, "seems to me to be like casting fishing nets in a hurricane. He who does so, and will not wait until the storm is over, destroys himself and his nets." Unlike Becket, who relied on charisma and his quicksilver oratory to get his own way, Henry was a bully relying on threats and taunts. The difference was reflected in their voices. Becket usually spoke in the softer, more measured tones that he had learned to overcome his stammer, whereas Henry's voice was harsh and cracked from constantly barking out orders on horseback.

Normally his wrath subsided as swiftly as it arose. If he bawled people out in the morning, he would carry on as if nothing had happened in the afternoon, especially if their failings had been for reasons beyond their control. Though often lenient toward honest opponents (on a few occasions, he caused himself a great deal of unnecessary trouble), he could not tolerate disloyalty or breach of trust. Once his enmity was stirred, he would never forgive and forget. "If he once forms an attachment to a man," says Peter, "he seldom gives him up. If he has taken a real dislike to anyone, he rarely admits him afterward to any familiarity." Disloyalty not only rankled, it caused him to brood. His tirades against "traitors" were legendary; he would shout and swear and throw things around the room, as at Caen in 1166, when he upbraided the constable of Normandy, Richard de Humez, who had dared to speak in favor of someone with whom he had just quarreled. Burning with rage, he "tore his hat from his head, undid his belt, hurled his cloak and the clothes he was wearing far away from him, tore the silken covering from the bed with his own hand, and began to eat the straw on the floor, as if he were sitting in a ditch."

Henry's most shocking vice was sacrilege. He visibly lacked piety and was said to enter his private oratory to sketch or whisper to his friends instead of to pray. And he was more than happy to take a solemn oath without much intention of keeping it. His oath breaking would first come to light in 1157, when he did it three times. On the first occasion, he stripped Stephen's younger son William of those castles and estates guaranteed to him by the oaths linked to the Treaty of Westminster. Skillfully exploiting William's ongoing feud with Hugh Bigod, he confiscated all his properties without warning, returning only those that William had possessed on the day of Henry I's death. He afterward softened the blow somewhat with smaller marks of favor, knighting William when he fell back into line, but nothing could cloak his perjury. When he then refused to restore Devizes Castle to Jocelin of Salisbury in defiance of his oath before Theobald, it seems as if a pattern had been established.

In July of the same year, he broke another oath, made before he had become king, to cede Newcastle and the whole of Northumbria to Scotland in return for aid against Stephen. When the day of reckoning came, he chose to default and was lucky to get away with it when the Scottish king rode south to redeem the pledge. Henry put it to him bluntly, man to man, that he either had to break the oath or abandon his plans to restore the status quo as it had existed in his grandfather's lifetime. "Necessity," he said, required the former, claiming that his "ancestral rights" could not be alienated and that he had an overriding duty to protect them. Grudgingly accepting the earldom of Huntingdon as a consolation prize in the hope of better things to come, the Scottish king swore fealty to him and became his vassal, a result that was typical of Henry's flair for talking his way out of trouble.

VERY LITTLE BEYOND legends can be discovered about Eleanor's personality and daily life, despite more than a hundred references to her in the chronicles, more than 150 charters issued in her name, and several dozen accounts of her expenditures. Such perennially fascinating questions as whether she was a bad wife and mother, whether she liked vernacular French poetry and so was an eager patron of Poitevin poets like her grandfather, and how large her independent household was, are as impossible to answer as whether she was ever truly in love. Romantic fictions about her abound, returning to haunt her from generation to generation like trick birthday candles that cannot be extinguished. One claims that she presided over "Courts of Love" at Poitiers, pronouncing verdicts on the correct behavior for lovers according to the rules of courtly love. Another is that she led a battalion of three hundred women dressed as Amazons into battle in the Second Crusade.

Her charters and the fiscal evidence confirm that she was an extraordinarily wealthy woman. Besides her income from "queen's gold" (a levy of 1 mark of gold for every 100 marks of silver on certain payments to the king) and the revenues of Exeter in Devon and Waltham in Essex, she had lands in Hertfordshire, Berkshire, and Hampshire. That Henry granted her an independent household, which unlike his own included Poitevins, is almost certain, since his payments to her for its maintenance ran at around £600 a year, a substantial sum and far more than could be collected in annual rent from thirty fertile manors. Such payments suggest that she lived in extravagant luxury, spending significantly on herself, her children, her knights and ladies, her children's nurses, and her household servants. She paid regular salaries to her chaplain, chamberlain, steward, constable, almoner, and clerks. She had building projects carried out on her chapel, houses, and gardens, and she spent money on clothing and shields for her attendants. She even had her own ship on standby ready for Channel crossings.

She clearly liked clothes. Vast sums were spent in acquiring and transporting them on her behalf. She may also have enjoyed dicing, as one of her clerks had to pay her an annual rent of three ivory dice for lands he held from her. Otherwise, her most frequently itemized purchases, apart from furnishings for her chamber, included incense, pepper, wine, cinnamon, almonds, and chestnuts.

She did play an independent role as a literary patron. An Anglo-Norman translation of Geoffrey of Monmouth's *Historia Regum Britanniae* (*History of the Kings of Britain*), known as the *Roman de Brut*, was dedicated to her in 1155. Mingling the fiction of the Celtic legends of King Arthur with the known facts of pre-Conquest Britain, it was scripted to provide Henry and his immediate predecessors with a genealogy older and more distinguished than that of the Frankish rulers descended from Charlemagne, so poking the Capetian monarchy in the eye. In addition, the celebrated Poitevin poet and troubadour Bernard de Ventadour came to England to address his lyrics to her and Henry. Such works were probably sung or read aloud on long winter evenings, even if the record of a grant of land Henry made in Suffolk to a jester called "Roland the farter"—for making a leap, a whistle, and a fart annually at Christmas—gives a more accurate impression of his own preferences.

Although Eleanor's experiences were unavoidably conditioned by such male stereotypes as her fecundity, religious devotion, and works of mercy and piety, she broke this mold at several key moments in her married life with Henry. While Becket was alive, however, her influence was neither uniform nor complete, operating chiefly as an adjunct to her husband's kingly power. When she and Henry were together, her independent influence was minimal. When he was away on the Continent and she stayed in England as regent, she had more power. Theobald reports her anger when her word was doubted or her wishes frustrated, but this scarcely touched Becket, since if, while he was chancellor, Henry went abroad, Thomas would accompany him, and the two were seldom apart. One day Eleanor would shake the Angevin empire to its very foundations, but it would be as regent in Aquitaine, mainly after Becket's murder, that her political ambitions would most sensationally come to the fore.

THE FIRST LETTER that Becket discovered in his in-tray after arriving at court was from Arnulf of Lisieux, to whom Theobald had appealed for assistance in his efforts to secure Becket's appointment. No one understood Henry's psychology better, for Arnulf, a slippery courtier-bishop, had been his chief adviser in Normandy for more than four years. But if few knew more about the backstairs politics of a princely court, with its many fawning flatterers and backstabbing cliques and factions, none except Thomas would have a more chastening experience there. Within a few years, Arnulf would be severely castigated by his colleagues in the church for placing royal interests ahead of theirs. Even so, Henry would never fully trust him, since during the civil war Arnulf had attached himself to those who had questioned Henry's mother's legitimacy by claiming that she had been dragged from a nunnery, a slight against his ancestry that the Angevin king could not forgive.

Arnulf's letter, whatever his true motives for writing it, could not have appeared friendlier or more genuine. He well understood, he said, that he and the new chancellor could easily have become rivals, but Becket had assured him of his goodwill in an earlier letter (now lost)—one with which Arnulf professes himself delighted. Your cordiality, he unctuously insists, "seemed to me to drop honey and be redolent with the sweetness of affection. I was delighted to find that I had not lost the privilege of our early intimacy either by the wide distance which now separates us or by the pressure of business in which you are involved." But he also strikes a note of caution:

> Friendship is a rare virtue . . . and nowhere is it more rarely found than between those who are invited to give counsel to kings and to direct the affairs of kingdoms. To say nothing of other difficulties, ambition sits with a heavy weight upon their minds and as long as each fears to be outstripped by the vigilance of the other, envy springs up between them, which, before long, does not fail to become open hatred.

In idioms all too redolent of those Becket would use to his own followers ten years later, Arnulf—himself always jealous of the intimacy that sycophants enjoyed with the king—warns him of the dangers of smiling faces at court and of relying too much on Henry's confidences, since the minds of rulers can be fickle: "If the favor of the prince is changed and he begins to look on a man with a furrowed brow, all the deference and support of his erstwhile colleagues will disappear and the applause and obsequiousness with which they once showered him will wither."

No reply survives to this fascinating letter of advice, and what Becket's reaction was, we can only imagine. Arnulf did his best to heed his own advice, but despite giving his undivided allegiance to Henry in his efforts to marginalize Thomas once Becket's struggle with the king began in earnest, he would one day himself be driven from court, and the king would conspire with the clergy of his own cathedral in forcing him out of his bishopric. Unlike Thomas, however, he would die in his own bed.

9
ROYAL MINISTER

HENRY II BEGAN HIS REIGN AS HE MEANT TO GO ON, MAKING his own luck while playing for the highest possible stakes. From the outset, he planned to reintroduce what he would always like to call the "ancestral customs" of his grandfather. This involved reversing the losses the Crown had suffered during King Stephen's reign, while repudiating many of the concessions Henry had himself made as part of his succession bid. Once he was enthroned, his resolve was never seriously in doubt, however ingeniously he behaved in seeming to act only with the "advice and consent" of the magnates while in reality playing them off against one another. His own rhetoric considerably understated the case. While he imagined himself as simply returning to the governing ideals of the past, he was as much an innovator as a restorer. Three generations removed from William the Conqueror and brought up in Anjou, he had a fresh vision of the monarchy. He would boast that his grandfather had been "king in his own land, papal legate, patriarch, emperor, and everything else he wished." His worldview would steadily emerge over a decade and more. Ironically, Thomas Becket, as the king's chancellor, would play a crucial role in shaping these pretensions, for he would be at Henry's side, whether in England or on the Continent, for the whole of the first eight years of king's reign, apart from a few special assignments rarely lasting more than a few weeks or months.

Becket too began as he meant to go on, assisting Henry during his first year with the pacification of England and continuing the work he had begun as Theobald's fixer. As he rode nonstop around the country with the king, he drafted or witnessed a flurry of charters from places as far apart as London, Lincoln, York, Worcester, and Burton-on-Trent in Staffordshire that restored lands or castles to their rightful owners. Giving Henry the benefit of the doubt, the chronicler Gervase of Canterbury describes how he wished "to eliminate every reason for the resumption of warfare and to sweep away all incitements to mistrust." His earliest proclamations, which Becket may have drafted, set a time limit for the departure from England of Stephen's hated Flemish mercenaries and for the demolition of more than a hundred illegally built castles. His next moves were to build new fortifications from scratch, beginning with Orford Castle in Suffolk with its magnificent polygonal keep modeled on that at Gisors, a fortress meant to defend the coast and keep Hugh Bigod in check, and to reclaim lands and fortresses once belonging to his royal predecessors that had slipped into private hands during the civil war.

Faced with such a demonstration of raw power, Hugh de Mortimer, who had illegally occupied Bridgnorth Castle in Shropshire during the civil war, was one of only a handful of barons prepared to fight. "Estimating the king to be a mere boy and indignant at his activity," he fortified Bridgnorth and refused to obey the proclamation, provoking Henry to lay siege to his three castles. After they had fallen one by one, Hugh submitted at a great council attended by the bishops, earls, and barons, with Becket handling the paperwork. It was a cautionary tale, and with the prospect of losing his own castles, Bishop Henry of Winchester decided he had had enough and went voluntarily into exile. Last spotted at the royal court in March 1155, he left for his old abbey of Cluny before Christmas, first sending on ahead his treasure and fine collection of antique sculptures. Although the bishop reconciled with the king two years later, his influence would be greatly reduced, and on returning to Winchester, he would rarely be seen outside his palace or cathedral, where he would occasionally entrance his visitors by showing them Domesday Book and pointing out to them what his ancestor William the Conqueror had achieved.

* * *

BY CHRISTMAS 1155, Henry felt more secure in England than on the Continent, where he was threatened by a revolt led by his younger brother Geoffrey of Anjou and by Louis VII's refusal to recognize him as Duke of Aquitaine. Still resentful over Henry's marriage to his ex-wife, Eleanor, Louis was intensely jealous of her fecundity with Henry, for the birth of their first son, William, had been swiftly followed by another, named Henry after his father and great-grandfather, bringing to an abrupt end Louis's hopes that one day his daughters by Eleanor might succeed to her inheritance in Aquitaine. Leaving Eleanor to govern England as regent during his absence, Henry rode with Becket to Canterbury, crossed from Dover to Wissant, and finally reached Rouen on February 2, 1156. Once there, Thomas settled down again to his paperwork, sealing a series of charters, notably one to Merton Priory, where he had first attended school and where he had persuaded Henry to pay for the completion of the nave in the priory church.

The chancellor then set about raising the money needed to finance the king's campaign against Geoffrey. Wars were increasingly fought by professional soldiers, and Henry had thought it wise to hire an army of mercenaries locally in Anjou rather than summoning the feudal host in England and transporting it across the Channel. To fill his war chest, Becket helped Henry revive an unpopular tax called "scutage," or "shield money." First levied in his grandfather's reign to pay for mercenaries, scutage amounted to a tax in lieu of military service, allowing tenants in chief to pay a set amount rather than provide knights and equipment for the king's army. But Becket's war tax was doubly controversial, since to cut corners he imposed it at a flat rate of 20 shillings (around £600 today) on each knight's fee regardless of how many soldiers were owed. While raising more than enough money to pay Henry's troops, he elicited howls of protest, including one from Theobald, who petitioned for an exemption but was refused.

With his brother Geoffrey protesting against the size of his inheritance and speciously arguing that he alone was rightfully ruler of Anjou, Touraine, and Maine according to their father's will, Henry summoned a family conference at Rouen in an effort to settle their differences. It was very much in his interests to do so, since if his aggrieved overlord,

King Louis, were to recognize Geoffrey as Count of Anjou while Henry was still pressing his own claim for recognition as the new Duke of Aquitaine by virtue of his marriage to Eleanor, he could have been forced to defend much of his empire to the south of Normandy in battle.

Fortunately, Louis did not want to fight either. So after messages had been exchanged, Henry met Louis in the Vexin and did him homage for the whole of Normandy, Anjou, Touraine, Maine, and Aquitaine, outmaneuvering and isolating Geoffrey, whose allies promptly deserted him. When at the end of February the king's younger brother fortified his castles and summoned his retinue to battle, few answered the call. Henry then surrounded his brother's fortresses at Chinon and Mirebeau and dug in with more than enough provisions for lengthy sieges. Geoffrey had no choice but to submit, renouncing his claims in return for a generous pension. Only Eleanor seems to have resented this outcome, which she saw as a further move toward absorbing her ancestral duchy of Aquitaine permanently into the Angevin empire.

With his inheritance apparently secure, Henry decided to intervene in the disputed succession in the duchy of Brittany. He was eager to expand his influence westward into the rich lands that the dukes of Normandy had long claimed as a feudal dependency, especially coveting the port of Nantes, the gateway to the Loire. By skillfully exploiting a civil war begun there after Duke Conan III's death eight years before, he was able to persuade the citizens of Nantes to elect Geoffrey as their count and the Breton barons to choose one of his own Norman vassals, Conan IV, as their new duke. Gervase of Canterbury reports that the idea of resettling Geoffrey at Nantes had all along been Becket's. If so, it was a helpful one, giving Henry's disgruntled sibling an opportunity to redeem himself rather than encouraging him to rebel again by disowning him completely.

In June 1156, Henry's first daughter was born and named Matilda after his mother, through whom he had inherited his claim to the English throne. Just as soon as Eleanor had recovered from her delivery, she crossed from England to join her husband at Rouen, and their combined entourage began a leisurely journey first to Anjou, where they stayed for a while and where the abbot of Battle tracked down Becket with a petition, and afterward to Aquitaine. There they ejected a rebellious viscount from his lands and razed his castles before celebrating Christmas at Bordeaux, attended by the barons of Aquitaine, who swore oaths of fealty and paid homage to them jointly—a conciliatory move on Henry's part, since without Eleanor's consent, it is unlikely that these barons would have agreed to acknowledge him as duke. With his reach now extending as far south as Bayonne on the borders of Navarre, Henry had every reason to see his marriage as a great asset. Even so, because he had no intention of allowing Eleanor to rule her ancestral lands in Aquitaine herself, he was storing up trouble for the future.

Becket on this occasion had accompanied the royal family only as far south as Limoges, also shuttling to and from England, where he traveled around the countryside hearing legal cases. Among his other, more important solo duties around this time was the entertainment of visiting diplomats. William fitz Stephen records how he greeted the ambassadors of the king of Norway, lavishing on them everything they needed for their stay. He then received envoys from the German emperor, Frederick Barbarossa, and from the Moorish king of Valencia and Murcia. Welcoming the Germans, who wished to pay their respects to a king who was clearly going to be one of the future arbiters of Europe, Thomas gave them a gift of gold coins together with four prize gyrfalcons. The Valencian ambassadors brought gifts of gold, silk, and other precious wares from Africa and the Middle East, hoping to negotiate a league with Aquitaine in a war against the North African sect known as the Almohades, who had conquered Granada and were threatening to overwhelm both Christian and Muslim Spain. Unable to give them an answer on his own, Becket had to send them back across the Channel to Henry, who thrust gifts on them in return but was otherwise noncommittal.

Such encounters, however glamorous, were soon to be eclipsed by the crucial part Becket would come to play as a peacemaker with France. When Henry and Eleanor returned north from Bordeaux in January 1157, there was still unfinished business with King Louis. This centered on control of the perennially disputed frontier territories of the Vexin, for Louis had been given firmly to understand that Henry had paid him unconditional homage for his continental empire only on the condition that the old Norman lands ceded to France by the Angevins during their struggle against King Stephen would one day be restored to him. When the royal couple were greeted by Becket at Falaise, the preliminary negotiations with Louis had already begun. Becket and Eleanor crossed the Channel to England during February, leaving Henry to follow with the rest of the court in early April. At first the diplomacy with France went slowly. The breakthrough came in the spring of 1158, when Louis and his second wife, Constance of Castile, had a daughter, whom they christened Margaret.

Barely was Margaret out of her cradle than Becket led a magnificent embassy to Paris. His instructions were to forge a dynastic alliance by betrothing the infant to Henry's son and heir, the younger Henry, still under four, on the understanding that her dowry would be the lands of the old Norman Vexin. After debating the betrothal with his barons, Henry deputed his chancellor to arrange everything. For his part, Thomas meant to spare no expense in demonstrating to the world all the luxury and ostentation that the Angevin empire could provide—a display of splendor and opulence worthy of a king who ruled territories stretching a thousand miles from Northumbria to Gascony.

With more than two hundred mounted followers in his retinue—including knights, clerks, stewards, servants, esquires, and young pages, all fitted out in costly apparel, each according to his rank—Thomas traveled to Paris in style, equipped with twenty-four changes of clothes. Most of these he wore only once or twice and then gave them away as either presents to Louis's counselors or gifts to the poor. Very few of his possessions escaped this extraordinary exhibition of philanthropy—neither his rare furs, rich silks, and expensive cloaks, nor his tapestries, carpets, and bed-curtains. For his own recreation and further to impress his hosts, he also took with him several packs of hunting dogs, together with falcons, hawks, and exotic birds of every kind from his mews and aviaries.

To transport the mountain of baggage needed for such a spectacle, every one of the departments of Becket's household was allocated its own wagons, each drawn by five horses comparable in size and strength to warhorses. Each horse had its own groom walking alongside the wagons, sporting a brand-new tunic, and each wagon had its own driver and guard. Two were laden with the finest English beer, others with clothes, furniture, cushions, bed linen, food and drink, kitchen equipment, and so on. And each one had chained to it a great mastiff as strong as a lion or bear, fierce enough to frighten away thieves or marauders.

Behind them in the caravan came twelve packhorses, each once again with its own groom and with a monkey on its back. These packhorses bore bundles containing the most valuable items: the ornaments and vestments of Becket's chapel, rare books and manuscripts, gold and silver plate, money, vases, bowls, goblets, flagons, basins, saltcellars, spoons, and plates.

Whenever the cavalcade approached a French village or castle, it would form itself into a procession to impress the gawping onlookers, to whom free English beer would be distributed. First walked the footmen, around 250 of them in groups of six or ten or more, filling the width of the road and singing as they went. Behind them were Becket's hunting dogs and greyhounds, on leashes and chains, with their keepers. Then came the wagons, covered with hides to protect the luggage, followed by the packhorses, now ridden by their grooms. The incredulous villagers would flock from their houses to see what the approaching din was all about and to whom this astonishing retinue belonged.

Becket always had a well-developed theatrical streak to match his talents as a power broker. Little did the wide-eyed villagers know as they turned their heads toward what they believed to be the rear of the parade that the star of the show was still to come. A short distance behind the main column were the esquires, carrying the shields of their knights and leading their chargers; next came their young pages; then the falconers, each with a hawk on his glove; after them the clerks, stewards, and lesser functionaries of Becket's household, riding two by two. Last of all, flanked by a small group of bodyguards, was the chancellor himself. When the villagers asked who this great man could be and were told it was the English king's chancellor going on an embassy to their own king, they all exclaimed, "If this is the chancellor and he travels in such great state, how much greater must the king himself be!"

Nor was this the full extent of Becket's dramatic art. It was the custom of the Capetian kings to offer unstinting hospitality to their guests, and as Thomas approached Meulan in the French Vexin, some thirty miles from Paris, Louis issued a proclamation forbidding the sale of any victuals whatsoever to the chancellor or his servants during their stay, since he would provide them. Determined to upstage his hosts, Becket sent his purveyors ahead in disguise, using false names, to all the markets and fairs in the vicinity of Paris. There, on his instructions, they bought up such a supply of bread, meat, fish, and wine that when he arrived at his lodgings at the Temple, he found it stocked with three days' provisions for a thousand men.

Thereafter, Becket showered every imaginable courtesy upon his hosts. Each member of the French court, from the grandest aristocrat to the humblest servingman, received a token of the chancellor's wealth and generosity. Knowing no bounds, his gestures of liberality included gifts to all the masters and students in the schools, where he had once been a student. Such was his desire to make a splash that everyone would remember, he even included the landlords and creditors of all the English students in his largesse.

When Louis promised his daughter's hand to Henry's son and the terms of a dynastic treaty were agreed on, Becket's efforts and colossal expenditure were rewarded. Such was the increasing rapport between Thomas and Louis, the Capetian king could not see that the English chancellor was beguiling him into believing that a rapprochement with the Angevins would increase his security. By the terms of the marriage treaty, Becket secured a written undertaking that the lands and castles of the whole of the Norman Vexin would be restored to Henry on the day of his son's wedding, and in return Margaret would receive a settlement of £2,000, the revenues of the cities of Lincoln and Avranches, and lands sufficient to support five hundred knights in England and Normandy. Thomas also obtained confirmation of Henry's ancestral claim, as Count of Anjou, to be hereditary high steward of France, a brilliant move that within a few weeks would prepare the way for the near annexation of Brittany. On his journey back to England, Thomas had an unexpected opportunity while out hunting to show off his riding skills by chasing after and capturing an incorrigible Norman rebel, Guy of Laval, who had so far evaded Henry's clutches and whom Thomas put in chains. When he greeted Henry on his return to Westminster, his prestige had never been higher.

* * *

ON JULY 27, 1158, Henry's younger brother Geoffrey died at the age of twenty-four, throwing the Bretons into turmoil. Conan IV, the vassal whom Henry had imposed as Duke of Brittany, promptly seized the county of Nantes, usurping his overlord's right to dispose of it as he thought fit and reneging on their pact made two years before. Henry's retribution would be swift, for this amounted to a declaration of war. Leaving Eleanor as regent in England, a furious Henry set sail for Normandy. But to avoid jeopardizing his treaty with France, he first consulted Louis. Meeting Henry between Gisors and Neufmarché on August 31, Louis charged him as his hereditary high steward to pacify the Bretons and arbitrate the rival claims as he saw fit. It was a virtual invitation to conquer Brittany, and at Argentan, on September 8, Henry summoned the feudal host of Normandy to muster in three weeks. Meanwhile, he rode to Paris, where he was fêted by Louis and the betrothal was ratified. Two weeks later, Henry secured the guardianship of the infant French princess, who was placed in the household of Robert of Neubourg, the high steward of Normandy, and his wife, where she was to be brought up until she reached a marriageable age.

In a striking contrast with Becket's recent embassy, Henry avoided pomp and show, declining much of the lavish entertainment that Louis thrust upon him and presenting himself as a pillar of moderation and self-restraint. He had no desire for a protracted stay. All he wanted was to obtain the guardianship of his son's future bride and then turn his mind to conquering Brittany. As it turned out, a conquest would not be necessary, since when the feudal host of Normandy duly assembled on September 29, Conan IV surrendered. Realizing that he stood no hope of defeating Henry in battle, he threw himself on the king's mercy and was confirmed as the client-duke of Brittany in return for ceding the town of Nantes. Already Henry's liege man for his lands in Normandy and heavily outnumbered by his vastly superior forces, Conan had no choice but to yield.

After taking possession of Nantes in October, Henry went on to besiege Thouars, where its castellan had rebelled against him. In November he met Louis again at Le Mans and escorted him on a triumphal progress around Normandy. Resting overnight at Bec Abbey on their way to Mont-Saint-Michel, they were greeted by the monks and led in a solemn procession to mass, where Louis was overheard saying that there was no one he more highly esteemed than the king of England. "*Mirabile dictu*" (Wonders never cease), observed the Bec Abbey chronicler sardonically. So stunned was Gervase of Canterbury by this newfound amity, he reported that "an earthquake was felt in various places in England and in London the Thames dried up, so that it was possible to walk across it without getting wet feet." In the minds of the chroniclers, political events of seemingly cosmic significance were always associated with miracles or unexplained phenomena such as comets or earthquakes, ghostly apparitions or monstrous births.

Now back in Normandy and accompanying the two kings on every stage of their circuit of the duchy, Thomas Becket confidently believed that his intimacy with Henry had never been deeper. As he stood beside the two kings at the abbey of Mont-Saint-Michel, he may even have believed his international standing to be secure. In December, after Louis had returned to Paris, Thomas spent Christmas with Henry and Eleanor, and when the queen retraced her steps to England to resume her duties as regent, he rode with Henry to Rouen.

Little did he know that unpredictable, dramatic events would shortly occur that would throw his position and all his achievements so far dangerously into jeopardy.

10

BUREAUCRAT AND JUDGE

BESIDES BEING CHIEF CUSTODIAN OF THE KING'S SEAL, Becket managed the royal scriptorium and sat in the Exchequer and the royal courts of justice. In the Exchequer (its name was derived from the black checkered cloth spread over the table on which the sheriffs' accounts were audited), he had to work alongside one of the two chief barons, but he could authorize payments in his own name. He was also in charge of the king's chapel, where the royal collection of saints' relics, some of them going back to the pre-Conquest era, was kept. When Henry traveled around the countryside, these relics went with him, carried in special coffers. For all his lack of genuine piety, he was eager to invoke the miraculous powers and sacral mystique surrounding English kingship, making a pilgrimage to the shrine of St. Edmund, the ninth-century king of the East Angles killed in battle fighting the heathen Vikings, and vigorously supporting the efforts of the monks of Westminster Abbey to secure the canonization of King Edward the Confessor.

Although there had been a king's seal and a chaplain or keeper in charge of it since the tenth century, Becket would transform the chancellorship into something far closer to the great office of state it afterward became, dramatically increasing the number of clerks in the scriptorium, where he was in charge of translating the king's will into charters, letters, and writs. Before 1154, the chancery clerks—no more than two to four during Henry I's reign and a maximum of eleven during Stephen's—were often called away at the direction of the king or his senior officials to other tasks, imperceptibly merging with other clerks who had no fixed duties. Beginning with sixteen clerks after he was appointed chancellor, Becket poached scribes from the church and its courts, making them his own loyal servants and familiars, until the number rose as high as fifty-two. Aware of their potential as future diplomats and royal bureaucrats, Thomas looked for bright young men, whom he lodged and trained in his own household. He also brought back several of the best of the older clerks whom Stephen had ousted, notably "Peter the Scribe," a masterful calligrapher who had migrated to Archbishop Theobald's service, which is where Thomas had first got to know him.

Like many a talented bureaucrat, Becket was eager to raise the status of the office he held, making it "second only to the king." After living in Paris as a student for just over two years, he was fully aware of the pomp and pageantry of the Capetian chancellor, which he clearly sought to imitate. His program of building repairs and improvements at the palace of Westminster—said to have been completed within six weeks by a vast army of masons and carpenters specially conscripted for the purpose—may chiefly have been intended to provide Henry and Eleanor with lodgings comparable in luxury and sophistication to those of the French king on the Île de la Cité in Paris. But these renovations almost certainly included the provision of dedicated work space for himself and his clerks when they were in London. Up until then, the chancellor's clerks had worked largely from home or wherever they could find a vacant spot to set down their pens, penknives, and inkhorns in the great hall of a royal palace or the refectory of a monastery. In France, the chancellor was already providing his clerks with basic office accommodations, and Becket may have aimed to do the same.

THE EXCHEQUER, whereby custom the chancellor gave precedence to one of the chief barons, was the place where the regular tax, or "farm," from the shires and towns was collected, along with other taxes such as scutage, feudal dues, or fines and amercements. Each sheriff came twice a year at Easter and Michaelmas to account for what he owed, once to make a payment and afterward to be audited and to settle the balance of his account. Sometimes the Exchequer sat at Winchester, Oxford, Northampton, or Gloucester, but more often it was based at Westminster.

Becket's baronial colleagues there were both much older than he was. Robert de Beaumont, Earl of Leicester, was sixteen years older, the son of a Norman knight ennobled and richly rewarded by William the Conqueror after fighting valiantly at the battle of Hastings. A genuine heavyweight with an aristocratic lineage going back several generations, he was one of the most powerful barons on either side of the Channel. Educated at Abingdon Abbey, where he had studied more than enough Latin and moral philosophy to astonish the diplomats and cardinals of Pope Calixtus II on the eve of the sinking of the *White Ship*, he had become one of King Stephen's staunchest supporters but was among the first to come to terms with the Angevins in the spring of 1153, which is when Becket first encountered him. His relations with the new chancellor were good, even warm, but his unusually vocal support for the theory of the divine right of kings—his favorite phrase was that the king ruled "in the image of God himself" and he would repeat it to anyone who would listen—meant that he held views about kingship closely resembling Henry's own, which would lead him one day to clash diametrically with Thomas.

Richard de Lucy was of a different type. Six years younger than de Beaumont, he was harder, more unflinching, and less flexible, remaining loyal to Stephen after many of his fellow barons had switched sides. A self-made man, he lacked a pedigree and a formal education; his wealth and achievements owed everything to his own efforts and almost nothing to those of his ancestors. First granted land in Suffolk by Henry's grandfather, he was the son of an ordinary Norman knight and had risen high mainly through his military skills, ably supported by his kinsmen, who had their own semi-independent network of clients and hangers-on. From the very beginning, there was a degree of tension between Thomas and him, for de Lucy was none other than the chief henchman whom Stephen had sent to demand Theobald's submission after he had defied the king and attended the Council of Rheims with Becket in tow.

More often than de Beaumont, de Lucy presided in the Exchequer, although both took their turns, sitting at the head of the table flanked by Becket, two chamberlains, and the marshal. To their right sat the treasurer and his scribe, the chancellor's scribe, and one of the chancellor's clerks. To their left sat the senior clerk and another official appropriately known as the calculator. Spread over the table in front of all of them was a black cloth divided by lines into rows or columns, representing pounds (in rows of tens, twenties, hundreds, thousands, and tens of thousands), shillings, and pence. When a sheriff or other debtor came to render his account, the calculator placed silver pennies used as counters in piles in the appropriate columns to indicate how much in total was owed. He placed a second set of counters to indicate the payments that had already been made. This made it easy to work out everyone's debit or credit balance. The chancellor's scribe and the treasurer's scribe recorded every aspect of the day's business on long, narrow parchment sheets, and Becket's principal duty was to challenge any entry that he believed to be mistaken or ambiguous.

Thomas also sat with the barons and bishops to decide legal cases in the *curia regis,* or "king's court" (meaning both a court of law and the central administration as a whole), also serving during Lent and in the summer as one of the so-called itinerant justices—panels of circuit judges traveling around the countryside. Henry intended to resume his grandfather's attack on serious crime and disorder, increasingly claiming an exclusive jurisdiction over treason, homicide, theft, and rape, and seeking at least to oversee, if not actively monopolize yet, other types of litigation usually heard in the feudal or local courts that he believed affected his rights, chiefly land disputes. As in France, where the activities of an energetic chancellor named Hugh de Champfleury had greatly expanded the work of the judiciary in a relatively brief period and so increased royal income from fines, Henry expected Becket to blaze a trail.

Very few judicial records survive before the reign of King John (1199–1216), allowing only occasional snapshots of Becket's attitude toward justice. But in the few reports that remain, he appears more as a peacemaker than as a ruthless manipulator, prepared to help in reconciling to Henry those who had somehow offended the king, rather than seeking their prosecution and punishment to the extremity of the law. If this was indeed the chancellor's approach to justice, it resonates with the principles of "equity and reason" he had learned while studying Roman law at the law schools of Bologna and Auxerre. In one of the very few cases he decided for which written evidence is available, he successfully reconciled a litigant to the king after Henry had sequestered his property and padlocked his house, so that he and his family were cast onto the street. After Thomas intervened to propose a settlement, the man's property was fully restored to him.

Another case, the most important heard while he was chancellor, appears to show him in a markedly less favorable light. The case began in May 1157, while Henry and Becket were traveling around East Anglia. Thc plaintiff was Richard de Lucy's brother Walter, abbot of Battle, who sought a remedy against Bishop Hilary of Chichester. Bad blood had long existed between the parties, whose attitude toward justice was typical of what any independent-minded judge would have been up against in Henry's law courts if he wished to act fairly and honestly. Walter, a Norman monk who had followed his brother across the Channel in Stephen's reign, had been appointed to the plum post of abbot of Battle, the Sussex monastery founded as William the Conqueror's penance for the blood spilled at the battle of Hastings. Later, he had been a candidate for the bishopric of London, from which he hoped one day to leap into the primate's chair. But Bishop Hilary had refused to recommend him. And then Hilary had claimed a right of supervision over the morals and discipline of the abbey, which lay within his diocese, greatly annoying Walter and his monks and provoking them to resist Hilary tooth and nail.

By 1157, their dispute had long reached fever pitch, with the bishop excommunicating Walter for refusing to obey him and the abbot exploiting his political connections to denounce Hilary for exceeding his authority. The abbot's trump card was a charter he claimed had been granted by William the Conqueror, exempting Battle Abbey from all episcopal interference. There was indeed a copy of a charter to this effect, which it seemed both William Rufus and Henry I had confirmed. All the abbey's early charters had been preserved in pristine condition, which, with hindsight, is hardly surprising, since it turns out that all of them were ingenious forgeries. But at the time, nobody suspected this; the Battle Abbey charters were not denounced as forgeries until 1234, a verdict that was not to be scientifically proved until 1932. The issue for the judges was therefore simple but explosive. Did the king of England have the power to exempt the monks from the bishop's jurisdiction? The abbot and his brother believed that he did. The bishop, though in other matters loyal to Henry, insisted that this right was the pope's alone.

Henry convened his judges to decide the case at Colchester Abbey in Essex on the morning of Friday, May 24, 1157, after mass. Founded by Eudo the Steward in 1096 and consecrated in 1104, the abbey was dedicated to St. John the Baptist and sat on fourteen acres of grounds. Presiding himself in the chapter house, situated off the cloister on the south side of the abbey church away from the noise and bustle of the town, Henry was flanked by Robert de Beaumont and Richard de Lucy, Becket and Richard de Humez, the constable of Normandy. From this point on, the Battle Abbey chronicler is the chief, often the only, source for the proceedings. First, Richard de Lucy, who acted as his brother's legal advocate while retaining his seat on the bench, gave the opening speech, after which Henry told the abbot to produce his charters, which Becket read out to the court. After closely inspecting them, Henry swore, "By God's eyes, if ever I were to found an abbey, I would have for it none other than the liberties and privileges of Battle Abbey." Becket then asked the abbot if he had anything further to say. Walter denied that he had done anything to offend the bishop and was supported from the bench by his brother, who ended the first day's hearing with a long panegyric praising Battle Abbey as a monument to Norman daring and achievement.

The case resumed on the following Tuesday with Theobald, Roger of Pont l'Évêque, and several other bishops and abbots now reinforcing the permanent judges. Becket brought everyone up to speed by reading once again the abbey's charters, before inviting the bishop to set out his defense. Hilary's speech instantly touched a nerve with Henry, since he delivered a lecture extolling the values of the ascetic reform movement in the church and the power of the papacy. Though a brilliant canon lawyer, who had made a reputation for himself in cases heard before the pope, Hilary had one major failing. He could never stop himself from saying too much. And now he claimed that the church and the bishops should be free of all secular control, remarks that enraged Henry. "The church of Rome," Hilary said, "marked out by the ordained successors of the Prince of the Apostles, has achieved so great and so marvelous a preeminence throughout the world that no bishop, no ecclesiastical person at all, may be deposed from his position without its judgment and permission."

"Very true," snarled Henry through his teeth. "A bishop may not be deposed, but see (and at this he gave a violent shove with his hands), with a really good push, he could be thrown out!" Everyone burst out laughing, but Hilary was unabashed. He bravely reiterated his main argument that it was impossible for any layman, even for the king, to dictate the terms of the privileges and exemptions to be allowed to churches or monasteries except by the pope's permission.

Henry had heard enough. "You are plotting," he accused Hilary, "to attack the royal prerogatives given to me by God with your crafty arguments. So by your fealty and your binding oath to me, I command that you undergo just legal judgment for presumptuous words against my crown and royal prerogative."

A buzz instantly went around the room. Would Henry now accuse Hilary of treason? The Battle Abbey chronicler's story is that Becket sharply rounded on the bishop, saying, "You have forgotten your allegiance to the king, to whom you have, we know, taken an oath of fealty. You should therefore be prudent." Hilary, realizing he had crossed the line, began again. "My lord," he said, addressing Henry, "if I have been tactless toward your royal majesty, I declare before God in heaven and your royal dignity that I meant no crafty attack upon you or your royal prerogative." But the king was unmoved. "As everyone is aware," he retorted, "your fawning, lying words are meant to destroy the prerogative that by God's grace has been handed down to me from the kings, my ancestors, in hereditary right."

Hilary stumbled through the rest of his case, but Henry cut him short, declaring, "We have heard something of a marvel here: something to be exceedingly wondered at, that the charters of the kings my predecessors . . . have been adjudged too drastic by you, lord bishop." And he issued a warning: "May it not come to this. May the splendor of my reign never see a time when things I decree, as dictated by reason and by the counsel of my archbishops, bishops, and barons, are to be criticized or judged by you and your ilk."

Seeing the king and the judges about to retire, Walter spoke again, for his rival had made serious allegations against him, and he wished to clear his name. But Henry silenced him. This case was no longer to be about the privileges of Battle Abbey. "From now on," the king retorted, "it is I who must defend this case as my own personal and royal business."

Hearing this, Richard de Lucy asked permission to withdraw and take counsel with his brother while Henry went to mass. By the time the service was over, at least if the Battle Abbey chronicler is to be believed, Becket, as the king's chancellor, had taken de Lucy's place as the prosecutor, purportedly introducing devastating new evidence exposing Hilary as a hypocrite, who professed his fealty to the king but who, three months before, had appealed to Rome behind Henry's back and obtained a papal decree imposing canonical obedience on the abbot, which Walter had refused to obey.

Glaring straight at Hilary, Henry barked, "This decree that was mentioned. Did you ask for it? By your oath of fealty to me, I order you to tell me the truth."

Terrified, the bishop lied. "By the oath of fealty which I took to you as my lord," he replied, "I deny that I or anyone to my knowledge asked for this document."

Immediately, Theobald, who knew differently, crossed himself in holy terror. Henry then retired with his judges and the bishops to the monks' cemetery, and when they returned, the parties stepped forward. No judgment was delivered, because Hilary already knew what he was expected to do. Henry nodded for him to begin, and Hilary read out a written statement in everyone's hearing amounting to an abject, humiliating surrender. He withdrew all his claims against the abbot, adding at Henry's express command that he did so "voluntarily" and "not under any compulsion." At Theobald's urging, the king then gave him the kiss of peace, and Hilary did the same to Abbot Walter and his brother. While everyone kissed, the archbishop made the sign of the cross over them in a final benediction. The Battle Abbey chronicler was exultant.

He and his fellow monks set out for home in triumph to Sussex, praising God and St. Martin, their patron saint.

AND YET NOT every impression left by written sources created nine hundred years ago may be true. In 2001, a leading expert, Professor Nicholas Vincent, proved that large chunks of the Battle Abbey chronicle are as spurious as the abbey's forged charters. The chronicle was previously thought to be an accurate representation of Abbot Walter's famous victory over Bishop Hilary, but it now turns out that the key passages were manufactured afterward to provide a context and a background for the forged charters rather than reflecting what was actually said in court. The episode seems to capture exactly Henry's attitude toward the church and the power of the papacy, but was Thomas Becket just as strident and exacting in his demands?

Writing to the pope ten years later, the former royal chancellor would take a very different view from that put in his mouth by the chronicler, citing Henry's conduct in this famous case as one of the more scandalous events of recent times. "What progress," he asks, "could the bishop of Chichester make against the abbot of Battle, despite having apostolic privileges on his side?" Had he not been forced to make a humiliating submission? "For thus," insists Thomas, "it pleased the king and the court, which dared to contradict him in nothing."

Unlike all the other evidence in this case, Becket's letter of 1168 is a wholly genuine document. Its provenance has never been challenged or suspected, whereas the Battle Abbey chronicler is now exposed as a forger on the grandest scale. And there are other unresolved puzzles. It seems distinctly odd that Thomas should have introduced such deadly testimony about the papal decree so late in the day when, according to the abbey chronicler—who failed to notice how this jars—Abbot Walter and his brother had known everything about it from the outset but never referred to it in court. Becket's shocking revelation, had he been the one to make it, would have caused a sensation, and yet the abbey chronicler's account of his lethal strike is uncorroborated. Neither John of Salisbury, usually the most prolific source of news, nor any of Becket's early biographers even mentions the chancellor's role in the Battle Abbey case or felt the need to explain away his actions or rebuke him. The whole affair was far deeper and murkier than it appears to be.

Such questions become compelling when we realize that the case documents were not copied into the abbey chronicle until long after Becket's murder, when the old dispute with the bishop of Chichester would reignite. The narrative we now possess is actually a composite version of several different manuscripts, some genuine, some forged, once kept separately then subsequently edited and recopied, until they were finally bound up together as one consolidated document that has all the appearance of a systematic unity but that in reality is a hybrid.

Nothing, therefore, about the case as recorded in the chronicle can be accepted as fact. All that can be said with certainty is that Thomas witnessed a document drafted by Theobald recording Bishop Hilary's "voluntary" submission to the king. After Becket's murder, what purports to be his speech in their favor gave the monks of Battle the invincible authority of a canonized saint; the fact that he seemed to be arguing the precise opposite of one of the chief points for which he would be assassinated was immaterial to them. Their undivided allegiance was to the king because of their special history as William the Conqueror's foundation. So narrow was their mindset that such a glaring discrepancy was of little concern to them. The long-term result of their spin was one day to make Thomas appear to be an even greater hypocrite than Hilary in the eyes of his detractors, but at the time the monks' sole purpose was to vindicate their forged charters. Perhaps Thomas did indeed make some sort of speech on their behalf. It can never be known for certain. But even supposing he had been willing to collude with Henry in what amounted to a show trial, was that something that he could go on doing forever?

11
WARRIOR

AFTER LEAVING COLCHESTER IN MAY 1157, HENRY AND Becket spent a further six weeks in Essex, lodged, among other places, at Waltham Abbey—close to where Eleanor had some of her lands and where the clerk collecting her "queen's gold" came from—before riding sixty miles north to Northampton. There, at a great council of the barons beginning on Wednesday, July 17, Henry announced a summer campaign to crush the most powerful of the northern Welsh princes, Owain of Gwynedd. Only partially colonized by the Norman settlers after 1066, Wales had been pacified up to a point by Henry's grandfather when several of the local princes had done him homage. But little of his authority had survived the anarchy of Stephen's reign, especially in the north. Only in Powys in central Wales had the princes been willing to make terms, and with Owain taking the lead in harassing the settlers, it was time to teach him a lesson.

Becket strongly supported this declaration of war but was clearly anxious about it. The venture was risky, and to John of Salisbury's unconcealed disgust (since he loathed such people), his friend consulted soothsayers to advise on the most propitious moment to attack. On their advice, Henry and Becket ordered the feudal host to muster on the saltings south of Chester within two weeks. From there it was to march up the coast of the Dee estuary while a fleet quietly shadowed it offshore and carried its provisions and equipment.

Edward Grim ruefully reflects on the change whereby, over the next two years, Becket would reinvent himself as a swashbuckling warrior. "Who can tell," he asks, "how many suffered death at his hands, how many the loss of all their wealth? Surrounded by a valiant body of knights, he came to attack whole states, destroy cities and towns, give villages and farms to the devouring flames without one thought of pity, and prove merciless to the enemies of his lord the king." But such sentiments are anachronistic. Becket surely took as his working model the example of the Capetian chancellors, who assumed a command in the army as easily as they sat in judgment in the royal courts. And there was a notable English precedent. Early in Henry I's reign, the warrior-chancellor Waldric, who also loved hunting and falconry, had put on chain mail and fought at the battle of Tinchebrai, personally taking Robert Curthose prisoner—this despite being ordained a deacon like Becket. Even after his consecration as bishop of Laon in Normandy, Waldric could not stop fighting, culminating in his murder in his cathedral close, where an angry citizen of the town, Bernard des Bruyères, sliced off the top of his head with an ax. Nor while at the Council of Rheims with Theobald in 1148 could Thomas have failed to notice the fabled Albero von Montreuil, archbishop of Trier, seated in a place of honor by Pope Eugenius despite his having led knights bravely into battle in Italy and northern Germany earlier in his career.

Sorely disappointed with his friend, John of Salisbury fell back on his wit, joking ironically that even such important Angevin saints as St. Martin, the patron saint of Tours, had gone into battle—knowing very well that Martin, according to one account, had been forcibly conscripted into the Roman army as a teenager under the emperor Julian, but when put to the test as a Christian and ordered to fight had declared himself a conscientious objector. In a closely related vein, John renewed his criticism of his friend for his love of blood sports. The church frowned on hunting almost as much as it frowned on warfare, arguing that far from being the sport of kings or gentlemen, it undermined human reason as powerfully as madness or intoxication and debased human nature, encouraging men to kill one another instead of beasts or fowl.

* * *

AS JOHN HAD predicted, Becket's soothsayers were fraudsters, their prophecies no more than empty words. Henry's fleet, looking for plunder, was severely mauled when it put into Anglesey, and the king, who had marched his army into Flintshire, was ambushed in the pass of Coleshill, a densely forested, marshy area. Several barons were slaughtered when the Welsh, with the most terrifying shrieks and cries, leapt from the trees that lined the steep, rocky sides of the narrow pass and bombarded Henry's men with rocks, arrows, and other missiles. Henry of Essex, the royal constable and standard-bearer, made a bad situation considerably worse, causing a sudden panic by casting aside his banner, taking to his heels, and proclaiming to all he met that the king had been slain. The Welsh swiftly moved in for the kill, and only Henry's sudden reappearance after desperately fighting his way out of the thickets averted a massacre. The army then advanced more cautiously along the seashore, avoiding the higher ground, while Henry sent out raiding parties to cut down trees and carve out fresh paths, enabling his troops to crisscross the countryside without exposing themselves to further unnecessary danger.

As Henry began advancing deeper into Snowdonia, the Welsh decided to sue for peace, and in August their leaders came to his camp under a safe-conduct. Handing over hostages, including his son, as a gesture of good faith, Prince Owain did homage for his lands in Gwynedd, satisfying Henry's demands for overlordship. Becket, on this occasion, could not have marched very far with the royal army. While Henry was receiving Owain's homage, his chancellor was still busy handling paperwork in Chester. The Welsh chronicles are silent as to his role in the fighting. Two years later, however, he would be in the vanguard of the army, fearlessly leading his own contingent of knights into battle. The flash point was Aquitaine, where Henry, to Eleanor's delight, at last meant to attempt to enforce her ancestral claim to possession of the city and county of Toulouse.

Herself one of the driving forces behind this new campaign, Eleanor had first raised the matter with Henry some years before, after the powerful Languedoc warlord, Count Raymond V, who occupied Toulouse, had married King Louis's sister Constance, the widow of King Stephen's son Eustace. With Louis as his ally and no fewer than three young sons by Constance available to succeed him, Raymond felt supremely confident that he could hold the Angevins at bay forever. Not without reason, Eleanor could see the opportunity to regain her lost territory fast slipping away. For her, it was a case of now or never to reclaim her rightful inheritance. Henry agreed, especially while she was continuing to play her own queenly role to perfection. Well aware of the dynastic significance of her fecundity, she would bear him seven surviving children over the course of little more than a decade: Henry and Matilda, born respectively in 1155 and 1156, Richard born in 1157, Geoffrey in 1158, Eleanor in 1161, Joanna in 1165, and finally John two years later.

As in 1156, Henry chose to lead only an elite cohort of around 1,500 knights across the Channel on the first stage of their long journey south and to place a greater reliance on the mercenaries he would be able to hire closer to the seat of the action. The feudal hosts of Normandy, Anjou, and Aquitaine supplied further reinforcements, which, when everyone assembled at Poitiers in midsummer 1159, made up a combined army perhaps amounting to more than 4,500 knights with some 10,000 supporting troops, who would have needed more than 1,500 wagons for their tents and equipment and another 600 for their supplies of food and barrels of beer.

Before unleashing his forces, Henry met Louis at Tours, urging him to advise his brother-in-law to surrender peacefully while he still had the chance. He then took a detour to Blaye on the Gironde estuary, some thirty miles north of Bordeaux, to make a pact with Raymond's bitter rival, the Count of Barcelona. When these moves failed to impress Raymond in the slightest, Henry, flanked by Becket, led his troops at a leisurely pace through Périgord in the direction of Quercy, a county famous for its rolling countryside and fertile soil, traditionally part of the duchy of Aquitaine but cheekily claimed by Raymond. He meant to overawe this upstart count, showing him that he had more than sufficient forces to annihilate him whenever he so chose.

After halting briefly at the town of Périgueux about June 30 to obtain fresh provisions, Henry marched south to besiege the ancient walled citadel at Cahors. An old Roman fortress set on a rocky height overlooking a wide bend in the river Lot, as it meandered slowly down through

Quercy toward the Garonne, Cahors had once been defended by its towering barbican and encircling walls, but these had fallen badly into disrepair. In consequence, the citizens opened their gates without a fight. Unwilling to waste time there while Raymond gathered his forces, the Angevin king continued on swiftly south toward Toulouse, where by the second week of July he had pitched his camp outside the southern walls of the cité, possibly near the Porte Montoulieu about five hundred yards east of the Château Narbonnais.

With Henry keen to make the expedition a speedy success, Becket had thrown himself into his new military duties with gusto. A select force of seven hundred knights from the chancellor's own household was among Henry's crack troops. While the army waited for its orders, Louis arrived to parley. He proposed acting as an impartial umpire, but when Raymond denounced Henry as the aggressor and appealed to his brother-in-law to save him and his three young sons from capture and ransom, the Capetian king put his family ties before his obligations to Henry, withdrawing his offer and disappearing without more ado inside the cité, where he took charge of its defenses.

This move deadlocked the siege. With neither an army nor weaponry at his disposal, Louis might have been overwhelmed, but he was Henry's feudal overlord. Militarily, it could also have been extremely dangerous, since to besiege Toulouse was no simple task. Protected on one side by the river Garonne and on the others by high brick walls, ditches, towers, and fortified houses, the cité was virtually impregnable and its citizens well prepared. Siege weaponry—such as battering rams and high platforms on wheels, trebuchets and mangonels to sling heavy rocks against and over the walls—would have been required. It may well have been around this time that Becket sent for the duplicate copies of the famous classical manual on military tactics and siege warfare, *The Art of War* by Flavius Vegetius (which often included diagrams), later discovered in his library. Even had Henry's army been able to penetrate the cité, there were chains at every crossroads, with catapults stationed on the tops of the towers guarding the narrow cobbled streets. The Château Narbonnais, to which Louis had retreated, was a notoriously difficult target. A formidable fortress, it was integrated into the walls of the cité, further protected by massive earthen ramparts.

Henry faced a stark dilemma. If he risked an attack and stormed the cité, he could incur huge losses, only to end up saddled with his overlord as his prisoner. With his treaty with Louis only recently concluded, he had his dynasty's succession to the French throne through his young son's future bride, Louis's infant daughter, to consider, since the Capetian king still had no male heir. This was hardly the moment to turn his newfound amity with France upside down.

A serious quarrel—the first in their relationship—now took place between Becket and Henry. The occasion was a council of war attended by all Henry's barons and captains, at which he stated his dilemma baldly. Should he attempt to storm the cité or watch and wait to see if Louis would withdraw? The barons veered strongly toward the side of caution, but Becket accused them of cowardice, believing them to be deceiving Henry to save their own skins. Concerned also for the effects on his own seven hundred knights of idling away in the blistering summer sun, he argued that Louis had forfeited his rights as a feudal overlord by openly supporting Henry's enemies. "By standing against him there," he insisted, "the king of France has abdicated his position as his [Henry's] suzerain." The attack should go ahead.

Henry sided with the barons, and when Becket stood his ground, believing his arguments were valid, the king ordered him to be silent. Only when French reinforcements arrived was the matter put beyond all doubt. Determined not to waste any more time, Henry ordered his army to decamp, besieging other castles and towns in the vicinity of Toulouse and razing them to the ground, laying waste the countryside as he went along in the hope of tempting Louis to leave his lair. He then faced a second major setback when his army became ravaged by dysentery and malaria. In late September, he retreated first to Cahors and from there back to Normandy, but he left garrisons in several of the hilltop towns he had captured in Quercy. Louis, for once, had successfully outwitted and outmaneuvered Henry, judging correctly that, for all his weaponry, he would not dare to attack his feudal overlord.

After making emergency repairs to the walls of Cahors, Henry entrusted the citadel to Becket. But the town remained difficult to defend, and the assignment was a poisoned chalice. Moreover, still smarting from his chancellor's outspoken objections in the council of war, the king denied him the money he needed to pay his troops or buy provisions, merely offering to lend it to him instead for repayment at a later date. He assigned overall command of his other Quercy garrisons to his disgraced former standard-bearer, Henry of Essex, strongly reinforcing the idea that he meant such a task to be more of a punishment than a privilege. Yet because these towns and castles were all that King Henry had to show for his herculean effort and colossal expenditure and he did not want to lose any of them, Becket was left under no illusion as to what was expected of him.

"All the other barons had excused themselves" when asked to take on these commands, a rare insight into the internal politics of the council of war, itself nothing less than the king's great council on the march. Luck, fortunately, was on Becket's side. In his zeal to guarantee the security of Cahors, he took an extraordinary personal risk, suddenly leading his knights out of the citadel and storming three heavily fortified castles nearby in helmet and hauberk, riding at the head of his own troops and galloping after his opponents to the far side of the Garonne without adequate protection in the rear. His bravery has all the thrilling echoes of an action movie, but the reality is more chilling, for he risked leading his crack troops straight into an enemy ambush. His irrepressible urge to win his spurs in a decisive encounter further illustrates his inexperience in the practical art of warfare. The same tendency had almost cost him his life as a teenager after he fell into a millstream while out hawking with Richer de l'Aigle. Once again, it seems he was a newcomer aspiring to be an insider.

BECKET DID NOT rejoin Henry in Normandy until the county of Quercy had been secured, by which time another difficult challenge awaited him. As he crossed the Norman frontier, he discovered that fighting had resumed between Louis and Henry in the Vexin and that French troops had invaded Normandy. Henry had retaliated by invading France, razing the town of Beauvais to the ground before laying siege to the castle of Guerberoi and leveling it. He then attacked Count Simon of Évreux, forcing him to abandon his castles at Rochefort, Épernon, and Montfort, which effectively sliced the French royal demesne in two, giving the Angevins control of the main road between Paris and Orléans.

As soon as Becket reappeared, Henry sent him to join the fray. He could not seriously have expected to hold such an exposed position for long, but with a series of sharp frosts already announcing the arrival of an unusually cold winter, he was determined to grab whatever he could before a truce was negotiated. The chancellor was assigned 1,200 mercenaries to supplement his own 700 knights, plus around 4,000 others hired to serve them and attend to their horses. As in Quercy, the costs of so large a battalion quickly rocketed, since each knight required £3 per day for the keep of his men and horses. Becket had to borrow heavily again, this time from a Jewish moneylender on Henry's guarantee. As before, he had little choice, but these obligations, together amounting to 1,000 silver marks (around £400,000 today), proved to be a serious liability for him, as he never repaid them and Henry would never forget them.

Quite what Becket's men did in the Vexin campaign is not clear, since a gap exists in the sources. But on at least one occasion, Thomas repeated his recklessness at Cahors, riding at a gallop at the head of his men toward the enemy, with his spurs digging into his horse's sides and his sword raised. Engaging a famous French knight, Engelram of Trie, in single combat, Becket succeeded in knocking him off his horse and claiming his charger as a prize. With his adrenaline high and his concentration closing out everything but his desire for victory, it seemed as if warfare was becoming his true vocation.

When spring returned and the temporary truce expired, a peace was concluded. Thomas led the negotiations on Henry's side, exploiting his cordial relationship with Louis to secure terms that were extraordinarily favorable in the circumstances. The Capetian king first confirmed to Henry all his conquests in Quercy in return for withdrawing his occupying forces from France. He then did what Henry had always really wanted, returning the lands of the old Norman Vexin to him, holding back only Gisors and some other strategically important castles. Summoning to his presence three leading Knights Templar who were already familiar figures in Paris and London—Richard of Hastings, Osto of Saint-Omer, and Robert de Pirou—Louis swore them to act as neutral guarantors of the peace, holding the coveted castles in trust until his daughter's wedding day, when they would revert to Henry as the final element of her dowry settlement.

In this way, Becket salvaged the dynastic alliance on which he had spent so much time and effort, although Louis clearly did not expect his daughter Margaret, who was still barely two, to be married for another ten years or more. Henry, however, was never one to be content with a settlement, however generous, that did not give him everything he wanted, and he still had Gisors to reclaim. The chronicler William of Newburgh describes him as "impatient with delay" over the return of the Vexin. Now twenty-seven and supremely confident of his ability to gain his aims, he intended to strike, to win a fait accompli—even if he used underhand methods. Nothing, simply nothing, could be allowed to stand in his way. All he needed was a pretext.

He got his excuse in September 1160, rather sooner than he expected, when Constance of Castile died and Louis announced within a fortnight his decision to take a third wife, Adela of Blois-Champagne, King Stephen's niece. Determined to father a son and heir as soon as possible, Louis had chosen a bride from a family able to trace its descent from William the Conqueror and so stake a claim, however flimsy, to the kingdom of England. Inflamed by this provocation, Henry meant to answer in kind. Canon law strictly forbade weddings of children under twelve, but Henry would engineer one, extorting a clandestine license from papal representatives. On November 2, the younger Henry would marry Margaret in Normandy, where she had been living for the past two years as Henry's ward and where she would continue to live until the age of twelve. In consequence, the Knights Templar, according to their oaths, were honor bound to hand over the castles in their care to Henry, who was triumphant. Louis, however, was indignant, accusing Henry of fraud and the Templars of "outright treachery." Assisted by his new wife's relatives, he crossed the frontier and harried Touraine, but Henry stormed the castle of Chaumont-sur-Loire, and the result was a draw.

Becket, meanwhile, whose rash choices on the battlefields of Quercy and Normandy had paid handsome dividends, had safely come through what may have seemed, after his searing experiences at the gates of Toulouse, more like a baptism of fire. Thanks to him, Henry's territorial gains in Quercy had been secured, while after the peace settlement, the king—using methods as foul as they were fair—had recovered the whole of the Norman Vexin as he had long sought to do. Against this, the original aim of the campaign had not been achieved. To Eleanor's increasing dismay, Henry would gradually allow her claim to outright possession of the lands occupied by Count Raymond to fall into abeyance, replaced instead by a more nebulous demand for homage and proving that, where his continental empire was concerned, he would always put Norman interests ahead of Poitevin ones.

But the pulp had gone out of Henry and Becket's relationship, even if the chancellor was hardly to blame for what had gone wrong. Thomas retained much of his old influence, but he found that after their quarrel in the council of war, Henry would deploy many of the same controlling tactics against him that he used against everyone else. In the short term, Becket's reputation would recover, and it would seem to the world as if all was well. He sat in a place of honor at Prince Henry's wedding and was still sufficiently high in the king's favor that the boy would now be placed in his household to be educated with the other sons of the leading barons who served as pages there. It may even be that his jingoistic behavior and ostensible lack of moral scruples at Toulouse had persuaded Henry of his lack of religiosity, foreshadowing things to come.

But if Thomas found himself in another tight corner, would he have sufficient wiggle room to escape? Perhaps, but only if Henry was content to play by the normal rules. And as the king matured and discovered not just what he ought to do but what he was able to do, that was likely to become an increasingly tall order.

12

A SOLITARY MAN

THOMAS BECKET'S CHARACTER AS IT HAS BEEN UNDERstood for nine hundred years has a riddle at its heart. If his clerk and fellow Londoner William fitz Stephen is to be believed, it would seem that Henry and his chancellor were always the best of friends, working and playing together, fighting and hunting, eating and drinking, sharing every secret thought—as inseparable as lovers or blood brothers. And yet Thomas's brutal humiliation in the council of war at Toulouse suggests something rather different. Even if his judgment had been found wanting on this occasion, it was decidedly unusual for Henry to react so roughly to someone speaking from the heart, as long as the person was making an honest mistake and not plotting something.

A closer examination of the sources shows that other contemporaries are decidedly more measured. They recognize a close rapport but give it a far less euphoric spin. According to Robert of Cricklade, Thomas proved himself to be shrewd, ingratiating, and disciplined as chancellor, but he was also well aware of the limitations of his position, "doing nothing which might offend the king." Combing the book of Genesis for a suitable analogy, Edward Grim describes Thomas as "a second Joseph in Egypt," which superficially seems a highly positive remark but when unpacked is strangely ambiguous, since while Joseph won the highest favor and trust from Pharaoh, rising to be chief governor of Egypt, he was certainly not Pharaoh's near equal or anything like it, and he was in fact there only because his brothers had sold him into slavery.

Moreover, when fitz Stephen does finally spice his narrative with a fully developed illustration of the unique familiarity he had imagined, he fatally subverts it. One cold winter day, he says, as the king and his chancellor were riding together through the streets of London, a shivering beggar appeared before them clad only in rags.

"Do you see him?" said Henry.

"Yes, I do," answered Thomas.

"How poor he is, how frail and thinly clad," said the king. "Wouldn't it be a great act of charity to give him a thick warm cloak?"

"It would indeed, and it behoves you as a king to think and act so," replied Thomas.

As they reined in their horses, the beggar stepped forward, and Henry asked him if he would like a fine new cloak. At first not recognizing them, the beggar thought the offer a cruel taunt. Suddenly Henry turned toward Thomas. "This great deed of charity," he said gleefully, "shall be yours." And grabbing hold of Becket's cloak by the hood, the king tried to pull it off him. But Becket resisted angrily. It was a brand-new scarlet cloak lined with gray fur that he loved and did not want to lose.

An unseemly commotion ensued as Henry snatched at the costly garment and Becket battled to retain it, each man using both hands and narrowly avoiding tumbling off his horse. Seeing what appeared to be a scuffle, the royal bodyguards rushed forward but were ordered back. The scene was turning very ugly indeed when Becket, visibly piqued, finally allowed a triumphant Henry to overpower him and seize the garment. Handing it over to the wide-eyed beggar, the king explained what had happened to the onlookers, and all except Thomas laughed uproariously, some courtiers mocking the chancellor by offering him their own cloaks or capes. As to the beggar, he slipped quietly away to sell his prize to the highest bidder, praising God and thanking his lucky stars.

Interpreted by one romantic historian as "a charming joke" designed to force Becket into showing deference and generosity to his social inferiors, the story of the beggar has a more menacing edge, vividly illustrating the inequality and social distance between the king and his middle-class chancellor, showing that even when a disagreement arose between them on so trivial a matter as possession of a cloak, Henry had to win and be seen by all to do so. Willful, autocratic, and capricious, he was a ruler with an innate appreciation of his awesome powers as a divine-right king. He would regularly cut his courtiers and officials down to size, ambushing them, reducing them to jelly, exposing in calculating, humiliating, unexpected ways exactly where they stood with him.

Henry's conduct invites a more skeptical hypothesis running along the lines that as a younger man while he was still carving out a path for himself, he found Becket useful, amusing, and companionable, indulging him and treating him as a favorite, but knowing that such privileges could always be withdrawn. For his part Thomas, especially in this earlier phase of their intimacy, was naïve and inexperienced enough to believe it was something unique, even a relationship of near equals, whereas in reality it was a partnership of convenience, enabling Henry to settle the boundaries of his empire and begin to achieve his more specific aim of restoring the "ancestral customs" of his grandfather while keeping Theobald and the church firmly on the same side.

Arnulf of Lisieux, the insinuating insider who had been first to congratulate Thomas on his promotion, supports this harsher interpretation. Writing after the relationship had broken down but before it reached its lowest point, he commiserates with Becket as to how difficult it had been from the outset for him to function as chancellor, when his authority had stemmed not "from his own name" but "from the hazard" of Henry's will, on which Thomas had been utterly reliant. Far from this being a friendship of near equals, Henry was so obsessed with his own dignity that it made him almost impossible to advise. Only Becket's skill in ingratiating himself and his talent for engaging with such a complex, forceful intelligence had enabled him to operate as he did. Alone of those in Henry's inner circle, he could interpret the king's mood, judging "all the movements of his heart, what mildness there may be in him, what courageous action he might risk attempting," and while it suited him to do so, Henry had reciprocated, valuing Thomas's "consummate prudence" because it was so far removed from the usual, unvarnished forms of sycophancy.

Thomas himself neatly captured the king's psychology when recounting to a papal envoy what later would turn so sour:

> If he senses that he can corrupt you by promises or frighten you by threats so that he can obtain something against your honor and some security for himself in the matter, from that moment your authority with him will utterly vanish, and you will become contemptible, a mockery and a laughingstock to him and his. If, on the other hand, he sees that he cannot turn you from your intention, he will first fake fury, he will swear again and again, he will imitate Proteus,* and finally come back to his senses; and thereafter, unless you get in the way, you will always be like a god to Pharaoh. For among the many things for which he is renowned by his familiars and those close to him, that man boasts especially that he is a tester of character. . . . On all matters, therefore, he should be approached with the greatest restraint and an avoidance of too much talk.

When Becket says "that man boasts especially that he is a tester of character," he is speaking from hard-won experience. More likely than a friendship of near equals, Henry's rapport with his chancellor was built on the latter's willingness to endure in good spirit the frequent challenges that Henry set for him. Hungry for power and influence, Becket was still sufficiently malleable. Arnulf, however, put his finger on the problem. One day, he warned Becket, circumstances may arise in which "you do not wish to abandon your aims or he to derogate anything from the royal dignity." Surely then, a right royal battle must arise.

JOHN OF SALISBURY, the contemporary who knew Thomas longest and best, always believed that his friend had an ascetic, rebel's impulse within him, springing from his origins as a middle-class Londoner and giving him a divided consciousness at the courts of princes. Better-placed than most to know the true facts, John confirms that the chancellor *always* found his relationship with Henry difficult. Kings like Stephen and Henry, he explains, were "arbitrary rulers" and "slaves of their own passions." Courtiers, despite their winning ways, were like "untamed beasts": wanton and greedy, treacherous and lawless, frivolous and drunken.

* A sea god in classical literature who could change his shape at will.

"Right from the start," he recounts, "the chancellor carried the burden of so many and such great necessities of various kinds, he was exhausted by so many labors, almost crushed by so many afflictions, assailed by so many traps, exposed to so many snares by the spite of courtiers, that often on certain days . . . he would despair of living. . . . He was every day forced to contend as much against the king himself as against his enemies and to evade innumerable crafts and deceits."

Developing his opinions mainly for his own eyes in a semifictional verse satire titled *Entheticus de Dogmate Philosophorum* (*An Abstract of Wise Men's Doctrine*), John portrays the royal court as a place of intense personal rivalry, even homicidal feuding, painting a picture in which the chancellor strove to do his best against the odds, comparing Henry's claims to be merely "restoring the customs of his grandfather" to the tricks of a circus performer. In this fascinating jeu d'esprit packed with insights that could not otherwise be voiced for fear of retribution, John picks out three leading courtiers of a tyrant-king named "Hyrcanus" who are surrogates for real-life figures.* The specialty of "Mandroger," a parasitic astrologer, is attacking the church. He exalts the king's sovereignty at the expense of canon law, boasting that "he alone preserves the crown and is the father of the laws of the kingdom," while pillaging the church like a robber. "Antipater" does the same, but more blatantly, attacking the church by stealing its property and imposing taxes. His friend "Sporus," an effeminate eunuch, extorts protection money under the guise of "gifts" and is the most crafty and insidious of the "beasts," cloaking his villainy under the guise of "friendship."

"Mandroger" is generally agreed to be Robert de Beaumont, "Antipater" is Richard de Lucy, and "Sporus" is Richard de Humez. In the Battle Abbey case, all three had purportedly expressed views very close to those lampooned by John. All too had played prominent, if Janus-faced, roles in the transition of power from Stephen to Henry, when a secret pact of friendship bound together de Lucy, his brother Abbot Walter, de Humez, and Earl Reginald of Cornwall, one of Henry I's illegitimate children by a woman named Sibyl.

* To achieve the effects he required, John conflated the real John Hyrcanus (r. 134–104 B.C.) with John Hyrcanus II (r. 67–63 B.C.). In the writings of the historian Flavius Josephus, both were rulers of Judaea before the arrival of the Romans.

In John's satire, "poor England" is rescued by the chancellor, Thomas Becket, a virtuous man known as the "protector" and "defender of liberty." But to outsmart the "untamed beasts," he has to work circumspectly. He is forced to dissimulate, to pretend that he is one of them. To survive at Henry's court, he is forced to become a chameleon, to take the part of the enemy, "but only in appearance so that he may learn with equal zeal how to love God." John describes his friend's tactics as a form of "virtuous deceit" or "pious deception" (*pia fraus*). Such dissimulation in a higher cause, approved by authorities as varied in their beliefs as Cicero and St. Augustine, says John, is the only way that a man like Thomas could gain enough clout with a king as dangerous as Henry to be able to steer him away from evil paths.

Whether John ever showed his (seemingly unfinished) satire to Becket or kept it buried in his private papers will never be known. However, a shorter poem capturing the spirit of the longer one is copied neatly into the front of John's presentation copy of his great treatise on statecraft and politics, the *Policraticus,* delivered to Becket during the Toulouse campaign, where it takes the form of a 306-line personal dedication. Here John depicts Thomas as Henry's only honest counselor. Among a greedy bunch of flatterers, he alone is a "lover of truth." A man of "justice and equity," Becket "cancels unjust laws." If anything is detrimental to the ordinary people or a threat to morality, "through him it ceases to be hurtful."

John was never a blind sycophant, candidly conceding in one of his later letters that Thomas, for much of his time as chancellor, had been "a mighty trifler in the court," where "he seemed to despise the law and the clergy, while he followed low pursuits with the magnates." And yet even that way of putting it is deeply intriguing. He had only "*seemed* to despise the law and the clergy." Unlike his letters, most of which are newsletters to be circulated among his friends, John's poetic and satirical writings are a complicated mixture of fact, fiction, homily, and wishful thinking. Using language and the power of his imagination, his claims for Becket's virtues may be rhetorically inflated, but they do suggest he had seen something special in the man. Those who take appearances purely at face value, he gleefully assures us, will shortly be in for a sudden, dramatic surprise.

* * *

IF BECKET'S FRIENDSHIP with Henry was indeed shallower, more ambiguous, and less sincere than the stereotype suggests, can it be that he was also less self-possessed and convivial as a royal intimate than he appears to have been and rather more of a solitary man? Whereas Henry had the confidence of a born aristocrat, the manners of a schoolyard bully, and the stomach of an ox, Thomas, who had been closest to his mother as a child, was always anxious and insecure by temperament. Never able to manage stress well, his digestive ailment began to trigger intermittent bouts of colitis. Severe mental strain linked to overwork would cause it to flare up, leading to short but agonizing bouts of pain.

Unlike Henry, he was extremely devout, praying regularly and allowing himself to be scourged, retaining two priests specifically for this purpose while he was chancellor and receiving their discipline in secret, "his back stripped for whipping." He did not wear a hair shirt yet—that would come much later on—but he believed that he needed a sharp dose of physical pain before attending confession and mass as an antidote against the sin of pride and to warn him against the devil's temptations. Such behavior does not hint at sadomasochism and has to be seen in the context of his age, not ours. The value of experiencing pain as an aid to penance or devotion was deeply etched into medieval society, regarded by devout Christians as an essential prop to all laity and clergy—not just something reserved for monks or hermits, but potentially of value to everyone.

Robert of Cricklade was among those aware of Becket's hidden piety, describing how a close kinsman had told him about a friend with some important business who had decided to ask for Becket's help. Arriving at the town where he was staying late in the evening, the man decided to wait until the next day before approaching him, but rose at daybreak to meet him. Passing beside a church along his way, he looked inside through the open door and saw a pilgrim prostrate on the floor in prayer. Quietly observing him for a few minutes, the man suddenly sneezed, disturbing the pilgrim, who ended his prayers and set off home. Pausing only to note the pilgrim's unusually splendid attire, the man then sought out Becket's lodging and awaited his turn for admission. No sooner had he gained entrance than he saw from the chancellor's clothing that he and the mysterious pilgrim were one and the same.

The early biographers make no bones about their distaste for Becket's venial sins. "Many times and in many places he did wrong on the king's behalf," one of them says, "but he used to make amends privately to God at night." The difference between Becket and Henry and his courtiers is that he was also known to be chaste. "Proud he may have been," says Guernes of Pont-Sainte-Maxence, "and given to vanities as far as worldly affairs go and in outward show, yet he was chaste in body and healthy in soul." William fitz Stephen insists that "from the time he became chancellor, no lechery polluted him," a singular achievement in royal palaces, where whores crowded expectantly around the gatehouses and fornication was the norm. When Henry actively incited Thomas to join in the fun "and so laid snares for him day and night," he refused, for "he was a chaste man who hated indecency and depravity." Thomas also made sure that his standards were enforced within his own household, so that when one of his clerks, Richard of Ambly, seduced a friend's wife by convincing her that her husband had died overseas, Thomas dismissed him and cast him in chains into a dungeon at the Tower of London.

A vivid anecdote concerns one of Henry's discarded lovers, a highborn woman named "Avice," described as "the most beautiful lady in all his empire." When his lust for her was satiated and he wished to palm her off, he thought of Thomas, who was then staying at Stoke-on-Trent. The lady, taking her cue, sent many messengers to the chancellor's lodging, arousing the suspicions of his host, a clerk named Vivian, who saw an opportunity for blackmail. One night after Thomas's bed had been carefully prepared with a silken valance and the finest linen sheets, this man set a trap, waiting until he felt sure that the couple were enjoying illicit sex before bursting into the chamber with a lantern. To his astonishment, the bed was empty and the sheets undisturbed. Instead, he found Becket alone and asleep on the floor, covered only by his cloak and with bare legs and feet. He had worn himself out with work and prayer and had lain down there too exhausted to move. Avice, it was discovered, had never set foot in the house.

But can all these stories really be true? While making many of the same points, Edward Grim adds an intriguing qualification. Becket, he says, "kept his body chaste, although some think differently about that" (*licet aliter aliqui aestimaverint*). Someone fitz Stephen trumpets as one of his sources—Becket's confessor, Brother Robert, whom he had first encountered while a pupil at Merton Priory and whom he appointed as his confessor shortly after he became chancellor—is equally guarded. While sure that "from the time he became chancellor, no lechery polluted him," he is deafeningly silent about Becket's earlier lifestyle.

There is, of course, a semantic point at stake. According to canon law, the "true servants of God" were chaste, meaning that they did "not endanger their souls by fornication." Fornication means illicit sex; therefore married couples who slept only with each other were also "chaste." What counts is the nature of the relationship. Where single men and women were concerned, a hierarchy of tolerance and condemnation existed. Although celibacy was the ideal, it is also true that infrequent intercourse between single people of the opposite sex could be excused in the confessional. Both parties could be absolved and given penance unless either had taken a vow of chastity, in which case fornication was a mortal sin. Monks and nuns were in a special category, since both had taken these vows. Even where ordinary priests were involved, the church took a realistic view of what they could be expected to achieve. A double standard prevailed, since regardless of canon law, doctors overtly prescribed occasional sexual release as essential to bodily health. Once the pressure had begun to mount on Becket during his exile, his own physicians strongly recommended an active sex life for the benefit of his health—advice that he declined on the grounds that such medicine would prove harmful to his soul.

It is highly improbable that even if Thomas was celibate later in life, he had managed this as a student in Paris, where, if the satirists are to be believed, most of his fellow students had sex on the brain and the tavern prostitutes or *fillettes* outside the city walls were readily on hand. His friend John of Salisbury, who had lived in Paris much longer than Thomas, more or less admits this outright, reporting that as a younger man, Becket "indulged in the rakish pursuits of youth. . . . He was proud and vain, and silly enough to show the face and utter the words of lovers." Almost certainly, when the early biographers emphasized his "chastity," they meant the word to be a metaphor for the far bigger idea that, for all his apparent pride and vanity as the king's chancellor, Thomas remained pure of heart. That said, the overwhelming impression is that once he entered Theobald's service as a clerk, he attempted to repress his sexuality, certainly in comparison to those around him.

THAT STILL LEAVES open the question of sexual orientation. Was Thomas Becket uneasy in the company of women? Were his mother and the Mother of God the only important women in his life? His adolescent friendship with Richer de l'Aigle clearly worried his mother as much as it worried Robert of Cricklade, who says with calculated ambiguity that in Richer's company, "the world offered him her sweetness somewhat more freely than before."

Authors floating theories about Becket's sexuality include Jean Anouilh in his 1959 play *Becket; or, The Honor of God*. Turned by Hollywood into an award-winning feature film in 1964 starring Richard Burton and Peter O'Toole, the action centers on an unfulfilled homoerotic relationship between the two main characters. Henry, in Anouilh's dramatic realization, has a bad case of thwarted homosexual love, while Thomas is an earthbound man in search of his true identity. The truth is considerably more complex. On the one hand, homosexuality (or lesbianism) in the twelfth century was not merely a mortal sin; it was "the sin that should not be named"—a crime against God. On the other hand, the boundaries typically were porous. Love and friendship between males were often thought to be superior to the love between men and women. Kissing was the normal way of greeting people or taking one's leave. Holy men kissed holy men on the mouth; laymen of equivalent social status did the same, while inferiors received a kiss on the cheek; the rituals of homage and fealty between a lord and his vassal ended with a kiss on the mouth. Many popular songs had racy lyrics describing the love of two knights for each other. Monks, even abbots, wrote baldly erotic poems in the style of Ovid addressed to young boys, which was risqué but not condemned outright.

The acid test was whether such encounters led to sexual activity or abuse. Teenage males were expected to bond spiritually with one another, but not to have sexual relations. Young knights would eat together, sleep in the same chamber, and spend every waking hour in one another's company. Often led and inspired by an older man, they were taught to love one another as brothers. But such love had to be "virtuous." Kissing was allowed, but sexual desire had to be checked, since in the eyes of the church, the sole purpose of sexuality—with the possible exception of older people on grounds of mutual love and affection—was the procreation of children.

Whether Becket's adolescent intimacy with Richer included a homoerotic element we can only imagine, but the mature Thomas could not have been homosexual, since if he had been, he would have been unable to keep it a secret during the bitter propaganda war that was unleashed by his final quarrel with the king. The church regarded homosexuality as a crime against nature as well as God, condemning those who engaged in same-sex relationships to a special place in hell, where hideous demons would torture them for all eternity. In a futile attempt to deal with them on earth, Archbishop Anselm in 1102 had issued a decree ordering them to be excommunicated and—if they were clergy or freemen—degraded from their place in society and outlawed. It was even claimed by canon lawyers that sodomy was a more heinous crime than raping underage girls on the grounds that "at least" forcible sexual intercourse with a woman was heterosexual.

Had the slightest doubt existed about Becket's sexuality, it would have been turned against him by the royal propagandists when his breach with Henry became so vitriolic that all the normal rules of polemic were abandoned and anything that could be slung against an opponent, fair or foul, was used. Just such an exposé would befall Roger of Pont l'Évêque, the new archbishop of York. During the mutual recriminations after Becket's murder, John of Salisbury would publish for all to read how Roger, while still archdeacon of Canterbury and one of Theobald's clerks, had dabbled in pedophilia. He had seduced a beautiful young boy named Walter and repeatedly sodomized him, but when the boy grew older and tried to expose his tormenter, Roger had him blinded. Then, when he complained to the secular court, Roger—on the principle that dead men tell no tales—bribed the judges and had the boy sentenced to death and hanged. "Thus," waxes John, "he rewarded the long complaisance of his old love. First he seduced the wretched youth; then to make him more wretched still, because he repented his consent to such sordid and filthy behavior, he mutilated and blinded him; finally, to bring his wretchedness to its height, because he made such noisy protest as he could of his misfortunes, he had him murdered by hanging on a gallows."

To our eyes, this exposé redounds badly against Becket too. For Roger, the documents reveal, had escaped punishment only because, at Theobald's request, his fixer Thomas had hushed everything up in the interests of the church's reputation and, perhaps more important, those of Theobald himself, in whose household the boy's seduction had first taken place. Thomas, who in this disreputable affair had shown himself to be a man of unrivaled efficiency, had recruited Bishop Hilary of Chichester to assist him, with the result that Theobald had successfully exploited a special legal immunity clause to hear Roger's confession in a secret, unrecorded ceremony in a monastic chapter house. Thereafter, Roger had gone to Rome, where by bribing many of the more influential cardinals, he had once again escaped punishment.

Since Roger came to regard Becket's quarrel with the king as his golden opportunity to trump a hated rival, John of Salisbury believed after his friend's murder that Roger's hands were stained with the blood of an innocent man who had once taken pity on him out of Christian charity, saving him from the ignominy he rightly deserved. Modern readers will think differently about it, viewing the episode with loathing, for John's account makes it crystal clear that Becket had helped to conceal a shocking case of sexual abuse. Had it come to light at the time, it would have caused a scandal rocking the English church to its foundations, perhaps forcing Theobald to resign. By the standards of the day, Becket had done what he had been instructed to do by Theobald, and John too had kept his silence for many years.

What, however, this sordid episode makes starkly clear is that had comparable ammunition against Becket been available to them, Roger's friends would have struck back once John had published his exposé, even if they too had previously held their tongues. No holds were barred in this exchange, which took place a year before Thomas was canonized by the pope and at a moment after his assassination when it was still possible to criticize him. If he had been a closet homosexual, Roger and his friends would have said so.

An incidental repercussion of these disclosures, furthermore, is how curious it is that Becket was so friendly with Hilary of Chichester at the time of the cover-up that he could confide in the bishop and rely on his discretion in a matter of such potentially explosive sensitivity. And yet, during the Battle Abbey case, if the abbey's chronicler is to be believed, he would be so contemptuous of the bishop's reputation that he would make a speech in front of Henry stage-managed in such a way as to inflict maximum damage on Hilary. That dissonance too may be significant, casting further doubt on the credibility of the Battle Abbey chronicler's account of Becket's speeches in court and reinforcing the already strong suspicion that this section of the chronicle is a forgery.

Given the often intractable nature of sources written nine hundred years ago, some things can never be proved one way or the other. But the mistake is surely never to ask the awkward questions in the first place. Not just a legend, Thomas Becket was also a man, however repressed his sexuality, however ambiguous his relationship with Henry.

13
RENDER UNTO CAESAR

ARCHBISHOP THEOBALD HAD PLANTED HIS PROTÉGÉ AT THE heart of Henry's court as the churchmen's defense against the predatory barons. A strong king, he fervently believed, could only be a blessing for the church after the pillaging and looting of King Stephen's reign. And yet the primate, now in his mid-sixties and eager to devote what was left of his life to his pastoral work, also knew that Thomas had to satisfy a willful, imperious, mercurial king determined to restore the power of the monarchy. A high price would have to be paid for the king's cooperation in defense of the church. What was Caesar's must be rendered unto Caesar. But in Theobald's eyes, it would always be worth it—if, that is, Thomas could put the clock back to something approaching the golden age of Lanfranc, restoring the king's traditional role as a patron and protector of the church.

Nothing short of a high-wire act would be needed, and in the churchmen's eyes Becket often failed to pull it off. Charged by Henry in 1159 with levying fresh scutage assessments to replenish the war chest for the Toulouse campaign, he earned widespread opprobrium, setting the basic rate as high as 2 silver marks for each knight whose service was owed and so leaving the wealthier bishops and abbots liable for sums in excess of £80. Even worse, he shifted the burden of taxation disproportionately to the church by demanding supplementary levies euphemistically called "gifts" (*dona*), by far the largest from the higher clergy, so that five bishops (York, Durham, Lincoln, Bath, and Winchester) were assessed at the astronomical sums of £333 each and three (London, Norwich, and Worcester) at £133, while the abbots and abbesses paid between £5 and £146.

According to the chronicler Gervase of Canterbury, the combined yield of Henry's war taxation was a punitive £180,000, or more than £95 million today. That figure—like many of the large numbers given by chroniclers—is not entirely to be trusted, but however the amounts are calculated, the church paid six times as much as before. Defending Thomas from the accusation that he alone was to blame, John of Salisbury retorts, "I know it to be false—since I know that at that time he did not follow the counsel of greed, but the dictates of necessity." But he adds, "I do not doubt that he was the servant of wickedness, and I judge him to have fully deserved to be punished." While acknowledging that his friend was only following Henry's orders, John does not attempt to deny his culpability. By consenting to such punitive taxation on the church, he had "put the king before God."

On the other side of the ledger, Becket enjoyed some success in talking Henry into making appointments to vacant bishoprics and abbeys promptly instead of freezing the posts for several years to enjoy their revenues. Even after their quarrel in the council of war at Toulouse, Thomas still had more than enough influence to handle a particularly tricky situation in a manner that Theobald could only applaud. It arose when Henry sought to appoint Henry, dean of Mortain, to the bishopric of Exeter. An illiterate nonentity, the dean was the illegitimate son of Robert fitz Harding, a baron to whom Henry owed a favor and who sent his men to badger the aging archbishop about the case while he was sick in bed. Theobald wanted Bartholomew, archdeacon of Exeter, one of his former clerks and a friend of John of Salisbury, to have the post, but he was getting nowhere until Becket went into action, arranging for Bartholomew's consecration. Other worthy candidates whom Thomas assisted included Robert of Melun, his old Paris teacher, who was made bishop of Hereford, and William, prior of Saint-Martin-des-Champs near Paris, who became abbot of Ramsey.

While he was working his magic for Bartholomew, Thomas attempted at some personal risk to block a scandalous marriage between Matthew, younger brother of Henry's cousin and former ward Count

Philip of Flanders, and Mary of Blois, King Stephen's daughter. Always on his guard where the house of Blois-Champagne was concerned, Henry wanted Mary safely married off to someone he could trust. A fine catch, she had become sole heiress to the county of Boulogne after her brother William, many of whose castles and estates Henry had already confiscated, had died of malaria on his way home from the Toulouse campaign. If the marriage went ahead, Count Philip's brother would become the new Count of Boulogne in the right of his bride, enabling Henry to interfere in Picardy and Boulogne. The difficulty was that she had become a nun. Rising to be abbess of Romsey in Hampshire, she had taken a vow of chastity, which required a dispensation from the church to override.

When Becket protested against the wedding plans, calling them "profane" and "abominable," Henry ordered him to be silent. No more was the king going to be lectured on an inconvenient point of canon law than on military strategy outside the gates of Toulouse. Judged as equivalent to incest, the marriage plan aroused a chorus of opposition from the church, but Henry insisted on having his way, and the marriage took place in May 1160, when Mary was dragged from her convent.

More successfully, Thomas pulled strings to help John of Salisbury when he fell afoul of Henry for getting too close to Pope Adrian IV. The only Englishman ever to occupy the chair of St. Peter, Adrian—born plain Nicholas Brakespeare, the illegitimate son of a priest from Abbots Langley in Hertfordshire—had been chosen a fortnight before Henry was crowned, creating a unique opportunity for the new king, who sent a high-level delegation led by Arnulf of Lisieux to him. Naturally, Henry had a hidden agenda, this time in Ireland, where the Normans had so far rarely ventured except to deal with pirates and buy furs. Building on his mother's ties to Dermot MacMurrough, king of Leinster, Henry sought the overlordship of Ireland for his youngest brother, William, floating the idea at a great council at Winchester in September 1155 but soon realizing that for it to succeed, he would need the backing of the papacy, just as the pope had backed the conquest of England in 1066.

Theobald, meanwhile, had already sent John of Salisbury to Adrian, who was then at Benevento, a papal enclave in southern Italy, sixty or so miles northeast of Naples. Just as he had planted Becket at Henry's court, so he also aimed to plant John at the curia to win concessions for the English church, and since John and Adrian were oldest and best of friends, John dined at the pope's table throughout his stay, enraging Henry's ambassadors, whom he completely outshone.

Unfortunately for John, Arnulf was his inveterate enemy, his "hammer of iniquity," as he puts it. At first their squabbling seemed to be rather a joke, but when Arnulf sent back scurrilous reports to Henry, John started to panic. As he complained to Peter of Celle:

> The indignation of our most serene lord, our all-powerful king, our most unconquerable prince, has grown hot against me in full force. . . . I alone in all the realm am accused of diminishing the royal dignity. When they define the act of offense more carefully, these are the charges that they hurl upon my head. If anyone among us invokes the name of Rome, they say it is my doing. If the English Church ventures to claim even the shadow of liberty in making elections or in the trial of ecclesiastical causes, it is imputed to me, as if I were the only person to instruct the lord bishop of Canterbury and the other bishops what they ought to do. On these counts my position is shaken to its foundations, and they are so pressing that it is thought that I am in danger of banishment.

John's chief offense was that to score points off Arnulf, whose diplomacy was floundering, he had secured from Adrian a green light for Henry's plans in Ireland, but on terms that the king found obnoxious. Claiming that the papacy had an ancient jurisdiction over all islands that could not be revoked, Adrian declared that Henry could colonize Ireland and possess it by hereditary right, but only as a vassal of the pope. To this end, he gave Henry a gold ring along with a parchment authorizing his investiture as "lord of Ireland." Perhaps a little anxious from the outset at the wording of this document, John had the ring specially adorned with a fine emerald at his own expense, crossing his fingers that all would be well.

But if Henry pocketed the ring, he refused—on Arnulf's urging—to accept the parchment. Not simply did he repudiate the idea that the pope had jurisdiction over island kingdoms, which he saw as a threat to his sovereignty, but he refused to demean himself by becoming a vassal to one of his own subjects—and an illegitimate one to boot—even if this man happened to occupy the stellar position in the church. For Henry, the social divide alone was far too great. At least the chancellor, lowborn as he was in the king's eyes, had been born in lawful wedlock.

Inflamed by Arnulf's reports, Henry raged against John, calling him a traitor, even threatening to put him on trial. Unable to extricate himself by throwing himself on the king's mercy, John turned to his friends. Besides seeking Theobald's assistance, he appealed to Becket. "If the memory of our old familiarity still counts for something," he pleaded, "if the onslaught of fortune does not undermine the loyalty of a tried and trusted friendship, then do what you can to assuage the indignation which our most serene lord the king has conceived against me without a cause, so that I may make good my innocence in his sight."

Problems of distance would make John's efforts to rehabilitate himself doubly difficult. When he sent out his appeal, Becket was in Normandy and Henry was with Eleanor in Aquitaine, where they had hastened after suppressing the revolt of Geoffrey of Anjou. Becket's answer to John has not survived, but the uneven and haphazard way in which letters were dealt with when the court was on the move makes it unlikely that it would have. But another of John's letters to Peter of Celle reveals that as soon as Thomas returned to England, he reassured his friend that he would survive his chastening experience more or less unscathed. He had even managed to get Eleanor on John's side, for she too told him that "the storm . . . has abated," suggesting that this may have been one of the very rare occasions on which the chancellor was able to play Henry off against his wife. Ordered never again to enter Henry's presence unless accompanied by an official minder, John was allowed to retain his post in Theobald's household and his salary as a canon of Exeter—until Becket quarreled with the king in earnest. Then John would show himself the first to reciprocate for earlier kindnesses.

POPE ADRIAN'S DEATH in September 1159 marked the beginning of a long struggle for supremacy in Italy. At its heart was Frederick Barbarossa, the Holy Roman Emperor, who had once supported the pope against King Roger II of Sicily and his son, but more recently, fearing encroachments on his own territories, had steeled himself against the claims of the ascetic reformers, modeling himself on his great-grandfather, Henry IV, who had defied Pope Gregory VII. In the papal election, Frederick ordered his supporters to choose Cardinal Octavian, who took the name Victor IV, only to find that his enemies had successfully voted for Cardinal Roland Bandinelli, a leading canon lawyer, who took the name Alexander III. The result was a schism, with a pope and an antipope vying with each other for the right to succeed Adrian.

In such circumstances, it was the right of every secular ruler to recognize the pope of his choice. Thirty years before, Henry I had claimed such a right, which Theobald had no stomach to contest, since he saw that Christendom would be rocked to its foundations by a divided response to a schism. Quickly asserting his authority, Henry forbade the bishops of England and Normandy to approve either claimant until he should give his final decision. Opinion gradually shifted in Alexander's favor, and within six months Theobald was ready to endorse him, recommending him to Henry as the "more virtuous, more prudent, more learned" of the rival candidates and advising him that a majority of the French bishops had already abandoned Victor.

In July 1160, shortly after Becket had sealed the peace between the two rival kings following the Toulouse campaign, Henry met with Louis at Beauvais to agree on a coordinated response, but then he stalled for another four months, insisting that their decision be kept secret. To Theobald's dismay, Henry was conducting his own backstairs diplomacy, refusing to recognize Alexander until the pope's representatives agreed first to approve the long-delayed canonization of King Edward the Confessor to bolster the English monarchy's divine-right credentials. And by the time the favor was conceded, Constance of Castile had died in childbirth, and Louis had decided to marry Adela of Blois-Champagne, the cue for Henry to storm back to Alexander's envoys to demand immediate approval for his young son's wedding to Louis's infant daughter as a further precondition to recognizing the new pope.

Becket at first saw no reason to meddle in the politics of the papal endorsement, unaware as yet that Theobald blamed him more than anyone for permitting Henry to extort what amounted to a ransom from the new pope. But as the episode dragged on, he went out on a limb, taking sides with two Norman prelates, Giles of La Perche, archdeacon of Rouen, and William, bishop of Le Mans, who had refused to condone the king's behavior and spoken out, leaking news of the decision in Alexander's favor prematurely, for which Henry ordered the immediate destruction of their property.

Thomas appealed to Henry to relent, saving the archdeacon's house from demolition by pretending that it was where he himself stayed when in Rouen. He could do nothing to rescue the bishop's house in Neufmarché, which was ransacked and his goods thrown into the street. But he would prevent the burning of William's castle at Le Mans, even though Henry had already dispatched fast riders armed with writs that he had first brandished in the faces of his terrified courtiers, shaking his fist while shouting, "Forsooth, let the citizens of Le Mans know of the infamy of their bishop." Behind the king's back, Becket ordered these messengers to take four days for their journey instead of the usual two. The next day, he sent a delegation of bishops to intercede with the king, but they were rebuffed. Undaunted, he returned himself again and again, until finally, on the third day, Henry yielded, if only because he thought that enough time had already elapsed for his officers to raze the castle.

Instantly, Becket's own couriers galloped nonstop to Le Mans. Arriving breathless and in the nick of time—for the king's writs had been handed that very morning to the civic authorities—the castle was saved. William fitz Stephen, ever partisan where Becket's reputation is at stake, claims that Henry, once he had cooled down, thanked his chancellor for sparing him the shame and embarrassment of a fatal overreaction. Perhaps, but whatever he may have said in public, in private he must have smoldered. Had a license not subsequently been granted by Alexander's representatives for the children's weddings, his reaction would have been far less benign.

BY JUNE 1160, Theobald was seriously ill and had to be carried about from place to place in a horse litter. Some years before, he had succumbed to a chronic disease described as "a grievous malady [that]

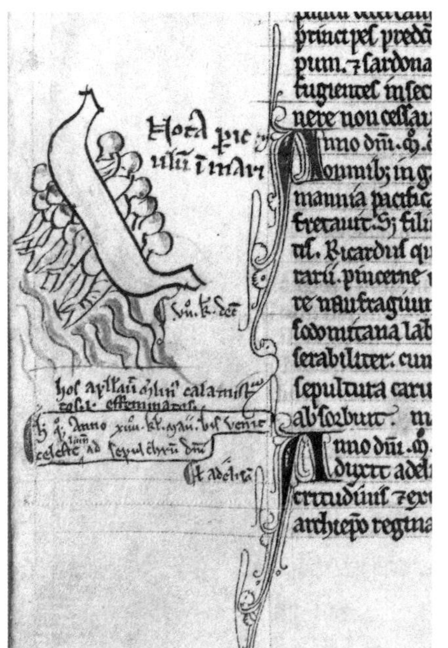

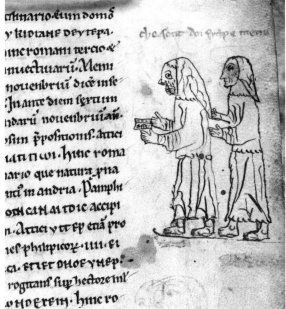

The sinking of the *White Ship*.

Poor scholars, one reading a book.

A queen greets her two sons as they prepare to fight for the throne after their father's death. An imaginary scene from the early fourteenth century.

Pevensey Castle, from where Becket rode out hunting and hawking as a teenager.

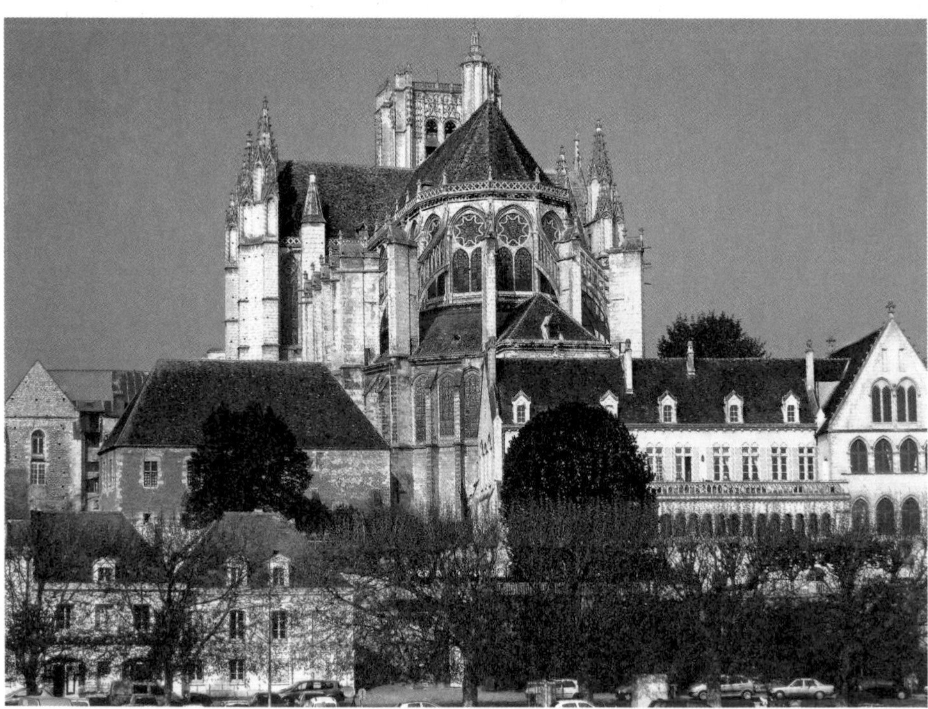

Auxerre Cathedral. Only the crypt remains the same as when Becket studied canon and civil law within the precincts.

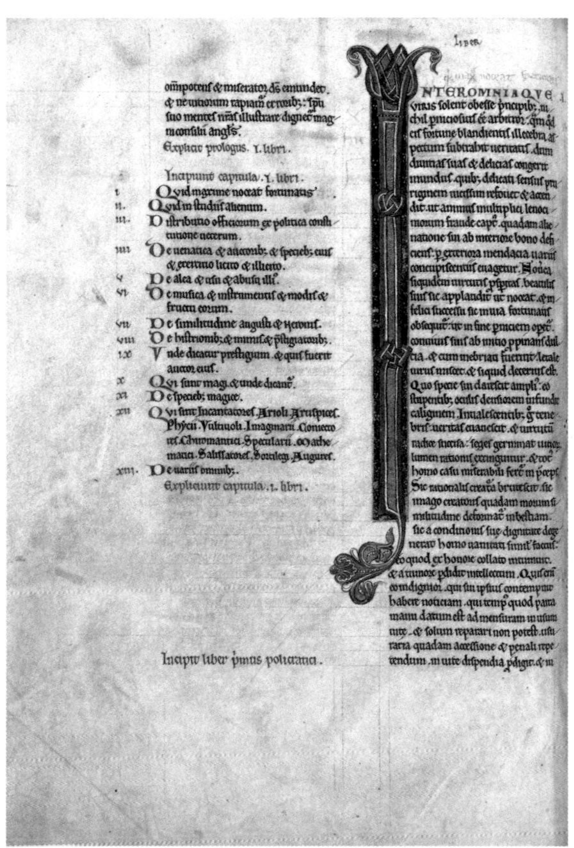

The opening of Book I in the copy of John of Salisbury's *Policraticus*, presented by the author to Thomas Becket.

Thomas Becket, a late twelfth-century stone relief, Sens Cathedral.

The monks' cloister at Canterbury Cathedral.

Henry II, an eighteenth-century engraving, with a panel showing Becket's murder below.

Pope Adrian IV.

Orford Castle, where the keep was modeled on that at Gisors.

The ruins of the monks' refectory at Battle Abbey.

Thomas Becket, a modern image made from fragments of thirteenth-century stained glass, Canterbury Cathedral.

Canterbury Cathedral. The nave and western towers were rebuilt in the fourteenth century.

The nave at Sens Cathedral.

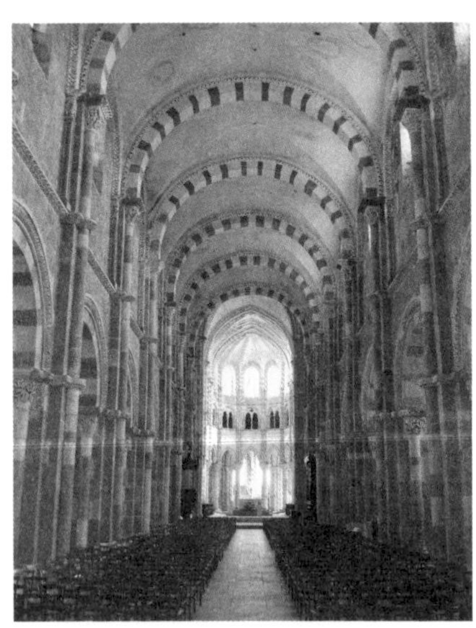

The nave at Vézelay Abbey.

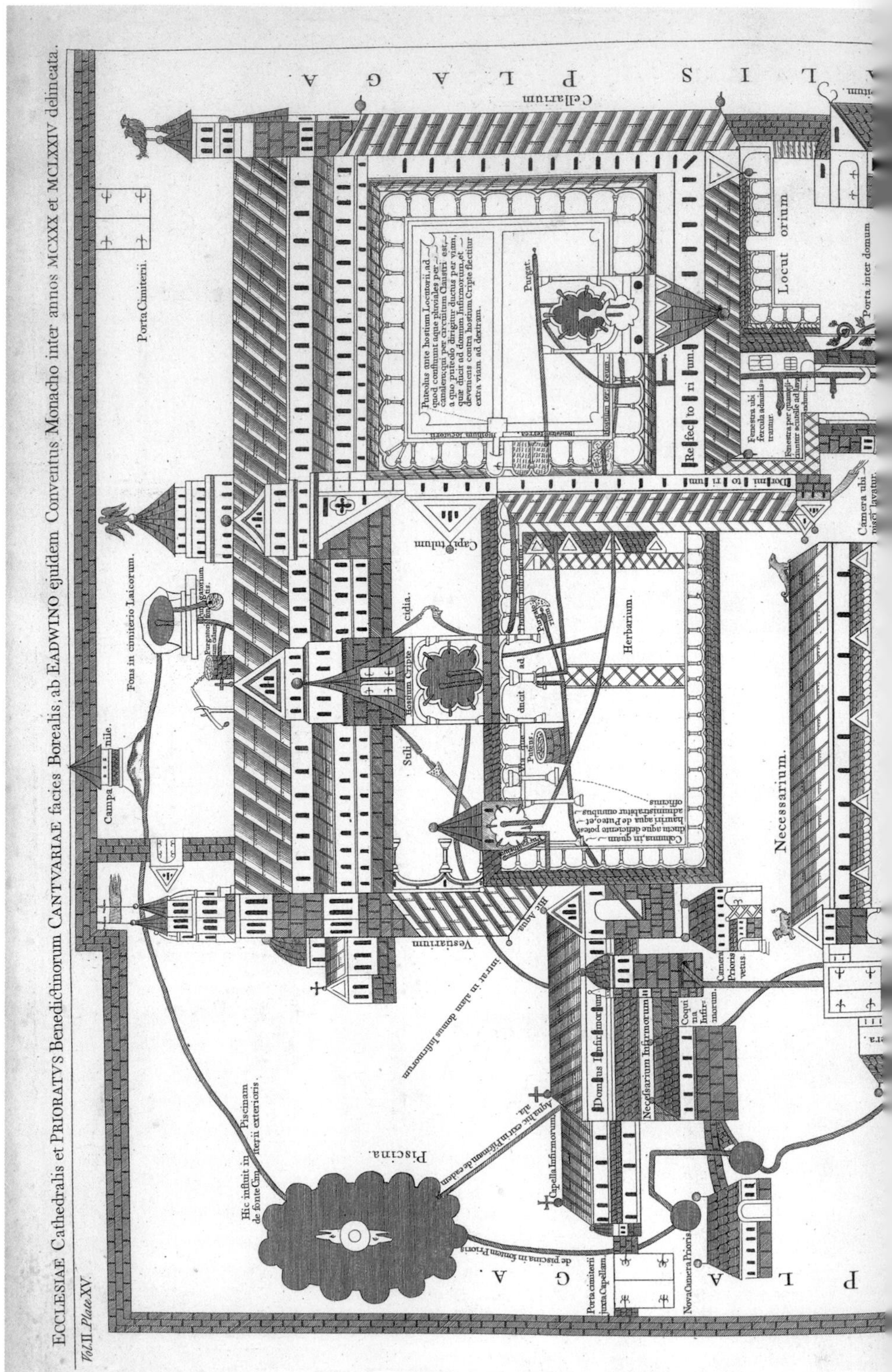

A plan of the priory of Christ Church, Canterbury, showing the cathedral and monastic buildings as they existed before the fire of 1174, including the hydraulic waterworks system installed c. 1155–67. The monks' cloister can

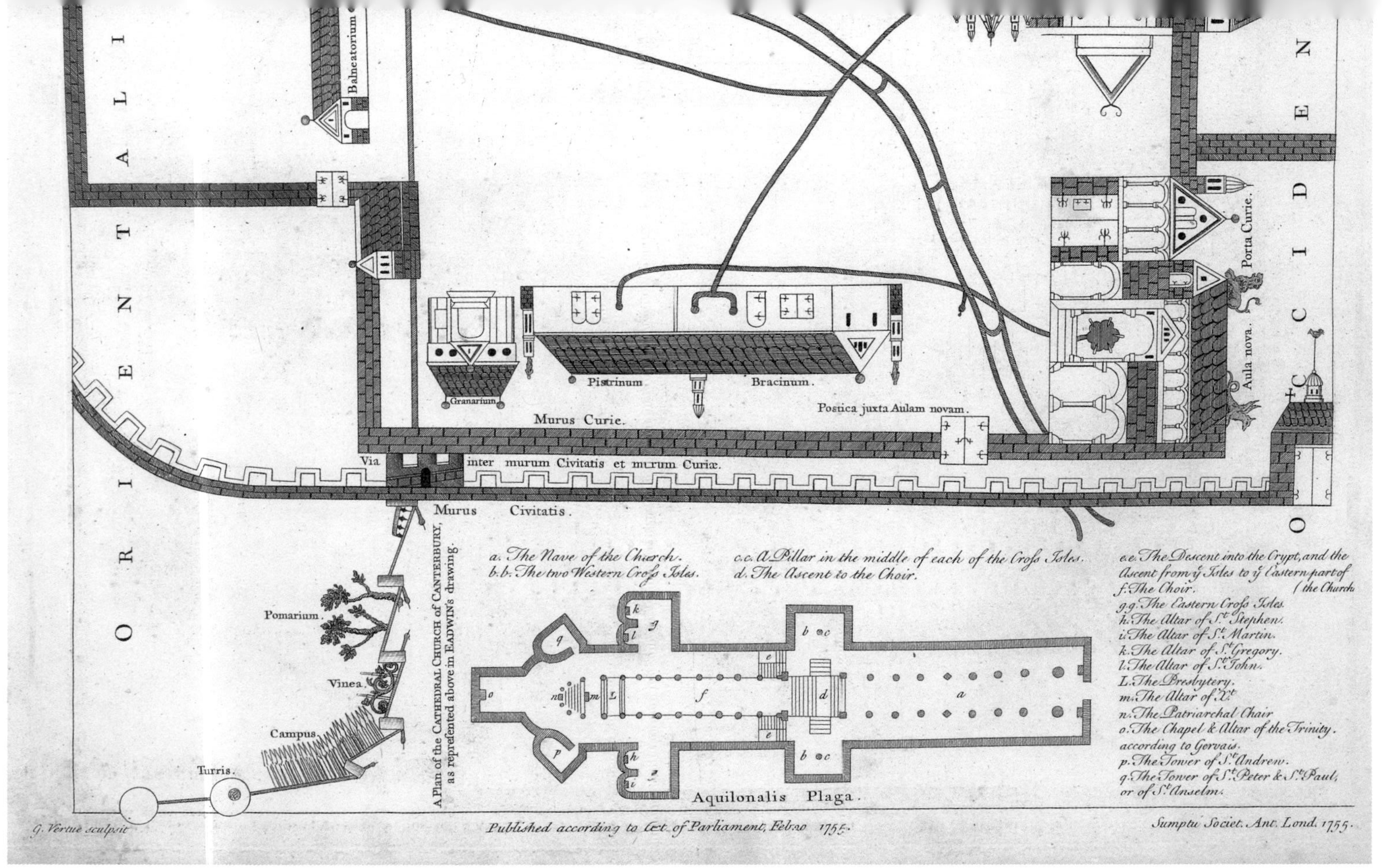

be seen beneath the cathedral, but the archbishop's palace is off the plan. From an eighteenth-century engraving.

The murder of Thomas Becket, showing Edward Grim attempting to deflect the knights' blows (thirteenth century).

The murder of Thomas Becket, from an engraving made at Venice c. 1660.

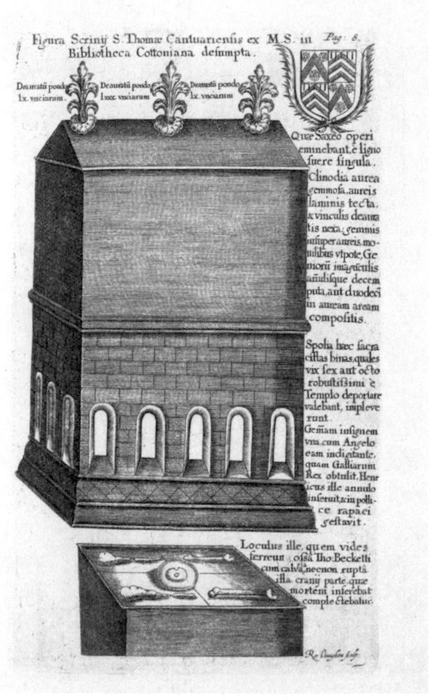

A clumsy seventeenth-century attempt to depict Becket's post-1220 shrine.

brought me nigh to the gates of death," a complaint diagnosed by John of Salisbury as a stomach ulcer. Seeing his end approaching, he vowed to make restitution to anyone he had wronged, "to make satisfaction," as he poignantly said, "to the Scourger and to avoid the everlasting scourge by chastisement." Soon afterward he wrote to Becket, saying that he wanted to abolish the bad custom of "second aids" introduced by his brother Walter while archdeacon of Canterbury. A discretionary levy on the incomes of parish churches for the archdeacon's personal benefit, second aids were lucrative, and Thomas, whose expenses by this time may have been exceeding his income, strongly resisted the suggestion.

On the move in Normandy when the archbishop's letter was dispatched, Thomas claimed that he did not receive it for several months. John of Salisbury wrote to warn him, "You charged me to watch over your interests. . . . Our lord archbishop has ordered that the tax which has been paid by his own churches should be withdrawn from you. Though others resisted me, I struck out in vain against the rushing stream." Theobald, however, was unmoved. He knew the levy was morally wrong. "What little," he insisted, "would it profit us if we should gain the whole world and lose our own soul?"

He particularly blamed Becket for not reproaching Henry for his delay in recognizing Pope Alexander, accusing him of betraying his trust and withholding essential information. Given that the chancellor had by now risked his position with Henry on several occasions to help the church, this seems unreasonable. What Theobald simply could not see was that Thomas had his own dire predicament to contend with. For he had been set by Theobald to serve two masters, a nigh-impossible task given Henry's character. In any case, triumphant from his success in extorting such large concessions from Alexander's representatives, Henry was daring to believe he had the new pope in his pocket, in which case anything Thomas said would be irrelevant.

Matters finally came to a head when Becket ignored Theobald's further appeals over second aids and the archbishop sent him a scathing rebuke. "You have often been recalled," he wrote, "and you ought to have returned in answer to a single summons of your father, now old and ill. Indeed it is to be feared that God may punish your tardiness, if you shut your ears to the call of obedience, forgetting the benefits you have received and despising your father whom you should have carried on your shoulders in his sickness."

Mindful that death was approaching, Theobald also wrote several times to Henry. "On every side," he protested, "we hear the clash of kingdoms, new shapes of things swim into view, and, owing to our sins, evil increases ever more and more." He implored the king that "since the evils of these days deny us your bodily presence, you would at least allow our archdeacon to return to us. . . . He ought to have come even without our summons and would have been convicted of disobedience before the eyes of God and men did not your needs excuse him."

But Thomas never came. John of Salisbury reports that Theobald had tried to summon him on pain of excommunication, but the order was countermanded after a royal messenger arrived to insist that Henry needed Becket constantly on the Continent and he could not be spared. The primate, rightly, smelled a rat. Henry and Becket, John hesitatingly dared to caution his friend, had offered different, potentially incompatible reasons for why Thomas could not return, suggesting that one of them was lying.

John was slower to doubt his friend, remembering his own bruising encounter with Henry over the Irish affair. "I think," he confided, "I have an inkling of the truth and realize almost as vividly as if I were on the spot what your situation is in the midst of your labors in a distant land." Had not St. Matthew hit the nail on the head in the New Testament? "No man can serve two masters. For either he will hate the one and love the other, or else he will hold to the one and despise the other."

John did not dare to complete the second half of the quotation, but his meaning is plain. Becket had begun his career in the church as Theobald's clerk and risen to be his fixer and right-hand man. He had been planted by the primate at court, where he had enjoyed the highest favor and the richest rewards. But as the years passed by, whether deliberately or not, he had weakened his ties to Theobald. He had very little choice in the matter after the pulp had gone out of his relationship with Henry at the gates of Toulouse, when he had become subject to many of the same controlling tactics that Henry used against all his courtiers. There was only so much that even an experienced high-wire artist could do.

He could help the church, as he had done several times, by mitigating royal policy at the margins, but that seemed to be all. The golden age of Lanfranc was no more. As Henry increasingly imposed his will on his chancellor, Thomas knew he would have to bend.

On April 18, 1161, Theobald died without ever seeing Becket again. His last remaining hours were spent with John of Salisbury, who sat faithfully at his bedside and fed him with a spoon. The chancellor, significantly, is not named as one of the executors of his will. He is not even mentioned in the document. Nor did he receive, as Henry himself would, a parting letter containing a final blessing and homily from the archbishop. So absolute was the rift between Theobald and his former favorite, it was as if Thomas had never been born.

14
ARCHBISHOP

WITH THEOBALD SAFELY RESTING IN HIS GRAVE, IT TOOK Henry a year to get around to choosing a successor. Becket, meanwhile, diverted the revenues of the vacant archbishopric into the royal treasury, while Walter of Rochester, Theobald's brother, performed the pastoral functions.

All along Henry, who believed he had brought Becket back into line at Toulouse, had it in mind to make him his next primate. But at first he was in no particular hurry, keen for a while to enjoy the additional income and the freedom of having no one of any great importance near at hand to give him moral criticism. At other times the chancellor had urged him to fill senior church appointments promptly, but on this occasion he said nothing, already aware that his own nomination was imminent. That information had never been a secret. As soon as the news of Theobald's passing had reached the royal entourage, all the courtiers "immediately began to place their bets, some whispering, some openly declaring that the chancellor would be the late primate's successor, and the people believed this too."

But Henry had other things on his mind, skirmishing in Touraine and the Vexin with Louis, who was still in high dudgeon over his infant daughter's wedding and over the fact that the Angevin king had failed to settle on her the lands and revenues he had promised. During the late spring, when Thomas lay sick at Rouen, both Henry and Louis came to visit him before agreeing to a truce in June. For the rest of 1161, apart from a brief visit to England to sit alongside Richard de Lucy in the Exchequer, the chancellor stayed in Normandy, while Henry was called away to smother a baronial uprising in Aquitaine.

For all his ambition and will to succeed, Thomas could not find it within himself to jump at an offer that he knew would shortly come. As his friend John of Salisbury relates, Henry wished Becket to combine the primacy with the chancellorship "so that he could more easily rule the whole of the English Church." After recovering the lands and castles that had been lost to him during the civil war and supremely confident that he had the new pope in his pocket, the king was turning his mind more toward the church. A cause célèbre arising in the Diocese of York had first focused his thoughts in that direction.

During a visit to Yorkshire three years before, a citizen of Scarborough had brought a petition before him. A rural dean, the man complained, had extorted 22 shillings from him by falsely accusing his wife of adultery on the evidence of a single witness. Henry had summoned him to appear before Richard de Lucy, sitting alongside Roger of Pont l'Évêque, the bishops of Lincoln and Durham, and John of Canterbury, now treasurer of York. Under questioning, the dean admitted that the woman had denied the charge, but when ordered to prove her innocence, she had asked her husband to bribe the dean to secure an acquittal. When John of Canterbury insisted that the dean be handed over to the church for punishment, Richard de Lucy cried out, "What share then in the decision will you allot to my lord the king whose authority the man has disobeyed?"

"None," replied John. "The man is a priest."

But de Lucy overruled him and referred the matter to the king, who scornfully denounced all those deans and archdeacons "who exercise tyranny, plague laymen with their calumnies and clerics with their unjustified extortions." And while holding his Christmas court with Eleanor at the castle of Falaise in 1159, he demanded that the testimony of neighbors enjoying good repute in their localities should be taken into account in all future cases coming before the church courts.

Henry's desire to restore what he always imagined to be the "ancestral customs" of his grandfather in cases involving the church was coming to the fore, but a primordial dynastic instinct also drove him on.

Increasingly eager to reduce the time he spent commuting across the Channel and to consolidate his power south of the Loire, he wished to designate his newly wedded son as his successor in England by crowning him. Deriving ultimately from the nomination by the Roman emperors of a successor or coruler who would bear some of the imperial titles, the custom had been unknown in England until King Stephen had attempted to crown Eustace, but it was common on the Continent, where rulers, notably in France and Germany, had their chosen heirs crowned in their own lifetimes to prevent a future civil war.

Having already placed his young son and heir in Becket's household to be educated, Henry planned either to make Thomas archbishop of Canterbury as well as chancellor, so that he would become a de facto viceroy for England and Wales until the younger Henry came of age, or to appoint a regency council led jointly by Becket and Robert de Beaumont. In either case, he meant to limit the possibilities for conflicts between church and state by making his chancellor and the new primate one and the same.

From Henry's point of view, the plan had the virtue of elegant simplicity. All Thomas had to do was obey, just as he had always done in the past—even during the Toulouse campaign when he had disagreed with the king's plans. The young prince was already forming a close bond with his mentor, so it made perfect sense to depute Thomas as his guardian while his father was abroad. In readiness for his son's coronation, Henry purchased fifty ounces of gold to make a crown and other regalia. And to provide for every possible contingency, he sought licenses from Pope Alexander, one ordering Roger of Pont l'Évêque to crown his son should this happen to be done during the vacancy at Canterbury, and another, which he held in reserve, allowing him to have his son crowned by any bishop he chose.

Becket knew of these plans in February 1162, when he met Henry at Rouen and was told bluntly that he was to be sent back to England as a prelude to his election as archbishop and to preside over the prince's investiture. Henry said he was relying on Thomas, doubtless recalling his part in the negotiations with the barons and King Stephen in 1153 that had made Becket a guarantor of the dynasty. Prior Robert of Cricklade, usually with his finger on the pulse, says that Henry strove to make

Thomas archbishop "because he trusted him beyond all men to aid his heirs to the throne in case he himself should be no more." But for some unknown reason, Henry had now decided that speed was of the essence, and Becket's indecision over the offer of the archbishopric caused the king to stumble badly. A majority of the bishops of the Canterbury province forcefully objected to a usurpation of the primate's ancient right of coronation. With Becket's promotion undecided but plainly in the offing, they refused to participate in a ceremony at which Roger of Pont l'Évêque or another stand-in presided. So to Henry's fury, the event would have to be downgraded into one of mere homage and fealty to the young prince—far less than he wanted or had demanded.

Unwilling to become archbishop simply on Henry's say-so, Becket was not easily budged. John of Salisbury suspected that he refused outright at first. "Being a man of great experience and well accustomed to measure the future," he says, "he had carefully considered the dangers of so great a charge, for by long familiarity he had learned what the burden and honor of that office comprised." As Theobald's clerk for nine years, he had observed every aspect of the job—and at a time in Stephen's reign when the church had been dragged into political affairs more than ever before. Hardly could he have forgotten watching Stephen pose as a protector of the church even as his reign degenerated into a tyranny, nor could he have forgotten fleeing across the Channel with Theobald in a fishing smack to attend the Council of Rheims and afterward seeing the primate narrowly escape assassination at the hands of a dozen of the king's armed knights.

Having served Henry as chancellor for more than seven years, Thomas may already have begun to fear that his royal master might soon end up as another Stephen. "He had," resumes John, "by now learned to understand the king's character and the wickedness and rapacity of his officials." He had concluded that "if he were to accept the post offered to him, he would lose either the favor of God or that of the king. For he could not cleave to God and at the same time obey the king's will or give precedence to the laws of the saints without making an enemy of the king."

Henry had taken Thomas quietly aside at Rouen and told him, "It is my wish that you be archbishop of Canterbury." Looking down with a smile at the fine clothes he was wearing, Thomas had retorted, "How religious, how saintly is the man you would appoint to that holy see!" But Henry had made up his mind and refused to listen. The more his chancellor prevaricated, the more insistent he became, until, refusing to be deflected any longer, he proclaimed to the whole court his instructions. Richard de Lucy and the other leading barons were to escort Thomas back to England. Once they had done homage and taken their oaths of fealty to the prince, they were to hasten to Canterbury and convene the monastic chapter in order to secure Becket's election as archbishop, a task that would tax all their powers of ingenuity, since Thomas was certain to meet resistance as a mere archdeacon who was neither a monk, as all but two of his predecessors had been, nor even yet ordained as a priest.

Finally Becket yielded, but only after his lingering scruples were overridden in an interview at Falaise with Henry of Pisa, one of the same papal representatives from whom King Henry had extorted a clandestine license for his young son's wedding. The suspicion must be that the elder Henry had extracted another big favor from the pope, since he immediately boasted that he had received official approval for Becket to serve as his chancellor-archbishop. Possibly he was bluffing, intending to seek papal approval for the election once it was a fait accompli. Either way, Becket's objections were overcome, and he boarded his ship for England with de Lucy and the others around the beginning of May 1162.

IN ITS TRUNCATED FORM, Prince Henry's investiture ceremony went off smoothly enough. Becket presided, leading the barons and bishops in taking the oath of fealty. Young Henry may even have worn a gold circlet for the occasion, but no coronation or anointing took place. From his father's perspective, therefore, the affair had been seriously bungled—and there was more. Roger of Pont l'Évêque, already Becket's jealous rival and smarting at the prospect of deferring to him, petitioned Pope Alexander for the right to have his cross carried before him throughout England in an attempt to claim equal status with Becket, and the right to crown the future king. In doing so, he ignited a slow fuse that would smolder for years, to explode some months before Thomas's assassination.

By comparison, the new archbishop's election went like clockwork. Richard de Lucy; his brother Walter, abbot of Battle; Hilary of Chichester; and the other bishops and barons whom Henry had commissioned as his agents did their job to perfection, winning over the monks of Christ Church Canterbury and fighting off some spirited resistance. As they explained it, the case for Thomas was that the English church would be assured of a safe and lasting peace "with such a welcome mediator between the king and the clergy." The case against him, the monks countered, centered (aside from the obvious fact that he was not a monk) on the prospect of the king pillaging the church through his chancellor-archbishop. How could it be right, they asked, that a man who had fought in wars and loved nothing better than to ride out with hounds and hawks, a man "with the appetite of a wolf," should become the shepherd of Christ's flock? But after voicing such objections, the monks did what was required of them and voted to a man for the chancellor.

Becket's election was ratified at a council held at Westminster Abbey on May 23, 1162, the Wednesday before Whitsunday. In the presence of the younger Henry, whom his father had appointed as his surrogate, the meeting was opened by Henry of Winchester, lately returned from his voluntary exile at Cluny after making his peace with the king. Following prayers and a short speech, the prior of Christ Church was asked to step forward to announce the chapter's choice and affirm that "by the inspiration of the Holy Spirit, Thomas, the chancellor of the realm, had been unanimously and canonically elected." After the king's representatives had duly confirmed the vote, a majority of those present nodded their assent, and the prince, though just seven years old, solemnly approved the decision in his father's name.

But not before a lone voice had spoken loudly in opposition. Gilbert Foliot, the bishop of Hereford and a former prior of Cluny and abbot of Gloucester, was a distinguished theologian; a strong-minded, traditional churchman; and a strict vegetarian. It might seem surprising that the scion of a noble Norman family, a former ally of Theobald, and one of the most active supporters of the claims of Matilda and the Angevin succession during the civil war now sought to frustrate the king's commands, but he believed that he acted purely out of principle. Exactly what he said would be airbrushed out of the records, but the gist appears to have been that it was sheer presumption that someone hardly fit to hold an oar should take the helm of the church. A brief summary of his speech by an anonymous Canterbury monk makes it likely that he also cast doubt on Thomas's display of reluctance to accept the primacy, calling it a sham.

Foliot's objections to Becket's appointment stemmed from his intense distaste at the prospect of being governed by a man whom he regarded as lowborn, smooth, gauche, mealymouthed, materialistic, and a lightweight. A dedicated professional who felt he had served his time, Foliot was consumed by a burning jealousy of a gifted and more successful younger man whom he regarded as unqualified. "The current opinion," almost all of the chroniclers and early biographers agree, "was that he himself had for a long time aspired to the archbishopric."

But he was shouted down. When someone cried out, "The voice of God and not man," he abandoned his protest, even if he was afterward still heard grumbling that Henry "had wrought a miracle by transforming a warrior and a man of the world into an archbishop." And yet his hostility may not have been untypical. In the "Thomas Saga Erkibyskups," the Icelandic author relates how the pope's representative, Henry of Pisa, had attended the assembly in an advisory capacity at the king's special request, sitting in the place of honor beside Prince Henry and ready to deal with any potential troublemakers. And far from his role being negligible, he had been forced to intervene more than once by hinting at the likely consequences should any of the malcontents go too far. "And now," says this anonymous author, "through his guidance they all say now 'yea' to Thomas being elected, although the hearts of some of them went right another way."

Taking all the evidence together, one can only conclude that a deep unease scarred the procedure for Becket's election, an unease covering a wide range of emotions, from seething resentment to cowed compliance. If the extract from the "Thomas Saga" is a fair reflection of the general mood as it purports to be, it would also seem likely that opposition to the new archbishop would be bound to resurface later in one form or another.

A closer look at Foliot reveals that he was ten years older than Thomas and an ally of Roger of Pont l'Évêque. Trained under Peter the Venerable, one of the shining lights of the ascetic reform movement in the church, Foliot led as upright a personal life as would be expected of a former prior of Cluny, a position to which he had been appointed at the remarkably young age of twenty-five. Unlike Thomas, who still showed occasional traces of his youthful stammer when under pressure and who had always preferred to ride or hunt in his spare time, Gilbert—an expert in logic and rhetoric besides theology—was a skilled Latin orator. On first becoming abbot of Gloucester, he had been famous for giving regular pep talks to his monks. The one blemish in his otherwise exemplary character was that he had written to Pope Eugenius III testifying to his friend Roger's sound morals, disregarding the evidence to the contrary.

Becket would sincerely attempt in the early months of his archiepiscopate to reconcile himself to Foliot. Both he and Henry may have felt that some form of consolation prize was owed to him, and within a year Thomas would recommend him for the vacant bishopric of London, at which he promptly jumped. If, however, the new archbishop thought that he might somehow appease Foliot and win him over to his side, he seriously miscalculated. Whatever his hopes for a rapprochement may have been, when Thomas most badly needed his support, Foliot—far from reciprocating—would step forward to lead the opposition. By then he would be Becket's most deadly and effective rival, the "Judas" in his life.

ONCE BECKET'S ELECTION as archbishop had been confirmed, he set out with his clerks and a large retinue for Canterbury, following the same road that he had first taken as a young man of twenty-four on his way to join Theobald's household. The crowds were already thronging around the precincts of the cathedral to welcome him, among them fourteen bishops and a large number of abbots, monks, and barons. Prince Henry too was keen to see his mentor consecrated as primate and insisted on attending.

As Thomas approached the gates of the city, the bishops came out to meet him, "acclaiming him with a heartfelt joy and high honor" and leading him inside the walls. The primate-elect, however, paid little regard to the pomp and ceremony laid on for him, dismounting and entering the city on foot like a poor pilgrim. First impressions matter, and he was eager to create the right one.

But before he could be enthroned, he had to be properly ordained as a priest. This was done on Saturday, June 2, by his old ally and protector Walter of Rochester. As to his consecration, with the vacant bishopric of London not yet filled by Foliot, there could be no agreement as to which of the bishops had seniority. Both Walter and Roger of Pont l'Évêque staked their claims but lacked enough support, leaving Henry of Winchester to officiate. The next day, Trinity Sunday, the day already chosen by the Christ Church monks as their patronal feast day, the ancient ceremony took place.

The order of service can be found in the pages of a surviving fragment in the British Library. At an early hour, and in full view of a large congregation gathered in the nave of the cathedral, the air thick with incense as the monks chanted the hymn "Veni Creator Spiritus" ("Come, Holy Ghost"), Thomas came out of the vestry, wearing a black cope and a white surplice as befitted a humble priest. He moved slowly up the steps of the choir to the high altar, where he knelt quietly in prayer. From there he was led back to the steps of the choir, where he was released from all secular obligations in the name of the church of Canterbury. With this part of the service completed, Bishop Henry began the solemn rite of consecration, in which he laid his hands on Thomas before giving him his pastoral staff, miter, ring, and gloves, acclaiming him as the archbishop of Canterbury and primate of all England.

Only one glitch marred the proceedings. It was traditional for a newly consecrated bishop to have a copy of the Gospels opened and held on his head and neck, after which a verse would be chosen at random that would serve as an omen, or "prognostic," of his future achievements. For example, at a consecration service conducted by Lanfranc in 1077, the first words to catch his eye had been, "Bring hither the best robe and put it on him." Unfortunately, the random text chosen at Becket's consecration was a well-known passage from St. Matthew in which Christ cursed a barren fig tree: "Never shall fruit be born of thee throughout eternity; and it was forthwith cast into the fire." At this, Foliot could not contain his glee. In fact, our only information about the mishap comes from a vituperative attack he delivered against Becket four years later. Since, however, the text was read from the Vulgate, perhaps only the clergy and monks in the choir and those sitting at the front of the nave who understood Latin would have been aware of it.

After the consecration, the final step was to ask Pope Alexander to grant the pallium, a "stole," or long scarf, of white wool to be placed around the shoulders of a metropolitan bishop. Usually a suppliant traveled to obtain it in person, but Henry forbade such a visit for reasons that he took to the grave. As his proxies, Thomas sent John of Salisbury and John of Canterbury to the papal curia—now hounded out of Rome by Frederick Barbarossa and at Montpellier, in the county of Toulouse, on its way to seek refuge in France. With the pope's entourage constantly on the move, it took the two Johns six weeks to track it down, but the job was done by the beginning of August, when they carried the precious garment home to Canterbury.

On August 10, Becket again mounted the steps of the choir in his cathedral, this time with bare feet. Approaching the high altar, he took up the pallium with his own hands and waited until it was carefully placed around his neck by the monks. A low-key affair to the few onlookers, the bestowal of the pallium marked the moment that Thomas's spiritual powers came fully into effect and was of the highest significance for him, for it was a day on which he can only have felt he stared God directly in the face. The questions in so many minds as they watched him on that warm summer day were, How would it change him? Would he be able to juggle the rival claims of church and state? Or would he sooner or later end up frustrating either Henry or the pope in the same way he had ended up disappointing Theobald?

There would be ample time to find out, for the new primate was not yet quite forty-two. To the hundred or so Christ Church monks packed into their stalls in the choir on August 10, 1162, it must have seemed as if Becket would be their pastor and spiritual leader for at least the next twenty years, perhaps even longer.

How wrong they were.

15
A BROKEN RELATIONSHIP

AS WHEN HE HAD BEEN APPOINTED CHANCELLOR, THE NEW archbishop's first letter of congratulation came from the wily Arnulf of Lisieux, ramming home the point that Thomas would now have to learn how to balance a courtier's role with that of a holy pastor. "We beg," declared Arnulf sanctimoniously, "that he who chose you"—it is left deliciously ambiguous whether "he" is God or Henry—"will so govern the estate of the dignity you have received, that your holiness will not dim your grandeur nor your grandeur diminish your holiness, but each with equal steps will keep pace with the other."

Becket, however, preferred not to linger in a no-man's-land where divided loyalties could lay him open to attack from every side. As archbishop, his pastoral responsibilities and obligations to the church gave him a distinctive identity. He was also experiencing his first taste of power, with no one immediately above him except Pope Alexander, himself an exile in France. Soon comfortably settled into the archbishop's palace at Canterbury, Thomas decided he was no longer willing to go on vacillating between self-assertion and dishonest compliance. He had no further wish to be chancellor, and in the autumn of 1162, only some four or five months after his consecration and without waiting for Henry and Eleanor to return from the Continent, he resigned, claiming that his pastoral duties were too onerous for him to occupy both positions.

His worst offense was not to consult Henry first. All that the king thought he knew of Thomas had so far led him to believe Becket would be unlikely to surrender a highly prestigious, lucrative office that, all over Europe, was routinely held by a bishop. The speed of the decision took Henry completely by surprise. His darkest suspicions were aroused, so that when the archbishop's messenger first delivered the news, he swore, "By God's eyes," then flew into a fury, unleashing a diatribe accusing Thomas of betraying him.

That Becket meant to act without fear or favor, signaling his unswerving spiritual commitment, is shown by one of the very first letters he wrote from Canterbury, in which he ordered his consecrator, Henry of Winchester, to restore a gold cross he had (allegedly) removed without permission from his cathedral. "We know how numerous and serious are the problems which are disturbing and troubling you," he began ingratiatingly, before changing his tone and delivering the sternest of rebukes. "We have learned that you have alienated the gold cross from your church. . . . We direct you by the virtue of obedience to strive by every means possible to restore it . . . within forty days from the receipt of this letter failing which you should not put off coming to our presence within two months from that fortieth day to make satisfaction."

He then announced his intention to resume Theobald's work by recovering lands or castles pillaged by the marauding barons from the church of Canterbury in King Stephen's reign, a high-profile campaign closely resembling Henry's own after his coronation, in which Becket had been his hard-nosed assistant. William fitz Stephen, one of the trained lawyers handling this work, claims that Thomas had secured Henry's blessing for the plan. If so, it did not last long. Becket's zeal far exceeded the more politic Theobald's, and it soon appeared to those on the receiving end that he was using the same autocratic methods he had learned as chancellor when fighting in Henry's corner. Roger of Clare, a powerful baron from whom Thomas claimed the honor of Tonbridge in Kent, was among those refusing to yield. After much haggling, the baron grudgingly gave Becket much of the land he claimed, but refused to do penance or acknowledge any blame, not at all what Thomas seemed to expect.

Among other contested properties were the lands of William of Ros and the castles of Rochester, Saltwood, and Hythe. In his efforts to recover Rochester, the new archbishop was able to produce one of Henry I's charters to back his claim, but in the case of Hythe, he lacked written proof and merely hoped to regain possession of the castle on the basis of his say-so. The case of Saltwood was the trickiest of all. Rightfully belonging to Theobald, the castle had been illegally occupied in the closing months of the civil war by the royal standard-bearer Henry of Essex, one of the greatest landowners in Essex, who was busily expanding his sphere of influence across the Thames into Kent. But after the standard-bearer's disgrace for cowardice in north Wales, King Henry gave the castle to his doorkeeper and official whoremaster, Ranulf de Broc. At the time, Becket had said nothing, but now he objected that the Crown had no right to give away estates that lawfully belonged to the church of Canterbury. The trouble was that de Broc was one of Henry's cronies. Where he was involved, might was right. The archbishop's claim led only to angry exchanges of words. Becket would lose this round resoundingly, since de Broc and his allies, backed by Henry, remained firmly in control of Saltwood, which rankled like a running sore.

Not taking pause for thought from his mixed success so far, Thomas next revoked summarily those leases of the Canterbury demesne lands that he considered to have been granted out too cheaply or for too long. Rightly believing that Theobald had been coerced into making many of these agreements during the civil war and that they were far too favorable to the beneficiaries, who in some cases were claiming to own church lands by hereditary right, he acted aggressively, expelling either the tenants or their farmers. Then, when sued in the royal courts by those he had dispossessed, he refused to enter a plea in his defense or even to appear in court, claiming that anyone with a grievance should bring their petition to the archbishop's court at Canterbury.

Although viewed as unfair and dictatorial by those occupying church lands, Becket's actions were justifiable by canon law. One of the more paradoxical and disruptive consequences of the triumph of the ascetic reform movement in the church was the fast-evolving idea that in the cause of moral regeneration, the ministers of the church were answerable only to God and the pope. A century earlier, the reformers would have relied on secular rulers to assist them, but with the pope and cardinals now regularly deciding lawsuits and hearing appeals from all over Europe, the church authorities had begun to bypass lay rulers completely and assert their immunity from secular jurisdiction. Theobald, who belonged to an older generation that had placed a far higher value on cooperation between church and state, had trodden warily in his own efforts to recover church property. That said, he had been spectacularly unsuccessful at recovering more than a small proportion of what the church had lost in Stephen's reign, and what Becket was now attempting had merit even if it was impolitic.

At first muffled because of the extraordinary favor in which Thomas was still presumed to be held, howls of protest soon reached Henry's ears in Normandy. His abrupt resignation of the chancellorship, coupled with the reports of the king's shocked reaction, greatly emboldened these petitioners. Had Thomas thought more carefully about it, he might have delayed resigning until more of the contested church lands had been recovered. By quitting when (and in the manner) he did, he not only incensed Henry but also lost a good deal of his authority over the landowners of southern England. Fast making enemies among them, he would shortly discover one of the most threatening was someone well-known to him: John the Marshal, a seasoned courtier and veteran of the civil war, who had lost an eye fighting for the Angevins.

Serving Henry since the beginning of his reign as the hereditary marshal in the Exchequer, John had sat regularly on the bench in this court just a few places along from the chancellor. A fearless warrior no more fazed by litigation than by battle, he did not stand idle when Thomas demanded back some lands in South Mundham, Sussex, which formed an ancient portion of the archbishop's demesne manor of Pagham but which John believed were his own. When he sued Becket in the archbishop's court, his case backfired. Despite claiming he had inherited the lands, he could produce no charter to justify his claim. So Becket threw out his petition, at which John produced a mass book, or troper, from under his cloak, on which he swore that he had been robbed. Beyond this, for the moment he held his fire. Coolheaded and ruthless, whether in battle or bargaining, he was a man who knew when to attack and when to retreat. "Silence or I will slay thee with my own hands," he had once famously exclaimed to his blood-spattered comrades while masterminding a retreat. Now he chose to retreat again, but he stayed on the alert, awaiting his opportunity for revenge. Henry had clearly not yet made up his mind whether he would support Becket or disown him. All eyes were on the king.

ONLY A SERIES of particularly violent winter gales prevented Henry and Eleanor from returning to England in time for Christmas 1162. After celebrating the festival at Cherbourg, they finally arrived at Southampton on January 23, 1163. Becket and his young charge, Prince Henry, whose relationship was still close, were waiting to greet them. Herbert of Bosham, one of the archbishop's clerks and an eyewitness, believed nothing was amiss. "The king and archbishop," he says, "kissed and embraced, each trying to outdo the other in giving honor. So much so that it seemed that the king was not effusive enough toward his son, being entirely effusive toward the archbishop." Over the next few days, the king and his archbishop met again repeatedly, riding out unaccompanied, dismissing their usual attendants, so that it seemed as if their familiarity was as strong as ever. Seeing and hearing this, the disgruntled barons and petitioners "soon made themselves very scarce indeed."

On the surface, all seemed unchanged, but some could see that the archbishop no longer had the full extent of the king's love. Not only that, but John the Marshal was seen loitering nearby. And within a few days, Henry would demand that Thomas give up the valuable archdeaconry of Canterbury, which he continued to hold in addition to the primacy. Only with some difficulty was he persuaded to part with it. All who watched closely could not fail to notice how, step by step, Henry began to withdraw the license he had previously granted to his chancellor, reestablishing a distance between them.

In April 1163, Becket sailed from Romney in Kent to Gravelines on his way to a church council that Pope Alexander had summoned to meet at Tours. The capital of Touraine, Tours lay in a fertile plain on the left bank of the Loire, just inside the Angevin dominions and directly across the frontier from France. With a general council of the church meeting for the first time on his territory, Henry's influence over the pope would never be stronger. Unlike his experience in 1148, when he had crossed the Channel ignominiously with Theobald and John of Salisbury in a fishing smack to attend the Council of Rheims, Thomas would travel to Tours at the head of an entourage whose splendor, if not perhaps its size, echoed that which had accompanied him on his embassy to Paris in 1158.

Halting at all the more important towns and villages as he rode through Normandy and Maine, he was received by the nobles and leading citizens with as much honor as if he were a king himself. "Approaching Tours," says an eyewitness, "the city was immediately roused." Even the cardinals came to join the crowds thronging outside the gates to welcome him, before escorting him to the temporary papal residence at St. Martin's Abbey. There Alexander, "who seldom got to his feet for anyone, came to meet the archbishop and hastened to show him reverence."

With the pope himself stepping forward to greet him, Becket became the most fêted prelate at the council, not for his own merits as he may naïvely have supposed, but because he was still judged by the world to be Henry's man, the most trusted confidant of the most powerful ruler north of the Alps, and the ruler most conspicuously seen to be supporting Alexander in his struggle against Frederick Barbarossa and his antipope. The assembly at Tours was about to become a carefully choreographed showcase for Alexander, but it would also become one for Henry, in whose mind a model of a regional church by papal concession under royal control was fast coming into view. His language proves it, since—with one eye on what he believed to have been the established norm in his grandfather's day and using words that would soon become mantras in his dealings with Becket—he had already cautioned the pope that, whatever else happened at the forthcoming council, the "dignity" of his kingdom should in no way be diminished and "no new customs" enacted.

For unbeknownst to the English chroniclers, perhaps unknown even to Thomas himself, secret negotiations had taken place between the pope and Henry before he and Eleanor had returned from Anjou and Normandy. On leaving his safe haven at Montpellier, the pope had ridden by way of Clermont to the Benedictine abbey of Notre-Dame du

Bourg-Dieu at Déols, near Châteauroux, where for three days in September 1162 he had conducted face-to-face talks with Henry. No one revealed what was said between them, but clearly the pope was emollient. Showered with gifts and bribes, he and his cardinals were led in a grand procession into Tours, continuing on briefly to Paris, then returning to Tours for the opening session of the council.

With Henry invisibly pulling the wires and laying down his terms in secret, it was a foregone conclusion that the business of the council would be minimal. Once prayers had been said and a Gospel reading proclaimed, a decree excommunicating the antipope's supporters was pronounced. Otherwise, some jurisdictional disputes between monasteries and their local bishops were settled, and two further decrees were passed tightening up the procedures for recovering church property embezzled by the laity, a move that Becket would strongly have approved.

But Thomas's role at the council was restricted to lobbying—vigorously but unsuccessfully—for the privileges of his own church of Canterbury and for his distinguished predecessor Anselm's canonization. In a failed bid to whip up votes for the man who had defeated Henry's grandfather in the struggle over "lay investiture," Becket laid before the cardinals a "life" of Anselm specially compiled for the occasion by John of Salisbury. But there were already too many candidates for sainthood, and Anselm's case was ignored. Pope Alexander was so wary of irritating Henry, he may even have vetoed the proposal.

Undeterred, Becket basked, as he believed, in Anselm's reflected glory. At the suggestion of Henry of Pisa, who lionized him if only out of deference to Henry, he was seated at the pope's right hand and from this prominent position was able to build up useful connections among the seventeen cardinals and more than one hundred bishops who attended. And yet he was still somewhat out of his depth. Stephen of Rouen, a monk of Bec, whose verse history of the house of Anjou gives one of the fullest accounts of the council's proceedings, says that when Alexander suddenly turned to Becket and invited him to give one of the opening addresses, Thomas had embarrassingly to decline because his impromptu Latin was not yet sufficiently fluent.

If that were not enough, Roger of Pont l'Évêque then stood up, determined to pursue his vendetta. Now his claim was that since he had been consecrated as an archbishop before Becket, he should take precedence over him in the official seating plan. Since he and Thomas were beyond English shores, right was on his side however petty or technical his grievance, but he wrong-footed himself by speaking on the topic at excruciating length, so that everyone shouted him down.

No sooner was he silenced than Gilbert Foliot, the newly consecrated bishop of London, caused an ugly scene. Still burning with jealousy, he was refusing to make the usual profession of subjection to Becket as primate, claiming that in his earlier capacity as bishop of Hereford, he had already made one to Theobald. Pope Alexander, to whom the matter was referred, promptly backed him to gratify Henry, ruling that it was not the church's custom to demand a profession of obedience to be repeated, a decision that left Thomas feeling wounded and humiliated. Was he yet aware that Henry had already sent for Foliot and appointed him to be one of his spiritual confessors, inviting him into his inner circle as an adviser on church affairs? So rapid an ascent to favor for a man who, scarcely a year before, had caused considerable embarrassment and inconvenience to Henry by his blistering attack on Becket at the ceremony ratifying his election as archbishop surely illustrates the direction of the king's thoughts.

On returning to Canterbury, Becket must have felt decidedly let down. Superficially, his appearance at the council had been a resounding success. He had been seated in a place of honor. His name and face would now be known to the entire college of cardinals and other dignitaries of the church. When in the following year his quarrel with Henry would lead to his sudden flight into exile, his cause would come to electrify those who had seen him there. But he also must have felt deeply dissatisfied at his own shortcomings and more than a little unsettled by the sniping of his two most senior subordinates. If he ever felt himself a newcomer and an outsider trying to become an insider, this would have been the moment.

THE FIRST OF a fresh series of squabbles began on July 1, 1163, at a great council summoned to meet in the "new hall" at Woodstock in Oxfordshire, built by the king's grandfather to transform one of his favorite hunting lodges into a royal palace not far from where he had created a menagerie of exotic wild animals, including leopards, lions, camels, lynxes, and a porcupine. Henry's youngest brother, William, was there, as were Richard de Lucy, Richard de Humez, and many of the other leading barons. Gilbert Foliot, as bishop of London, joined Becket at the head of the church's delegation, and all went smoothly until Henry raised the issue of taxation. He had refused to replace Becket as chancellor and was managing his own finances, ingeniously attempting to develop a new system of taxation that could be levied in peacetime and not simply in times of war or revolt. The new tax was designed to replace an old Anglo-Saxon tax known as the "danegeld," originally levied annually in peacetime to buy off the invading Danes. This ancient levy had been continued by William the Conqueror, but though once lucrative, it now fell mainly on the peasantry and so raised a maximum of only £5,000 before deducting the expenses of collecting it.

Henry's new tax was to be levied at the rate of 2 shillings for every "hide" (roughly 120 acres)—enough to buy a team of oxen and two hundred pigs—which potentially could have raised three or more times as much revenue in total as the old one. But so as not to increase the overall tax burden, he wanted it to subsume the customary "sheriff's aid," collected annually by the sheriffs for their own expenses. Under the king's plan, taxpayers would pay exactly the same amount to the sheriffs as before. The losers would be the sheriffs themselves, who would have to pay the full amount of the new tax to the Exchequer without deductions, leaving them to fund the genuine costs of local administration out of their own pockets.

Becket led the opposition. As the son of a former sheriff of London and the secretary to another for just over two years before entering Theobald's service, he knew the likely impact of stripping the sheriffs of their only legitimate source of funds. He told the king that the church would continue to make its usual payments to the sheriffs on a voluntary basis, but if the money were to be appropriated as royal revenue, not a penny would be paid to the sheriffs in future. To this Henry angrily retorted, "By God's eyes, it shall be given as revenue and written down as such in the royal records." To which Becket swore back in a fit of pique, "By the eyes by which you swear, never while I am living will this money be given from my land."

The two men then clashed over another marriage license. One of the richest heiresses in the kingdom, Countess Isabel de Warenne, the only surviving child of William de Warenne, Earl of Surrey, had been widowed when her husband, King Stephen's younger son, William, had fallen mortally sick on his way home from the Toulouse campaign. Still relatively young and childless, the countess was being wooed by Henry's brother William, who was head over heels in love with her. His suit was supported by his brother, who relished the thought that on the strength of a simple exchange of wedding vows, the Angevins would be able to recover control of the vast Warenne estates in England and Normandy. The only obstacle was that the couple were third cousins and within the prohibited degrees of marriage. William had to obtain a license to marry her, but Thomas opposed the request, following canon law to the letter as he had done before as chancellor in the case of Mary of Blois. His decision could not reasonably be criticized, except that coming hard on the heels of his resistance to the revamping of the sheriff's aid, he was taxing Henry's patience to the limit.

On this occasion, Henry bided his time, waiting until he was able to recover the Warenne estates by a different route a year or so later, when he arranged for Isabel to marry his illegitimate brother, Hamelin of Anjou, since in his case consanguinity did not arise. But if the king was satisfied with the outcome, his brother William was not. From this moment on, he and his close friends, including John the Marshal, harbored a grudge against the new archbishop that would fester until the day it could be avenged.

Henry and Becket, meanwhile, had begun arguing over the church's claims for the immunity of the clergy from secular jurisdiction. First visible in his searing attacks on Hilary of Chichester during the Battle Abbey case and then resurfacing in the case of the citizen of Scarborough from whom a bribe had been extorted, the king's distaste for what he saw as the unaccountability of the clergy to himself and his judges was on the point of exploding into a major quarrel. Fueled by the spiraling breakdown of his intimacy with Becket, this situation, which so far had seemed like tit for tat after the new archbishop had begun his high-profile campaign to recover lost church lands, would gradually turn into a major clash over fundamental issues of principle.

The crux was how to deal with criminous clerks (priests, deacons, and others in minor orders, such as subdeacons and acolytes) who were convicted of a serious crime against the king's peace, such as murder, robbery, larceny, or rape, for which, if the offender were a layman and not a clerk, the punishment would be death or mutilation. According to Henry, the royal judges had complained that more than a hundred homicides by those who claimed exemption from trial in the secular courts had gone unpunished on account of their holy orders. Church courts did not inflict capital or corporal punishments "lest in man the image of God should be deformed," preferring instead to impose unfrocking, imprisonment in a bishop's prison, confinement to a monastery, penances, or pilgrimages, either alone or in various combinations.

On the king's side was the fact that the church's claims for immunity from royal justice were a relative novelty. There had been few exemptions before the later years of his grandfather's reign, but the rise of the ascetic reformers in the church, combined with the uncontrolled reception of canon law in England during the anarchy of Stephen's reign, had changed all that. In particular, Gratian's *Decretum,* now the standard textbook in the church courts, included a clutch of canons forbidding the accusation or trial of churchmen before a secular magistrate and insisting that no punishment could be inflicted on them without the church's consent.

By far the greatest myth surrounding this topic is that the church courts were a soft option. That this was not necessarily true is proved by one of the first cases in which Henry took an interest, that of a priest accused of homicide in Bishop Jocelin of Salisbury's court. Although the priest denied the charge, he was unable to prove his innocence, but neither could the accusers prove his guilt, so the bishop sought Becket's ruling. His decree, which he published as a precedent for his whole province, was that in such a case, a clerk was to be unfrocked, stripped of his living, and imprisoned in a monastery, where he should do penance in relation to the gravity of his crime. In this instance, Becket envisaged a harsher sentence than would have come from a trial in a secular court, where if an accused person was unable to prove his innocence but could not be convicted, he had to be acquitted, since it was a rule of English common law that a prisoner was always to be judged innocent unless convicted by a jury.

Henry then actively intervened in the case of a priest caught stealing a silver chalice from the church of St. Mary-le-Bow in London. On Becket's orders, the priest had been unfrocked and stripped of his living, but Henry wanted mutilation or the death penalty. Although the church courts rejected capital or corporal punishment, canon law allowed an unfrocked priest in a few exceptional cases to be returned, at the bishop's discretion, to the secular power for punishment. Henry knew this rule and demanded that it be applied to the priest, even though the mere theft of a chalice was not at all the type of crime envisaged in the canon, which was meant to apply only to cases so notorious that the spiritual welfare of an entire community was judged to be at risk, such as heresy or witchcraft. "In order to placate the king," Becket on this occasion gave in, agreeing to hand the priest over to the sheriff to be branded as a convicted felon. But soon he would have second thoughts.

What lay at the heart of Henry's objections to clerical immunity was that where an offending priest was found to be guilty of a serious crime, the church courts would spare his life, while the royal courts would not. In the next case over which he and Becket quarreled, the archbishop refused to allow the royal judges to try a priest accused of murdering a Worcestershire man in order to sleep with his daughter. Instead, Becket put him in the bishop's prison until he could be tried in a church court, where if convicted, he was to be unfrocked and dismissed, imprisoned, exiled, or sent on a lengthy pilgrimage to Jerusalem. Regardless of what other punishments he received, his life would be spared. Only if he committed another felony after he had been unfrocked could he be hanged, since an unfrocked priest became a layman again and thus could be tried for any future offense in the secular court.

Today the debate would most likely be couched in terms of the merits of capital punishment, but for Becket the type of punishment meted out was not the point. In his mind, the only issue at stake was the liberty of the church. From Henry's standpoint, this was not only an affront to royal justice but also an abuse hindering the execution of his coronation oath to do justice. From Becket's, it was a cardinal rule of canon law to which he now owed fealty as archbishop. And far from earning opprobrium for merely casting around for a convenient way to dress up a personal vendetta against Henry, he would be loudly supported in the earlier stages of the quarrel over criminous clerks by his bitterest rivals, Roger of Pont l'Évêque and Gilbert Foliot, both of whom ardently believed that churchmen were exempt from trial and sentence in any other tribunal on earth except a church court until they were unfrocked. Had Thomas been speaking merely out of pique or self-interest, such jealous rivals would never have backed him as they did.

Although Henry, who claimed to have consulted his own canon lawyers, strained every nerve to create the impression that he was occupying the high moral ground, his motives appear far less savory when a landmark case buried deep in the papers of John of Salisbury is considered. Dating back to 1156, these documents prove that before he began quarreling with Becket, Henry had himself forcefully defended the church's exclusive right to try criminous clerks for their first offense. The documents relate to the alleged poisoning of King Stephen's unpopular nephew William fitz Herbert, the deposed archbishop of York. Osbert of Bayeux, his archdeacon, stood accused of the crime, and Theobald was bracing himself for it to be heard in the king's court. To his delight and astonishment, Henry, after debating the point at exhaustive length with his barons and lawyers, decided that canon law took precedence and so Osbert would be tried in the church court.

Having once set the precedent, Henry now sought to overturn it. For this he was warmly applauded by the lay barons, who John of Salisbury says had fiercely resisted such concessions to the church all along. But if the king had really felt so strongly about criminous clerks as an issue of principle as he now claimed, he would surely have allied with these barons and sought to reintroduce the so-called "ancestral customs" of his grandfather into the church much earlier in his reign. Now, after allowing such an important precedent as the trial in the church court of Osbert of Bayeux to be put on record, it would be harder for him to turn the clock back. In short, the punishment of criminous clerks in the royal courts—however much of a no-brainer by modern ethical standards it may appear—was always going to be an exceptionally difficult battle for

Henry to win when the rest of Christendom stood against him. In choosing this as the ground on which he meant to fight Becket, he was unconsciously exposing how personal their quarrel was fast becoming.

Had Henry only approached the matter in a more balanced frame of mind, for example by suggesting a compromise by which unfrocked priests, after conviction in the most heinous cases in the church courts, could be handed over to the secular power for punishment with the church's consent, his argument would have had some valid foundation in canon law. Then, he might first have isolated Thomas before following his usual tactics of divide and rule. But this is not what he intended to do. For after his new archbishop's return from the Council of Tours, he was not thinking straight. Demanding all or nothing, he was spoiling for a fight. It seemed as if his former chancellor could do nothing right and that the issue of criminous clerks was the stick that he had chosen to beat Becket with.

For his part, Thomas, fresh from sitting at the pope's right hand and in awe of his new spiritual responsibilities, intended to defend the liberties of the church, great or small. He was eager to prove himself a champion of the church, and after resigning the chancellorship, his hands were free.

He would not have long to wait.

16
CONVERSION

NO ASPECT OF THE PSYCHOLOGY OF BECKET'S JOURNEY from the worldly warrior-chancellor to the conflicted, brave, otherworldly priest and victim of his later years is more intriguing than the metamorphosis he is alleged to have undergone after his consecration. Several of the early biographers report him as experiencing something close to a Damascene conversion, seeing him as a second Saul in the Acts of the Apostles. "Touched by the hand of God," they say, "he put off the old man and put on the new," a line most effectively dramatized by Alfred, Lord Tennyson, in his play *Becket*, published in 1884 and first produced in 1893, with the virtuoso Henry Irving making his last stage appearance in the title role:

I served our Theobald well when I was with him;
I served King Henry well as Chancellor;
I am his no more, and I must serve the Church.
This Canterbury is only less than Rome,
And all my doubts I fling from me like dust.

His character was turning, but the biographer's trap is to look for a decisive moment of change—to do that is to write the history of the saint without his shadow. Rather than being two distinct individuals before and after a watershed, Becket had a divided consciousness as chancellor, displaying worldly ambition and acquisitiveness on a grand scale while keeping his body chaste, saying his prayers regularly, and allowing himself to be scourged before attending confession and mass. Yet given his attitude toward his intellectual development so far, it is a little unrealistic to imagine that the ideas fast breeding in his highly receptive brain as archbishop had been gradually absorbed over many years. The chances are that they had been put there recently by someone and that he resumed his studies neither for pleasure nor to satisfy his teachers, but to gather texts and arguments that would justify his cause.

If we are to believe his early biographers, visible changes in Becket's lifestyle immediately accompanied his consecration. He abandoned hunting and falconry. Instead of wearing the finest silks and the costliest furs, he put on a monastic garb beneath his outer clothing and mortified his flesh with a hair shirt. It is even claimed that he was wearing the habit of a monk beneath his outer vestments when he was invested with the pallium in his cathedral. Not content with this, he adopted Theobald's old habit of rising with the Christ Church monks at around 2 A.M. to say his daily office before washing the feet of thirteen poor men in secret and then returning to bed until about 6 A.M., when he studied a varied selection of devotional works to prepare himself for mass, which followed at around 8 A.M. The biographers concede that, unusually for an archbishop, he did not say the service daily himself, but they argue that this "was not through neglect, but through extreme reverence." On the days when he did consecrate the host, he would first study Anselm's prayers. He would then hear legal cases in his court of audience from about 9 A.M. until dinner, which was eaten between noon and 2:30 P.M., depending on the season. During the meal, his crossbearer and sacristan, Alexander Llewelyn, would read aloud passages from scripture or some Latin work, as was customary in a monastic cathedral setting. Once the plates had been cleared, Thomas would retire to his private chamber with his clerks and some specially invited guests. Passages from scripture or the church fathers would be debated, giving him a welcome opportunity to try out his ideas informally.

A closer examination reveals that the early biographers handle this material in markedly inconsistent ways. Such inconsistencies are extremely damaging, since they tend to throw everything into question. To begin with, Becket abandoned hunting and falconry only little by little. That he rose every day in the early hours of the morning to say his prayers with the monks and wash the feet of thirteen poor men seems unlikely but is impossible to verify. And where his dress is concerned, little or no change occurred during his first year as archbishop. Only after some fifteen months, and perhaps even longer, did he finally decide to cast off his silks and scarlet in favor of a simple dark robe or mantle lined with nothing more luxurious than lambskin. As to his alleged hair shirt, no solid evidence can be found that he ever considered wearing one before fleeing into exile in France.

The biographers come even more embarrassingly unstuck when describing the new archbishop's alleged change of eating habits. According to their stories, "He now partook of the sparest diet and his favorite drink was water in which fennel had been boiled." Merely sipping out of courtesy the wine he served to his guests, he only picked at the dishes set before him, preferring to dine on plain bread.

This is palpable fiction. Thomas was often abstemious, but chiefly for dietary reasons. His colitis had meant that for the past ten years or so, he had eaten and drunk only in moderation. He also continued to insist on the finest and most delicate food. Herbert of Bosham, who was present throughout and alone gives a faithful account, admits that his table still glittered with gold and silver plate and that the food served in his great hall was the best that his purveyors could find. Among other costly specialties, venison, boar, and pheasant were regularly on the menu. Such luxury naturally exposed him to criticism. These provisions could have been sold and the money given to the poor. An anecdote survives of how he one day justified himself to a gluttonous abbot who sneered at him for eating game during Lent. "If I mistake not, brother," he had retorted, "there is more greed in your eating beans than in my eating pheasant." His logic was that he might be eating richly, but at least he was eating less.

But if the notion that Becket underwent a conversion overnight from Saul to St. Paul is far too crude, there were discernible changes in him. Soon after his consecration, he chose Herbert of Bosham to be his divinity tutor. Thereafter, as Herbert himself recounts, he was "like a man awakening from a deep sleep." He began to study in depth, and out of this process of prayer and self-examination, he was able to reanimate the spiritual side of his character. As time went on, "the new man hungered to be revealed and would let himself be hidden no longer." Thomas increasingly "embraced the holy image-bearing scriptures with deep attention and devotion." He sought eagerly "by his new learning to shake off the old ignorance which long occupation with the world had brought, so that he, a new bishop, should be reformed to the new image of a bishop." In particular, he mastered every conceivable detail of the case put forward by the ascetic reformers for the immunity of the clergy from secular jurisdiction: "Touch not mine anointed" (Psalm 105:15) was one of several biblical mantras to which Herbert introduced him.

That Becket took his biblical studies extremely seriously can be verified. The earliest fruits can be detected in his correspondence, where he began quoting scripture constantly. In perhaps his earliest surviving letter written as archbishop, the one in which he ordered Henry of Winchester to restore a missing gold cross to his cathedral, he wove together multiple quotations from Isaiah, Psalms, the book of Wisdom, and Song of Songs. Another letter to Gilbert Foliot, congratulating him on his enthronement as bishop of London, is built around material from Psalms and the Gospels. Paraphrasing the passage in the Sermon on the Mount in which Christ compares his disciples to "the light of the world," Thomas declares that, with Foliot's promotion, "the lighted lantern which lay as if hidden under a bushel has now been placed on a lamp stand, so that it can spread its light far and wide through the house of the Lord." Such a clumsy attempt to mollify his rival would only earn its author a further dose of hearty contempt, but the letter proves handsomely Becket's increasing familiarity with key passages from the scriptures.

Other signs of his intellectual reawakening can be observed in the contents of the library he would gradually begin to amass. After his murder, his personal possessions became the property of the Christ Church monks, one of whom cataloged his collection of seventy or so books as it existed in the early fourteenth century. Many of these manuscripts would be purchased after his final breach with Henry, but Thomas had acquired a dozen or more earlier. One of the very first people he would ask for help in tracking down a copy of a book after his consecration was John of Salisbury's friend Peter of Celle, from whom he requested the sermons of Gebuin of Troyes, a disciple of St. Bernard.

As archbishop, Thomas was said to carry a book in a pocket of his outer garments, even when on horseback. Roughly one-tenth of the actual volumes from his collection can still be traced today, dispersed when the monasteries were suppressed by Henry VIII and now hidden away in Oxford or Cambridge libraries. Most were deluxe productions, two still in their original bindings and with a note of Thomas's ownership on the flyleaf. Whether he was chancellor or archbishop, it seems that when he wanted something, it always had to be the best that money could buy. Before printing with movable metal type was invented, books had to be copied and illustrated by hand. Extremely expensive if they also included color illustrations, as several of Becket's certainly did, they would have been treasured and studied, not merely tucked away in his traveling coffers as cultural trophies after a single cursory browse.

Organized around four main themes, most likely under Herbert's influence, Becket's collection, according to the fourteenth-century inventory, brought together scriptural and devotional works, moral and political philosophy, canon and civil law, history and rhetoric. A small section of works on classical history and on military and physical science, including duplicate copies of *The Art of War* by Flavius Vegetius, had probably been previously acquired while he was chancellor, those on military science doubtless around the time of the Toulouse campaign.

The first category is by far the largest. As would be expected of a newly appointed archbishop, Thomas purchased copies of the Vulgate, together with a variety of commentaries on nearly all the individual books of the Old and New Testaments. As a novice obliged to preach in his cathedral on the major church festivals, he also acquired a set of preaching or devotional aids, including Gebuin's sermons and a popular commentary on the story of Noah's ark. He dipped extensively into the church fathers, notably St. Isidore of Seville, St. Cyprian, and St. Gregory of Nazianzus, chiefly their scriptural paraphrases or writings on the obligations of the ministry, but his copy of the famous *Apology* of St. Gregory of Nazianzus, a largely autobiographical work, would have struck an immediate chord with him. Ordained a priest against his will at an early age, the young St. Gregory had been nominated archbishop of Constantinople on the insistence of the emperor Theodosius, had reluctantly yielded, and was initially acclaimed as the hero and restorer of Christianity, only to be attacked, denounced, and ridiculed within months for his ignorance and inexperience. After surviving for a year in the face of fierce rivalry and opposition from his fellow bishops, he had resigned, retiring to his family estates in Cappadocia.

Overall, Herbert of Bosham steered his pupil toward an understanding of the plain texts of scripture. Far less time must have been allocated for deeper, abstract theology, since such genuinely heavyweight church fathers as St. Augustine and St. Jerome were not on Becket's reading list. Herbert did introduce him at some stage to one leading manual of scholastic theology, Peter Lombard's *Sentences,* but since this was the latest and most fashionable work on the subject, he may have acquired it more for the sake of appearances.

Of the books Thomas had already collected as chancellor, the most interesting is the handsome presentation copy of John of Salisbury's *Policraticus,* now safely preserved in the library of Corpus Christi College, Cambridge, which his friend had dedicated to him and delivered to him by courier while he was still camped with Henry's army outside the gates of Toulouse. A copy of Livy's *History of Rome,* acquired in Italy and now in the library of Trinity College, Cambridge, was another of John's gifts, and to complement it, Becket purchased Cassiodorus's *Variae,* which continues Livy's story to the end of the classical era. He owned a popular *History of Troy* and its companion, *The Life and Deeds of Alexander the Great,* by Quintus Curtius Rufus. For insights into the physical and natural world, he turned to Gaius Julius Solinus's *Polyhistor,* an encyclopedia often found in cathedral or monastic libraries, much of which is plagiarized from Pliny's *Natural History.*

Thomas had already encountered Gratian's *Decretum* and Justinian's *Code* and *Institutes* as a young clerk in Theobald's household, and as archbishop he would soon purchase his own working copies of these standard works. Lastly, to hone his preaching and oratorical skills, he obtained a copy of the famous handbook of the first-century rhetorician Quintilian, *The Training of an Orator,* besides what is likely to have been a well-thumbed copy of an anthology of the *Attic Nights* by Aulus Gellius, a second-century author famous for his wordplay, conceits, and racy anecdotes.

THE IDEA of a Damascene conversion peppers several of the early biographies, but it is significantly missing from John of Salisbury's earliest vignette of Becket in the form of an open letter circulated among his friends within a few weeks of the murder. Between friends there is no need for pretense. John had known Thomas from his earliest days as a clerk in Theobald's household, unlike so many of the other early biographers, and he was under no illusions that his friend's career would be something of a roller-coaster and that Thomas was far from an obvious candidate for sainthood; in fact John would have considered utterly absurd the whole idea of Becket's future canonization by the pope.

Chief among Thomas's critics in the same year as he was consecrated archbishop was Peter of Celle, who at his abbey of Saint-Rémi at Rheims scribbled innuendos against him in the margins of a manuscript of Lactantius, a third-century Christian apologist persecuted by the emperor Diocletian. Unimpressed by Becket's search for a copy of Gebuin's sermons, Peter was scandalized by what he believed to be his fondness for grand gestures. "Hear, Thomas" and "Nota," he scrawled alongside several passages of Lactantius warning that generous gifts to and from the rich and powerful, or to those from whom something is expected in return, are unworthy of the name. Always the force of these annotations is the same: Becket's life shows that he is little better than a charlatan. His faith is superficial, his behavior is driven by pride and ambition, and by mingling with the great and good with such relish, he is helping the wicked to flourish at the expense of the just and innocent.

No more could Peter be convinced by changes in outward appearances. Although he still addresses Becket as chancellor, as Thomas continued to hold that office until the autumn of 1162, his letter in answer to the request he had received for a copy of Gebuin's sermons must have been written after Thomas's consecration as archbishop, for why else would Becket need a preaching crib? Despite promising to send the sermons, Peter's response is icy. Somewhat cheekily, Thomas had asked to be admitted into his intimate circle, effectively to become one of his pen friends, for nothing in the eyes of Christendom could have done more to advertise a fledging archbishop's claim to piety and spirituality. Peter, whose galaxy of celebrity correspondents had included Peter the Venerable and St. Bernard, brutally snubbed him in return:

> What common ground is there between the abbot of Celle and the chancellor of the English king? Who does not know that you are second only to the king in four realms? Who does not count me first in the sufferings of our brothers? My words are carefully weighed, for to the degree that I find you more and more excellent, I realize myself to be all the more worthless. By no means, then, shall I extend to you the hand of friendship, but if we were to become mere acquaintances, I should be flattered.

Peter, who during these years rarely strayed far from his comfortable cloister, where he was busy directing the rebuilding of the abbey church, was as yet unaware that his friend John of Salisbury had rallied to assist Herbert of Bosham in revitalizing the moral side of Becket's character. Still not allowed into Henry's presence without an official minder but steadily recovering royal favor after his disgrace in 1156–57 for meddling in Irish policy, John had no appetite for a second brush with the king, but he would steadily warm to the new archbishop to the point where he willingly consented to assist him by performing duties similar to those he had undertaken for many years for Theobald.

John's cooperation was not lightly to be assumed. A candid critic as well as a dutiful friend, he had severely rebuked Thomas for "putting the king before God" when imposing scutage on the church as chancellor. Moreover, once he took the plunge and joined the new archbishop's household, his relationship with Becket's divinity tutor would be far from smooth. Herbert of Bosham was something of a zealot who allowed his pen and his tongue to run away with him. He and John often sharply disagreed, but generally only over timing and tactics. On basic principles, they tended to agree. In particular, a close affinity existed between them over the punishment of criminous clerks. On that explosive subject, they spoke, and would continue to speak, as one.

If Herbert's influence chiefly came to bear in the sphere of scripture and knowledge of the church fathers, John's was in assisting Becket with intelligence gathering across Europe using his legendary networks of friends and correspondents, in helping with the drafting of correspondence and ensuring its delivery, and in stimulating Becket's interest in his moral obligations as a minister of the church, notably in relation to Henry. John wholeheartedly agreed with Herbert that any infringements of the church's liberty were an affront to God. Already in the final chapters of his *Policraticus,* completed in 1159, he had carefully built on Robert of Melun's theories of resistance to a tyrant, agreeing with him that the officers of the church, not least an archbishop, had a duty to impose sanctions, but taking the argument considerably further by claiming that a good pastor should resist a wicked ruler who stubbornly refuses to mend his ways, even to the point of martyrdom.

When the squabbling with Henry over criminous clerks turned into something far more dangerous, Becket would begin to draw heavily on these ideas. John's influence, felt as early as 1163 and 1164 and in full flood by 1165 and 1166, is apparent from what appear to be Thomas's own marginal notes in his presentation copy of the *Policraticus*. Chiefly comprising the letters *a* and *b* and also a small banner or flag, ranked according to a system in which the flag appears to indicate the most significant passages and *a* and *b* the next most important, these annotations have never previously been noticed and can only be satisfactorily observed with the assistance of high-resolution digital photography. Most appear in John's account of how tyrants are to be called to account for their transgressions, many of them where he discusses the extreme difficulty of distinguishing when a tyrant is condemned by God from when his tyranny is merely a manifestation of God's providence in the world, sent to scourge the people for their sins. Also greatly troubling the annotator is the extent to which a tyrannical ruler can be disciplined by someone already tied to him by a bond of fealty, as Becket was. Tyrants may be brought to account by the church and perhaps also by the community, but they are to be punished without loss to religion and honor, hence a man who has sworn an oath of fealty to a tyrant may already have disqualified himself from being an agent of divine retribution. Often the safest method of dealing with a tyrant, the annotator observes, is through prayer and penitence in the hope that punishment might be inflicted on him by the visitation of God. The classic dilemma is whether action should be taken or the remedy left to God's providence.

If Thomas really is their author, these annotations suggest that he was indeed undergoing something of a conversion, but chiefly inside his own head. With Herbert and John as his most trusted counselors, he would soon acquire a clear vision of the world, one he would find utterly compelling, even if the reasons that had driven him to acquire it in the first place were another matter. Now scripture and the church fathers, papal decrees and canon law, would become the acid test of his relationship with Henry, whom he would paint in the colors of a tyrant for his determination to subjugate the church. Soon the new archbishop would be proclaiming to Pope Alexander and to anyone else who would listen that "although the king must be obeyed in many things, he must not be obeyed in those things which cause him not to be a king." While it remains true that "what is Caesar's must be rendered unto Caesar," rulers who seek to subordinate the church to the secular power are tyrants, whom the church must resist. Anything appropriated by the secular power over and above its lawful entitlement "belongs not to Caesar but to a tyrant."

Such ideas would gradually come to furnish Becket with what he would regard as a supremely convincing narrative justifying his quarrel with Henry, enabling him to interpret the past and the present in a coherent way so as to create a clear message for his supporters and for posterity. If the king wanted to attack the church, Thomas would be forced to rebuke him as John the Baptist had once rebuked King Herod.

If the early biographers thought they had observed a metamorphosis in Becket, surely this was it.

17
THE CLASH

IN LATE JULY 1163, WHILE HENRY AND BECKET WERE IN LONdon together, the archbishop preached a fiery sermon before the king, taking as his text "'Look, Lord, here are two swords.' And he said to them, 'It is enough'" (Luke 22:38). This text had been a classic way of discussing the respective powers of kings and popes since Peter Damian, one of the most powerful advocates of the ascetic reform movement, had first used it a century earlier. According to the Gospels, the disciples showed two swords to Christ immediately after the Last Supper, before he went up to the Mount of Olives to pray. He said, "It is enough," and afterward in the garden of Gethsemane, he commanded St. Peter to sheathe one of these swords.

When Lanfranc was alive, the allegory was taken to mean that the pope governed in partnership with secular rulers, the one tending to the needs of the spirit, the other to the needs of the body. But Becket, following the militant church reformers, interpreted it to mean that the pope—as the vicar of St. Peter—had a controlling authority over both church and state because the material sword must be unleashed by the secular ruler at the pope's command. His sermon in July 1163 is another landmark in his intellectual development, since under Herbert of Bosham's direction, he had now secured a copy of a letter of St. Bernard to Pope Eugenius III, otherwise known as the *Exhortation,* in which on the eve of the preaching of the Second Crusade, the saint had famously declared: "Both swords must now be drawn in the passion of Christ, for

Christ is now suffering again where he suffered before. By whom are they to be drawn, if not by you? Both are St. Peter's, and are to be drawn when necessary, one by his own hand, the other at his beckoning."

It was not in Henry's nature to pay much attention to sermons, but this was different. As Becket's argument unfolded, the king "took note of each of his words and . . . did not receive his sermon with a placid spirit." He saw instantly how far his archbishop had shifted from his earlier opinions as royal chancellor.

A few days later, king and archbishop quarreled over the case of Philip de Broi, a priest whom Thomas had first got to know at the end of King Stephen's reign. A fellow prebendary of Lincoln Cathedral, he had been accused of murdering a knight but had been acquitted in the bishop of Lincoln's court. At first both Henry and the victim's relatives had accepted this verdict, and the matter appeared to be closed. Then Simon fitz Peter, one of the circuit judges for Bedfordshire, where de Broi had his main home, sought to reopen the case. Summoned to appear before him, de Broi refused to enter a plea, and when ordered to do so, he hurled abuse at Simon, who rode posthaste to London to complain to Henry.

With the words of Becket's sermon still ringing in his ears, Henry chose to interpret the insults leveled against Simon as a personal attack on himself. Swearing his familiar oath "by God's eyes," he ordered a new trial, but Becket intervened, saying, "This will certainly not be done, for laymen cannot be judges of clerks and whatever this or any other member of the clergy has committed should be judged in a church court."

Stifling his objections for the moment, Henry grudgingly agreed to commit de Broi for trial before a committee of bishops at Canterbury. There the accused priest successfully pleaded that he was not obliged to enter a defense for the murder, since he had already been acquitted in a previous trial. But he refused to answer to the charge of insulting a royal judge, claiming that it was "beneath his dignity to engage in this quarrel, for he was a great man and from a great family."

At this, Henry's lawyers leapt forward, crying, "We demand judgment upon an evident injury that has not been denied." The archbishop reluctantly agreed, sentencing de Broi to be deprived of all his church livings for two years and the income given to the poor. He was to serve his sentence in exile and before leaving the country was to be handed over to the sheriff of Kent, to receive a public flogging in the presence of the judge he had defamed.

Such a harsh punishment ought to have been sufficient for opprobrious words, but Henry was spoiling for a fight. He ranted and raged, crying, "This judgment has failed to respect my honor." He demanded nothing short of the death penalty, and on failing to obtain it, he rounded on Gilbert Foliot, causing him to squirm: "By God's eyes, you are going to confirm to me on oath that you have given a true judgment and have not spared this man because he is a clerk." But by calling for such an oath from both Foliot and all the other bishops, he went too far. It was almost as if he was making what he knew to be an unreasonable demand in the expectation that the bishops would refuse, since when they agreed to take the oath, he became even angrier. "He did not know what to do or to whom to turn for fury." Finally, after consulting the barons, he resolved to settle the matter of criminous clerks in his favor once and for all.

But before he could do so, tempers rose even further. As archbishop, Becket claimed the right to appoint new priests to all the vacant churches on his manors and hence had given the church living of Eynsford in Kent to a clerk called Lawrence. When William of Eynsford, one of Henry's tenants in chief, objected and expelled Lawrence's men, Becket excommunicated him, knowingly flouting William the Conqueror's decree that a tenant in chief could not be sentenced by the church unless royal consent was first obtained. Speechless with rage when he heard the news, Henry was now willing to communicate with Becket only through intermediaries. Thomas had little choice but to absolve William, since his episcopal colleagues were unwilling to support this sort of outright defiance. Soon after this latest spat, Henry rode to Windsor, where he said of Becket, "Now I have no more love for him." Their dueling would soon begin in deadly earnest.

HENRY STRUCK at a council of the English church convened at Westminster Abbey on Sunday, October 13, 1163, the date chosen for the removal of the body of King Edward the Confessor from his existing tomb beside the high altar to a reconstructed shrine on the same spot, but aboveground rather than below, following his canonization in partial exchange for Henry's recognition of Pope Alexander. With Edward's remains freshly exhumed and wrapped in a precious silk cloth, Henry and eight leading barons came into the abbey and watched while a new wooden coffin was sealed. Bearing it on their shoulders in the presence of the monks, they then processed around the cloisters before placing it safely in its shrine.

No better piece of theater could have been choreographed by the king. The ritual made it plain that his royal predecessor was a saint who the pope had confirmed could work miracles. Who could doubt that such a sacred monarchy was well suited to preside over the English church? Becket was deliberately sidelined at this event. The master of ceremonies was the abbot of Westminster; the principal actors were the king, the barons, and the monks. Perhaps steeling himself for what he knew was still to come, Thomas sought comfort from a holy relic that he requested as a gift from the abbot: the stone to which it was believed St. Wulfstan's pastoral staff had once been transfixed. His choice was significant: St. Wulfstan was the one Anglo-Saxon bishop who had successfully resisted William the Conqueror's attempts to oust him. According to a legend of the Westminster monks, Wulfstan had come to Edward the Confessor's tomb and said, "Edward, you gave me my staff and now I cannot hold it because of the king, so I commit it to you." He had rammed the staff into the gravestone, where it had miraculously stuck until Wulfstan himself had released it.

Little good would the relic do Becket. When at last the business of the council began, Henry made a threatening speech upbraiding the bishops for their lack of respect and demanding that the secular judges punish criminous clerks in the future. Becket withdrew with his colleagues to consult, and soon disagreements arose among them. A majority, for once rallied in Becket's support by Roger of Pont l'Évêque and Gilbert Foliot, fully agreed with Thomas that the church courts alone should continue to try the cases of criminous clerks, but some of the more timid bishops argued that canon law already permitted a convicted priest to be returned for punishment to the secular arm at the bishop's discretion in cases so notorious that they endangered the entire community.

Determined to give a firm lead to the waverers in the face of Henry's bullying, Becket went on the offensive, moving into hitherto uncharted waters, seeking to close a possible loophole in canon law by citing the maxim "God will not judge twice for the same offense." Here he had moved on considerably from his earlier thinking, claiming that "double jeopardy" in cases involving criminous clerks was *always* morally wrong. The maxim had never been part of strict canon law, but this did not stop Thomas from citing it now in ways suggesting that it had. Deriving not from a papal decree or decision of a church council, but from a commentary by St. Jerome on a passage in the Greek Septuagint* saying, "A mere man should not exact a twofold vengeance for one single fault, when God, judge of all men, as it is written, judges no one twice for the same offense," it was a theological, not a legal, argument.

His critics regularly assert that Thomas plucked this general rule against double jeopardy out of the air. In reality, the idea had already been planted in his brain by Herbert of Bosham and John of Salisbury; all he had to do was pick it up and run with it. Herbert, who agreed with the most zealous of the ascetic reformers that the clergy formed a separate order of society accountable to Christ alone, turned to a theological argument in the absence of a legal precedent. John's precise reasoning remains unknown, but discussing the penalties for criminous clerks four years before in his *Policraticus,* he had forcefully argued that "it always obtains that no one is to receive two punishments on account of the same case."

But by voicing in public an argument he had so far been debating with his advisers only in private, Becket had come to deny what he had previously once allowed: the transfer of criminous clerks from the church court to the secular court after conviction for further punishment, with the bishop's consent, in a few exceptional cases. Now such transfers should always be prohibited.

* A translation from Hebrew into Greek of portions of the Old Testament made in about 250 B.C.

With his fellow bishops rallying behind him, the archbishop returned to the king. "Let it be our unfeigned desire," he said, "to honor and worshipfully to heed your will in all things, my good lord, if it turn not against that which is right. But if it setteth itself up obstructively against the will of God and the laws and dignity of the holy church, we neither may nor dare give our assent to it."

Seeing that he was outmaneuvered, Henry decided to pursue a different tack. He knew that most of the bishops were weak: "not pillars, but reeds that swayed and quivered in the wind." If pushed, and especially if questioned individually, they might give way. Holding in his hand a charter of Henry I for maximum effect, he therefore demanded that they answer on their allegiance "whether they would obey his ancestral customs." This put an entirely different, far more sinister spin on the matter. It was a much broader question, which it could be treasonable to answer in the negative.

After taking counsel, Becket replied, "Yes, in every way—saving our order" (*salvo ordine nostro*). It was a bold, defiant answer implying that anything contrary to canon law or to his position as a churchman would be excluded from his assent.

Henry then put the same question to each of the bishops individually, who all gave the same answer, except for Hilary of Chichester. On the receiving end of Henry's fury in the Battle Abbey case, he lacked the stomach for further resistance and so substituted the words "in all good faith" (*bona fide*) for "saving our order." But if he hoped to mollify the king, he abjectly failed. Henry burst into a tirade, before turning to Becket and accusing the archbishop of conspiring against him. "Poison lurks in that phrase 'saving our order,'" he snarled. "It is nothing more than sophistry." He demanded that all the bishops should absolutely and unreservedly swear to observe the "ancestral customs." "By God's eyes," he expostulated, "you shall not say anything of 'saving your order,' but shall agree outright and expressly to the customs."

Becket tried in vain to remind Henry that the very same proviso was already etched into the oaths each of the bishops had taken to him before their consecrations, when they had sworn fealty to him "in life and limb and earthly honor saving their order," and that the words "earthly honor" already covered the ancestral customs. But Henry would not listen, repeating his demand for compliance. When Becket refused, the king turned on his heel and left the chamber without bidding farewell.

The next morning, Henry shamed the archbishop by ordering him to surrender all the castles and estates that he held from the Crown and by removing Prince Henry from his household, much to the eight-year-old boy's distress. The king then departed for the Midlands, leaving the bishops in disarray. Bishop Hilary was in the worst case, since besides being snubbed by Henry, he was rebuked by Becket for unilaterally altering the formula agreed on by his colleagues.

IN LATE OCTOBER, Henry tried again to cow Becket by summoning him peremptorily to a rendezvous outside Northampton—possibly the ground beside the river Nene still known today as Becket's Park, close beside Derngate—refusing him entry to the town on the grounds that it was already full with his own courtiers and their servants. At first they could not even approach each other easily. Both rode stallions that reared and pranced until they were forced to change mounts. Once new horses had been found and they had separated themselves from the gathering crowd, Henry reproached Thomas for his ingratitude, using arguments he would repeat again and again over the next few years. "Have I not raised you from a poor and lowly station to the pinnacle of rank and honor?" he began. "How comes it that so many benefits, so many proofs of my love for you, well known to all, have so been erased from your mind, that you are now not only ungrateful, but obstruct me in everything?"

"Far be it from me, my lord," answered Thomas. "I am not unmindful of the favors which, not you alone, but God, who dispenses all things, hath condescended to confer on me through you. Wherefore, far be it from me to show myself ungrateful or to act contrary to your will in anything, so long as it accords with the will of God."

Barely were the words out of his mouth than Henry cut him short. "I don't want a sermon," he snapped. "Are you not the son of one of my villeins? Answer me yes or no."

"In truth," said Thomas, stung by the swipe at his middle-class ancestry, "I am not sprung from royal ancestors, but neither was St. Peter, the prince of the apostles, to whom the Lord deigned to give the keys of the kingdom of heaven and the primacy of the whole church."

"True," said Henry scornfully, "but he died for his Lord."

"And I," retorted Becket, "will die for my Lord when the time comes. . . . I trust and rely on God, for cursed is the man that puts his hope in man." Or this, at least, is what the hagiographers claim that he said. Maybe he did, but if so, he spoke in the heat of the moment, and there is no reason to believe he was making a serious threat or courting martyrdom, for he still believed that he could win. Calming down after a few moments, he added more soberly, "I answer, as I did before, that I am ready to please and honor you saving my order."

The interview continued in this vein for about an hour until Henry, wholly exasperated by hearing the archbishop's proviso repeated like a mantra, lost his temper and insisted that it "be entirely dropped." When Becket refused, the two men spurred their horses and rode away.

Now Henry began to show his true colors. He had been provoked but had himself behaved in ways that were highly provocative. The quarrel had become personal, but after considering the matter more soberly, he believed that many, perhaps most, of the bishops could be suborned. Most had been seriously alarmed by the turn of events at the Council of Westminster; many regarded Becket as at best unqualified and at worst a cuckoo in their nest, and it should not take much to silence them.

Henry's agent was the slippery Arnulf of Lisieux, who advised him to court the bishops assiduously as the prelude to Becket's isolation and suspension by the pope. With his finger firmly on the pulse, Arnulf knew that Roger of Pont l'Évêque had his eye on an appointment as a papal legate so that he could laud it over the primate, while Gilbert Foliot sought Becket's suspension or deposition so that he could replace him at Canterbury. Hilary of Chichester was another who could easily be suborned, as was Robert of Melun. Clearly, Robert had decided that his revolutionary ideas of resistance to tyrannous rulers were only for use in the classroom, after all. John of Salisbury was scathing in reply. Such men, he insisted, were careerists consumed by ambition and with "the face of a whore." He also denounced Robert as a man he had always secretly suspected to be an academic fraud, a sycophant deluded by pride.

With the nucleus of a royalist party established, Henry sent Arnulf to the papal curia, now in sanctuary at Sens, in French territory, beyond the Angevin king's reach. Crisscrossing the Channel as many as six times, Arnulf put in train a flurry of diplomacy aimed at securing Pope Alexander's approval of Henry's so-called ancestral customs. To counter this, Thomas sent two of his most trusted friends and allies, John of Canterbury (now bishop of Poitiers) and Henry of Houghton, to lobby the pope and cardinals. His letters to Alexander around this time reveal his talent for vivid, fiery oratory. "We see nothing but shipwreck hanging over us," he begins one of them somewhat melodramatically, "and no course left, except to arouse Christ, seemingly asleep in the vessel, by calling out with all our strength, 'Save us, O Lord, we are drowning.'" When explaining why Henry was a dangerous man, he says, "That which Jesus Christ has purchased with his blood is being torn from him; secular might is stretching forth its hand to Christ's own inheritance." In his mind, the struggle was fast turning into a battle to protect the Christian faith itself.

Whereas Henry managed to stay cool and calculating, Becket's responses were rooted more in his emotions. For all his fabled tantrums, the Angevin king could usually curb his passion when it was really necessary. His next move was to send Hilary of Chichester to visit Becket at his manor of Teynham in Kent. After first threatening him, warning him that the king already had the power to do as he wished, Hilary adopted a softer tone, saying enticingly that if Thomas would agree to honor the ancestral customs, Henry would consent never to enforce them in a manner detrimental to canon law.

To this Becket retorted shrewdly that it was an empty pledge, for while the king could hold the clergy to their promise, neither they nor anyone else would be able to hold him to his. Under John of Salisbury's influence, Thomas was already beginning to debate whether Henry was becoming a tyrant who merely pretended to champion the law but in reality meant to subvert or ignore it whenever it suited him. "Justice" might be his slogan, but his intentions were thoroughly evil. To treat with him would be to sup with the devil. "Far be it," Thomas exclaimed, "that I buy back the favor of an earthly king through such a bargain!"

Hilary protested, "I ask you, what is this evil that is so great and appalling that you alone see and understand it, and no one else?" But Becket would not budge. He thought he knew Henry better than anyone, certainly better than Hilary. "For this," he added with a conviction based on his eight years' experience as chancellor, "you will most certainly discover, that the king exacts from you whatever you promise him, but you cannot force him to stick to his own promises."

But even if Becket was for the moment intractable, the ground was shifting beneath his feet. Superficially, his envoys at the papal curia appeared to be successful. John of Canterbury relayed to him Pope Alexander's satisfaction that at last someone was prepared to speak honestly to the princes of this world, but John warned him that Henry was still in high favor. "So far as human aid is concerned," he said, "you should not expect from the curia anything that might offend the king." From the pope's viewpoint, Becket was indeed something of a liability. Alexander even wrote to Gilbert Foliot, urging him to use his influence with the king to settle the dispute swiftly. He also wrote to Thomas, commending him for being such "a steadfast and able defender of the church" before ordering him to lie low. "We direct and order your fraternity," he said, "to return to the church of Canterbury and travel as little as possible about the country, and keep with you only the smallest number of attendants which you absolutely need." And he concluded worryingly, "We are giving you this particular advice so that you may not be compelled to renounce the rights and dignities of your church by any fear or misfortune which may befall to you."

That did not bode well. Thomas was already feeling vulnerable when, in December, Alexander sent an envoy—Abbot Philip of L'Aumône near Blois, a prominent Cistercian who had been prior of Clairvaux under St. Bernard—to visit the archbishop at his manor house at Harrow. Carrying letters from Alexander and the cardinals that begged Becket to reconcile himself to the king and escorted by Robert of Melun and the same Knights Templar who had taken custody of the disputed Vexin castles in 1160, the envoy had already called on Henry, who, as he reassured Thomas soothingly, had said he would now be willing to accept a simple verbal assent to the ancestral customs rather than an oath.

All Becket had to do in return was to abandon the proviso "saving my order." "If that were done," Philip said, "he and the English church would gain the king's full peace and favor," and a crisis would be averted.

The offer seemed almost too good to be true, but such were the papal envoy's credentials that Becket was persuaded to yield. He agreed to go with Philip and his fellow intermediaries to meet with Henry at Woodstock. There, in a highly emotional speech, he first begged the king "to destroy and abrogate forever the abuses of tyrants and strive to associate himself with the merits and company of saintly kings," before promising, without reservation, "from now on to observe the customs of the realm in all good faith and to obey the king in what is right (*in bono*)."

A considerable effort was needed on Becket's part to say this, since not only did it mark a humiliating retreat, but it also required a high degree of trust, because no satisfactory method had yet been determined for defining the ancestral customs. By promising to observe the customs "in all good faith," he used the same phrase for which he had recently upbraided Hilary of Chichester. He had buckled under pressure from the pope's representative, gaining little in return, and he would be stunned when Henry's response was to double the stakes.

Far from regarding Becket's submission as putting an end to the affair, the king declared that since the archbishop's initial refusal to accept the customs had been in public, his assent to them must be equally so. "Everyone," he said, "knows how stubborn you showed yourself by using that proviso and how much you offended my honor by your defiance." He gave orders for a fresh council to be convened in late January 1164 at his palace of Clarendon, three miles southeast of Salisbury, where all the bishops and abbots, and all the magnates and royal judges, could hear Becket's words of unconditional surrender for themselves.

With that, Henry closed the interview, riding pointedly away to spend Christmas with Eleanor and their children in unusual splendor at Berkhamsted in Hertfordshire, one of the castles he had stripped from Becket the day after the Council of Westminster. All his old affection for his former chancellor was gone, and with Pope Alexander not daring to offend him for fear of Frederick Barbarossa, he was determined to show who would be the master. Thomas himself suspected it and sent John of Salisbury across the Channel posing as a traveling scholar, instructing him to recruit allies and prepare an escape route should he decide to flee into exile.

John did his work well, arranging for an initial safe haven, should it be needed, at the abbey of Saint-Bertin, where Theobald had taken refuge after being sent into exile after the Council of Rheims in 1148. He then rode to Paris, taking comfortable lodgings in accordance with Becket's instructions and seeking King Louis's aid. In what may have been his earliest report from France, John informed Thomas, "I went to the French king and expounded your case to him in full. Need I say more? He feels for you, and promises assistance. And he told me that he has written to the pope on your behalf, and he will write again if need be."

By sending John to make these preparations, Becket was taking a massive risk, for Henry considered his tactics to be nothing short of treason. On his friend's advice, John had gone to visit Eleanor to see if she would mediate, or at least grant him a license allowing him to leave the country legally, but she had flatly refused, complaining to Henry, who had promptly seized John's revenues, leaving him almost destitute. Believing the pope still to be in his pocket, Henry sent Arnulf of Lisieux back across the Channel. Under his malign influence, Pope Alexander—here John, in describing his own reception at Sens, did not mince words—was visibly veering over toward Henry. John had even heard it said in mockery that "the pope will visit Canterbury Cathedral to knock your candlestick out of its place."

Poverty did not agree with John. There was a gaping gulf between his strident demands for the liberty of the church and his willingness to suffer for the truth. Forced to sell his horse to pay his rent, he implored Becket to settle with Henry if he could bear it.

But he pleaded in vain. When Thomas had been catapulted into the archbishopric by Henry, he had thought initially that he would be forced to choose between the values of his king and those of his new position. After their latest round of clashes, he would come to think that it would not be that simple, because he was also beginning to convince himself that he was choosing between the values of tyranny and justice. Henry, meanwhile, had questioned his new archbishop's loyalty and would never accept that there might be a code of conduct different from his own. Once Thomas understood this, the ascetic, rebel's impulse in him, always there since his adolescent years, would reassert itself, after which he would steel himself to impose a moral principle on the world. Whatever his intentions had been as chancellor, now he would struggle as archbishop to become exactly as John of Salisbury had once imagined him: the "defender of liberty" and the man "who cancels unjust laws."

18
CLARENDON

WHEN HENRY CONVOKED THE COUNCIL OF CLARENDON, he knew exactly what he intended to do. He meant to reverse his setback at the Council of Westminster and force Becket and the bishops to concede publicly his right to govern the church in accordance with the ancestral customs. The proviso "saving our order" was to be dropped, and the archbishops and bishops were to promise to uphold the customs "in all good faith," the formula first used by Hilary of Chichester in an attempt to satisfy the king.

The palace, one of Henry's favorites, which he had gradually transformed from a hunting lodge set deep in the royal forest into a fine residential complex of flint rubble and stone around a central courtyard, stood on a hill overlooking Salisbury. The great hall—where the council would assemble, warmed by blazing logs in a huge central fireplace—occupied the north range next to the king's chamber, itself close to the east end of the hall. Set around the courtyard were smaller chambers for the king's barons and knights, for his chaplains and confessors, and for the more important royal household officials. Nearby were a mews and the stables, an almonry, a bakery, and the kitchens. Some years later, the great hall had a roof held up by rows of stone pillars decorated with elaborate Romanesque sculptures, and the palace complex would include separate queen's apartments, a chapel, and apartments for Prince Henry. It may well be that these already had their simpler precursors when those summoned made their way through the snow to the palace a fortnight after Epiphany 1164.

Beginning on January 25 and lasting three or four days, the council was unusually well attended. Almost all the bishops were there, notably Roger of Pont l'Évêque and Gilbert Foliot, and as many leading barons and royal officials as could conveniently be gathered in one place. Those whom John of Salisbury called the "untamed beasts" of the court—Robert de Beaumont and Richard de Lucy, together with the king's uncle Earl Reginald of Cornwall, the most powerful men in England—took their places close to the king. Richard de Humez is not mentioned in the sources, but as he had sailed from Normandy shortly before the council and would return there soon afterward, the chances are that he too was present. Also in attendance was John the Marshal, still seeking revenge for the archbishop's seizure of his lands.

Flanked by Prince Henry, who was almost nine but must have felt utterly confused by the treatment meted out to his old mentor, the king opened the proceedings by asking Becket to redeem the promise he had made at Woodstock before Abbot Philip of L'Aumône "to observe the customs of the realm in all good faith and to obey the king in what is right." The king's peremptory tone put Thomas on his guard. Knowing Henry as he did, he was quick to suspect a trap. He had to convince the bishops to think and act unanimously; discord within their ranks would play into the king's hands. What happened next is uncertain, since the sources give wildly conflicting versions, but it looks as if he turned for advice to his episcopal colleagues, only to be met by a sullen response. They did not want to change their earlier replies at the Council of Westminster, which had included the "saving our order" proviso. If Thomas now wanted them to submit to Henry unconditionally, he would need to say so, "because he was their head, and they were afraid to advise him to give way."

This impasse caused a lengthy delay. Becket's relations with his colleagues had rapidly deteriorated since the earlier council. They felt that he had boxed them into a corner, so it was up to him to lead them out of it. If Gilbert Foliot is to be believed, Henry had the bishops locked up together for two full days in an attempt to cow them. His bullying was in vain. With Foliot urging them on, all stood firm, apart from Jocelin of

Salisbury and William of Norwich, who begged Thomas to yield, protesting that the king already had grudges to settle with them and that they would be the first to suffer his reprisals.

Henry, meanwhile, was in a fury. He threatened to castrate or summarily execute anyone who resisted him, sending a cohort of royal knights and henchmen into the room where the bishops were confined. Menacingly "throwing off their cloaks and thrusting out their arms," they shouted violent threats. Robert de Beaumont and Earl Reginald came next to browbeat Thomas. When he stayed resolute, the king tried a different tack, sending the same Knights Templar who had accompanied Abbot Philip on his visits to Harrow and Woodstock to beguile him with honeyed words. "For we know," they said, "that the king is planning neither fraud nor deceit against you, but to him it seems too harsh and unbearable if he is seen to be disobeyed by you over this formula." Repeating the papal envoy's avowal that if the bishops were to satisfy the king verbally and "in all good faith," they would "never again hear mention of these customs which you recoil from and detest so much," the Knights Templar even went so far as to stake their eternal salvation on Henry's honesty. Why they would be willing to do this is difficult to imagine, but bribery or threats may be suspected. Their leader, Richard of Hastings, the master of the English Templars, was a kinsman of Ralph of Hastings, one of Eleanor's leading household servants, and of William of Hastings, one of Henry's own inner circle. Henry was himself a patron of the English Templars, giving them gifts of gold and the land in London on which they would shortly build their "New Temple" to replace the "Old Temple" in Holborn.

During the later stages of his quarrel with the king, Becket could sometimes act impulsively, jumping prematurely to the next level of hostilities in his attempts to force matters to a head, but not at Clarendon. After informing his fellow bishops that his decision was to obey the king, he bowed before Henry, saying, "I freely consent to your demands and I declare that I will keep the customs of the realm in all good faith." It would turn out to be one of his biggest regrets of his life. For Henry had lied, and despite all Becket's experiences of the king's oath breaking, the former chancellor had been too trusting to see what was coming.

Triumphant at his success, the king ordered the bishops to follow suit, which they all did. They had little choice, since their leader had cut the ground from beneath their feet. But no sooner had the last man finished speaking than Henry doubled the stakes again, demanding that a delegation of senior barons should "go outside with my clerks and make a record of the laws and customs of my grandfather, King Henry. And when they have been carefully written down, let them be brought quickly to me." His reassurances to the pope's representative and the Templars that a simple verbal assent to the customs would suffice, and that once it had been given the matter would never be heard of again, had been hollow. He had all along intended to put everything into writing.

The barons and clerks withdrew and soon returned with a memorandum. Richard de Lucy; John of Oxford, a royal chaplain; and Jocelin de Bailleul, a knight formerly in the service of Henry's mother and now a key figure in Eleanor's household, took the lead. For their pains, Becket would later excommunicate all three. Maybe a working template had been prepared in advance, since the memorandum was ready at lightning speed. Henry even ordered it to be read aloud without reading it first himself, saying, "See, these are the customs which have been conceded to me. Therefore, lest a disputed point arise from now on in relation to them, or perhaps new points of law emerge, we now wish the archbishop to affix his seal to them."

As the clerk read through the document, Becket's face turned white. Although a number of the clauses were genuine customs, others were innovations in whole or in part, ingeniously constructed to create the impression that each of them had the ring of authenticity. Collectively, they amounted to a flagrant attack on the church. Far more corrosive, however, was the fact that they were now codified in written form, expertly crafted by de Lucy and his legal team so as to forge general rules out of exceptional instances and exploit every loophole and ambiguity in canon law and feudal custom in Henry's favor.

On the most contentious issue of criminous clerks, the phrasing was as slippery as it was ambiguous, but no one could doubt that its effect would be to emasculate the church's claims. According to this clause, all priests or clerks accused of crimes against the king's peace should first be summoned before a royal court, where their cases were to be registered, and from there be sent to the church court, where they were to be tried, unfrocked after conviction in the presence of a royal officer, and then sent back under guard to the king's court to be punished as laymen. Henry's intention was to win control of both the opening and closing stages of every trial and to make unfrocking and delivery of criminous clerks to the secular power for capital punishment or mutilation the automatic and invariable sentence, so that the royal judges should not be handicapped by the church in any way. What had very occasionally been allowed in highly exceptional cases was now to be turned into a general rule. From the church's viewpoint, this was not a compromise but a rout.

As to the remaining customs, they included draconian restrictions on the church courts in cases involving debts or church livings, which were to be settled exclusively in the royal courts. Other cases involving the property rights of the higher clergy were to be subject at all times to judicial review in the royal courts. Appeals to the pope were to be severely curtailed and not to proceed without the king's license in every case. Sentences of excommunication or interdict against the king's tenants in chief were not to be given without royal approval. No bishop or priest was to travel overseas without first obtaining a royal license and giving security that he would attempt nothing against the king or the kingdom. The revenues of vacant bishoprics and abbeys were to continue to be disbursed at the king's sole discretion. Elections to vacant posts were to be held in the king's own chapel and only with his consent, placing novel restrictions on the process. Lastly, the sons of villeins were not to be ordained without the consent of the feudal lords on whose lands they were born, a maverick clause likely to have been inserted by the barons to prevent labor shortages on their estates at harvesttime.

As the wider implications of this mischievous document began to sink in, Becket started to panic. He knew that Roger of Pont l'Évêque and Gilbert Foliot in particular would believe he had betrayed them, since in their earlier discussions they had vehemently opposed several proposals similar to those now read out. So he leapt to his feet, playing for time by protesting that he was unsure of how to respond to some of this material. He was too young, he said, to have sufficient knowledge of the ancestral customs and would need to take advice. Since the hour was late, the session was accordingly adjourned.

But this was simply a breathing space. Henry returned to the attack the next day, demanding that Becket seal the memorandum without further debate. Faced by intimidation on this scale, the rebel's impulse in Thomas took over, and he cried out, "By Almighty God, never while I am living will my seal be put to these!" And yet no sooner had the words left his lips than he began to have second thoughts. He had already promised on his word as a priest to observe the customs. It appears that he vacillated for several hours, consulting the distraught bishops again but finding them obdurate, as they claimed that a written document did not need to be sealed when their earlier, verbal agreement to the customs—foisted on them by Becket himself—had bound them hand and foot.

This left Thomas trapped in a vise. Outflanked and outgunned by Henry and unable to take the pressure, he was finally realizing the gravity of his position and badly wanted to draw a line under the affair. Misled by the entreaties of the pope's representative and the Knights Templar, he had allowed his heart to rule his head and been outwitted. He had promised verbally to follow the customs "in all good faith," but he had taken that decision unilaterally, losing the support of his fellow bishops. Now he was on his own and had to choose. Should he retreat and change his mind, in effect committing perjury, or be accused by his rivals of betraying the church into slavery?

Henry, ironically, offered what at the time Becket naïvely regarded as a lifeline. He ordered his clerks to prepare a chirograph—a type of legal or diplomatic document that did not need to be sealed in order to be valid—in which a record of the council's business, including the memorandum of the customs, was written out three times on a single skin of parchment, with the word CIROGRAPHVM in block capitals separating the individual copies. The scribe then cut horizontally across each example of the separating word with a knife, making a jagged edge along the parchment so that anyone questioning the authenticity of any of the copies would be able to see if it fit back neatly together with the others. A tripartite format was the most common, and as everyone made ready to leave the palace on January 29, Henry handed one copy to Becket and one to Roger of Pont l'Évêque, keeping the third for himself.

By receiving a copy of this record from Henry's hands, Becket was understood to have approved it, since both canon and common lawyers agreed that the mere physical acceptance of such a document by an interested party was legally binding. Afterward, Thomas claimed that codifying the customs in writing after he had undertaken to observe them verbally had violated every promise that had been given to him, entitling him to change his mind. He took the document purely for information and for use as evidence in his future appeals to the pope. As Roger of Pontigny reports his words, he told Henry, "I accept it not as consent or approval, but as precaution and defense of the church, so that by this evidence we may know what is to be done against us."

But this is shameless spin, devised retrospectively to exonerate Becket. Not even his staunchest supporters would find it easy to condone his acceptance of the chirograph. Several compare it to the fall of St. Peter, who after leaving the Mount of Olives denied Christ three times before the cock crowed the next day. Nevertheless, Henry came out worse from the encounter. He had sorely deceived the pope's ambassador at Woodstock. He had either bribed or threatened the Templars. Vivid proof of the significance of the distinction between a verbal and a written undertaking comes from a remarkable letter Becket would afterward receive from Nicholas of Rouen, who with Herbert of Bosham would show Becket's copy of the chirograph to Henry's mother, Matilda, in Normandy.

When Nicholas read the document to her in Latin and then translated it into French, she remarked that it had been a great mistake ever to put the customs into writing and require the bishops to swear to uphold them. "That woman comes from a race of tyrants," declares Nicholas triumphantly, but despite praising her son for his zeal for justice, she "disapproved of many of the clauses, and she was particularly displeased that they had been set down in writing . . . for this was not required of earlier bishops." Her view was that Henry's personal loathing for Becket had caused him to bungle the affair. He should, she said, have handled it "in such a way that the ancient customs of the realm would be observed without formal promise or written record, and with the addition of a balancing proviso that the secular judges would not take away the church's liberty, nor the bishops abuse it."

AS BECKET RODE home with his clerks from Clarendon, he was uncharacteristically silent, not speaking to anyone as he went over and over the events of the council in his mind. Asked what the matter was by Herbert of Bosham, he replied, "I begin to see that it is through me, and because of my sins, that the English church is reduced to slavery." He bitterly regretted where his initial naïveté had led him. His most serious mistake had been in accepting a copy of the chirograph, which had allowed Henry to believe that he had capitulated and would lead to accusations of treason and betrayal afterward. He must also have reflected ruefully on how he had alienated his fellow bishops by first cutting the ground from beneath them and then changing his mind. Yet his offenses were vacillation and weakness rather than deliberate perfidy. He had never meant to commit perjury, but this is what he believed he had done, because deep down in his conscience he knew that the ancestral customs were wrong.

A number of his clerks were equally dispirited, beginning to murmur against him and preparing to leave his service. His crossbearer, Alexander Llewelyn, remained loyal but voiced his opinions freely. "The secular power," he said, "disturbs everything. Iniquity rages against Christ himself. The synagogue of Satan profanes the sanctuary of God. Princes have sat and gathered themselves together against the Lord's Anointed. No man is safe who loves equity." These were extreme opinions characteristic of the Cluniac wing of the ascetic reformers, but Llewelyn came closer to the mark when he asked, "What virtue is left to a man who has betrayed his conscience and his reputation?"

For his humiliation, Becket blamed Hilary of Chichester, who by first offering to obey the customs unconditionally at Westminster had put the idea in Henry's head. When on the road home Herbert of Bosham pointed out Hilary to Thomas, he turned directly toward Hilary, saying, "Get thee behind me, Satan." But he chiefly blamed himself, fasting, doing penance wearing sackcloth and ashes, and suspending himself from saying mass. This was to become one of the lowest points in Becket's career before his murder, a cathartic moment he would never forget and in which he discovered how genuinely ill prepared he had been for the role of a pastoral leader.

He did, however, reluctantly join Henry and Roger of Pont l'Évêque in asking Pope Alexander to confirm the customs. With no other option available to him, there was always the hope that Alexander would refuse, lifting the burden from his shoulders. To this end, he sent the pope a letter of his own, confessing his mistakes. The papal curia was still in sanctuary at Sens, so Becket's messenger returned quickly, bringing with him a letter that must have brought him both hope and relief. "We direct and order," wrote Alexander, "that if the illustrious English king has at any time required from you anything hostile to the liberty of the church, you should not attempt to render it to him in any way. . . . If, however, you are aware that you are bound to the said king in anything of this kind, you should not in any way observe your promise, but rather take care to revoke it and strive to make your peace with God."

The pope gave Becket a clear line to follow. He also dealt unwaveringly with Henry's messengers, condemning as "obnoxious" all the disputed customs that he believed infringed the liberty of the church and neatly sidestepping the king's request that Roger of Pont l'Évêque be appointed a papal legate with authority over the primate. A separate decree instructed Roger not to have his cross carried before him in Becket's presence, a calculated snub of the king as well as of Roger. But Alexander did not make either of these crucial decisions public, for he did not wish to provoke Henry unnecessarily. Unwilling to throw the Angevin king into the arms of Frederick Barbarossa, he even hinted that he might one day tolerate a handful of his customs, although not those involving criminous clerks, ecclesiastical appeals, or the right of the prelates to visit the papal curia.

Alexander, now settled safely under King Louis's protection, was learning how to survive and thrive, carving out a path that kept as many forces as possible at bay for the longest amount of time. To weather the storm himself, Thomas would need to follow his example. "Since the desires of princes should be respected," the pope cautioned him, "we advise, counsel, and exhort you, as a prudent and discreet man, to weigh the danger of the times and truly consider what is necessary to protect yourself and your church from harm." This, he absolutely insisted, meant keeping the lowest possible profile, striving not to offend Henry, and even deferring to him, "saving the honor of your ecclesiastical status."

But if Alexander clearly regarded Becket as a loose cannon, he never doubted his integrity and dedication to the cause of the church and its freedom. "As soon as I can," he concluded, "I shall do whatever is possible to increase your honor and standing in the eyes of the king and ensure that the rights and dignities of your church are preserved."

As Easter drew near at Canterbury, Alexander quietly absolved Thomas of his failure of leadership at Clarendon, and the archbishop resumed saying mass. "What proceeds from the exercise of free will," the pope wrote, "is recognized to be different from that which proceeds from ignorance, as it is called, or the compulsion of circumstances." "Ignorance" and "compulsion" had been the causes of Becket's misjudgments, but God would forgive him, and his conscience could be set at ease by confessing his sins to a priest.

Within a month, the pope's own potential for exercising decisive leadership in the church would be dramatically transformed when his rival, the schismatic Victor, died suddenly at Lucca. A gleeful John of Salisbury, who had traveled from Paris to Sens, wrote to Becket with the news. Victor had lost his wits for a fortnight before he died and was so deranged, he could remember neither God nor his own name. At first no one had been willing to bury him, but at length his body had been taken to a monastery outside the city walls.

John, however, was pessimistic about the future. The pope, he thought, might be his own master for the moment. Frederick Barbarossa was sick with a virulent strain of malaria, but what would happen when he recovered? Who could tell whether a new antipope would be elected and which way Henry's mind would turn? John believed the king's latest envoys at the papal curia, sent to replace Arnulf of Lisieux, were masters of deception. Spreading lies far and wide about Becket, they were also sending scurrilous reports to Henry about how recklessly he and his friends were slandering the king. "I urge and advise," John fearfully pleaded, "that no matter what the twisted mind of wicked men contrives against your honor, you should strive to obtain and keep the king's favor for yourself as far as you can. . . . I cannot see that you can achieve anything worthwhile as long as things remain as they are and the king opposes you in everything—especially since the Roman church can receive nothing from you except words, and whatever loss it suffers on account of others it ascribes to you."

John was never the stuff of which martyrs are made. Nor at this stage was Thomas. In July he rode again to see Henry at Woodstock in an attempt to patch up their relationship, but the gates were slammed in his face. The court was in mourning for the death of the king's youngest brother, William, who allegedly had pined to death at Rouen as the result of Thomas's refusal to license his wedding to the widowed Isabel de Warenne. His loss had crystallized Henry's hatred for his archbishop. William had been a favorite of both the king and his inner circle; they could never forgive Thomas for what they saw as an action equivalent to poisoning.

Now Becket resumed his earlier inquiries into possible escape routes into exile, listening carefully to his friend John of Canterbury, who a month or so earlier had identified the Cistercian abbey of Pontigny in northern Burgundy, thirty miles southeast of Sens, as an ideal refuge. "I advise you," said John, "to establish a closer friendship with the abbot of Pontigny, either in person, if you can come to France yourself on the pretext of pursuing your case, or at least by letter if you cannot secure a license to leave the country." The abbey "is ready to serve you even in temporal affairs if it should be necessary." John added in a confidential aside he marked as for Becket's eyes alone, "I have chosen Pontigny as my own place of exile, when I am no longer able to bear the torments of our torturer."

With nowhere else he felt he could turn, Thomas by the beginning of August had decided to take this advice. From his manor of Stowting, near Hythe in Kent, he rode early one morning before dawn with Herbert of Bosham and a few trusted companions to Romney, where he hired a ship and attempted to cross the Channel. But when the vessel was some way out to sea, the sailors under the command of Adam of Charing, a well-known figure in Kent and founder of the leper hospital at New Romney, mutinied, fearing Henry's reprisals. Becket was given the excuse that the wind was in the wrong direction, and the sailors put back into port. No more successful was a second attempt. Thomas had no choice but to retrace his steps to Canterbury, which he found almost deserted, as most of his clerks had returned to their own homes on discovering their master gone.

The next day, the king's henchmen arrived at the palace, declaring that they had heard of the archbishop's flight and had come to confiscate his goods, but they withdrew in confusion when he suddenly appeared to greet them. Henry was furious at Becket's efforts to abscond, "for he greatly feared that by his going to the lord pope, the kingdom would be placed under an interdict." Adam of Charing would shortly pay a hefty fine of 100 silver marks for his role in the affair. Although Becket's attempted flight had directly contravened the clause of the ancestral customs that required any bishop or priest who wished to leave the country first to obtain a license from the king, Henry chose this time to step back from the brink. Instead, he summoned Becket to return to Woodstock, where he entertained him for several days in a display of studied politeness. His only reference to the escape attempt was to inquire sarcastically, "So, my lord, you wish to leave my kingdom: I suppose it is not large enough to hold both of us?"

But if Becket thought the matter had been overlooked, he could not have been more wrong. On the contrary, Henry was biding his time, avoiding a clash with Alexander, who at last was free to censure him if he attacked the archbishop on a matter connected to the ancestral customs or the liberty of the church. Henry had to choose his moment and his pretext carefully. And he did not have far to look or long to wait. John the Marshal was standing nearby and (probably with Henry's connivance) took his opportunity to appeal to the king against Becket's handling of his case to recover his lands in South Mundham. John relied on the clause of the ancestral customs that made the property rights of the higher clergy subject to judicial review in the royal courts, obtaining a writ summoning Becket to appear before the king and his judges on September 14.

Thomas refused to appear to answer the summons, sending four knights with letters from himself and the sheriff of Kent, pointing out the "wrongs" committed by John the Marshal and the inadequacy of his pleadings in the archiepiscopal court. It was not nearly enough, for

Henry was bent on bringing the quarrel to where he could control it in person as decisively as in the Battle Abbey case. Presiding in court on the day on which Becket had declined to appear, he ruled, after bawling out the archbishop's messengers, that since Thomas had neither answered the summons in person nor sent a valid excuse, he had insulted the king. For this he should be severely punished and John the Marshal granted a fresh writ, ordering Becket to appear again on October 6 at a great council at Northampton. There, before all the barons, bishops, and great men of the realm, he was to be put on trial in a blaze of adverse publicity.

Henry had decided to humble Becket as he had humbled Hilary of Chichester in the Battle Abbey case. Both men had clearly changed with age. Now in his early thirties, Henry was more obstinate and capricious than before, while Becket, in his early forties, had decided that he could not go on vacillating as he had at Clarendon. Henry believed he had been deceived; Thomas believed Henry had become a tyrant. Henry meant to break Becket, if possible by convicting him of a serious crime, for his conduct in John the Marshal's case was still only a pretext for the new council. The king's officials were already trawling back through the records of Becket's seven years as chancellor, digging for dirt.

And they intended to find it.

19
NORTHAMPTON

THE GREAT COUNCIL THAT GATHERED AT NORTHAMPTON Castle on Tuesday, October 6, 1164, was a grand theatrical display, the equivalent of a state trial. If Becket refused a second time to submit unequivocally to Henry and in a form that was legally binding, the king meant to try him for treason. Little would be left to chance, as Thomas must have guessed almost as soon as he and his retinue of knights and clerks approached the gates of the outer bailey. A number of his worried servants, sent ahead to prepare his chamber, were waiting there to tell him that his usual quarters at the castle had already been taken by the royal squires. Nothing could be done to evict them that day, since Henry was out hawking. Thomas was forced to find new lodgings for himself and his clerks at the nearby priory of St. Andrew, a Cluniac house of about twenty-five monks founded in about 1100, which had spacious buildings and was situated on the northwest side of the town, abutting the town walls and bordering on the river Nene.

Early on Wednesday morning, he rode to the castle, where Henry was attending mass in the chapel. On climbing the stairs to the royal chamber on the first floor, he offered the customary kiss of greeting—but Henry rebuffed him. Without attempting further courtesies, Becket asked that the squires be expelled from his quarters, and Henry agreed. The squires, however, did not move out, and the archbishop stayed at the priory for the remainder of the council. He then asked Henry for a license to travel to Sens to consult the pope but met with a sulfurous refusal. "You shall first answer me," the king snarled, "for the injury which you caused John the Marshal in your court."

No such answer could be given that day, since John had not yet arrived at the castle. Purportedly busy in the Exchequer on the king's affairs, he would in fact never arrive, further suggesting that his case was trumped-up. By Thursday morning, the more important barons and prelates were assembled and ready to begin, apart from Richard de Lucy, who was on a pilgrimage to the shrine of St. James at Santiago de Compostela.

Charged first with contempt of court for disobeying the king's writ on September 14, Thomas chose not to plead illness or the constraints of his pastoral duties. Still determined to hold his ground, he said only that he did not believe he was legally bound to account in a royal court for his actions as archbishop.

A murmur of disquiet resounded around the castle's great hall. Though far from unjustified in the circumstances, Becket's plea smacked of arrogance. William fitz Stephen, a trained lawyer and one of Becket's advisers throughout these hearings, says, "Everyone believed that, out of respect for the royal majesty and because of the strict obligation created by the liege homage which the archbishop had done to the king . . . his defense or excuse was insufficient." Indignant that Thomas had disobeyed him, Henry called for judgment, and it was decided that the archbishop should forfeit all his movable property.

The first glitch in Henry's plan then arose. The barons clashed with the prelates as to which of them should deliver the sentence. Keen to involve the clerics in the issue, the barons argued that since Becket was a churchman, it was for his own colleagues and not for laymen to sentence him. "Not so," replied a bishop, "this belongs rather to your office and not ours, since this is not an ecclesiastical but a secular judgment." Angered by the squabble, the king ordered Henry of Winchester to give the sentence. Becket, meanwhile, was sorely tempted to claim immunity from secular jurisdiction and appeal to the pope, but he was dissuaded by the bishops, who—Gilbert Foliot apart—stood as sureties for a fine of £500.

Called upon next to answer the substance of John the Marshal's appeal, Thomas pleaded that he had no case to answer since the suit was frivolous. Not only had John signally failed to prove his right to his Sussex lands in the Canterbury court, but he also had resorted to subterfuge in complaining to the king, swearing that he had been denied justice in Becket's court only on a mass book produced from under his cloak and not on the Gospels or the relics of a saint as the law required.

Now vigorous nods of assent could be seen all around the hall. Becket's was a winning argument, because the wily barons could see exactly where this case might lead. If John the Marshal was allowed to appeal to higher authority in a feudal land claim on the strength of an unlawful oath and without even turning up in court to justify his plea, a precedent would be set for any member of the baronage to lose control over his tenants. To his obvious chagrin, Henry had to let the matter drop, leaving Becket as the victor.

But Henry never allowed an inconvenient setback to deflect him. As he had proved in the Battle Abbey case, this was his court, and he intended to condemn Becket one way or the other. He moved quickly on, changing tack by posing new and searching questions about Becket's fiscal administration as chancellor, showing his intention to level charges of embezzlement and false accounting against him. Thomas was not prepared for this sudden shift of direction, but Henry was. His men at the Exchequer (not least the ubiquitous John the Marshal) had already worked out which fiefs or vacant bishoprics had been granted to Becket and for which he had been legally accountable.

The fiscal accounting system functioned in such a way that the chancellor had been expected to make fixed annual payments to the Exchequer but not to file detailed accounts. To fund his independent household, he had been allowed to retain the surplus—should there be one, as often there was—between the revenues he managed to secure and the sums he really owed. He was also allowed to deduct disbursements legitimately incurred on the king's behalf from the sums he credited to the Exchequer, which is where most of the trouble set in.

Had Thomas been able to produce official receipts for his deposits into the Exchequer and copies of the warrants for his expenditures on Henry's behalf, all would have been well. But he could not. At the time, such a scrupulous regard for paperwork had seemed unnecessary. In any case, Thomas had almost certainly "declared" his annual accounts verbally and informally to Henry and secured a verbal "discharge." Only now, after the king had quarreled with him, was a formal, written confirmation of his authority for his financial transactions suddenly, and retrospectively, needed.

Henry began by asking Becket to account for around £300 for the castles of Eye and Berkhamsted. He was testing the waters, waiting to see what Thomas would say, not letting him guess yet that these were specimen charges and far larger demands were waiting round the corner. Becket protested that he had received no warning of these charges and had been summoned only to answer to the suit of John the Marshal. He also protested (apparently correctly) that he had been freed from any outstanding debts relating to his chancellorship when he had been appointed archbishop. But in an effort to mollify Henry, he answered that he could remember spending that sum and a great deal more on building repairs at these castles and at the palace of Westminster. The refurbishment of Westminster Hall alone had been especially costly.

His plea would fail abysmally. In fact, nothing he could say now or subsequently would make any difference, since Henry denied that he had either authorized the expenditure or exonerated Becket from his debts. It was his word against the archbishop's. Still not seeing clearly where all this was leading and unwilling to pick a fight on what appeared to him to be a side issue, Becket rejoined that he could not allow a dispute over money to undermine their relationship, and he found three sureties to guarantee the reimbursement, one being Earl William of Gloucester, the king's cousin.

Night had fallen, and the session was adjourned. Becket returned to his lodgings at the priory, where the barons and knights no longer came to visit him. Such was the atmosphere of fear and suspicion that Henry had created, they dared to have no further association with the disgraced archbishop, for fear that they would be regarded as his aiders and abettors. They too were likely to owe money to the Exchequer, albeit on a far smaller scale.

On Friday, Henry intensified his attack, claiming the sum of 1,000 silver marks that Becket had borrowed during the Toulouse campaign of 1159, half from him and the other half from a Jewish moneylender on his guarantee. As on the previous day, Becket protested that his writ of summons had not mentioned charges like these, but he was willing to answer them off the record. The amounts he conceded, but he claimed that both sums had been written off, which Henry vehemently denied.

When Thomas was unable to offer any written evidence in his support, a fresh verdict was given in the king's favor. Once more Henry demanded sureties, and when Becket airily replied that his assets would be more than sufficient to meet the demand but he needed more time to realize some cash, the king snapped back that since the bulk of his wealth had already been confiscated, he must immediately find sureties or go to prison.

The sureties were found, but to little avail. Not after money or a forensic victory in a court of law, but out to humiliate and destroy Becket, Henry next showed the full extent of his spite and vindictiveness by requiring him to account for all the other revenues that had passed through his hands as chancellor, however briefly, including those of the archbishopric itself. Since he may have handled in excess of £30,000 in cash in this way, the scope for a shortfall was vast. And if as a result of yet another judgment he should be bankrupted or fail to find sureties for his fine, the penalties could be life imprisonment or sequestration of the lands of the archbishopric. If that happened, much of the property belonging to the church of Canterbury could fall into Henry's hands for many years, or perhaps even be forfeited to the Crown forever.

Becket asked for time to consider his response, and the court was adjourned while he took counsel. On Saturday, all the bishops and abbots came to visit him at the priory. Henry of Winchester, who steered these discussions, began by saying he thought it worthwhile to make the king an offer of 2,000 marks to settle the charges. His idea, unrealistic as it was, quickly gained support, and a pause ensued while he rode back to the castle to negotiate. But King Henry refused the money, ordering the bishops to be locked up to hurry along their deliberations, so triggering a long and impassioned debate.

Gilbert Foliot began by warning Thomas of the catastrophe that was fast approaching. Should he not consider humbling himself by resigning in the hope that Henry would restore him to favor? Hilary of Chichester seconded Gilbert, saying bluntly, "Would that you could cease to be archbishop, and become plain Thomas." Others agreeing included Robert of Lincoln and (more reluctantly) Bartholomew of Exeter. Since the times were "evil," suggested Bartholomew, maybe it would be better to make a tactical retreat by sacrificing one archbishop rather than selling the whole church into slavery.

Others strongly disagreed, chiefly Henry of Winchester. "If," he countered, "our archbishop and the primate of all England were to follow that advice, resigning the cure of the souls committed to him at the nod and threat of a prince, what can we expect but that the whole state of the church should be forever subjected to the king's will?"

But Hilary, who had taken on the mantle of leader of the royalist party, would have none of this. Rounding on Becket, he issued a chilling warning. "The king," he said, "is reported to have said that there is no place anymore for both of you in England, he as king and you as archbishop. It is safer to leave everything to his mercy and so to avoid, God forbid, the king detaining you or laying violent hands on you as his chancellor and one accountable to him . . . under the laws on extortion, for that would bring great hardship on the church and disgrace to the kingdom."

In reply, Bishop Henry urged Becket to stand his ground. Speaking from his own bitter experiences during the civil war in his brother's reign, he knew that it was a mistake to put one's trust in princes. He recognized a tyrant when he saw one and with hindsight had come to appreciate Archbishop Theobald's genius for safely steering the church through terrible storms. He thought that Thomas, as Theobald's former fixer and spokesman, should receive the benefit of the doubt. Only fear and old age, Bishop Henry knew, would prevent him from telling King Henry so to his face.

SUNDAY WAS MEANT to be a day of rest, but Becket spent it at the priory in earnest, anxious conclave with his clerks. "Scarcely," reports William fitz Stephen, "was there a free hour to breathe and take sustenance. The archbishop did not leave his lodgings all day." The psychological and emotional pressure was mounting. Thomas, facing the crisis of his life, could not have failed to be deeply apprehensive. As dusk fell, the strain became unbearable, and later that night, his colitis flared up in a highly aggravated form. "He was struck by an illness that is called a colic," says Herbert of Bosham. "His loins were shaking with cold and pain," resumes fitz Stephen, "and it was necessary to keep his pillows warm and replace them regularly."

On Monday morning, he was unable to ride to the castle, but Henry and the barons suspected a feint. "They considered this sickness to be a fiction," says Herbert, "and sent some of the leading barons to investigate the claim." Meanwhile, rumor had it that Henry had been overheard swearing that if Becket did not yield, the king would have him executed or thrown into a dungeon to rot. Whether this was playacting or merely arose from the febrile atmosphere at the castle over the weekend is unknown. But the story reached the ears of Thomas's clerks.

On Tuesday, the archbishop awakened feeling better. Barely had he dressed when the bishops reappeared to report that Henry had resolved to try him that day as a traitor. They begged him to resign or submit unconditionally to the vengeful king. Stunned by their defeatism, Thomas wondered why so few of them were guided by principle or love of the church; why so many acted simply out of ambition, fear, or a mixture of the two. He believed that by interpreting the dispute purely as a personal quarrel between himself and Henry that could be ended by his resignation as if at the stroke of a pen, his colleagues were missing the point. Even if they did not like him, he was their spiritual leader. If they allowed him to be crushed, they and the church would go down with him. Henry, he had come to think, wished to subjugate and enslave the church. His view of the king as a tyrant had recently received what seemed to be the strongest possible endorsement, in the shape of a letter from John of Canterbury warning him that Henry was already attempting to extend the ancestral customs across the Channel to all his continental dominions. Becket knew that he had to make a stand, even if his colleagues deserted him. On no account was he going to allow their counsel of despair to dampen his resolve.

Becket most likely met his fellow bishops in the Lady Chapel at the priory, a place well-known to several of them, since the Benedictine monks of the Canterbury province held their triennial gatherings there. Suddenly finding new reserves of inner strength, Thomas raised himself to his full six feet before addressing them. "Brethren," he began, "as you can see, the world rages against me and the enemy rises, but what I deplore most tearfully . . . is that the sons of my own mother [i.e., the church] fight against me. Even though I shall keep quiet about it, future centuries will tell how you have abandoned me in the struggle." Twice already, he said, the bishops had joined with the barons in convicting him in a secular court. "And I understand from your words that you are now ready to judge me again there, not only in a civil but also in a criminal case."

Thomas then uttered the words that would dictate the future shape of his collision with the king and alter his relationship with his colleagues forever:

> By virtue of your obedience and at the peril of your order, I prohibit all of you from taking any further part in any future judgment where my person is at stake, and to make sure that you abide by this, I appeal to the Roman church, our mother and the refuge of all the oppressed. And if, as it is already said among the people, it should come about that secular men lay their violent hands upon me, I order you by virtue of your obedience to me that you shall excommunicate those responsible. . . . Know this, that although the world rages, the enemy rises, the body quivers, and the flesh is weak, I shall, God willing, never give in shamefully or commit the offense of abandoning the flock that is entrusted to me.

No sooner had he finished than his enemy Gilbert Foliot made a counterappeal to the pope. A committed royalist who had been one of the king's spiritual advisers for more than a year, he likely had already prepared for this eventuality and obtained Henry's encouragement, since the customs codified at Clarendon dictated that no appeal to the pope could be begun without express royal consent. With matters at a stalemate and Thomas now a pariah for making his appeal, the bishops left hurriedly for the castle, apart from Henry of Winchester and Jocelin of Salisbury, who lingered for a while to talk things over further.

Setting out himself for the castle an hour or so later, Becket stopped at a nearby church, possibly St. Peter's close by the castle, where, somewhat provocatively, he put on the pallium, the defining symbol of his office as primate, and said the special mass used on St. Stephen's Day in honor of the first Christian martyr, in which the introit was a passage from Psalms beginning, "Princes also did sit and speak against me" (Psalm 119:23). After the service, he continued on to the castle, carrying secretly in a pocket of his cloak a wafer of the Eucharist, arming himself with the holy body of Christ for the fight he knew was about to begin. Before him, bearing his archiepiscopal cross, rode the faithful Alexander Llewelyn.

As soon as their horses were inside the castle yard, the porter slammed the great gates behind them. Dismounting, Becket took the cross in his own hands and, brandishing it like a weapon, strode boldly toward the doorway of the great hall, as if he were once again a warrior riding into battle in Quercy or the Vexin. His audience was thunderstruck, believing that he intended to challenge Henry in some unforeseen way, perhaps even to excommunicate him.

Observing his arrival from the window of an upstairs chamber, the king flew into a fury. As Becket approached the entrance to the great hall, one of his clerks said to Gilbert Foliot, "My lord bishop of London, how can you stand by while he carries his own cross?" Gilbert answered, "My dear fellow, he always was a fool and always will be." All the same, he rushed forward and tried to wrest the cross from the archbishop's hands. There was an undignified scuffle as Thomas pushed him away.

"If the king were to draw his sword as you have now done with your cross," Gilbert jibed, "what hope can there ever be of bringing about peace between you."

"The king's sword is an instrument of war," Becket retorted, "but my cross is a sign of peace for myself and the English church."

While Thomas sat in a small antechamber adjacent to the great hall on the ground floor of the castle, waiting for Henry to descend the staircase, Roger of Pont l'Évêque arrived, deliberately late for the day's hearing so that he might not be suspected of plotting against Becket with the "untamed beasts" upstairs. His cross too was carried before him—illegally, since Pope Alexander had forbidden him to flaunt it in front of the primate.

A crier then announced the resumption of the court, and Henry summoned the bishops upstairs. He had originally meant to revisit the matter of criminous clerks, but advised (probably by Foliot) that this would be the one and only issue capable of reuniting the bishops with their primate, he had decided to get Friday's unfinished business out of the way first. Now his aim was to convict Becket of embezzlement and false accounting, before charging him with perjury and treason for prohibiting the bishops from sitting in judgment on their archbishop and appealing to Pope Alexander without prior royal assent, thereby breaching his promise to observe "in all good faith" the customs published at Clarendon.

And yet Henry could not have been totally confident. Waiting anxiously downstairs, Becket's clerks could hear angry voices in the chamber above, and while this terrified them, it also gave Thomas a glimmer of hope. So awesome was the power of religion or the threat of an archbishop's curse and so potent was the cross as a symbol that for the remainder of the council, Henry refused to confront Becket face-to-face in open court, fearing that the archbishop might excommunicate him. Excommunication was precisely the course of action recommended by Herbert of Bosham, who was spoiling for a fight, but a worried fitz Stephen took a more cautious line, continuing to believe the dispute could be settled by compromise and negotiation. From his viewpoint, there was still everything to play for.

At last Henry sent a deputation of barons and bishops led by Robert de Beaumont and Reginald of Cornwall to treat with Thomas, asking him whether he was ready to produce his financial accounts as chancellor and whether he was responsible for the prohibition and appeal to the pope of which the bishops had complained. Becket answered confidently, doing everything he could to recover some of his dignity and authority by making the sign of the cross and deliberately sitting down while the others were left standing so as to underscore the distance between them.

"Men, brothers, earls, and barons of the lord king," he began, "I am certainly bound to our liege lord the king by homage, fealty, and oath, but the principal attributes of the priestly oath are justice and equity." He again protested that his trial was an abuse of legal procedure, since the king's writ had summoned him only to defend himself against John the Marshal's accusation. He emphasized once more that he had been exonerated of his worldly obligations as chancellor by Prince Henry and Henry of Winchester at Westminster Abbey when his election as archbishop had been ratified in 1162. "Although," he continued, "the king now denies this, it is known clearly to many among you and to all the clergy of this kingdom."

As to the prohibition and appeal that he had made that morning, he meant to stand by them. "I admit," he said, "that I told my fellow bishops that they condemned me with undue severity and contrary to custom and precedent, and for this I have appealed against them and forbidden them, while this appeal is pending, to judge me again in any secular suit, including one arising from the time before my assumption of the archiepiscopal office. I still appeal, and I place both my person and the church of Canterbury under the protection of God and the lord pope."

With the gauntlet thrown down, Thomas ended his speech. A resounding piece of oratory, it had reduced half the deputation to complete silence and provoked the others to cry out, "Behold, we have heard the blasphemy proceeding out of his own mouth." After the members of the deputation had trouped back upstairs, the debate continued in the king's chamber. "King William who conquered England," said some of the barons, "knew how to tame his clerics." They suggested that Becket be castrated or thrown into a pit, but Henry was more concerned that the bishops should ignore the archbishop's prohibition, since for the sake of legitimacy he wanted them to join with the barons in pronouncing judgment on Thomas for daring to appeal to the pope. With the bishops on his side, it would be harder for Pope Alexander to retaliate, or for Becket's supporters to call the king a tyrant.

But the bishops (as they themselves said) were between the hammer and the anvil. To obey the king would be to contravene canon law and their own convictions, while to defy him would be to risk sharing in the archbishop's fate. They were also bitterly divided, with some sympathetic to Thomas and others determined that he should resign or be deposed. Tempers rose as the barons lost patience and called on the bishops to end their bickering and obey the king. In an effort to break the deadlock, a delegation of bishops went downstairs, some in tears, hoping to persuade Becket at least to withdraw his prohibition and appeal.

As the delegation entered the lower chamber, a scene of black comedy ensued as Roger of Pont l'Évêque and Thomas raised their crosses against each other like lances in a tournament. But before they could come to blows, Hilary of Chichester rounded on Becket, saying that all this trouble had started when he had ordered them to follow his lead at Clarendon and then changed his mind. The result was that he was now ordering them to go against their promise to the king. But Thomas refused to budge. Whatever had happened at Clarendon and whatever mistakes he may have made there, the disputed customs had afterward been condemned as "obnoxious" by the pope. "If we lapsed at Clarendon, if the flesh is weak, we must take heart again and with the strength of the Holy Spirit fight the old enemy who hopes that those who stand will fall, and those who have fallen will not get up again." Hilary, bruised and battered in the Battle Abbey case, had become a turncoat, and Thomas had no time for him anymore. Looking him straight in the eye, he told him that no one was bound to keep an oath he should not have taken in the first place. "If we yielded and in good faith swore what was untrue or made unjust promises, you well know that an unlawful oath is not binding."

After more scurrying to and fro of courtiers upstairs and down, some carrying rods and sticks, Gilbert Foliot finally broke the deadlock, suggesting that if the king would excuse them from sitting in judgment on the archbishop, they would lodge a joint appeal to the pope against him, this time asking Alexander to depose him for perjuring himself at Clarendon. A flimsy idea, it was just enough to satisfy the bishops, who returned upstairs.

Henry by this time also wanted to draw a line under the secondary issue of who sat as judges in his court. Aiming to destroy Becket, not to make enemies of all his bishops and the pope at the same time by forcing them to judge him, he accepted Foliot's proposal, sending the bishops back downstairs to rejoin Thomas, who sat motionless as if turned to stone, awaiting his trial by the barons alone in the upstairs chamber and in his absence.

To give the court's verdict a greater semblance of legality, Henry summoned the knights and sheriffs of the shires to the upstairs room to reinforce the barons, then called on them all to make haste, as the day was almost past. The climax was fast approaching. None of the sources says precisely what the sentence was, but Becket was condemned, almost certainly to life imprisonment. He was still seated and holding his cross when the barons and knights came down the stairs for the last time, leaving Henry alone upstairs. As they entered the lower chamber, Thomas refused to rise and sat stony-faced waiting for Robert de Beaumont to do his worst.

Robert began haltingly, reminding Thomas of Henry's generosity to him as chancellor and of the great debts and obligations Becket owed the king for raising him up from nothing. But Thomas had heard all this before. He had also often sat in court beside Robert himself and knew him as well as anyone. He could read in Robert's face his disquiet at what he had been asked to do, and Thomas meant to turn it to his own advantage. Before the earl had got properly into his stride, Becket interrupted him and forbade him or anyone else present to judge him. Visibly shocked, de Beaumont falteringly began again but quickly started to ramble. Becket waited until it appeared that he was going to be sentenced. He then leapt to his feet, raising his cross high above his head and exclaiming, "It is not for you to judge your archbishop for a crime!"

Uproar ensued as some barons shouted "perjurer" and others "traitor." Reginald of Cornwall tried to carry on with the sentence, but he too fluffed his lines. Attempting to assert control, Hilary of Chichester cried out that the treason was clear and Thomas must hear the sentence. But Becket was having none of it. Rising to his feet, he strode toward the door, carrying his cross. Further hoots and cries of "perjurer" and "traitor" greeted him as he passed back through the great hall, where not looking properly where he was going, he stumbled over a pile of firewood. Regaining his balance, he heard Henry's cronies Ranulf de Broc, the royal whoremaster, and Hamelin, the king's bastard brother now married to Isabel de Warenne, joining in the chorus. Rounding on them, he shouted back, "If only I were a knight, my own fist would give you the lie."

In the castle yard, he swiftly mounted his horse, scooping up Herbert of Bosham into the saddle behind him, but the gates of the outer bailey were still locked. The porter was absent from his post—he was said to be beating a boy—but a bunch of keys was seen hanging from the wall. One fit, and the archbishop, closely followed by the rest of his clerks, escaped through the town. As they rode back to the priory, Thomas veered wildly from side to side; he could scarcely control his horse and carry his cross at the same time. But he was euphoric. Not only had he escaped from Henry's clutches, but an admiring crowd was also following him in triumph from the castle gate to his lodgings, cheering him as a hero who had resisted a tyrant-king and praising God and the saints for his safe deliverance.

On reaching the priory, he immediately said vespers with his clerks, then walked round the cloister to the refectory, where his retinue were eating their meal. On seeing him sit down to eat, many of them came to his table one by one, asking to be discharged from his service for fear of the king. This prompted Herbert of Bosham to jest, "A friend is someone who eats your food, but does not stay on in the hour of need."

After supper, Thomas sent a message to Henry asking for a safe-conduct for his journey back to Canterbury. The reply, delivered by return, was that a decision would not be made until the following day. The tone of this communication aroused Becket's worst fears. Henry was said to have proclaimed that he was not to be molested within the precincts of Northampton, but the risk of arrest elsewhere was high. Taking no chances, he decided to put John of Salisbury's escape plan into immediate effect. Only three trusted attendants from his retinue, whom he chose as guides, were let into the secret besides the loyal Herbert, whom he sent to Canterbury to gather as much cash and silver plate as he could find before traveling to Saint-Omer for a rendezvous. To allay suspicions at the castle, Becket declared his intention of spending the night in the priory chapel in vigil and prayer. The monks made up a bed for him behind the high altar and later saw him there, pretending to be asleep, when they passed by to sing their night offices in the choir.

An hour or so before dawn, still in pitch-darkness and during a torrential rainstorm that cloaked the clatter of the horses' hooves, Thomas, disguised as a lay brother, rode out of the priory with only his three guides as companions. Mounted on borrowed chargers, they made their escape through the north gate of the town, which they already knew to be unguarded. When early the next morning Henry of Winchester called at the priory to ask the archbishop's chamberlain how Becket was, he received the reply, "He is doing rather well, since he left late last night in a hurry and no one knows where he has gone."

The king's response to Becket's disappearance would be very different. *"Nondum finivimus cum isto,"* he barked. We've not finished with this wretched fellow yet.

20
EXILE

USING THE ALIAS BROTHER CHRISTIAN, BECKET TOOK A CIRcuitous route to the south coast after leaving Northampton, evading the pursuit by first riding almost one hundred miles in the opposite direction to Grantham and Lincoln, then hiding out in the fens for several days with the assistance of some Gilbertine monks. To make themselves inconspicuous, he and his companions traveled only by night, hiding themselves by day. Sailing in the cadaverous early morning light of November 2, 1164, from the tiny port of Sandwich in Kent in a skiff without any luggage, they crossed the Channel, landing at dusk on the seashore at Oye, four miles from Gravelines. Weary, afraid, and distinctly queasy from his buffeting upon the waves, Thomas was unaccustomed to walking on the shingle and fell exhausted to the ground. One of his companions managed to find a packhorse for him to ride, a miserable beast with only a rope of straw around its neck for a bridle, but which enabled him to reach Gravelines an hour or two after nightfall.

He quickly found that keeping himself concealed would be a wise decision, since his disguise was wholly unconvincing. For someone so often castigated by his modern biographers as an "actor-saint," he was an extraordinarily bad actor. No sooner had he sat down to eat a simple meal of bread, cheese, nuts, and fruit at a wayside inn than he betrayed himself. His fluent speech and polished diction; his refinement and air of authority; his sophisticated manners; his unusual height, broad brow, and thin face; his clean, smooth hands with their long, elegant fingers, all gave him away, for the news of his escape had spread like wildfire, and everyone knew he either had landed somewhere along the coast or was shortly about to.

Rising at daybreak, he set out on foot in the direction of Saint-Omer, once more intending to make a success of his disguise but again failing abysmally. Not far along the road, he passed a young knight with a falcon on his wrist. A lifelong expert in falconry, who had abandoned the sport only when he had resigned the chancellorship, Thomas was famous for being able to spot a prize gyrfalcon at twenty paces. He had only to take a single appreciative glance at the stranger's fine bird for the knight to see through his disguise and call out, "Either that's the archbishop of Canterbury or his double!" To which Thomas or one of his companions lamely answered, "Do you really think that the archbishop of Canterbury travels in this style?"

Now treading warily for fear of the soldiers of Henry's cousin Count Philip of Flanders, Thomas made his way in the rain and hail along a muddy road toward the Cistercian abbey of Clairmarais, three miles northeast of Saint-Omer. There he kept his rendezvous with Herbert of Bosham, who was waiting for him. Unable to lay his hands at Canterbury on more than 100 marks and a few silver cups, Herbert was shocked at the sight of the gaunt, blistered, unshaven, stooping figure who greeted him. They eagerly exchanged news, some of which was alarming, since Becket had discovered along the road that a deputation from Henry to the pope at Sens to plead for his deposition or suspension had crossed the Channel on the same day as he had. Led by Gilbert Foliot, Roger of Pont l'Évêque, Hilary of Chichester, and William d'Aubigny, Earl of Arundel—who had been briefly married to Queen Adeliza, widow of Henry's grandfather—these envoys were even now lodged in the castle at Saint-Omer. Anxious to avoid them, Thomas fled across the marshes in a row boat to a hermitage called Oldminster, where, surrounded by water, he concealed himself for three days. Emerging only when he thought it was safe, he retraced his steps to Saint-Omer, recovering his spirits at Saint-Bertin's Abbey, where he was given a hero's welcome by Abbot Godescal and his monks.

One ugly incident gave a brief foretaste of what was still to come. Hearing a report that Thomas might be found at Saint-Bertin's, Richard de Lucy, on his way home from his pilgrimage to Santiago de Compostela, came to visit him and begged him in the name of friendship to submit to Henry's will. Thomas refused, leading to an angry scene in which de Lucy declared that henceforward he would forever be Becket's sworn enemy.

Becket answered, "You are my vassal and shouldn't say such things to me."

"In that case I'll take back my homage," retorted Richard.

"It wasn't meant as a loan," Thomas snapped back.

A fascinating exchange, it shows that de Lucy, who had once accepted a sizable grant of Canterbury land and become one of Thomas's vassals on account of it, saving only his liege loyalty to Henry, had now defied his lord, as feudal custom allowed when relations broke down. Effectively, he had declared war on Thomas.

AFTER LEAVING THE castle, Henry's envoys divided themselves into two groups. While the main party rode directly to Sens to prepare for their meeting with the pope, Gilbert Foliot and the Earl of Arundel sought an audience with King Louis at Compiègne, fifty miles northeast of Paris, where they handed him a letter from Henry explaining how Becket, now described as "formerly archbishop of Canterbury," had "fled from the kingdom like a felon." Henry wanted the French king, his feudal overlord, to assist him by denying Thomas refuge. But Louis, despite their dynastic alliance, was still brooding over the manner in which his upstart vassal had double-crossed him over his daughter's marriage and the recovery of the disputed Vexin castles. He had got over the embarrassment of losing Eleanor of Aquitaine to him, but his marriage to his third bride, Adela, had not yet produced a son, and he was in no mood to be compliant. He kept asking who precisely had deposed Thomas if he were no longer to be styled archbishop. And when the envoys appealed to him to write to Pope Alexander on Henry's behalf, he refused and wrote in Thomas's favor instead.

After the envoys had departed, Herbert of Bosham, who was doggedly on their trail, arrived to give Louis Becket's side of the story and obtain a safe-conduct for his onward journey to Sens. Louis, who had always warmed to Thomas and whose piety was shocked at his rough treatment, then rode to Soissons, where the archbishop came and knelt before him, receiving a promise of his goodwill and financial support for as long as he might need it. Despite this generosity, Becket's position was far from strong. While it might suit Louis to cut Henry down to size, he had no intention of offending him so deeply that he would break their alliance or wage war. A few desultory frontier raids against Henry in the Vexin was as much as Louis would be willing to attempt. Otherwise, he would blow hot and cold, telling John of Salisbury that as a loyal son of the church, he felt the deepest sympathy for Becket and loved him dearly, but he feared that if he were to encourage the pope to quarrel with the English king to the detriment of the church, he himself would get the blame. In short, Louis would walk a tightrope, granting Becket sanctuary in his territories and offering him fair words and a degree of protection, but no more.

As to what Becket might expect from Pope Alexander, the chief obstacle was the revival of the papal schism, since it did not take Frederick Barbarossa long once he had recovered from malaria to replace the deceased antipope, Victor IV, with Guy of Crema, who took the name Paschal III. The entry onto the stage of a fresh rival backed by German silver would greatly limit the pope's freedom of action. Even though a majority of the German bishops now opposed the schism and the communes of northern Italy would rise in open revolt against the emperor, Alexander worried that Frederick might suborn either Henry or Louis to support Paschal.

In a characteristically unctuous letter to Becket describing the political and diplomatic scene, Arnulf of Lisieux offered the pensive archbishop both a harsh reality check and some of the shrewdest insights into Henry's psychology that anyone would ever put down on paper. For Arnulf knew that however much Henry would like to outmaneuver Louis or the pope in his efforts to rid himself of Becket, he would manage to stay cool and rational. "You are dealing," he said, "with a man whose cunning frightens distant people, whose power overawes his neighbors, whose sternness terrifies his subjects." His consistent run of good fortune since his adolescent years had so bolstered his ego that "whatever does not yield to him, he considers unlawful." But if rarely headstrong or impetuous in war or politics, and indeed a man who could be patient and relatively humble if approached in the right way, Henry was easily inflamed and difficult to mollify once aroused. Above all, he would never yield to pressure, least of all to force. "Whatever he does," said Arnulf from almost twenty years of experience, "should appear to have proceeded from his will rather than from his weakness." If Becket wanted to recover his position as archbishop, he had to offer a solution that Henry believed was really his own, for "he seeks fame rather than profit" and knew he could secure it. Such was the state of play in and around his vast territories that "he has neither superior who can frighten him nor subject who can resist, nor is he attacked from outside." And this, concluded Arnulf prophetically, would become Becket's problem for the duration of his exile if he did not trim his sails to suit the wind. However loyal or committed to his cause his supporters might appear, before long they would simply tire or melt away.

SENT ON AHEAD to Sens by Becket and arriving a few hours after Henry's envoys had regrouped there, Herbert of Bosham met Alexander in private and again rehearsed the archbishop's side of the story while the pope listened intently and sympathetically, nodding from time to time.

The next morning, the king's men appeared before the cardinals in a full consistory, but Herbert had done his work well. When Gilbert Foliot, who spoke first, criticized Becket, Alexander sharply rebuked him, accusing him of spite, so that he became confused and gave way to Hilary of Chichester, who fared no better. As in the Battle Abbey case, he got carried away in the heat of the moment, showing off his Latin and making elementary mistakes in his verb conjugations that caused the cardinals and their clerks to fall about with laughter. Roger of Pont l'Évêque spoke less pretentiously, but no more effectively. The Earl of Arundel, who admitted that he knew no Latin and spoke in colloquial French, did the best, avoiding criticizing Thomas directly and emphasizing in velvet tones how valuable it would be for Alexander to retain Henry's friendship.

Following their instructions to the letter, the envoys proposed that if the pope was unwilling to depose or suspend Becket, special legates should be appointed to judge his case in England without any right of appeal. But their petition was roundly rejected. "When he is to be judged," said Alexander, "he shall be judged by us: for it were against all reason to send him back to England to be judged by his adversaries and among his enemies." The bishops' vitriol had undone them, for Alexander could plainly see that Becket would never be allowed a fair hearing in England. He also greatly resented Henry's insistence that on no account should the main case against the archbishop be decided at Sens, which he believed was prejudicial, arrogant, and insulting.

Disappointed at their failure and after spending three days vainly distributing gifts and offering bribes, the envoys had no choice but to pack their bags and set out home for England.

On the following day, Thomas rode into Sens on a great white charger lent to him by Miles of Thérouanne, an Englishman by birth. His theatrical instinct had come to his aid, and he had mustered a following, even if William fitz Stephen's claim that it included a detachment of three hundred horsemen, presumably lent to him by King Louis, must be rejected as hyperbole. Evading Henry's spies, Alexander Llewelyn, the archbishop's crossbearer; Robert of Merton, his confessor; Master Ernulf, his secretary; and another twenty or so of his clerks and attendants had made their way from Northampton or Canterbury to join him, and all found lodgings in the town.

After a preliminary interview with Alexander and some debate among the exiles as to who should be the archbishop's advocate, Becket decided to plead his case before the consistory in person. This was an arena in which he already had some experience as Theobald's spokesman and in which he knew he could shine; he meant to deliver a virtuoso performance.

Early the next morning, Thomas gave a full explanation of the reasons for his flight to a conclave of the pope and cardinals in the papal chamber. His actual words are recorded in a copy of a rough draft of the speech that he put together the previous night. "I lamented," he began, "that the liberty of the Church was gradually being destroyed and its rights dispersed to the avarice of princes, and I believed that the coming assault should be resisted." He believed that if the church's freedom was to be restored, no alternative had been open to him other than to resist the king at Clarendon and Northampton, and then to flee from a ruler who had been misled by his lay barons into becoming a tyrant. Mindful of John of Salisbury's advice, he knew that the prudent course was always to blame the "untamed beasts" of the court if he could, rather than criticize Henry directly. "I am not surprised," he concluded, "that evil laymen have constructed such a plot against the clergy." What had shocked him most was the lack of support he had received from his fellow bishops, who had been prepared to side with the courtiers. "Nothing of this," he avowed, leaving the door firmly open to a settlement, "should be imputed to the lord king, for he is the servant of this conspiracy rather than its author."

Then, falling on his knees before Alexander, he spread out before him the parchment chirograph of the disputed ancestral customs devised by Henry and his lawyers at Clarendon. "See," he said, pointing to the crucial passages, "what the king of England has set up against the liberty of the Catholic Church." He read aloud the disputed customs one by one, explaining the iniquity of each in turn, after which Alexander condemned those he found "obnoxious" for a second time. He also—as Becket afterward reminded him—absolved the archbishop of his obligation to keep the customs and "forbade that we should ever again bind ourselves to anyone in a similar case, except saving God's honor and our order." A bishop, Alexander had insisted, "should not make any undertaking, except saving God's honor and his order, even to save his life."

The theatrical effect of laying out the chirograph for the cardinals to see was considerable. Several were reduced to tears at the thought of the archbishop's ordeal. "They who earlier seemed to disagree about this case," he said, "were now united in one opinion that they ought to come to the aid of the universal church in the person of the archbishop of Canterbury."

Becket had a secret audience with Alexander and the cardinals on the following day in which he made a shorter, even more compelling speech, cutting the ground from under his opponents' feet by admitting his faults and volunteering to resign. "I willingly confess," he began, "that these troubles have befallen the English church through my own wretched fault." He continued:

> Although I accepted this burden unwillingly, nevertheless it was the will of man and not the will of God which induced me to do so. What wonder then if it has brought me to this misfortune. Yet, had I, at the threat of the king, renounced the jurisdiction of episcopal authority conferred on me as my brother bishops urged me to do, it would have been an evil precedent. . . . I therefore delayed to do so until I should appear before you. But, recognizing that my appointment was far from canonical and dreading lest the issue should become even worse for me . . . I now resign into your hands, Father, the archbishopric.

To the utter dismay of those of his clerks who were watching from the back of the room, Thomas then pulled the archiepiscopal ring from his finger and gave it to the pope.

Alexander withdrew to an inner chamber with his advisers, where some of the cardinals—Alan of Tewkesbury calls them "the Pharisees"—strongly urged him to accept Becket's resignation, seeing it as the best way to achieve a speedy reconciliation with Henry. Could Thomas not be moved, they argued, to a different position in the church and another, more experienced primate appointed?

After considering the matter at some length, Alexander rejected Becket's offer. Summoning Thomas before him, he said, "Now at last, brother, it is plain to us what zeal you have shown, and still show, for the house of the Lord, with how clear a conscience you have stood as a wall against adversity, and how pure a confession you have made since your appointment: these things can and ought to wipe away all blame of wrong." But while reinstating Thomas as archbishop, the pope forbade him to return to England until the dispute with Henry had been settled. Instead, as John of Canterbury had initially proposed, he was to live in seclusion with just a few of his closest friends and companions at the abbey of Pontigny, where he would have to learn to live without the affluence and luxury that he had enjoyed for the past ten years. In exile among the Cistercians, as Alexander clearly thought but did not say, he would encounter hardship and have plenty of time for quiet contemplation and reflection. With luck, he would soon even see himself that reconciliation with Henry was essential for the sake of peace. Otherwise, he could be in exile for a very long time.

SET IN WHAT was then a densely forested area of northern Burgundy in the winding valley of the Serein, a tributary of the Yonne, the abbey of Pontigny had been founded in 1114 by Hugh of Mâcon, another disciple of St. Bernard. Only twelve miles to the northeast of Auxerre, where Thomas had studied canon and civil law as a young clerk in Theobald's household, it was an area he already knew quite well. After staying at the papal curia for just over a fortnight, he and a dozen or so of his followers reached the place on St. Andrew's Day (November 30) and would remain there for almost two years. It was an isolated spot, for the Cistercians sought to return to a strict observance of the Rule of St. Benedict, choosing lonely sites in which to settle where they could be self-sufficient. Ideally they wished to create small islands set apart from the world, where they could worship God both as a community and as individuals, shielding themselves from the cares of everyday life. Whenever possible, they chose a deserted river valley where there was a ready supply of fresh water and firm, dry ground on which to build their large, plain abbey church, in which all pomp and pride would be avoided. Their dress was of the simplest kinds: habits of unbleached wool, vestments of the plainest white fustian or linen unembroidered. Their rituals too were unadorned. No precious metal was allowed, except a few silver vessels such as chalices or incense boats for use at the Eucharist. Wall paintings, carvings, and other decorations were forbidden in their churches; the windows were to be of the simplest geometric shapes, similar in scale to those of early Gothic churches but filled with clear glass; and no high towers were to be erected.

Work on the great abbey church at Pontigny had begun in 1140, replacing an earlier, smaller building. Some 390 feet long, with a transept 190 feet long and 65 feet high, it was designed for several hundred monks. One of the largest Cistercian edifices still standing in France and radiantly white inside, it is a place of quiet, haunting beauty. Built of limestone brought by river and oxcarts from Tonnerre, some eighteen miles to the east, it was still under construction when Becket was there. The rectangular porch, wide nave, and side aisles, where the architect achieves a perfect balance of line and light, had largely been completed by 1164, but the chancel and ambulatories, with their fine ribbed vaults and monolithic pillars, would not be finished until 1185. Fresh from enjoying the lavish hospitality of the papal court, Herbert of Bosham would be shocked—despite the warmth of the welcome he received from Abbot Guichard, a good friend of John of Canterbury—to find much of the place a building site, with stones and construction debris lying everywhere and the living quarters unheated despite the onset of winter. John of Salisbury would not even visit Pontigny, preferring to stay in his comfortable lodgings in Paris until his lease expired and advise Thomas from a distance.

Within a week, the exiles had been given small, individual cells scattered across the conventual buildings—Herbert calls them "little rooms in Noah's ark." The majority quickly adjusted themselves to the daily routine of the monastery, but Herbert never felt that he belonged there. Following the Rule of St. Benedict, the monks did not eat meat, preferring fish, cereals, vegetables, dairy products, and exceptionally honey. During Lent and Advent, they avoided eggs and dairy products; in winter, which they interpreted as running from mid-September to Easter, they ate only one meal a day. Abbot Guichard generously allowed his guests to vary this frugal diet, permitting them to be served meat and some other delicacies. But for Herbert, a man who enjoyed his creature comforts, everything was a struggle. Soon he was complaining that he had been "banished" to live "in solitude among the stones and the monks," and he took himself off on a visit to Auxerre, where he cheered himself up by dining with friends and buying a fine green tunic and long matching cloak, which "he wore after the German fashion, from his shoulders down to his ankles, with suitable adornments."

Becket, in contrast, seems to have regarded the privations of the cloister as the penance for his perjury at Clarendon. Never inclined to half measures when he felt he had something to prove, he insisted on sharing the same food as the monks and undergoing the same physical and spiritual trials. He ate only vegetables and ordered the meat and delicacies laid before him in the refectory to be given to the poor. He wore a hair shirt and monastic underclothes, almost certainly for the first time: Abbot Guichard is said to have invested him with them at a secret ceremony witnessed only by Alexander Llewelyn. Regularly saying mass and helping to sing the daily offices with the monks, he also kept vigil at night in prayer and contemplation, often rousing his confessor, Robert of Merton, at midnight with orders to scourge him and plunging himself at daybreak into an icy stream that ran beside the workshops of the monastery. Soon he made himself ill, developing an infection that led to abscesses and mouth ulcers. Finally, he became delirious, experiencing a series of hallucinations in which he found himself pleading his case before the pope, this time with "the Pharisees" attempting to gouge out his eyes with their fingers as he spoke.

At last persuaded that his abstinence was the cause of his decline, he resumed his normal diet. Herbert of Bosham led the way, artfully producing a sermon on the evils of excess and how extreme penances could be the work of the devil. Once Thomas was eating and resting again, he gradually recovered his strength, and instead of assigning himself more tasks of physical endurance, he returned to his books, "giving himself wholly over to the study of literature and especially theology." To this end, he made a special study of the Psalms and the Pauline Epistles, asking Herbert to prepare for him a complete edition of Peter Lombard's *Great Gloss* on these books. A complete edition was needed because Peter, once Abelard's pupil, had died before he could finish his own, and Becket knew that Herbert was the ideal man to do it. As one of Peter's former pupils, Herbert knew his work extremely well.

Herbert's magnificent manuscript, in four volumes, still survives, split today between Oxford and Cambridge libraries. By the imaginative use of colored inks and tinted line drawings, fine illuminated initial letters with the heads of lions or snakes set into them to grab the reader's attention, his scribes succeeded in making the text attractive and accessible. Other wonderful and costly books that Thomas commissioned at Pontigny, borrowing the money to pay for them, include copies of the Gospels, the Old Testament Prophets, and the book of Isaiah. Full of colored pages decorated with expensive, sparkling gold initials and using the purest blue pigment made from lapis lazuli, they illustrate, among other things, a tonsured man at a writing desk with his inkhorn, penknife, and ruler; a monkey reading a book; another monkey blowing a horn beside a man playing a rebec (a three-stringed instrument played with a bow); a mysterious blue man wrestling with a lion; and a naked man wrestling with a bear.

Thomas also began a fresh study of canon law, choosing as his teacher a learned canonist of Piacenza, a man called Master Lombard, who had reputedly been with him at Northampton and followed him into exile. What emphasis he brought to Becket's studies is not recorded, but to supplement the archbishop's working copy of Gratian's *Decretum,* he commissioned from Herbert of Bosham a deluxe edition of this classic text, perhaps the brilliantly illuminated manuscript now at the J. Paul Getty Museum in Los Angeles, or perhaps a broken manuscript from which important fragments survive at the Municipal Library at Auxerre and the Cleveland Museum of Art.

At Pontigny, Becket was quickly to become a connoisseur of the fine illuminated manuscripts for which its scriptorium was renowned. He had books copied from all over France, adding to those the exiles had by now recovered from among his personal possessions left behind at Canterbury. Hearing of his friend's sudden zest for learning, John of Salisbury begged him to spend more time on the Psalms and works of moral philosophy, and less on canon and civil law. He recommended St. Gregory's *Moralia,* a difficult commentary on the book of Job that emphasizes the liberating nature of adversity and exile, but Thomas appears to have restricted himself to that author's easier *Homilies* and potted extracts from it compiled by Garnier of Saint-Victor. In this respect, his old habits would die hard. He did, however, buy on John's advice St. Ambrose's *On the Duties of Ministers,* which gives a strong Christian emphasis to Cicero's classic handbook of moral and political philosophy, *De Officiis*. And he secured copies of Seneca's moral essays, especially *De Clementia,* which is dedicated to the emperor Nero and discusses in depth how a good ruler should behave and an honest citizen conduct himself under tyranny.

The topicality of such works for an embattled refugee cannot be overemphasized. Whereas Cicero and Seneca had placed a community of good citizens at the heart of their ethical models, St. Ambrose had placed the Christian church there. It followed, as Becket's old tutor Robert of Melun had long ago argued in his lectures, that the responsibility for disciplining a tyrant on moral grounds lay with the ministers of the church. St. Ambrose had also discussed the nature of true friendship, concluding that ethically it should always give place to honesty. No man should favor his friend when he is in the wrong. Just as he ought to vindicate him when he is innocent, so he must rebuke him when he is in error. With an uncanny resonance to Becket's current attitude toward Henry, Ambrose had said that nobody can be a true friend to someone who attacks or defies the church.

When Thomas chose to read and acquire his own copies of works like these, far more was involved than a basic desire for learning. At Pontigny and with the help of his friends, he set about equipping himself with all the books and information he thought he might need to carry on the fight against a king he had come to regard as no better than any of the biblical or classical tyrants. He meant to reinforce his sense of values and thereby equip himself to fight his corner while simultaneously guiding his flock, for he had no intention of abandoning the charge that had been laid upon him. If Pope Alexander could govern the Roman church from the sanctuary of Sens, why could Thomas not govern the English church from Pontigny?

At the very least, he was going to try. He would not let his enemies stand in his way if he could help it.

21

ATTACK AND COUNTERATTACK

NEVER ONE TO ACCEPT DEFEAT, HENRY STRUCK BACK WHEN his envoys returned empty-handed from the papal curia at Sens. After hearing their report on Christmas Eve 1164 at Marlborough in Wiltshire, he was indignant that Pope Alexander had thwarted him by allowing Becket to establish himself unmolested at Pontigny. He could be heard dropping broad hints that he was ready to renounce the pope and his "treacherous cardinals." And he decided to take vicious reprisals designed to irritate the pope and make the lives of Thomas and all those connected with him as miserable as possible.

On Christmas Day, he sequestered the archbishop's property and that of his clerks, taking the lands and revenues of the church of Canterbury into his own hands. Then, on St. Stephen's (Boxing) Day, he ordered the deportation and exile of Thomas's relatives and servants, whether men, women, or children, and anyone else who was known to have harbored or assisted him during his flight. All incomes owed to his clerks or family members were to be withheld, reducing them to penury. The receipts of all revenues due to the pope were to be frozen in the Exchequer, all appeals or visits without royal permission to the papal curia were forbidden, and anyone found bringing letters into England from the pope or the archbishop was to be summarily hanged or cast adrift by the sheriffs from the seashore in an open boat without oars.

Henry appointed his crony and whoremaster Ranulf de Broc as his chief sequestrator. Already illegally occupying Saltwood Castle, this flunkey had been among those shouting insults at Becket as he strode out of the great hall at Northampton. Wasting no time, de Broc; his nephew Robert, an apostate Cistercian monk; and their henchmen gleefully set to work the next day. Divided into small teams, they seized the Canterbury court rolls and organized a purge of Becket's relatives and servants, rounding up several dozen in London, including his married sisters, Agnes and Rose, and their children, whom they imprisoned in thieves' jails overnight or frog-marched directly to the coast. Put on board ships bound for the Continent, they were ordered to keep walking until they arrived at Pontigny. Those whom de Broc personally arrested were required to take an oath that they would not attempt to return. It was, says William fitz Stephen, "a most harrowing exodus," with infants—"some in cradles, others clinging to the breast"—treated as harshly as the rest. Only victims able to pay huge fines or bribes of £200 or 100 silver marks would be excused.

As many as four hundred people were deported, but few reached Pontigny, where guest accommodations were in short supply. When the exiles landed in France, many of the women and children were taken in by nuns, while their menfolk found employment with sympathetic bishops or nobles. To score more points off Henry, King Louis himself found places for a favored few; others, including one of Becket's nephews, a boy named Gilbert after his grandfather, took refuge as far south as Sicily. Faced by the prospect of a long and painful exile, some of Becket's servants decided to reconcile themselves to Henry, fitz Stephen among them. After much soul-searching, he knelt before the king in the chapel of a hunting lodge at Brill, near Aylesbury in Buckinghamshire, and presented him with a long verse prayer. Quite why this should have worked is hard to judge, since if Henry had bothered to read the prayer, he would have seen that in it he was made to confess to the sins of pride, adultery, and covetousness. That the gift was acceptable shows how eager he was to come to terms with those prepared to cut their ties with Becket. Not that fitz Stephen really did so, as a few years later on a mission to the pope he took a detour to visit Thomas. And late in 1170, he would switch sides again, being one of those closest to the archbishop in Canterbury cathedral when he was murdered.

* * *

WITH THE EXPULSION of Becket's relatives and supporters complete, Henry took the fight to the Continent. Unsettling him was the close entente between Louis and Pope Alexander that had led to both the pope and Becket taking sanctuary on French soil, which Henry meant to sabotage. He also harbored a deep and continuing resentment at the Capetian king's third marriage to Adela of Blois-Champagne, King Stephen's niece, which threatened his dynastic plans. In 1164, Louis had buttressed that threat by provocatively marrying his daughters by Eleanor of Aquitaine, Mary and Alice, to Adela's brothers, Count Theobald V of Blois and Count Henry of Champagne.

Sailing for Normandy in the latter part of February 1165, Henry was determined to pursue a two-pronged strategy. Hoping to win his cousin Count Philip of Flanders to his side, he meant to drive a wedge between Louis and Pope Alexander, but he also needed a quick result so he could return across the Channel, where Prince Owain of Gwynedd was in revolt again. To buy time before marching into Wales, he was willing to trade reconciliation with Becket for an Anglo-French peace. Seeing the diplomatic possibilities, Arnulf of Lisieux secretly urged Becket to settle the quarrel while he could. Henry, he said, "is coming, so they say, with a gentler mind than usual, because although he pretends otherwise, he thinks the omens for the future could be bad." Besides the rebellion in Wales, he faced fresh upheavals in Brittany, Poitou, and Aquitaine stirred by Louis. "Because of this," concluded Arnulf, "he has resolved first to approach the French king with certain proposals."

Precisely what these were, Arnulf would not say. But Becket, genuinely seeking a rapprochement, moved quickly, putting out feelers to Henry's mother, Matilda, asking her for help in brokering a peace. Now almost sixty-four, she had been seriously ill, but she agreed to mediate. Already dismayed (as she had told Herbert of Bosham and Nicholas of Rouen) at her son's attempt to codify the ancestral customs in a written document, she would first write to Henry to ask how he meant to proceed. "When I know his will," she said, "if I think that my labor can bear fruit, I shall strive as much as I can for the church's peace and his."

She was as good as her word. John of Salisbury, still in Paris and worrying about money but as busy as ever on his friend's behalf, reported that she had sent him a reassuring message. She "promises that she can easily induce the king of England to accept the pope's wishes if the pope is willing to make a treaty between the kings, as has long been sought." Louis, it seemed, had agreed to the plan, and Alexander had summoned him to Sens.

Becket turned next to his old secretary, Master Ernulf, in an attempt to arrange a meeting between himself and the two kings in the French Vexin. While Henry pursued his own diplomacy, Ernulf obtained an audience with Louis at Senlis in late March. There the idea of a conference was discussed, and Louis, after further consultations with Alexander, invited Becket to a rendezvous at the Cistercian abbey of Le Val Notre-Dame, near Pontoise. But the plan came to nothing. The pope rode to Paris in readiness; Becket also made the journey. But when Henry realized that the pope was likely to be present, he refused to proceed, leaving Thomas in limbo. It could hardly have been otherwise, for Henry feared that Alexander might repeat his condemnation of the ancestral customs or even threaten to excommunicate him if he failed to settle with Becket. To meet the pope, therefore, would be at best pointless, at worst counterproductive.

On April 11, Henry met Louis alone on the frontier at Gisors. He then rode to Rouen, where he took advice from his cousin Count Philip. But whatever Henry offered, it was not enough for Louis. No sooner had Philip gone home than Henry dramatically changed tack, aiming to spite Louis and the pope simultaneously by entertaining a magnificent embassy from the pope's archenemy, Frederick Barbarossa, led by the imperial chancellor, Rainald of Dassel, archbishop-elect of Cologne. He proposed a new dynastic alliance to counter his earlier one with Louis: his eldest daughter, Matilda, rising nine, was to be betrothed to Frederick's cousin Henry the Lion, Duke of Saxony and Bavaria; her sister Eleanor, not yet four, was to be betrothed to Frederick's son, another Frederick, as yet barely a year old, cutting Louis out of the picture completely.

Queen Eleanor also welcomed these ambassadors, but to Becket's delight her mother-in-law, Matilda, the Angevin matriarch, refused to receive them, protesting that they were schismatics and persisting in her efforts to mediate on the exiled archbishop's behalf. Her son was undaunted, binding himself on oath to fulfill the betrothals and sending John of Oxford, fast becoming one of his leading counselors, and Richard of Ilchester, archdeacon of Poitiers, to Germany, where they attended the schismatic Council of Würzburg. On May 23, these envoys, presumably egged on by Henry, even got sufficiently carried away to join in an oath renouncing Pope Alexander and recognizing the new antipope, Paschal, on behalf of Henry's territories.

Alarmed by the resulting furor that assailed him from all sides, Henry stepped back from the brink, firmly denying that any such oath had been taken, or if it had, his envoys had exceeded their authority. By then he had already returned to England, leaving Eleanor, who was pregnant again, at Angers. In an attempt to douse the flames, he ordered John of Oxford to swear that he "had done nothing against the faith he owed the church and the honor and advantage of Pope Alexander." But when Frederick, in a letter "to all people over whom our imperial clemency rules," gave him the lie and insisted that he had, Becket hit back, accusing John of "impious" and flagrant perjury.

On April 20, Alexander had left Paris on his way home to Rome. With Frederick's troops rampaging through Tuscany and the Roman Campagna, burning and flattening everything in their path, the citizens of Rome had begged him to return. As John of Salisbury informed Becket, the soldiers had devastated the countryside and set fire to the towns: "there is nothing left for the Romans beyond the walls of the city, neither in the fields, nor in the olive groves, nor in the vineyards." The citizens were preparing to oust the antipope from his palace at the Lateran, and Alexander's presence, he said, would make all the difference to their morale, since Frederick's power was not as great as he believed it to be.

Traveling by way of Bourges, Clermont, and Montpellier, Alexander had originally planned to sail with his cardinals directly across the Mediterranean to the port of Ostia near Rome, avoiding the coast of northern Italy. He already knew from his spies that the Pisans, the Genoese, and the pirates of Arles had received Frederick's orders to intercept him. Even despite taking all the necessary precautions, he would have the narrowest of escapes. When his vessels finally set sail, one carrying many of the cardinals was intercepted and boarded by Frederick's men.

In the nick of time, Alexander managed to flee in another, smaller boat to Messina, where King William I of Sicily gave him a military escort back to Rome.

Becket had left the abbey of Le Val Notre-Dame for Paris as soon as he had heard of Alexander's impending departure, riding south with him on the first stage of his journey as far as Bourges. As it slowly began to sink in that there would be no quick fix and that his exile could be a long and bitter one, his spirits flagged. Trapped in a dark hinterland from which he found it impossible to escape by his own efforts, he badly needed a psychological boost. He desperately wanted the pope to do more for him before disappearing into the abyss of Italian politics.

It was not to be. Like his ally King Louis, the pope had too much else on his mind. At their parting at Bourges, while the issues were still fresh in his mind, Alexander exonerated Thomas from the sentences pronounced against him at the Council of Northampton. And shortly after reaching Clermont, he sent a stiffly worded letter to Gilbert Foliot ordering him to instruct Henry to cease his attacks on the church. But as he approached Montpellier, he did a volte-face, urging Becket to reconcile himself to Henry and temporarily revoking the archbishop's right to impose sentences of excommunication on any of his opponents until Easter the following year, thereby rendering him powerless. Fast running out of cash as his entourage traveled south, the pope badly needed Henry to release the papal revenues he had frozen in the Exchequer. "Since these are evil times," he warned Thomas, "we ask, advise, counsel, and exhort you to act with caution, prudence and circumspection in everything concerning your own and the church's affairs. Do nothing hurriedly or precipitately, but only soberly and maturely, and labor and strive to recover the grace and goodwill of the illustrious English king by all possible means . . . while preserving the church's freedom and the honor of your office."

However unwelcome to Thomas, who looked for a far more decisive intervention from the pope, this would be sage advice, since the winning streak enjoyed by Henry for the past fifteen years was finally coming to an end. His second invasion of Wales, undertaken in July and August 1165, would turn into an even greater disaster than the first, eclipsing everything else on his mind for the rest of the year and sidelining his quarrel with Becket. After summoning the feudal hosts of England and Normandy and shipping in mercenaries from Flanders, Henry marched his troops through Shrewsbury and Oswestry into the Welsh mountains, taking the route traditionally known as the "English Road," until the Welsh, carefully tracking his position, blocked his path at Corwen at the westerly end of the Dee Valley. Between the two armies lay the densely forested Vale of Ceiriog, where a standoff ensued.

Attempting to profit from his earlier experience of fighting in the mountains, Henry ordered his troops to cut down the trees that separated the opposing armies in order to preempt an ambush. Instead the Welsh charged, and a pitched battle ensued. Both sides took heavy casualties, but the Welsh line held, forcing Henry to retreat into the Berwyn Mountains. Suddenly a torrential thunderstorm caused a flash flood that swept away his carts and left men and horses floundering in deep pools of mud and water. When his supply lines failed, he was forced to flee, with huge losses of men and equipment. In retribution, he ordered many of the Welsh hostages he had taken in 1157 to be castrated and blinded, among them Prince Owain's young son. Rather than blame himself for the calamity, he chose to turn his fury against his helpless captives.

After recuperating with the remnant of his army near Chester, Henry returned to London in September, where more bad news awaited him. Adela, the French queen, had given birth to a son named Philip. Gerald of Wales, then a student in Paris, relates that one hot Saturday in late August, he was awakened shortly after midnight by a cacophony outside his lodgings. Trumpets were blaring and bells ringing. At first he thought the city was on fire, but when he put on his shirt and leaned out the window, he saw citizens and students rushing toward the royal palace carrying lanterns and torches, shouting and cheering. Two old women, passing by with tapers, told him that the queen had borne a son. King Louis, who had longed for this day since he had first married Eleanor of Aquitaine, had at last settled the succession to his kingdom. Prince Henry's marriage to a French princess, purchased at such a high price, was now nothing more than a sideshow.

* * *

IN THE LAST WEEK of March 1166, when the Easter festival was approaching, Henry returned to Angers, where Eleanor had remained with their new daughter, Joanna. When the Easter candles were lit and mass celebrated on April 24, the pope's suspension of Becket's powers of excommunication expired, and he was once more free to strike. All efforts at mediation by the Angevin matriarch had failed, and in an attempt to assist Becket, Louis visited Henry. But the most that he could achieve was to persuade him to grant an audience to some of Thomas's clerks in the hope that they might be able to recoup their lost incomes.

John of Salisbury was the first to be seen. Never a willing exile, his hope, utterly unrealistic, was to regain Henry's goodwill and return to his old haunts (and church livings) without abandoning his friend or his ideals. As he informed the bishop-elect of Bayeux in a chatty newsletter, he would always keep faith with the exiled archbishop, but loyalty had its limits. "I am prepared to show," he said, "that neither the honor due to the king nor his interests have in any way suffered from me. . . . There is nothing consistent with the integrity of my reputation and my conscience which I would not do, and willingly, to make my peace and recover his favor."

A bruising interview on May 1 proved to him that this balancing act would be impossible. By demanding that John swear an oath to observe the customs published in the chirograph at Clarendon and break his ties with the exiled archbishop, Henry showed the true nature of what was at stake and gave a glimpse into the workings of his mind. Once again he was doubling the stakes, demanding fealty to the ancestral customs as well as to himself, using oaths to secure the allegiance not simply of the hearts of his subjects but also of their minds. A philosopher like John, for all his fear of physical violence, could never accept a demand like that in honor and good conscience. He told Henry that he could abandon neither the church of Canterbury nor Thomas; he could not agree to observe any customs not sanctioned by the pope or the archbishop. The most that he could do, he said, was "to accept what they accepted and reject what they rejected."

Hardly likely was it that Herbert of Bosham would succeed where John had failed. Now in his mid- to late thirties and as tall and svelte as Becket used to be before stress took its toll, he strode in wearing his new green suit and cloak, causing Henry to exclaim, "See, here comes a proud one!" Interviewed in a similar way to John, he gave the same answers until the subject of the customs arose, when he tried casuistry, saying, "He alone is faithful to the king who does not allow the king to err, when he can be restrained. For he who tries to appease the king when he speaks to him and glosses over his sin, if that is what it is, and supports it with silence, is not true to the king, but rather neglects faith."

A tactic tried a thousand times by philosophers and conscientious objectors from the era of the classical tyrants to the Renaissance, this had predictable results. After interrogating Herbert for twenty minutes or so to make quite sure he could not be persuaded to take the oath, Henry's patience snapped. "For shame," he expostulated to the barons around him, "why should my kingdom be disturbed and my peace unsettled by this son of a priest?"

To which Herbert indignantly rejoined, "It is wrong to call me a priest's son. I couldn't have been born to a priest, since my father wasn't ordained when I was born—just as it would be wrong to call someone a king's son if he wasn't born to a king."

Everyone held their breath, for this was an insult, a thinly veiled allusion to the fact that Henry's ancestors on his father's side had never been more than counts of Anjou and his hereditary claim to the English throne came only on his mother's side. In medieval eyes, he was not of royal birth. Herbert's riposte was cutting, clever, and exceptionally dangerous. As all those within earshot marveled at his wit and courage, whispering to their neighbors that they wished they had a son as brave as he, Henry fell silent, seething over the fact that he had been worsted in an argument by one of his villeins.

Herbert returned to Pontigny, but John of Salisbury retreated to the abbey of Saint-Rémi at Rheims, where his friend Peter of Celle had granted him sanctuary when the lease on his lodgings in Paris expired. With all hope of a speedy reconciliation with Henry gone, John threw himself into his books while still aiding Becket, attempting to distance himself from his friend's more unrealistic or extravagant claims, yet remaining a vocal, if dispassionate, supporter and a fierce critic of those who attacked the liberty of the church. A philosopher of a Stoic disposition, John believed that only studied objectivity and tranquillity of mind could give the victims of political persecution the inner strength to suffer tribulations while staying true to their beliefs. No longer did he see the contest as a struggle for power between individuals such as Henry or Thomas; in his mind it had become one between the cosmic forces of right and wrong, God and the devil. The righteous would one day have their reward, but they might have to wait for it until Judgment Day.

ARRIVING ON THE outskirts of Rome the previous November, Pope Alexander had made a triumphant entry into the city. Once reestablished in his palace at the Lateran, he felt able to take a tougher stand against Henry, whose eagerness to come to terms with the schismatic Frederick had put the pope's safe return in jeopardy. By the time his Easter deadline for the restoration of Becket's disciplinary powers had expired, he was feeling uncharacteristically bullish, actively encouraging Thomas to punish those illegally occupying his Canterbury lands, provided they had first been suitably cautioned. "By God's will," he reassured him, "we shall confirm and ratify anything you shall reasonably do in the matter." On May 2, 1166, he went even further, appointing Becket as papal legate for England on the same terms as those given to Archbishop Theobald in King Stephen's reign, enabling him to issue sentences of excommunication and interdict without prior approval from the pope. The only condition was that he was to have no jurisdiction over Roger of Pont l'Évêque or the Diocese of York, a restriction that had also applied to Theobald.

This move caused consternation at Henry's court, which had traveled from Angers to Le Mans, and from there to Chinon. At a council summoned in late May, the king took advice from the barons as to how to silence Becket. When no one offered a solution, he threw a tantrum, thumping the table with his fist and crying out that they were all traitors "who had neither the zeal nor the courage to rid him of a single man."

Henry knew Becket well enough to guess his likely intentions, and in the anxious days before the council, Thomas had sent him increasingly strident calls for repentance, the second with a gently chiding appeal to their old familiarity. "With longing," it began, "have I desired to see your face and speak to you, much indeed on my account, but more particularly on yours." If only they could meet in the flesh, said Becket, Henry would quickly recall Thomas's faithful and devoted service as his chancellor, while Thomas would once more be able to do his duty and offer his counsel as a loyal vassal. Abruptly shifting gears, Becket then sharply rebuked Henry for his predations against the church, using the vivid, fiery rhetoric that had become his trademark. Henry, he said, might be his liege lord, but as archbishop of Canterbury, he was the king's pastor and Henry was his "spiritual son." "I am bound," he said, "to reprove and restrain you by reason of my office." Rulers committing sacrilege or ignoring their religious duties and God's law would be severely punished like the wicked tyrants of the Old Testament. Their glory would be extinguished, their power stripped away.

When Henry manhandled Becket's courier, the Cistercian abbot of Cercamp, for his "impudence" in carrying such messages, Thomas decided to hit back. He had given the king fair warning, and with Alexander falling in behind him, he now had his big opportunity. Psychologically driven to counterattack, he was only too aware of the momentous implications. He had resolved on another of his grand gestures, but this time it was going to be different. Whereas before he had sometimes done things on the spur of the moment or without fully considering the consequences of his actions, this time it had been eighteen months since his relatives and servants had been frog-marched from their homes. What was about to happen was not the result of a decision taken on an impulse. John of Salisbury already had an inkling of it, since he advised his friend on no account to think of excommunicating the king himself for fear that he would come to regret it. Thomas knew that he had to make careful preparations for what he was about to do, choosing a time and place that would secure him maximum impact.

On May 29, after sending Nicholas of Rouen to explain to Henry's mother that, regretfully, the time for compromise had passed and that "shortly, very shortly, if we live and God aids us, we shall unsheathe the sword of the Holy Spirit," he left the cloistered serenity of Pontigny to ride 150 miles north to Soissons. There, among the pilgrims, he prayed for three nights at the shrines of the Virgin Mary, his mother's favorite intercessor; St. Gregory; and St. Drausinus, a seventh-century bishop who was the patron saint of those about to go into combat or fight a duel.

On June 3, he rode south again to Vézelay, only a day's journey from Pontigny but almost two hundred miles from Soissons. The Benedictine abbey was set on the summit of a hill, where it was visible from all four points of the compass. It was approached by a steep, straight path from the village below, just as it still is today. Boasting the relics of St. Mary Magdalene, the abbey church was a popular staging post on the pilgrim's route to Santiago de Compostela, and it had been from here that St. Bernard had famously preached the Second Crusade before King Louis and Eleanor of Aquitaine. Its Romanesque nave, narthex, and chapel of St. Michael had been recently completed and looked magnificent, but a fire in the crypt beneath the choir in 1165 meant that when Becket arrived, the place was once more something of a building site.

On Whitsunday (June 12), Thomas celebrated high mass inside the church, preaching a sermon to a packed congregation in which he gave the history of the quarrel with Henry and denounced the king for his attacks on the church and failure to respond to the archbishop's reprimands. "Speaking," says Herbert of Bosham, "as if a man possessed" (*miro modo compunctus*), he must have had something of the appearance of an Old Testament prophet, for loss of weight had made his cheeks hollow, and he had grown a beard. Suddenly, to the astonishment of his clerks—he had concealed his plan from all of them, even Herbert, for fear of leaks—he condemned the hateful customs published at Clarendon. They were, he said, "perversities, rather than 'customs,' by which the English church is thrown into disorder and confusion." His voice quivering with emotion as he fought back the tears, his youthful stammer perhaps briefly reappearing, he issued a general excommunication against everyone enforcing or defending the customs and released his fellow bishops from their obligation to observe them, while his audience gasped.

Individual excommunications followed: John of Oxford and Richard of Ilchester for their "vile oath" to the German "schismatics"; Richard de Lucy and Jocelin de Bailleul for inciting tyranny and drafting the memorandum of the customs at Clarendon with John of Oxford; and

Ranulf de Broc and his henchmen for their illicit occupation of Saltwood Castle and the archbishop's palace at Canterbury. By excommunicating de Bailleul, Becket made a lasting enemy of Eleanor, whose chief household knight he had become. In this comprehensive strike against the archbishop's foes, only the king was spared, possibly because of John of Salisbury's warning, more likely because a messenger from Louis had informed Becket during an overnight stop at Rigny on the road from Soissons that Henry was gravely ill at the castle of Chinon.

Before leaving the pulpit, Thomas called on the king to repent, "threatening to deliver sentence of excommunication against him shortly, unless he comes to his senses and makes reparations." After the sermon, he sent one Gerard, a barefoot monk, to Henry, this time with a letter containing a veiled but obvious threat. "If you are a good and Catholic king and desire to be one," warned Thomas, "it becomes you to follow the priests in ecclesiastical matters, not to go before them." History, as his old Paris master Robert of Melun had explained in his lectures, had compelling examples of the punishment of wayward kings and emperors. "Consider," concluded Thomas in a chilling memento mori, "where the emperors, kings, and other princes are, where the archbishops and bishops are who have gone before us. . . . Remember your last day, and you will not sin in eternity; and if you do sin, you will repent during the present life."

Becket believed this time he had the edge on Henry, that he could rely on Pope Alexander, who duly honored his Easter pledge by ratifying the Vézelay excommunications. But the pope's position was about to weaken once again, for Frederick Barbarossa was determined to unseat him in favor of his antipope. As soon as he had dealt with a popular uprising of the Lombard communes, Frederick meant to march his army south across the Alps. Henry, meanwhile, on recovering from his sickness, sent orders to Richard de Lucy that the English bishops should appeal Becket's sentences to the pope. He meant to confront Rome directly, asking Rainald of Dassel for a safe-conduct through German territories for a fresh embassy to the papal curia led by Roger of Pont l'Évêque, Gilbert Foliot, and John of Oxford. They were to give Alexander a verbal ultimatum, saying that if he did not agree to depose Thomas, revoke the Vézelay sentences, and recognize the ancestral customs forthwith, Henry would switch his allegiance to the antipope. In an accompanying letter, the king made his feelings all too plain, bluntly calling Thomas "my betrayer, formerly archbishop of Canterbury."

Not content with this, he wrote next to Abbot Gilbert of Cîteaux, an Englishman, roundly upbraiding him for allowing his order to offer sanctuary to Thomas at the abbey of Pontigny and otherwise assisting him. He threatened to expel every one of the Cistercians from England and seize all their property if the order did not swiftly mend its ways. He also demanded Becket's immediate expulsion from Pontigny.

Henry's renewed attacks on him incensed Thomas, who complained vociferously to Alexander and the cardinals. The king, he said, was "abusing the patience of the church" and "subverting justice under the guise of law." He accused Henry of hypocrisy for attempting to block normal appeals to Rome citing the ancestral customs, but himself ordering the English bishops to appeal to Alexander to revoke the Vézelay censures. It was time, said Thomas, to act—and yet he himself hesitated. Kings were called and anointed by God. When it came to it, not even Robert of Melun, whose lectures in Paris had argued that the ministers of the church were entitled to discipline evil rulers, would be willing to put his own theory into practice. Robert, quipped John of Salisbury, "was once thought to be the man who should have redeemed Israel, with his contempt of the world and his skill in letters." Now he was nowhere to be seen. He had, in fact, become a turncoat, joining Gilbert Foliot in setting his seal to the bishops' appeal to the pope.

The trumps were still in Henry's hands. By his retaliation at Vézelay, Thomas had precipitated a fresh crisis even greater than the first, merging his dispute with Henry into the wider conflict of the papal schism and ensuring his own speedy eviction from Pontigny. How Alexander would react to Henry's new ambassadors was not yet known, but with Frederick's troops about to cross the Brenner Pass, his nerve was likely to fail. After fleeing from Northampton, Becket had spent eighteen months on the defensive before fighting back. Now that he had done so, his position looked worse than it had at any time since he had crossed the frontier from Flanders into France.

The wheel had turned full circle.

22
SEARCH FOR A SETTLEMENT

SLOWLY BUT SURELY IN THE MONTHS AFTER THOMAS'S DEFIant run of excommunications at Vézelay, Henry regained the upper hand. With Frederick Barbarossa's troops advancing ever closer to Rome, an anxious pope knew he might soon face ignominious flight or a humiliating appeasement of the German emperor—and either would mean appeasing Henry too. While Becket had excommunicated some of Henry's staunchest supporters—notably Richard de Lucy, John of Oxford, and Ranulf de Broc—and had afterward sent a letter to Alexander describing the king as a "wicked tyrant," he had not excommunicated Henry himself. As his friend John of Salisbury had cautioned him, the prudent course was always to blame the "untamed beasts" rather than attack the king directly. Thus if Henry had erred, the fault lay more with his advisers than with himself. It was admittedly both a fiction and a pretense, but one generally adhered to in an era when the stereotype maintained that the king ruled in the image of God and his will was law. There were only so many shibboleths that Becket could challenge all at the same time.

Henry had no such scruples. When asked by his doctors how he was recovering from his sickness, he snapped back that his chief problem was Becket and that he could be cured only if they had a medicine that could soothe the "rancor and indignation" he felt because of him. His other problem sprang from his vassal Conan IV's inability to keep order in Brittany. After suppressing a baronial uprising there during the summer and early autumn of 1166, Henry lost patience with Conan, forcing him to abdicate and betrothing his own youngest son, Geoffrey, now rising eight, to Conan's daughter and heiress. On returning to Rouen, he signaled his contempt for Becket by imprisoning and torturing one of the archbishop's couriers, a young boy whom Herbert of Bosham had sent to him with a letter. His jailers clawed at the boy's eyes with their fingernails until the blood flowed, then poured boiling water into his mouth, scalding him and scarring him for life.

Not for the first time, Becket began to fear for his own safety. Henry, as John of Canterbury reported, had somehow managed to obtain a copy of the archbishop's letter denouncing him as a wicked tyrant. Now his aim was to capture Thomas and put him on trial again, not this time in a royal court as at Northampton, but before papal judges who would appear to be fair though in reality would be his own nominees. Eager for the trial to begin, Henry ordered his officials to start gathering evidence and searching for witnesses prepared to testify against Becket. "I counsel you," John of Canterbury urged his friend, "to take action by whatever means you can, while you still have time."

Henry, however, had been thwarted in his plan to send Roger of Pont l'Évêque and Gilbert Foliot to the papal curia, since both were unwilling to face Alexander in person. Instead, the more intrepid and irrepressible John of Oxford led a delegation asking for Becket to be deposed by the pope or else suspended until he could be tried and condemned before papal judges. While John was conducting his diplomacy, much of it through bribes, the king withdrew to spend Christmas at Poitiers alone with his children. Eleanor, who had left Angers in the autumn and returned to England, was pregnant again, giving birth to her youngest son, John, probably at Oxford, early in the new year. Something of a chill was developing in Henry and Eleanor's relationship. For his part, Henry powerfully resented the influence of his wife's maternal uncle Ralph de Faye, the high steward of Aquitaine, in reinforcing her commitment to a pro-Poitevin policy; on her side, she was finding it difficult to adjust to her husband's infidelities, fast increasing now that he was thirty-three and she approaching forty-five. Such burgeoning marital discord might have provided a wonderful opportunity for the exiles, but the cooling of Henry's passion for his queen would bring no comfort for them. By excommunicating Jocelin de Bailleul, Eleanor's leading household knight, for his share in drafting the memorandum of the customs at Clarendon, Becket had made as big an enemy of Eleanor as he had of her husband. "I wish you to know," John of Canterbury warned his friend, "that you can hope for no help or advice from the queen."

With Frederick's troops pouring into Italy and poised to march down the eastern route to besiege Ancona, Pope Alexander responded to Henry's intimidation in the only way he thought he could, granting him much, though far from all, that he had asked for: revoking the archbishop's powers of excommunication and interdict for a second time, absolving John of Oxford from his sentence at Vézelay, and commissioning two papal mediators. One was to be the king's first choice, William of Pavia, none other than one of the earlier papal emissaries who with Henry of Pisa had granted the license for Prince Henry's wedding to the French king's daughter while both parties were still children. His colleague, Otto of Brescia, whose commission gave him equal powers, was a more impartial choice, but Becket would soon be complaining vociferously that their mission could only turn him into "a figure of shame" and that all William was likely to offer was "the semblance of honey in the beginning, poison in the middle, and oil at the end."

To Thomas, Alexander wrote beguilingly, pledging a renewed effort to force Henry to the negotiating table. Until then, the exiled archbishop was to be patient and not act provocatively. His disciplinary powers, the pope promised, would be restored should Henry persist in his obstinacy, but as this fact was to be kept a closely guarded secret, it raised more fears than it dispelled—not least since, shortly after reading this letter, Becket discovered that the pope had written separately to Henry confirming the final arrangements for the mediators in such obsequious terms that Gilbert Foliot exclaimed with delight, "Thomas will no longer be my archbishop!"

Becket felt doubly betrayed, because Henry's attack on the Cistercians had yielded handsome dividends. On November 11, 1166, he and his fellow exiles had been politely but firmly expelled from their sanctuary at Pontigny and forced to seek refuge at the Benedictine abbey of Sainte-Colombe at Sens, under King Louis's personal protection. The exiles cried foul, excoriating Henry for his bullying and mocking William of Pavia, calling him a stooge and "the cardinal of St. Peter in Chains" (a pun on his official title of cardinal-priest of San Pietro in Vincoli). By the spring of 1167, such protests had moderated, for the exiles found the life of the Benedictines congenial, even luxurious, in comparison to that of the Cistercians. More important, Louis declared his hostility toward the papal mediators. Still blaming William of Pavia for granting the shabby license that had made possible his daughter's wedding at the age of two, he had denied them permission to enter his lands. He also had shown his contempt for Henry by stirring up more revolts in Brittany and Aquitaine and by raiding the Norman Vexin, prompting Henry to retaliate by burning the castle of Chaumont-sur-Epte.

As it turned out, the mediators, who finally left Rome on May 1, would be delayed for another five months. Otto had to bypass Frederick's armies as he made his way north, and William was diverted to Sicily to stiffen the resolve of the baronage against the antipope. With the imperial troops heading fast toward Rome, Alexander knew that he would soon have to flee south to Benevento. That moment came in July, when in a swift and decisive swoop, the city fell to superior German forces. After Frederick entered the holy city on July 22, the pope made his escape, enabling his rival, Paschal III, to be enthroned at St. Peter's Basilica. With Henry's daughter Matilda betrothed to Frederick's cousin and Saxon envoys preparing to escort her to Germany for her wedding, events were continuing to turn in Henry's favor. As soon as Alexander reached the sanctuary of Benevento, he urged his mediators not to be distracted from their task, since if the Angevins sided with the antipope, Christendom would be torn asunder.

Then exhilarating news reached Benevento. On August 2, a violent rainstorm followed by searing summer heat had accelerated a lethal combination of bacillary dysentery and the deadly malaria of the Roman Campagna, striking down the imperial forces as they camped in their tents. Among several thousand dead were the imperial chancellor, Rainald of Dassel, six other bishops, and a high proportion of the nobility. Frederick was forced to retreat over the Apennines with the enfeebled survivors, only to find the roads to the north barricaded against him by the rebellious Lombards. With great difficulty, he managed to reach the shelter of Pavia by alternative routes.

Becket, who received this news in late September or early October, was triumphant, seeing God's hand in the rout and interpreting Frederick's retreat in apocalyptic terms. "Look," he wrote triumphantly to Alexander, "at the man who did not make God his support, but relying on his own power, he expired in all his pride." Referring pointedly to the approaching mediators, he continued, "Who will dare in the future to obey the will of princes to the Church's shame, by not punishing wrongdoers? Let him dare it who will!"

Becket believed that the tables were about to be turned. Now was the time, he predicted, that "the presumption of tyrants, which seemed to have gained the day, may expire." The relief he felt was manifest, but would his optimism be justified by events?

BOTH SIDES PLACED their hopes on the papal mediators, but the negotiations were predestined to fail. Even before their meetings could begin, Henry was vehemently denouncing Becket as a traitor who had incited Louis to make war against him. And his refusal either to meet Becket or even to grant him a safe-conduct to enter his dominions meant that the mediators had to see him separately close to the Norman frontier, between Gisors and Trie. There, on November 18, 1167, they begged him to be reconciled to Henry without either preconditions or reference to the ancestral customs. The way forward, they suggested artfully, would be for Henry to quietly implement the customs and for Thomas to pretend not to notice them. Such conditions, they said, arose out of political necessity.

Herbert of Bosham, who alongside John of Salisbury and Alexander Llewelyn was representing the exiles at these preliminary conversations, was indignant. The customs, he insisted, "were the entire cause of the dispute [and] the root of all evil." At the Council of Clarendon, Becket "had been cheated and seduced to give his assent to them." Reconciliation could be achieved only by establishing "what had been wrongly done, according to the rule of civil law." So amazed was John of Salisbury at the idea that Becket should simply dissemble and tolerate the offending customs, he wondered whether the pope's envoys were being deliberately provocative, hoping that Thomas would lose his temper and so yield the high moral ground.

But if William and Otto believed they could cajole or bludgeon Thomas into submission, they would be disappointed. Set-piece encounters were the arena in which Becket had thrived since first representing Theobald at the papal curia in King Stephen's reign. Long accustomed to mingling with kings, popes, and cardinals, he relished this opportunity to state his case, speaking at length and in calm, eloquent Latin, offering to grant Henry whatever "was consistent with God's honor and the Church's liberty" before cutting straight to the heart of the matter.

The fact, he said, was that the king was seeking the confirmation of the ancestral customs, right or wrong. And yet none of Becket's predecessors as archbishop "had been compelled to make such a profession." Had not Pope Alexander condemned the most obnoxious of the customs at Sens two years before? "I have followed the pope's authority," Thomas declared, and will "never promise to obey customs patently opposed to God's law, repugnant to the privilege of the Holy See, [and] destructive of the Church's liberty." Nor would he accept a settlement that obliged him to turn a blind eye to the customs. "It is a proverb of our people," he reminded the mediators, "that 'silence implies consent,' and since the king would seem to be in possession of those customs, and would compel the church to observe them unjustly and by force if the onslaught on them already under way ceased by my silence . . . it would instantly appear to the king and to other folk that he had won his case." He then denied in the strongest terms that he had attempted to incite war between Henry and Louis as had been alleged.

Fresh from his canon law lessons at Pontigny with Master Lombard of Piacenza, Thomas then invoked an argument known as *exceptio spolii* (defense of despoliation) in order to checkmate Henry, claiming that he would not give any further answers until the sequestered lands and goods of the Canterbury exiles had been restored to them. When the king had made full restitution, he would gladly submit to whatever legal process the pope or his mediators decreed, but in the meantime he and his followers "could not be pressed to enter legal process, nor had they resources sufficient for the task." His plea stymied the papal envoys, who the next day sought an interview with Louis. The French king swore on oath that Becket, far from encouraging him to wage war, "had always given him counsel aimed at preserving peace." Unable to discredit Thomas by accusing him of disturbing the peace of Christendom deliberately, William and Otto had no choice but to return empty-handed to Henry, who had moved to Argentan. Hearing of their approach, he rode out to meet them, smiling broadly in anticipation of victory before escorting them to their lodgings. The next day, they were admitted to his chamber for two hours. On hearing how Becket had outwitted them, he was first speechless with rage, then flew into a blind fury before finally storming out, shouting, "I hope that I may never set eyes on a cardinal again."

Now the mediators saw Henry in his true colors. Left to find their way back alone to their lodgings on borrowed horses, they were all but imprisoned for several days, until on November 29—while the king deliberately went out hawking at the crack of dawn so as to snub them—a delegation led by Roger of Pont l'Évêque, Gilbert Foliot, and Hilary of Chichester arrived. Describing the scene with unconcealed relish, John of Salisbury says that Foliot delivered a violent, graceless, tactless speech attacking the incredulous William and Otto for their ignorance or incompetence in failing to call Becket to account. He added that Henry intended to take matters into his own hands by reviving his old charges of embezzlement and false accounting against the archbishop. As at the Council of Northampton in 1164, the king would demand £30,000—the entire sum that Thomas was believed to have handled as chancellor under the license allowing him to handle money without filing detailed accounts. In a clumsy attempt at black humor, Foliot quipped that Becket was so arrogant, he seemed to think that "just as sins are forgiven in baptism, so debts are waived on promotion." No one laughed, but when the mediators were at last permitted to leave on December 5 and Henry belatedly put in an appearance, weeping crocodile tears in one final effort to persuade them to depose or suspend Becket, Otto barely managed to suppress a guffaw.

The trouble, John of Salisbury warned Becket, was that it was no laughing matter. Even if Henry had been checkmated this time, it counted for nothing, since he was so angry, he "seems to want nothing else but your head on a plate." If anything, the position was worse than a year before. This really might become a struggle to the death. Otto wrote to Pope Alexander to say that he was so shocked by Henry's attitude, he would take no further part in any attempts to suspend or depose Becket. But the envoys, before they left, did succumb to Henry's plea to absolve those excommunicated at Vézelay without forcing them to restore the sequestered church property. To Becket, this was scandalous, but he could do nothing about it.

WHEN THE MEDIATORS departed, the initiative reverted to the papal curia. Becket could only watch helplessly from the sidelines as Henry was distracted throughout 1168 by fresh revolts in Poitou, where the barons resented his efforts to replace local administrators with his own officials and change their customs in favor of those of Normandy. Raising an army of mercenaries, Henry attacked the rebel strongholds, laying waste the countryside with fire and the sword before placing his garrisons in strategic places and returning to Poitiers. There he left Eleanor, now past the age of childbearing, to rule as regent in his absence under the watchful eye of Earl Patrick of Salisbury, one of the greatest landowners in the southwest of England, who had long supported the Angevins. As Easter approached, she was ambushed by the rebels while out riding. Saved by Earl Patrick's bravery, she managed to escape, but he was captured and assassinated—killed "the Poitevin way," by a sword thrust in the back.

In Italy, meanwhile, the Lombard League, opposed to the schismatic Frederick, gained in strength, culminating in an ambush on him by the citizens of Susa. Disguised as a servant, Frederick was forced to flee to Savoy under cover of night across the Mont Cenis pass. Still fearful for his own safety with the Germans on the loose, Pope Alexander would remain in the safety of Benevento for two more years, but his confidence was rising as support for the antipope, Paschal, waned. Beleaguered in Rome, Paschal was now at the mercy of the Lombard League. Seeing what was shortly to come, Frederick briefly contemplated switching sides. In the event, however, he decided to continue the schism, but when Paschal died and Calixtus III was nominated in his place, few votes would be cast in Calixtus's favor.

Frederick's enfeeblement further weakened Henry, enabling Alexander to fend off another of his embassies. The Angevin king's response was typically to bribe and threaten his way out of a corner, offering money to the cardinals and cities of the Lombard League, smooth talk and cash subsidies to the pope. When these failed, his ambassadors turned to threats and unashamed blackmail, pretending that Henry would convert to Islam if Thomas were not deposed or suspended as archbishop. Incensed by this, Becket sent two of his clerks to the papal curia to protest, but to his chagrin they too were kept at bay. Alexander still had to prevaricate. He was only strong enough to act as a juggler. To Henry, who faced yet another revolt from the Bretons after returning from the south, he offered just enough, extending the revocation of Becket's disciplinary powers for another year and wondering aloud whether he might be able to move him voluntarily to a different diocese. To Thomas, he gave a counsel of perfection. The archbishop was not to agree to anything "which leads to the abasement and reduction of the church's liberty." Instead, he must strain every nerve to make his peace with Henry and recover the king's love, surely impossible in the current state of play.

Resuming the search for a settlement on May 22, 1168, Alexander identified a pool of eminent monastic leaders to begin a fresh round of arbitration. Overseen chiefly by Simon, prior of Mont-Dieu and a friend and correspondent of John of Salisbury, and Bernard de la Coudre, prior of Le Bois de Vincennes, whom Henry already knew and respected, they were armed with letters that included a papal ultimatum, to be handed to the king at their discretion. But with the pope still in Benevento, Becket at Sens, and Henry with his army on the road, the time needed for couriers to shuttle between them all was several months. Even while the pope was still framing his plan and long before the necessary documents could be delivered, Henry was again at war with Louis, who had begun to cherish the hope of the disintegration of the Angevin empire by entering into a dangerous confederacy with his rival's rebels.

The breakthrough came at Epiphany 1169 (January 6–7), when Louis decided that Henry had pummeled him enough and the arbitrators brought Thomas before the two kings at their peace conference. Camping outdoors in a field beneath the hilltop frontier town of Montmirail, forty or so miles equidistant from Le Mans and Chartres so that neither would be dependent on the other's hospitality, the two kings pitched their pavilions on level ground at opposite ends of the field, aiming to settle relations between them for the next generation. Their retinues were camped in tents nearby, in the shadow of the castle, with its thick walls and notorious dungeons. The entire area was swarming with men, horses, carts, and equipment; the air for miles around was thick with smoke from the campfires, as it was a freezing winter.

Frederick sent a German delegation to the conference. It was led by Henry the Lion, Duke of Saxony and Bavaria, whose marriage to Henry and Eleanor's eldest daughter, Matilda, had now been celebrated. With the emperor lobbying for the Angevins, the pressure was on Louis to make concessions, but King Henry too wanted peace. Although only thirty-five and at the height of his powers, he was eager to settle the succession to his vast empire and had decided to divide it between his three eldest sons, who were all present. By artfully playing the role of a suppliant—offering to renew his homage for his continental dominions to the impressionable Louis, while ingeniously hinting that, if only a reconciliation with Becket could be reached, he would take the cross and journey to the East—he smoothed relations between them. The result was a dynastic accord whereby Prince Henry, rising fourteen, and his French bride would inherit England, Normandy, Maine, and Anjou. Richard, who was to be betrothed to Louis's daughter, Alix, sister of Prince Henry's wife, Margaret, would succeed to his mother's lands in Aquitaine. Finally, Geoffrey would have Brittany, but would first do homage for it to his brother Henry. In return, Louis agreed to legitimize Henry's conquests in Brittany and stop sending aid to his Poitevin and Breton rebels, while to put the seal on the settlement, Henry promised to expedite the coronation of Prince Henry and his wife.

Such a wide-ranging agreement promised the younger Henry and his Capetian wife the peaceful succession to all the Angevin territories except Aquitaine, while offering Louis the enticing prospect that his young son, Philip, would one day preside over a family consortium controlling a significant proportion of France. That is why, after a lull lasting just over a year, a reconciliation with Becket had suddenly become extremely urgent. It was the primate's undoubted right, despite Roger of Pont l'Évêque's counterclaims, to crown the younger Henry and his bride. Without this final piece of the puzzle, the terms of the accord would always remain contested and incomplete.

IN PREPARATION for his audience before the two kings, Thomas had to be carefully coached, for the papal arbitrators were painfully aware that Henry would insist that his "honor" be upheld. Becket would need "to submit himself in every way to the king's will and mercy . . . and unreservedly so." In particular, he had to agree—much against his better judgment—to observe the disputed customs, "if only verbally." Exerting maximum moral pressure on him while they had him in their care, the arbitrators kept insisting that the peace and security of Christendom, not to mention Pope Alexander's reputation, depended on his compliance. If things went wrong and Thomas fluffed his lines, there would be no safety net for the church.

Although by now physically and mentally worn down, the exiled archbishop was only too aware that this formula was exactly the same as the one offered to him at Woodstock by Abbot Philip of L'Aumône on the eve of the Council of Clarendon—which Henry had signally failed to honor—and arguably worse than the one suggested by William and Otto, who had recommended that he should simply turn a blind eye to the ancestral customs. So, mindful of Pope Alexander's counsel of perfection, he said he wanted to add the proviso "saving God's honor" to the words of assent. The arbitrators were dismayed, painfully aware from their discussions with Henry's advisers that he saw no difference between that phrase and "saving my order"—the mantra that had already driven him to apoplexy. After going round in circles with Thomas for several hours, with the arbitrators cajoling and threatening, wielding carrot and stick, they finally won him over.

He yielded only because, unlike William and Otto, these were spiritual leaders of genuine charisma and distinction, and because, after the long years and months since his flight from Northampton, he had become a shadow of his former self. Though but forty-eight, he was pale and gaunt-faced, thin as a knife, prone to bouts of depression, and ravaged by a crippling sense of failure and isolation. He also felt a deep sense of foreboding.

To Thomas, this was now only partly a dispute over the ancestral customs and increasingly a quarrel about Henry's innate assumption that his will was law. As Arnulf of Lisieux had observed, when the Angevin king considered something hotly contested—such as the ancestral customs—to be essential, he automatically assumed it must be legal. His speeches in the Battle Abbey case had already shown that he had a vision of the world in which the church, and perhaps even the pope, must submit to him whenever their opinions clashed with his own. Becket fervently believed that if someone did not take a stand, Henry's legacy would become a scourge to future generations. He had already told one of his clerks that if the king's ideas went unopposed, the fruits would be transmitted to his heirs, from whose hands it would be impossible to wrest them. "We do not know yet," he mused, "what the end of it will be . . . since there will be no one who can hold in check or limit the crimes of the tyrants, whose whole aim at present is to attack God's church and its ministers: nor will they desist until they have reduced them to slavery."

So when the time came for Thomas to be escorted down to the field to face Henry on his knees, in the presence of Louis and their assembled advisers, he knew that he had to be true to himself. When Henry said that no more was expected of him beyond his verbal consent to the ancestral customs, he began the memorized speech that had been so carefully scripted for him by the arbitrators: "On the subject which divides us, my lord king, I throw myself on your mercy and your pleasure, here in the presence of our lord king of France and the bishops, nobles, and others standing here." He said he was prepared to observe the customs to win peace and favor, and to do all that he could in accordance with Henry's will. But then, to general shock and astonishment, his tone of abject humility suddenly changed to one of defiance as the ascetic, rebel's instinct in him once more asserted itself, and he added the forbidden words "saving God's honor." Precisely when he decided to do this, we do not know, but it was probably at the very last moment after Herbert of Bosham whispered something in his ear.

Henry, feeling utterly humiliated, inveighed against him, bawling insults and accusing him of being proud, vain, and forgetful of the king's generosity. "I will never accept these words," he fumed, "or it will appear that the archbishop wishes God's honor preserved and not I—though I really want it preserved more than he does." Addressing Louis, he declared:

> See how foolishly and proudly this man has deserted his church, not driven out by me, but secretly running off by night. He would persuade you that he is a champion for the church, and by this ruse has deceived people both many and great. But I have always allowed and wished, as I still do, that he should hold and govern the church over which he presides in the full liberty in which any of his five saintly predecessors ruled.

He then called Becket a traitor. At this Louis scowled, seeing his daughter Margaret's coronation as a future Angevin queen fast disappearing into the distance. He asked Thomas tersely, "Lord archbishop, do you wish to be more than a saint?"

FOR A FLEETING moment until Becket uttered the fatal proviso, it had seemed to the exiles as if a settlement would be reached and they would be allowed home, but their hopes had been cruelly dashed. Aghast at the scene they had just witnessed, many burst into tears and criticized Thomas bitterly, but the truth is that failure was almost inevitable. Neither king nor archbishop had set eyes on each other since their fiery clashes in the great hall at Northampton. Neither was sufficiently prepared to set aside their differences, since neither could yet bring himself to modify his own preconceived vision of the world.

The negotiations continued until after dusk, which in early January fell shortly after four o'clock in the afternoon, but the papal arbitrators, whom Henry cursed for allowing Becket to get away with a volte-face similar to the one he had performed at Clarendon, failed in their efforts to save the talks. When it was too dark to see any longer, the two kings rose abruptly, mounted their horses, and rode from the field lit by torches. Thomas was left standing alone in the biting cold, for even his own clerks were reluctant to be seen in his company.

To Pope Alexander and the cardinals, Thomas gave a succinct explanation. It was, he said, a thing unheard-of that any bishop should be compelled to bind himself to a secular prince beyond the limits of the formula of fealty. "It will set a dangerous example for other princes, not only in our own time but in our successors' times. . . . If the customs which he demands were to prevail, it is clear that the authority of the Apostolic See would either disappear from England or be reduced to a minimum." Becket had formed a view of Henry's character that led him to believe it was the king's intention to dominate the church to a degree not achieved even by Frederick Barbarossa. Anyone who got in his way he would seek to have removed.

And yet Thomas still yearned for peace, for the sake of his companions and their families as much as for himself, but most of all for the safety of his beloved church of Canterbury, which he knew was being systemically despoiled by cruel, greedy men of the world like Ranulf de Broc and his nephew. With this in mind, he wrote humbly to Henry reiterating his willingness to serve him faithfully, "saving my order." "I remember that I am bound by my oath of fealty to preserve your life, limbs, and all earthly honor," he said, "and I am prepared to do whatever I can for you, according to God, as for my dearest lord. God knows that I have never served you more willingly than I shall in the future, if it should please you." The letter went unanswered.

Henry, predictably, cast all the blame onto Thomas. Since he had caused the wound, the king said, he should offer the cure. The trouble was that the latest deadline set by the pope for restoring the archbishop's disciplinary powers was fast approaching. What would Becket do? Would he make another grand gesture as at Vézelay, this time excommunicating the king? If he did, would Alexander support him, and if so, could he be outflanked? How would Louis react? And if the peace accord stayed intact, how was Henry to engineer his eldest son's coronation?

As the exiles rode away, battered and bruised, to their refuge at the abbey of Sainte-Colombe at Sens, they debated where they might seek shelter in the future, fearing that Louis would shortly withdraw his protection and expel them. The most popular suggestion was to move south to Provence in search of a sanctuary beyond either king's reach.

Suddenly, in what seemed like a miracle, a messenger arrived, summoning Thomas to the French court. Unbeknownst to the exiles, the peace accord was faltering, as Henry, believing Louis to be safely neutralized, began to exact vengeance on those of his rebels who had aligned themselves with the Capetian king. In Aquitaine, he stormed their castles, ignoring Eleanor, who was still technically regent, and leaving his prisoners to die of hunger chained to the walls of their dungeons, while on the frontier of the Vexin, he ordered his troops to dig a great ditch to secure his lands from border raids.

With Henry's stardust no longer in his eyes, Louis came to think that Becket had been right in the past to denounce the Angevin king as a man incapable of honoring the letter or the spirit of his agreements for longer than suited his purposes. Now he told Thomas that he believed the papal arbitrators at Montmirail, and perhaps Pope Alexander himself, had been equally blind or misled. "I promise you," he said, "I will not fail you or your people, as long as with God's favor I live." And to everyone's astonishment, he threw himself on his knees before the exiled archbishop, confessing that Becket alone had spoken the truth at Montmirail and requesting his forgiveness for having doubted him.

With Louis once more pledging his protection and fortune's wheel spinning round again, Thomas recovered his spirits. He knew that he might go down, but he would go down fighting. Soon he would be writing to his friends at the papal curia to say that in the cause of freedom, he would prefer to die in exile rather than see the church of Canterbury profaned, for in his mind Henry had become a latter-day King Stephen, and there was no more room for dissembling. When a "greed inflamed with avarice" like Henry's, he declared prophetically, was allowed to run unchecked, then "dissimulation" in the cause of peace, far from ending the dispute, would merely embolden the tyrant-king to engage in more of his evil deeds. "It would be better," said Thomas, "for us not to have been born than to have brought the contagion of so dangerous an example into the church."

The search for a settlement had failed; a trial of strength was still to come.

23

THE CASE AGAINST BECKET

WHEN THOMAS BECKET HAD FLED INTO EXILE IN HIS HASTE to escape Henry's clutches, he had crossed a second Rubicon even wider and deeper than the first when summoned to court to become the king's chancellor. At the Council of Northampton in 1164, he had appealed to Pope Alexander without first seeking royal approval as the ancestral customs codified at Clarendon had explicitly required, surely his most heinous offense in Henry's eyes. And by his indecision and sudden changes of tack at both Clarendon and Northampton, he had antagonized his rivals Roger of Pont l'Évêque and Gilbert Foliot, also severely testing the patience of those who would otherwise remain his supporters, such as Henry of Winchester.

Given the waves he had created, it is hardly surprising that the slippery Arnulf of Lisieux should now step out of the shadows to admonish him. Always eager to defend the liberties of the church while staying on the right side of Henry, he begins his widely circulated critique by praising Thomas for seeking to protect the righteous but ends by urging him to compromise, equivocate, and dissemble. Rebuking him for his sudden flight across the Channel, Arnulf mocks him for his naïveté in assuming that he had successfully made his escape through his own efforts. Had the king wished to prevent it, "no calm breeze, no favorable winds, no peaceful sea, no diligent sailors would have carried you away, for everywhere the hand of royal power would confront you." Arnulf urges

Becket to stop playing games and consider the awesome power of the ruler he has chosen as his adversary. Is he not aware that Alexander and the cardinals—far from being eager sympathizers set on joining him in his fight for "liberty"—find him to be tiresome, frankly a thorough nuisance, who has been a repeated obstacle to harmony between church and state?

Associating Henry implicitly with Christ himself, Arnulf asks how Thomas could turn against a divine-right king as if he were an unruly son rebelling against his father or a disobedient sheep rebelling against its shepherd, and with such uncloaked rancor. Does he not realize that if by any mischance, he were actually to gain his ends and successfully weaken or destroy Henry's kingship, neither the name of "liberty" nor any semblance of it would survive, since so much confusion would ensue that civil order would instantly yield to anarchy?

Becket, continues Arnulf, is doubtless aware that he has made himself into something of a people's darling for his outspoken resistance to the king. But he should never rely on the support of mere commoners. He should know that "none of them would dare to confess himself your friend." Instead, to avoid public outlawry or deportation like the exiles and Becket's own relations, "they will bring up old causes of enmity against you, so that their hatred of you will be more readily believed." As to the great and the good, upon whom Becket had lavished such care and attention as chancellor, he will never succeed in converting them to the vision of the world for which he stands, for they will form a "confederacy," stopping at nothing to advance their own interests or increase their wealth.

The archbishop's blind spot, Arnulf suggests, is that he simply cannot grasp how unwise it is to upset so many important people all at once. Invoking the old superstition that resistance to the king is both treason and sacrilege, he argues that after Thomas resigned the chancellorship and begged Henry to mend his ways, he should have left it to God to do the work of reformation. "Make peace with the king and do not appear to be quibbling in a pettifogging way" is the gist of his message. "Justice" and "virtue" are all very well, but "fortune" and "person" should also be taken into account. "If there is any debate about peace, do not discuss each clause with excessive subtlety, for exactness produces contention and contention excites and ignites the dangerous flames of hatred." Consider the bigger picture and the damage that will accrue to the church if you persist in your quarrel, he cautions. Otherwise, the inference will be that you are psychologically driven to make it appear that nobody is able to resist your power or will, and thus proving that you are as much a tyrant as you claim Henry to be, driven by the old pride and egotism of which you were once accused as chancellor.

THOUGH SEARING for its recipient, Arnulf's critique would be the mere tickling of a feather compared to that of Gilbert Foliot. Now Henry's chief spiritual guide and the most intellectually daunting of Thomas's opponents, Foliot was nicknamed "Judas" by Becket and compared to Achitophel, King David's wicked counselor in the Old Testament, by John of Salisbury. An archetypal villain driven by a mixture of jealousy and ambition, Achitophel had advised the king's son Absalom, to whose faction he defected, to commit open incest with his father's wives, followed by armed rebellion and patricide. When Achitophel knew his plot was doomed, he returned home and hanged himself (2 Samuel: 16–17). According to John, he had risen from hell in the guise of Foliot to plague the faithful.

For rather more than a year after his flight into exile, Thomas, despite their venomous clashes at Northampton, had nursed hopes of reconciling with Gilbert, attempting to appeal to the spiritual side of his character. "Choose to take pride in Christ rather than in the things of the earth, to put greater trust in the Lord than in the seductions of the world," he had entreated him early in 1166 from Pontigny. And there were reasons Foliot might have responded. Never an ultraroyalist, notably where criminous clerks were concerned, he shared many of the same principles as John of Salisbury and Herbert of Bosham and helped lead the assault on Henry's interpretation of the ancestral customs at Clarendon until Becket cut the ground from under his feet.

Personalities were the root of the problem. Foliot loathed and despised Becket, saying of him at Northampton, "He always was a fool and always will be." His enmity would prove lethal for Thomas, since (as contemporaries remarked) Foliot was "armed with eloquence." After the Vézelay excommunications in June 1166, when on Henry's orders he had led the bishops in appealing to the pope to annul Becket's sentences, he attempted to discredit the archbishop in the eyes of all Christendom, sending him a humble petition that in reality was a coruscating manifesto denouncing him. Widely circulated and surviving in multiple copies, this document purports to be a collaborative effort by all the bishops and clergy of England, but John of Salisbury saw immediately from its slick style and selective quotations that it was Achitophel's handiwork alone.

From its opening sentence on, the piece is thoroughly disingenuous—or at least so it appears now to anyone with access to all the available source materials. At the time, to the many uninitiated onlookers, and especially to those in the Angevin dominions who were able or allowed to hear only Foliot's version of the story, his arguments seemed devastating in their force. "We were hoping," his manifesto begins grandiloquently, "that what was thrown into confusion at the beginning of your unexpected departure to distant parts would, with the help of God's grace, be restored to its original serenity through your humility and prudence." Foliot explains how word has reached him that Becket is applying himself diligently to reading and prayers during his "self-imposed" stay at Pontigny, "redeeming the loss of past and present time with fasting, vigils, and tears." What a disappointment it is, therefore, to discover that, for some unknown reason, Henry has received a threatening letter from Thomas, followed by the unfathomable suggestion that he too might shortly be excommunicated.

How can that be, when Henry is the living embodiment of sweet reasonableness, a man renowned for his piety and gentleness, justice and courtesy, whose generous heart desires nothing more than to be told if and when he has done something wrong? "We do not say that the lord king has never sinned," claims Foliot in a much-vaunted passage taking sycophancy, understatement, and the art of rhetorical redescription to heights hitherto unexplored, "but we do say and confidently proclaim in public that he is always prepared to make amends to the Lord."

A well-connected Norman aristocrat with cousins in high places all over Henry's empire, Foliot concludes with a thinly veiled sneer at his adversary's lowly parentage. Everyone has heard "how kind our lord the king was to you; to what renown he raised you up from poverty and received you into his intimate favor." How can Thomas find it within himself to show such ingratitude in return? Would he not do better to resign his archbishopric and continue to be praised for "voluntary poverty" than to be universally condemned for hypocrisy? Has not Henry raised him up from nothing, hoping to thrive with his counsel and support? "If instead he receives a battle-ax where he was hoping for security, what reports of you will be on everyone's lips? How will the story of such an unprecedented betrayal go down in history?"

ON RECEIVING a copy of this feline document from a close friend, John of Salisbury did not mince words. How, he asks with knowing irony, could anyone find it in his conscience to be so bold, so impudent, and so meretricious with the facts as to maintain Henry's innocence, "when his injustices are in everyone's mouth, whose acts of craft and violence the whole world knows"? Such an author scripts lines that a professional jester cannot speak without shame. Achitophel, like his Old Testament counterpart, is so brazen, he condemns himself out of his own mouth.

John felt nothing but contempt that a man of Foliot's intelligence and erudition could seriously envisage anyone being simple or naïve enough to be fooled by his spiderweb of deception. Has he not the lewdness of a prostitute, the impudence of a charlatan, the hide of a rhinoceros not to blush when he proclaims that Henry desires nothing more than to be told if and when he has done something wrong, when his acts of oppression are abominated by the whole Christian world?

Reading Foliot persuaded John that Henry was being advised by wolves in sheep's clothing, men who would settle for nothing short of Becket's destruction and the church's enslavement, leading him to drop many of his earlier reservations about his friend's more impetuous or ill-advised actions. Unnerved by the lengthy diplomatic deadlock after the excommunications at Vézelay, he had been urging Thomas to recapture the initiative by summoning Henry of Winchester and some of the other more sympathetic bishops to his presence, so he could explain to them face-to-face the frustrations he had suffered in his efforts to bring Henry to the negotiating table, while at the same time educating them in the king's many tricks and subterfuges.

Becket, however, was ahead of him, publishing his own *pièce justificative* that answered Foliot's accusations one by one, and in the process giving a long and detailed history of the quarrel since its inception. This he quickly followed up with a shorter, more personal letter, a document he made sure would be leaked by his clerks so that everyone could read it, ratcheting up the pressure by including a vitriolic accusation of cowardice against Achitophel that, more than anything else he had said so far about him, was meant to lance. What it seems had stung him most were Foliot's swipes at his parentage.

"It's a matter of the greatest astonishment, stupefying in fact," Thomas begins, "that someone like you, a prudent man, ostensibly learned and a monk, should so blatantly—not to say irreverently—deny truth, resist justice, and in every possible way ignore the difference between right and wrong." You call yourself a follower of Christ? You will find that it is not so. "A fierce storm is violently shaking the boat. I hold the tiller and you call me to sleep. You conjure up and place before my eyes the favors conferred on me by our lord the king, and you remind me that I was raised up to the heights from poverty." What poverty is Foliot thinking of? What lowly ancestry?

As to the charge of ingratitude, "I call God to witness that I put nothing under the sun before the king's grace and salvation." Foliot, Becket avows, is like a blind man giving directions to the sighted. "You say that the king is ready to make amends and always has been: this you state with confidence, this you say you are proclaiming. So hold still for a moment and answer this question. In what sense do you understand your proposition that he is 'prepared to make amends'?" All the world, says Thomas, can see the treatment meted out to the exiles by Henry, who has dragged innocent orphans, widows, and children from their homes; sent priests and clerks penniless across the sea; and then pillaged their property. "You remain mute; you see your mother, the church of Canterbury, despoiled of her goods, and you do not resist. You see me, your pastor, having scarcely escaped the swords hanging over my neck, and you do not grieve—but what is far worse, you do not blush to stand with my persecutors against me."

* * *

NEVER A MAN to be reproached by anyone he regarded as an upstart, Foliot returned to the attack with a blistering broadside. Not rediscovered until the eighteenth century, it would first be published in full by George, Lord Lyttelton, in an appendix to the fourth and final volume of his *History of the Life of King Henry the Second* (1767–71). Since then it has been seized upon by generations of lazy historians, who ought to have known better, as a conveniently prepackaged, purportedly independent assessment of the Becket quarrel by an educated eyewitness. An anticlerical politician whose hero was Henry, Lyttelton could hardly believe his luck in being one of the first to stumble onto such a trophy in the voluminous collections of the famous Jacobean antiquary Sir Robert Cotton. He believed what the document said, but publication stirred up a hornets' nest, and its authenticity was hotly contested. Subsequently denounced by Catholic and Anglo-Catholic writers as a brilliant forgery, its credibility was questioned as late as 1943 by an eminent French scholar, who claimed it to be a parody or literary squib (possibly by John of Salisbury) in the style of Jonathan Swift. Only in 1951, when copies were traced back to reliable twelfth- and thirteenth-century manuscripts in Oxford and the British Library, was it finally accepted as genuine.

Presented in the form of a classical declamation or speech meant to win over its audience by its sheer force of eloquence, Foliot's tirade, usually known by its opening words, *Multiplicem Nobis* (A Labyrinthine Argument Before Us), is a triumph of the rhetorician's art. Unlike many of Becket's own more rambling narratives, its story has the beauty of elegant simplicity.

As Foliot claims, Thomas, after corruptly obtaining the chancellorship despite his lack of qualifications, coveted the primacy, persuading Henry to abuse his kingly power by ordering Becket's selection at unprecedented speed, so that someone whose chief credentials were to have "plunged a sword deep into the bowels of holy mother Church" by levying taxes and scutages to lead an army to Toulouse would be chosen. Thus it was that someone "fresh from the enjoyment of birds and hounds and the other delights of the court" would almost the very next day be celebrating mass in his own cathedral, presiding over the church courts, and issuing spiritual guidance to the most learned priests and bishops of the realm, despite his own fabled ignorance of theology.

Scarcely had a few months elapsed, resumes Foliot, than Becket—rash, brash, arrogant, and supercilious as he was—allowed his obsessions to run riot, turning everything topsy-turvy and creating sparks that soon flared up into an inferno. To calm things down, "meetings were assembled and councils called." Chief among these was the Council of Clarendon, where Henry attempted to restore order by calling for the observance of some "customs." These, Foliot candidly concedes, "appeared in some cases to stifle the liberty of the church," but Henry "vehemently demanded that we promise to observe them without any reservation." Accordingly, the bishops stood fearless and unwavering against them. Even when locked up for two full days and threatened with physical violence, they refused to bend. And yet, crows Foliot, "what was the response to this? Who fled? Who turned tail? Whose spirit was broken?"

Far from the bishops showing cowardice, it was "the captain of the army" who yielded to Henry's intimidation. "The leader of the camp fled, the lord of Canterbury withdrew from the association and advice of his brethren and, after reflecting on the matter on his own, he returned to us later and burst out with these words: 'It is Christ's will that I should forswear myself; I submit for the present and incur the guilt of perjury, to do penance in the future as far as I can.'"

Scandalous as that volte-face may have been, at least (Foliot maintains) it brought a prospect of peace, raising hopes that "what our lord king was demanding under the temporary sway of anger would be restored to a good state . . . when his passion had cooled." Becket, unfortunately, is a warmonger unable to restrain himself. Swiftly recanting his concessions and attempting to flee abroad, he flouted one of the cardinal customs to which he had just bound himself—that he should never leave the country without a royal license. No one, on hearing of this betrayal, could have been more taken aback or disappointed than Henry, not least since such a move could damage his own reputation. Would not the commoners, in their woeful ignorance, begin to wonder whether, in a fit of rage, he had become a tyrant and exiled his archbishop out of hatred for Christ? In reality, claims Foliot, the true extent of the king's moderation would be proved when, with the archbishop's vessel forced to return to shore by unfavorable winds (in reality, the sailors under the command of Adam of Charing had mutinied for fear of royal reprisals), Henry had welcomed him back "with kindness" rather than severity, allowing him safe passage home to his church at Canterbury, "honored with fitting respect."

"When," asks Foliot—now conveniently forgetting everything he has just said about Henry's bullying tactics at Clarendon—"did the king ever give way to his anger or his power or act unreasonably against you, or even say anything harsh?"

Foliot portrays Henry as an affable prince, "whom the sweetest children, the most noble and honorable wife, the many realms subject to him" could scarcely restrain from his overwhelming desire to abandon the world and all his goods and "go naked after his Lord Jesus carrying his cross." Such a man asks no more of his archbishop than that he should "show him the affection and kindness of his heart." Like a disobedient child, however, Thomas sulks and squirms, spoiling for a fight, so that when John the Marshal makes a "reasonable" claim in the Canterbury court, the archbishop brushes him aside like the autocrat he always is, forcing Henry to call him to account before a great council of the barons in the castle at Northampton.

Steadily moving in for the kill, Foliot slams Becket for submitting himself to the king's judgment and finding sureties in John the Marshal's case, accusing him of defying the very same principles on which Foliot and Thomas were once perfectly agreed—that criminous clerks are immune from secular jurisdiction. Foliot then harangues Thomas for failing to mollify Henry, as he ought to have done as a loyal archbishop and former chancellor, on the more serious charges of embezzlement and false accounting, before finally appealing to Pope Alexander.

Of course, there is a massive inconsistency here. If Becket goes against canon law by accepting judgment in Henry's court in John the Marshal's case, how can it also be that he is delinquent by refusing to be bamboozled by the king's trumped-up charges of embezzlement? How, likewise, can it be that if he is pusillanimous and subservient at Clarendon for yielding to the customs while the bishops stand firm like a rock, he is rebellious and intransigent at Northampton for standing his ground and appealing to the pope?

Foliot's most credible and cutting claim is that by impetuously fleeing into exile, in disguise and by night, abandoning his pastoral obligations while encouraging others to risk their lives to save the liberties of the church, Thomas has himself behaved like a coward. "What did you achieve by these actions, except that you very carefully avoided the death which no one thought to inflict?" Here the accuser has a palpable hit: Thomas is like a shepherd who refuses to lay down his life for his sheep. Relentlessly pressing home his advantage, Foliot adds that by his excommunications at Vézelay, it would appear that Becket is more concerned for his lost lands and revenues than with caring for his flock. "Are your annual revenues so important to you that you wish to acquire them by the blood of your brothers? Even the Jews spurned Judas when he came to them with the price of blood, throwing it back in his face."

Taking the high moral ground and assuming the mantle of peacemaker, Foliot urges Thomas—as it would seem more in sorrow than in anger—to reconsider the issues in a calmer, cooler, more discerning way. Surely, he insists, no question of faith or morals, ethics or the sacraments arises. Neither has heresy or schism. All that has really happened, he insinuates, is that Henry has sometimes allowed himself to get somewhat carried away by an innate but understandable desire to observe the customs of his grandfather. To these, he clings like a clam from a well-intentioned, if occasionally misguided, sense of honor. Is this, Foliot inquires, the cause for which Becket is willing to turn his country and much of the rest of Christendom upside down?

For most of his contemporaries, Foliot's argument would have carried immense weight. Few were sufficiently versed in the true extent of Henry's wheeling and dealing to be sure that Thomas had a genuine grievance. And by charging the exiled archbishop, here and elsewhere, with issuing threats and acting as tyrannically as he was himself accusing Henry of behaving, Foliot touched a nerve. In the eyes of many laymen, Becket's vulnerability was identical to that identified in the papacy by the more vocal critics of the ascetic reform movement. Although the popes since the time of Leo IX and Gregory VII had successfully rebranded themselves as the supreme leaders of a Christian community ordered by moral considerations, they claimed to be answerable to God alone for their own moral purity. They sought to liberate the church from any interference in its internal affairs by the representatives of society at large, while at the same time claiming the right to interfere in the affairs of the secular kingdoms on moral and spiritual grounds.

Arguing the case for the monarchy, Foliot echoes Arnulf of Lisieux by reiterating that Henry was a divine-right king responsible to God for maintaining civil order. As he pungently chides Becket, royal and priestly power, properly exercised, must complement and support each other. Delivering what he believes to be the coup de grâce, he says that Thomas is a bishop who lacks "holy humility." His zeal, his pride, his petulance, his obstinacy, his contempt for the views of others cause him to censure Henry for doing what any responsible ruler would rightly believe to be his prime kingly duty.

Written in energetic, forceful, supple Latin prose, Foliot's broadside is a bravura performance, refocusing the controversy from Henry's viewpoint and winning many of the waverers over to his side. Numerous facts are twisted, several arguments disingenuous or illogical, but the accusations leveled at the exiled archbishop that he was himself as cowardly and autocratic as he claimed Henry and his cronies to be would prove damaging and deeply embarrassing. Becket, so far as anyone is aware, simply refused to reply. Perhaps wisely, he realized that attempting to do so would only give wider publicity to Foliot's case for the prosecution. Perhaps he also accepted that as a less proficient rhetorician and Latinist than his rival, he was outclassed. He may have calculated that as the waverers came to understand Henry's true nature better in the stalemate years after the Vézelay excommunications, they would discover how misplaced, inaccurate, and fundamentally dishonest Foliot's underlying characterization of the royal tyrant really was.

Only John of Salisbury could have rivaled the ease and subtlety with which Foliot elides crushing attack with elegiac reproach, blending them like light and shade in the fashion of a landscape artist. But the closest he would come to referring to Foliot's diatribe was to declare of the Old Testament Achitophel that he "has had many successors in his counsels, who pervert the minds of princes and devise and proclaim a poisoned counsel against God." Such men were like Ahab and Jezebel when they persecuted Elijah. "Wickedness has many devices and wiles" and "works in the skin of a vixen." Such was John's opinion, but since the Machiavellian traducer was now Henry's chief spiritual counselor, he did not dare, for fear of reprisals, to attack him by name as he had done before. Only after Becket's murder would the tables be irrevocably turned, and Foliot's accusation of cowardice would look decidedly hollow.

24
CAT AND MOUSE

THE COLLAPSE OF THE PEACE TALKS AT MONTMIRAIL NEED not have been conclusive. With King Louis on Becket's side again, Prior Simon and the other papal arbitrators brought Henry back to the negotiating table on February 7, 1169, at Saint-Léger-en-Yvelines, near Rambouillet in the French Vexin. John of Salisbury, an eyewitness, says that Henry wriggled and squirmed, making "many diverse and inconsistent replies," denying that he had expelled Thomas from his lands, and saying that he would gladly take him back "if he is willing to do as his predecessors had done, and to promise as much honestly and in good faith." Code for "observing the ancestral customs," whether written down or not, Henry's words meant that for him, nothing had changed. As Becket ruefully reflects, "He is seeking nothing from us apart from the observance of his customs. . . . He indeed changed the word, but did not change his intention." So the exasperated arbitrators finally served on Henry the papal ultimatum they had so far withheld, ordering him to restore both peace and property to Thomas and the exiles without further delay or risk the consequences.

Becket had no remaining doubts. Surely the time for talking was over, and it was time to act. With the deadline set by the pope for the restoration of his disciplinary powers fast approaching, he made lists of those he intended to censure. He planned to replicate his actions at Vézelay, choosing as his theater the Cistercian abbey of Clairvaux, where St. Bernard, its founder, had preached so many of his famous sermons. Nestling beside a stream in a densely forested valley on the border of Burgundy and Champagne, near Bar-sur-Aube, Clairvaux was less than three days' ride from Sainte-Colombe. Thomas arrived there shortly before Palm Sunday, the day marking the beginning of Holy Week, one of the most significant days of the church's calendar. This is the day that commemorates Christ's entry into Jerusalem riding a humble donkey and cheered on by the jubilant crowds who had come to welcome him, only to meet his death on the cross five days later.

To win maximum publicity for what he was poised to do, Thomas could not have chosen a better stage or a more auspicious day. Pilgrims lined the route to the abbey, watching the grand procession in which a statue of Christ mounted on a donkey made its way toward the church and saints' relics were carried aloft. Once the procession had entered the nave, Thomas mounted the pulpit, the air still thick with incense, and solemnly excommunicated Gilbert Foliot, the leading signatory to the bishops' appeal against the Vézelay sentences, and Jocelin of Salisbury, another of Foliot's allies, who had appointed the hated John of Oxford to a deanery in defiance of a papal prohibition, much to Thomas's disgust. Next, he excommunicated the seven principal sequestrators of the Canterbury estates, beginning with Ranulf de Broc and his nephew and giving notice that another six miscreants, including Richard de Lucy and Richard of Ilchester, would be sentenced on Ascension Day (May 29) unless they returned their misappropriated church lands before that date and made reparations.

With Pope Alexander safely beyond Frederick Barbarossa's reach at Benevento, the English bishops were warier than before of ignoring their obligations to censure and cast out from their community those whom their primate had excommunicated. Besides Henry of Winchester, those publishing Becket's sanctions in their dioceses were William of Norwich, Bartholomew of Exeter, and (most encouragingly for the exiles) Hilary of Chichester. Together with Roger of Worcester, to whom Becket wrote a personal appeal for support, they found the latest sentences too serious to pretend not to see, splitting the episcopate down the middle. Even Roger of Pont l'Évêque wavered, preferring not to disobey Thomas in case the pope took his side. Foliot alone was unmoved, declaring that his own London diocese had ancient metropolitan status, making it superior to Canterbury, which if true would have exempted him from Becket's jurisdiction—a fraudulent claim, relying on a single line in a long-forgotten letter of Pope Gregory the Great, written in the year 601.

Thomas wrote to Alexander asking for confirmation of the Clairvaux sentences. Little did he know that two of Henry's youngest, supplest, and most ingenious and ingratiating envoys, Reginald fitz Jocelin and Ralph of Llandaff, had already reached Benevento to give a wholly misleading account of the failure of the peace talks. With their words ringing in his ears, the pope had backtracked once more, commissioning two new curial officials, Vivian of Orvieto and Gratian of Pisa, both expert lawyers, as replacement ambassadors to begin the negotiations all over again. On May 10, in what must have seemed to Thomas like a bolt from the blue, Alexander wrote to inform him of their imminent departure, reiterating his counsel of perfection. "We ask and admonish you, brother," he said, "carefully to bear in mind the difficulties and evils of the time and . . . to strive by every means possible to recover the grace and love of the king as far as it can be done, saving your order and your office." Thomas had heard all this before. It was easy to say, impossible to achieve; and since the pope also instructed him to suspend his Clairvaux sentences pending the arrival of the ambassadors, he could only have felt abandoned and humiliated. For what else could he reasonably be expected to do as long as Henry insisted that he yield to ancestral customs that Alexander himself had pronounced "obnoxious"?

Plainly driven by second thoughts, Alexander sent another letter the very next day, its tone entirely different from the first, reassuring Thomas that this really would be a final throw of the diplomatic dice, and that if Henry could be shown to have resisted or obstructed the newly commissioned ambassadors, "the severity of due vengeance" could be exacted and the king excommunicated. His heart leaping at this news, Becket eagerly looked forward to meeting the envoys. Vivian, a trusted servant of the pope, he found to be inscrutable, but Gratian, a nephew of Pope Eugenius III and a former student of civil and canon law at Bologna (not to be confused with the author of the *Decretum*), was well-known to the exiles and an old friend of John of Salisbury. They had first met during one of John's missions to the pope on Theobald's behalf in King Stephen's reign. Herbert of Bosham also knew him, rejoicing that the pope had sent "a man truly gracious in name and deed," who, he said, would refuse all Henry's bribes and blandishments.

The ambassadors had reached France by July 22, when John made a pilgrimage to Vézelay to greet them, chatting with them in the abbey's garden and establishing that, on balance, they favored Thomas and that should the new talks fail, his friend would indeed be free to strike against the king.

After meeting Becket at Sainte-Colombe in the last week of July, the envoys were forced to kick their heels until Henry, who was fighting again in Aquitaine, put in an appearance. Their first series of meetings with him took place at Argentan, Domfront, Bayeux, and Bur-le-Roi between August 15 and September 2, while the royal court wended its way slowly around Normandy. Ever restless, eager now to shift his attention to Brittany again and so looking for a quick fix, Henry at first took a gentler, subtler, more emollient line than he had before, winding and weaving, doubling and twisting his words like a silk maker to dazzle and beguile Vivian and Gratian into finding in his favor. A graphic narrative of the negotiations was sent to Becket by a sympathetic courtier, an eyewitness who wrote anonymously, wisely keeping his identity a closely guarded secret for fear his letter would be intercepted by Henry's spies.

Barely, it seems, had the serious bargaining begun than it was rudely interrupted by a carefully staged act of deliberate provocation in which the fourteen-year-old Prince Henry barged in with a band of his hunting friends, all blowing horns to announce the killing of a stag. The next day, the discussion resumed around 7 A.M., when the king, flanked by a contingent of his Norman bishops, demanded as a precondition that those sentenced at Clairvaux should be absolved without taking the usual oath to accept the archbishop's judgment on their crimes. The argument raged until sunset, when Henry stormed out, bitterly complaining that the pope never listened to him. "By God's eyes," he exclaimed menacingly, "I mean to do something about it!"

He was shocked to discover that Gratian was steelier than he had judged. "Do not threaten us, my lord," the envoy quietly advised him. "We come from a court that is accustomed to command emperors and kings." Henry was forced to apologize, but when the talking resumed, this time outdoors in a park, he threatened the envoys again, and when they rejected his demands, he ran back to his horse and in everyone's hearing swore of Becket, "For the rest of my life, I will never listen to anyone concerning that man's peace and restoration—neither the Lord Pope, nor anyone else."

And yet, when the ambassadors, unnerved by the prospect that their mission would fail even before it had properly begun, offered to meet him halfway by absolving those excommunicates who appeared before them in person and did penance, his response was like the calm after a thunderstorm. He agreed to reconcile himself to Becket and the exiles and restore them to their lands, but no sooner had this offer been accepted than he raised the stakes again, demanding in return that either one of the envoys or one of their clerks should take ship to England to absolve the others whom the archbishop had sentenced. When Gratian refused, Henry stalked out again, shouting as he went, "Do what you like: I don't rate you and your excommunications and doubt if they are worth an egg."

Scandalized, the Norman bishops cautioned him, saying that the envoys had in their pockets copies of a decree from Alexander commanding everyone to obey them on pain of excommunication. "I know, I know," he replied, "they will interdict my land. But cannot I, who can capture a well-fortified castle every day, capture a single clerk?" As dusk fell, he relented, summoning Vivian and Gratian to return and repeating his offer to settle the dispute on the terms he had previously indicated as if nothing untoward had happened.

Confident of success, the envoys next day absolved those of the Clairvaux excommunicates who appeared before them, in the belief that the game of cat and mouse would shortly be over—only to discover they were the mice and Henry the cat. For when the parchment prepared by the royal clerks recording the peace terms was submitted to them that evening, Vivian and Gratian saw to their dismay that Henry had deceived them, inserting a novel and belligerent proviso into the document— "saving the dignity of my realm" (*salva dignitate regni mei*)—clearly indicating that he still expected Becket to comply with the ancestral customs if he ever returned to England and putting the clock back to where it had originally started.

Gratian rejected this subterfuge, which he had no hesitation in denouncing as a trick. Henry was furious—so confident had he been of success, he had already written to Abbot Gilbert of Cîteaux giving his version of the peace terms, complete with the aggressive proviso. Unwilling to bend in the slightest degree, he sent Reginald fitz Jocelin and Ralph of Llandaff on yet another mission to the papal curia, with orders to seek approval for his own flawed version of the text.

Armed with his anonymous informant's report of the proceedings, Thomas wrote to Alexander and to his own envoys at the papal curia, urging them to "take the greatest care in our business, and exercise caution and unending vigilance against our enemies." He warned them especially against Reginald, a rising star who had served his apprenticeship in Becket's own household before defecting to Henry's. Reginald, he said, was the bastard son of Jocelin of Salisbury (the bishop's story was that he had been a student, not a priest, at the time of his son's conception), "who is everywhere dishonoring and blackening our name as far as he can, calling us a traitor."

Feeling it to be superfluous to wait for Alexander's replies, as it was obvious to him that Henry remained obdurate, Thomas first reinstated his Clairvaux sentences in spite of the pope's instructions to suspend them, and then he threatened to lay a general interdict on England. All church services would have to be suspended except for infant baptism and unction to the dying, which could continue but only in private. Monks alone would be allowed to carry on saying mass, and then in low voices, with the laity excluded and without any ringing of bells or other accustomed rites.

Henry's draconian riposte was to devise a set of preemptive ordinances—reported by Alan of Tewkesbury and a small army of feverishly excited chroniclers, including Roger of Howden and Gervase of Canterbury—that showed he was ready to go as far as a schism, breaking completely with the pope in order to defeat Becket. On September 29, he published this document, which was intended to sever all links between England and the archbishop and pope. Anyone caught with a letter from the pope or archbishop declaring an interdict was to be judged a traitor, and all those willing to obey an interdict were to be summarily deported with their entire families. All appeals to the pope or archbishop were proscribed, and the sending or receipt of letters or decrees to or from either was strictly forbidden. No priest or monk was to leave the country without a special passport. All clerks, including students, domiciled abroad but with church livings in England were to be recalled home. The goods of all those known to be the archbishop's supporters were to be seized. Lastly, every male over the age of fifteen in the entire country was to swear an oath to obey the prohibitions, especially those relating to an interdict.

With rumors flying thick and fast, Becket's first reaction to these ordinances was one of panic. His chilling claims that Henry meant to blind or castrate priests caught carrying letters from the papal curia and cut off the feet of monks were melodramatic, but since such men were to be hanged from the gallows instead, his fears were hardly groundless. To enforce the ordinances, Henry chose Geoffrey Ridel—a courtier whom he had appointed archdeacon of Canterbury over the archbishop's head and who was already performing many of the former royal chancellor's functions—who was to be assisted by Richard of Ilchester, one of the envoys attending the schismatic Council of Würzburg in 1165. As soon as they began their work, the ports were sealed, and the sheriffs started taking the new oaths of allegiance from males over age fifteen in their counties. But these measures triggered an almost immediate backlash. To the king's fury, Roger of Pont l'Évêque took the lead in this outspoken resistance. He might be Becket's sworn enemy, but Henry, he felt, was going too far. Outward conformity was not enough for the king. He was, in effect, attempting to police his subjects' thoughts, to look inside their minds and punish what he saw there as crimes, fueling Becket's determination to fresh heights—as indeed it would do four centuries later for Sir Thomas More when another Henry ordered him to take a not dissimilar oath on pain of death in the king's determination to break with Rome and marry Anne Boleyn. (More would famously choose death rather than capitulate.)

As Becket, in an anguished outpouring of pent-up grief and frustration, protested to an ally at the papal curia around this time, Henry had a project that struck at the heart of everything Christians believed in, changing the law of God "so that a tyrant's injustice may take its place" and aiming to create a regional church under royal and therefore his own personal control, enclosed within the ring fence of the coast and directed by a compliant archbishop of his choosing. Whether this had been his intention from the beginning, Thomas could not tell—nor did it matter, for it was his intention now. After some five years of near-constant humiliation in exile while the political battles between the pope and the German emperor, and between Henry and King Louis, were played out, the beleaguered archbishop felt he had to act decisively. In William fitz Stephen's ringing phrase, he knew the time had come "to put the ax to the root of the tree."

HENRY HAD ONE further game of cat and mouse to play out before the resources of diplomacy were spent. Thomas, who with his Canterbury revenues sequestered was increasingly unable to afford the intelligence networks needed to keep fully abreast of developments, suddenly discovered that as soon as Gratian, the more uncompromising of Alexander's ambassadors, had left France on his homeward journey to Italy, Henry had coaxed his more pliant colleague, Vivian, into convening another peace conference at the abbey of Saint-Denis north of Paris at Martinmas (November 11, 1169). Marking a last-ditch attempt to give substance to the Angevin-Capetian dynastic accord agreed on at Montmirail, a key agenda item of this round of talks would be the coronation of Prince Henry and his wife, hence the need to settle the dispute with Becket—if it could be done on terms as close as possible to the elder Henry's demands.

In the event, Henry and Thomas did not meet face-to-face. On Sunday, November 16, Louis entertained Henry sumptuously at the abbey, where the bones of kings would be preserved until they were thrown unceremoniously into trenches by the French revolutionaries in 1793, while Becket and his followers lodged with the Knights Templar, just outside Paris. It was agreed that on the following Tuesday, the archbishop would come to the Chapel of the Holy Martyr, built on an ancient site at the foot of the hill known as Montmartre, then the halfway point between Paris and the abbey, where intermediaries would shuttle to and fro between him and the two kings. When the day came and

Becket arrived, he was quickly shepherded inside the chapel, leaving Henry and Louis, their nobles and bishops, the papal envoy Vivian, and Archbishop Rotrou of Rouen, one of Henry's Norman advisers and former ambassadors to the papal curia, to congregate outside.

Most of the talking was done by King Louis and his advisers, who took on the role of intermediaries themselves, trying to broker a compromise. Henry began well enough, speaking in French for maximum clarity and offering—if in vague and general terms—to renounce "all the evil customs which might enslave the church" and to return the exiles' property. Thomas, beginning to wonder whether something genuinely constructive might be achieved this time, promised to defer to Henry as his king and "to render unto Caesar what properly belonged to Caesar." The rest of the day was consumed in discussing terms for the restoration of the archbishop's property. When challenged to produce a detailed inventory of the estates he claimed, Thomas wisely countered that he could not possibly know after so long an absence precisely which lands had been seized, but he wished to have everything returned to him that Theobald had once possessed, making particular reference to the lands that he had already contested with John the Marshal and others. Rather than abandon his rights to these, he said—rashly, although Henry, to his credit, did not rise to the bait—that he would prefer to stay in exile forever.

Much further haggling ensued over the reparations to be made for the exiles' lost revenues and arrears. Becket put his own losses at £20,000, a daunting but realistic figure, but generously offered to settle for just half that amount. Henry offered only 1,000 silver marks, around a thirtieth of what he owed, refusing to budge. Louis, with his own agenda of ensuring his daughter's coronation and his dynasty's potential claim to many of the present Angevin territories in years to come, eventually broke the deadlock, persuading Thomas that "it would be dishonorable and unworthy of him to obstruct the peace which was so necessary and desirable to the realm and the church for the sake of money alone."

Astonishingly, therefore, as it appeared to the weary group of bystanders, a settlement by late afternoon seemed close at hand. Since both sides had already been persuaded by Vivian and Louis to avoid any last-minute speeches or belligerent provisos that might alter the terms and so make a rapprochement impossible, all that remained was to seal the peace.

To the utter dismay and consternation of the exiles—this time not simply the moderates among them like John of Salisbury and Alexander Llewelyn, but even the most zealous like Herbert of Bosham—the negotiations foundered at the final hurdle. Not unreasonably, Becket asked Henry to seal the peace in the customary way by giving him the kiss of peace in public. The king promptly refused, claiming that he had sworn an oath in anger nevermore to give Thomas the kiss, "even if it happened that one day he should restore his peace and favor to him." Herbert reports that when Thomas had once consulted Alexander about exactly this sort of situation, the pope had advised him not to attempt to exact a pledge or an oath from the king as security, but to content himself with a kiss of peace. "The kiss of peace," said Alexander (or so claims Herbert), "should suffice of itself for a priest maintaining the cause of justice. Unless any other security is offered voluntarily, it should not be exacted." Regularly used to mark the confirmation of a legal agreement, a settlement by arbitration, or a reconciliation between parties engaged in a feud as at the conclusion of the Battle Abbey case, the kiss had its origins in the liturgy of the mass, where, according to the Roman rite, the clergy and congregation kiss one another after the prayer for peace has been said and the celebrant has kissed the altar.

Was Henry speaking the truth about his oath, or was he merely saving face, raising an objection to the kiss to avoid making it appear to his barons and courtiers that he had given in to Becket, despite the niggardliness of his offer to the church on reparations? Was his refusal more about his own cherished "dignity" than about an oath? If the oath was genuine, it was the only one he never broke. Equally, should Thomas have delayed his request for the kiss of peace until this late stage? Was he simply looking for another last-minute excuse to undo a settlement that left him ruinously out of pocket? Could neither of these two men bear to see the other one claiming a victory?

Do we even know for certain that Becket had discussed the matter of the kiss with the pope? Probably he had, since a similar contingency had been at the forefront of his mind when he had first appealed to Alexander at Sens shortly after his flight into exile in 1164. Alternatively, he may have raised the matter when he rode south with the pope from Paris to Bourges the following spring, on the first stages of Alexander's return journey to Rome. But the sources are ambiguous: Herbert of Bosham muddies the waters by claiming that Thomas had consulted Alexander on this question as recently as "a few days before" the Montmartre conference. That makes no sense, since it could—depending on political events in Italy and conditions on the Alpine passes—take a minimum of three weeks, and sometimes up to three months, for a courier to carry a letter from Sainte-Colombe to Benevento, and that is without allowing for a reply.

What seems likeliest is that the negotiations failed because of an underlying lack of trust between the parties. Becket felt that he could not agree to return to Canterbury without a guarantee of his security before witnesses as symbolized by the kiss; Henry's refusal to grant it shows that by the close of 1169, the quarrel had gone too far and ran too deep to be settled in a single day and without a face-to-face encounter. Historians since Lord Lyttelton have roundly castigated Becket for the failure, but at the time both Louis and Vivian put the fault squarely on Henry's shoulders. Herbert reports that when the French king first heard of his Angevin counterpart's reason for withholding the kiss, he suspected foul play, declaring that "beneath Henry's honeyed speeches earlier in the day lay poison." Becket adds that when the kiss was refused, Louis said immediately that not for all his weight in gold could he advise the exiles to return home. Count Theobald V of Blois shared his view. It would be exceedingly dangerous, he said, for Thomas to return to Canterbury without the kiss.

Vivian cast the blame on Henry alone. After talking privately to him again outside the chapel and pressing him to redeem a pledge he had earlier given to avoid last-minute obstacles, the envoy left the scene, telling anyone who would listen that he could scarcely recall ever seeing or hearing anyone who broke so many promises. "In the sum of my experience," he said, "that king lives and speaks more falsely than any other mortal man, so that he should be hateful to God and man."

Since dusk was falling and the two kings had agreed to lodge at Mantes, some thirty miles northwest of Paris, the conference ended, with no date set for a resumption of talks. With a long night's journey still before him, Henry cursed Thomas again and again while mounting his horse, "reckoning up and recapitulating the labors, vexations, and distresses he had caused him." As to Becket, he was finally poised to lay an interdict on England, perhaps even to excommunicate Henry if he did not repent, as it seems he had once planned to do at Vézelay before John of Salisbury's entreaties and the king's sudden illness had dissuaded him.

And this time, Pope Alexander was likely to take his side. In fact, the pope, his patience tested beyond endurance by Henry's tricks and excuses, threw aside caution and went much further than he ever had before, instructing two specially commissioned legates, Archbishop Rotrou of Rouen and Bishop Bernard of Nevers, that if Henry persisted in his contumacy, they were to impose a general interdict on his continental lands in concert with one laid on England by Thomas. Only if the king recanted and agreed to implement the peace he had offered at Montmartre before snatching it away, sealing it with the kiss of peace regardless of any oath he claimed to have taken, would the interdict be withheld. Nor was this the end of the matter, since even if Henry yielded, he was to be required, after a suitable interval had elapsed to spare his honor, to "abrogate entirely all those evil customs, and especially the ordinances that he has recently added which are contrary to his salvation and the liberty of the church." Should he refuse, both Thomas and the legates were to inform the pope, who would himself decide on what further sanctions should be imposed. The only olive branch Alexander held out to the king was that in return, Becket had to grovel, humbling himself in word and deed to a degree he never had before, "saving only the liberty of the church and the danger to himself and his companions."

At last, then, it seemed as if Henry's attacks on the church and the archbishop would be bridled. Thomas, who since his expulsion from Pontigny had begun to despair that he would ever return to Canterbury, relished the prospect, but he was painfully aware that the battle was still far from won. On the contrary, as he advised Bishop Bernard, one of the newly commissioned legates, "You will have to fight against beasts." For John of Salisbury had been right all along. Courtiers were sly, slippery, treacherous, lawless flatterers "who lull virtue to sleep." And the ruler of the "beasts" was the lion king Henry, seeking whomever he could devour: a "monster," a "tyrant," whose lies and deceits, smooth talking and false promises, were as vile as robbery or fraud. "Whatever he says and whatever appearance he assumes," warned Thomas, "both he and all who belong to him should be suspect, considered full of lies, unless their plain and open actions demonstrate their honesty."

With the thunder of Henry's antipapal ordinances reverberating in his ears, Becket's struggle with the king had become for him a cosmic battle between the forces of good and evil, "justice" and "tyranny," akin to a crusade against an infidel. For he was beginning to wonder whether Henry, in his headlong rush to defeat and destroy his once loved former chancellor and now despised archbishop, would next dare to defy even God.

25
A TRIAL OF STRENGTH

AFTER THE FAILURE OF THE CONFERENCE AT MONTMARTRE, the pace of events markedly quickened. Without further delay, Becket reaffirmed all of his Clairvaux sentences, adding five more names to the list, including John of Oxford, Ralph of Llandaff, and Geoffrey Ridel, whose influence he judged to be especially malign. He also gave the king an ultimatum, saying that unless he restored peace to the church by the Feast of the Purification of the Blessed Virgin Mary (February 2, 1170), a general interdict would be laid on England, and Henry himself—"as we have spared him until now at the risk of our salvation"—would be excommunicated.

In reply, Henry appealed to the pope—not without some success, since by deceitfully pretending to be willing to submit the entire dispute to Alexander's decree, he secured a temporary postponement of the interdict. Meanwhile, all his efforts were put into making immediate preparations to return with his whole court to England to engineer Prince Henry's coronation. Craftily throwing up a smoke screen that would fool his critics for months, he professed his ardor to accompany King Louis and the archbishop of Tyre on a crusade, suggesting Easter 1171 as the date he would embark for the East. "To lend greater color to his crusading zeal," says John of Salisbury, who saw through this charade from the outset, he made it known that he had "set aside all complaints

[and] all anger and animosity against the archbishop of Canterbury and his followers."

Henry knew that to crush Becket decisively after Frederick Barbarossa and his German allies had so conspicuously failed him, he needed to persuade Louis to withdraw his protection from the exiles, which meant implementing the terms of the dynastic settlement agreed on in principle at Montmirail. During the mission of Vivian and Gratian, the Angevin king had unsuccessfully sought Alexander's consent to have his son crowned by a hand other than Becket's in order to fulfill his bargain with the French. Now, in his eagerness to satisfy Louis before an interdict came into force, he meant to ignore the pope and have the coronation performed by Roger of Pont l'Évêque, the archbishop of York, relying on one of the papal licenses he had obtained to crown his son during the vacancy at Canterbury in 1161.

Although Henry did not doubt that a majority of the English bishops would refuse to usurp the primate's right to crown the heir to the throne, he also knew that Gilbert Foliot and Jocelin of Salisbury, both excommunicated at Clairvaux, would rally to his side if they could secure their absolution from Becket's sentences quickly enough. Foliot, in particular, saw his role in the coronation as the way to recover his special influence with the king. With his hated rival beginning to occupy the high moral ground in Pope Alexander's eyes, Foliot was feeling vulnerable, since his claim to metropolitan jurisdiction for the Diocese of London had fallen on deaf ears.

While Henry made ready to cross the Channel, chartering ships and summoning the barons to attend him in a great council to be held at Windsor at Easter, Foliot wound his way over the Alpine passes to petition Alexander to absolve him. He had tried to prepare the ground by sending his clerk, Master David, on ahead to plead his cause. Foliot was lucky. He met Master David by chance in Milan, finding him already on his way home from Benevento after successfully obtaining a decree addressed to the legates, Rotrou of Rouen and Bernard of Nevers, which granted his request. He was indeed absolved. So too was Jocelin of Salisbury, after his son Reginald fitz Jocelin, the rising diplomat, pleaded for him personally at the feet of the pope.

The timing was critical. Both requests were made just as Alexander was preoccupied with accepting an invitation from the leaders of the Lombard League to move back to the Roman Campagna, closer to Rome itself. It seems that the pope and cardinals were too busy packing their luggage to consider the wider consequences of absolving the English excommunicates. Realizing within days that a serious blunder had been made, Alexander tried to countermand his mandates, but he was too late.

Incensed and distraught over the absolutions, which he viewed as tantamount to yet another revocation of his disciplinary powers, Becket sent a blistering rebuke to the papal curia, tetchily accusing Alexander of rehabilitating men who were nothing more than unrepentant criminals. "Those loyal to you," he scolded the pope in Latin prose made more pungent still with John of Salisbury's help, "had advised you from the outset that the English king could more easily be defeated by a certain degree of severity, but never mollified by any mildness, services, or favors." Exonerating Foliot, he continued, was a scandal, since he was a devil incarnate, an unbound Satan, "the author of all these wickednesses," who had first tempted his episcopal colleagues into appealing against the Vézelay sentences and now rejoiced in his ability to defeat justice and render innocence captive. "I do not know," Thomas railed, his emotions surging within him like an erupting volcano, "by what compact the Lord's party is always slain in the curia, so that Barabbas may escape and Christ be killed."

Becket then vented his scorn on a faithful friend, Cardinal Albert de Morra, his old law teacher from Bologna, who—since he worked in the papal chancery—suddenly came into the archbishop's line of fire. "The exiles," Thomas mocked sarcastically, "are condemned before you for no other reason . . . except that they are Christ's poor and weak, and refuse to withdraw from God's justice. On the other side, the sacrilegious and the murderers, the robbers and the impenitent are absolved." And in an impassioned avowal, he professed himself willing to suffer martyrdom for the church's sake: "God knows and he must judge, but we are prepared to die for her. . . . By God's favor, I shall never withdraw from fidelity to the church, neither in life nor in death."

How serious he was is difficult to assess. He had scarcely talked this way since confronting Henry on horseback outside the walls of Northampton in October 1163 after their first chilling clash at the Council of Westminster. Then, assuming his words were reported accurately, he was reacting to Henry's swipe about his lowly ancestry—"Are you not the son of one of my villeins?" Becket's retort had been uttered for rhetorical effect in the heat of the moment. Now, however, bitterly frustrated and disoriented after almost six long years of kaleidoscopic but futile diplomacy, he came to wonder whether only through martyrdom might his cause be judged on its merits, with the politics stripped away. As St. Cyprian, a handsome volume of whose collected letters he had acquired at Pontigny, had many times written, it was a Christian's duty boldly to resist the heathen magistrate in the cause of faith. If that led him into martyrdom, he must accept the obligation, showing confidence, fortitude, and constancy. He should not fear to be killed.

HENRY RETURNED to English shores at Portsmouth on March 3, 1170, after a perilous crossing in which some of his ships were wrecked and his personal physician and up to four hundred others drowned. Determined not to lose a minute once his barons had met in council, he gave the orders for his son's coronation, which was celebrated in his presence and that of his whole court and the citizens of London at Westminster Abbey on Sunday, June 14. First Prince Henry, now turned fifteen, was knighted by his father, then crowned and anointed by Roger of Pont l'Évêque, assisted by Gilbert Foliot and Jocelin of Salisbury. Henry of Winchester, William of Norwich, and Bartholomew of Exeter were among those boycotting the event.

So eager was Henry to crown his son before papal or archiepiscopal prohibitions arrived, he closed the ports; forbade anyone he suspected of colluding with the exiles, such as Roger of Worcester, from crossing the Channel; and put Eleanor and Richard de Humez in charge of an aggressive purge of dissidents, a move suggesting that his wife was as keen as he was to suppress any opposition to their son's coronation. Amid all the commotion, his daughter-in-law, Princess Margaret, was entirely forgotten. Although she and her female attendants were furnished with expensive coronation robes paid for by the London citizens, they would not be worn. Left kicking her heels at Caen instead of riding in procession to the abbey with her husband, she angrily complained to her father, who raged furiously at the insult.

As it happened, Thomas beat the embargo, choosing as his trusted courier the nun Mary of Blois, former abbess of Romsey and King Stephen's daughter, who in 1160 he had unsuccessfully tried to save from the scandalous marriage Henry had arranged for her to Matthew of Flanders. After several years (and two daughters), the marriage had been dissolved, allowing Mary to return to her convent. A royal princess could safely slip through the blockade, and using the code name "Idonea" (meaning "the most suitable one"). Mary served copies of decrees from Pope Alexander forbidding a coronation—unless Becket presided—on both Roger of Pont l'Évêque and Gilbert Foliot. The documents were safely delivered, but their recipients chose to ignore them. John of Salisbury's response was to advise Becket to make an immediate appeal to the pope.

With his son and heir crowned and deputed to govern England with the assistance of Richard de Lucy, who was now appointed justiciar (chief judicial official) following Robert de Beaumont's death two years before, the elder Henry returned to Normandy, to find Alexander's special legates, Rotrou of Rouen and Bernard of Nevers, waiting for him. Reinforced by Archbishop William of Sens—a trusted confidant of King Louis and one of Becket's supporters, whom the pope had appointed to be "papal legate for France"—they were armed with fresh and peremptory papal instructions to impose a peace on terms similar to those agreed to by Becket at Montmartre, whether Henry liked it or not. By this time, the papal curia had resettled itself in the Campagna, perambulating between such hilltop towns as Veroli, Ferentino, Segni, and Anagni, where earlier popes had traditionally kept their summer residences. Believing himself to be more secure than at any point since his election, Alexander had given his legates the power to place interdicts on all of Henry's lands; any bishop not observing them would be suspended or excommunicated. In a brisk concluding paragraph, the pope even threatened that if Henry failed to put the peace terms into effect within forty days, Alexander would personally excommunicate him.

Armed to the teeth with their papal mandates and abandoning their "ant-like" crawl in dealing with the king (as Becket's old secretary, Master Ernulf, put it), the legates flung themselves into action, proclaiming a general interdict on Henry's continental lands, beginning with Aquitaine, while Thomas composed fiery letters addressed to Gilbert Foliot, Roger of Pont l'Évêque, and others, laying another interdict on England.

Becket's letters of interdict may never have been sent, but that was only because they were not needed. He had been right all along. The mere prospect of interdicts with teeth was enough to bring Henry to the negotiating table. After consultations between King Louis and the legates followed by separate discussions between the legates and Henry at Falaise in late June and between the legates and Becket at Sens on July 16, it was agreed that a final peace conference lasting three days would be held on the frontier beginning on Monday, July 20. Fréteval was the place chosen: an impregnable castle set on a narrow spur of high ground guarding the road from Châteaudun to Vendôme in Touraine and dominating the valley of the Loir (a tributary of the Loire). The castle had a circular central keep—the outer bailey protected by earthworks and a deep ditch, the inner bailey protected by an exterior polygonal wall flanked by five towers and itself enclosing a circular interior wall flanked by two towers. The arrangement was that Thomas would come there to receive Henry's peace on the third and final day, the Feast of St. Mary Magdalene.

Typically, Henry would outmaneuver the papal legates even before the conference opened. He would prevail in his renewed insistence that he would never offer the kiss of peace to Becket, despite the pope's instructions to the contrary, since he had sworn never to give it and did not wish to be known as a perjurer. This was all about saving face, but realizing how momentous the consequences for the church and his own followers would be if another attempt at reconciliation failed, Thomas agreed to dilute the preconditions he had himself proposed—that Henry should give a written statement of the peace, recorded in triplicate, which offered specific assurances concerning the release of the exiles from his enmity, the restoration of their property, and the kiss of peace—and would instead concede that he should agree to a settlement without the kiss. Becket made this generous offer when Henry, who at this point was more desperate for a settlement than he had ever been before, agreed to swear on oath that by refusing the kiss he was not laying a trap for Thomas, naming William of Sens as his surety.

THREE VIVID, eyewitness narratives of the Fréteval conference survive, the most reliable and informative by Becket himself in the form of a memorandum to the pope; the others by Herbert of Bosham and William fitz Stephen, the latter now writing as much from the royalist viewpoint as the archbishop's, given that he had made his peace with the king and traveled in the royal entourage.

On the opening two days of the conference, Henry parleyed at great length with Louis in the presence of the legates and afterward in secret, seeking to assuage the French king's anger over his daughter's exclusion from the coronation. Fitz Stephen drew a veil over this portion of the talks, but almost certainly Henry invited Margaret to join her husband as he began a royal progress around his new kingdom of England. Possibly he offered to crown her at Westminster or Winchester at a later date. Whatever he proposed, it was the bare minimum needed to satisfy her father, who stood down his troops from the borders of the Norman Vexin. It was also enough to encourage Henry to indulge in friendly banter when he emerged outdoors, saying to Louis, "Tomorrow your thief shall have his peace, and have it good."

"By the saints of France, what thief?" asked Louis.

"Why, that archbishop of Canterbury of yours," said Henry.

"Would that he was ours as he is yours," answered Louis. "You will have honor before God and men if you grant him a good peace, and we will be grateful to you."

But this, says Herbert of Bosham, was only for the medieval equivalent of the cameras. As soon as the two kings went indoors again, "they spoke their minds."

On the third day, once Louis had withdrawn, Henry rode from his lodgings to meet Becket. Their reconciliation, it had been agreed, should take place in the open air, midway between the towns of Fréteval and Viévy-le-Rayé, in a clearing within a forest known today as the Bois des Brûlons. Herbert described the meeting place as a rustic Arcadia. It was only long afterward that he discovered that from ancient times, it had been known by the local inhabitants as "Traitors' Meadow."

As Thomas drew close, flanked by William of Sens, Henry spurred on his horse to greet him, removing his hat as a conciliatory gesture. After exchanging a few pleasant words with his former chancellor in William's hearing, Henry led him aside toward a distant part of the field out of earshot, animatedly talking (as Thomas later told the pope) "for a long time and with such familiarity that it seemed there had never been any discord between us."

Delighted and greatly heartened by the warmth of his reception, Becket was overcome, perhaps even totally disarmed, for it seemed as if an evil spell had suddenly been lifted. Momentarily, he even found the idea of resisting Henry's tyranny somewhat absurd, since far from reciting a litany of his grievances as a prelude to their encounter as he had so often done before, the king quickly volunteered to restore his peace and favor to the church and the exiles and to return all their sequestered property. As Thomas later gushed excitedly to the pope, "He did not presume even to mutter the much-vaunted customs. He required no oath from us or from any of our supporters; he conceded to us all the possessions which he had taken away from the church."

It had been a brilliant start far exceeding anyone's expectations, and when Henry even indicated that at some unspecified time in the future after Becket had returned to England, he might—despite all he had said before—be induced to offer his archbishop the kiss of peace, "if indeed we wished him to be pressed so far," it may well have seemed as if nothing more needed to be said. Unable to overhear their words but seeing clearly from their body language the two men recovering something of their old chemistry, the onlookers were amazed. Many of them (and doubtless chiefly the exiles) wept unashamedly as they praised God and St. Mary Magdalene for bringing about such a miracle.

The two titans were on their very best behavior. After so many previous failures, the fundamentals of the peace had this time been all but dictated by Pope Alexander in his instructions and thrashed out before the legates in their meetings with both parties ahead of the rendezvous. Even a full list of the sequestered Canterbury properties had been drawn up and submitted in advance to the legates to avoid any subsequent misunderstandings.

Only one potentially explosive matter, at least on the exiles' side, had yet to be resolved. Prince Henry's coronation by Roger of Pont l'Évêque in violation of the rights and privileges of the church of Canterbury was, the archbishop believed, an "execration" requiring immediate penance and satisfaction. Declaring that he could not overlook something so heinous, Thomas "chided" the king, calling on him to make amends, asking in particular for his permission to punish Roger and those of his own subordinates (meaning Gilbert Foliot and Jocelin of Salisbury) who "in their exceedingly blind and bold ambition" had defied the pope's prohibition.

While Henry struggled to restrain his temper, Becket ranted against this "outrage" for well over an hour, citing innumerable historical precedents of the primate's ancient rights and culminating in an appeal to the king, "for the love of God, for his own salvation, and for the safety of his children, to repair the damage of the grave injury done to us and to make amends for the sin of such great presumption."

In answer, Henry deftly turned the tables, producing not (as Becket had obviously expected) the license in favor of the archbishop of York that he had obtained during the vacancy at Canterbury—for that license, it turned out, had been expressly revoked by the pope in 1166—but the other, secured at the same time and held in reserve, allowing him to have his heir crowned by any bishop he wished, a grant that had included no time limit. "We command you," Alexander had then written, addressing whichever bishop Henry might choose to perform the rite of coronation, "that whenever the king shall request it, you shall place upon the head of his aforesaid son the crown on the authority of the Apostolic See; and what therein shall be done by you we decree to remain valid and firm."

Understandably, Becket challenged the validity of this second license, but he was struggling. He therefore, somewhat rashly, chose to attack again, throwing back Henry's own words in his face, reminding him of one of their conversations at Rouen in 1162 around the time the king had been urging him to agree to accept the nomination for the vacant archbishopric. Then, Henry had confided to him in a rare moment when he had bared his soul that he disliked Roger so much, he never wanted him to crown his son. "Were you not accustomed to say openly at that time," remembered Thomas, "that you would prefer your son to be beheaded rather than that aforesaid York should place his heretic hands upon his head?"

Instantly realizing that he had gone too far, not least by casting doubt on the legality of the junior king's coronation, Thomas retreated, reassuring Henry that it had never been his intention to undermine or disparage his son. "We desire his success," he protested earnestly, "and the enlargement of his renown, and we shall labor in the Lord to bring it about."

In that case, said Henry icily, "if you love my son, you have a twofold duty to do what you are bound to do. For I myself gave him to you as a son and you received him from my hand . . . and he loves you with such great affection that he refuses to see any of your enemies in a true light. He would certainly have destroyed them already, if he had not been prevented by the respect and fear of my name."

As Becket nodded, recollecting with satisfaction how the young prince had begun his education in his household when he was chancellor, Henry resumed, on the surface maintaining his affable, familiar mood, but now layering the conversation with a subtly menacing tone. Speaking of the bishops who had crowned his son, he said, "I know you will avenge yourself on them even more harshly than is appropriate as soon as you have time and opportunity. I do not doubt that the church of Canterbury is the noblest church in the Western world, nor do I wish her to be deprived of her right. . . . On the other hand, to those who have betrayed you and me until now, by God's providence I shall pay them back according to the deserts of traitors."

At the time, Thomas took the king's speech purely at face value. Believing he had successfully extricated himself from a tricky corner, overcome with relief and gratitude and exultant in his apparent triumph over the delinquent bishops, he dismounted from his horse and humbly prostrated himself at Henry's feet. Bidding him to remount, Henry—who had himself dismounted—took hold of Becket's stirrup and held it for him as he raised himself into the saddle again, while the onlookers gasped in astonishment from the opposite side of the field.

But what did Henry's last speech really mean? Was it just his own courtiers or bishops whom he meant to punish for their bad advice, or was it also those on Becket's side who he believed had betrayed him? Did he not already believe in his heart that Becket was the greatest traitor in his empire?

ESCORTING THOMAS back toward the royal tents pitched at the opposite side of the field, Henry declared in the presence of all that the old affection between him and his former chancellor had been fully restored and that their enmity had ceased. He then withdrew, ordering the Norman bishops to thrash out all outstanding points of detail with the exiles. Now the trouble set in. After first listening carefully to the advice of William of Sens and his fellow exiles on several matters, and in particular that the vexed issue of the level of compensation payable for loss of revenues and damage to the Canterbury properties should be deferred in the interests of a speedy repatriation, Becket became overconfident. In his sheer elation at the apparent scale of his success, he began to insist that on no account would he or his followers actually cross the Channel until every single yard of sequestered ground had been restored to them. As he later told the pope somewhat regally, "It is not in our mind to return to him as long as he has taken away a single yard of the Church's land." So subsidiary matters that ought to have been cleared up swiftly—perhaps better handled in their entirety by advisers such as Herbert of Bosham or John of Salisbury—took longer than the earlier, more critical interview with the king.

By late afternoon, when it was time for vespers, Thomas—to judge by his own account of the proceedings—had grown weary and was less psychologically in control as stress and exhilaration took their toll. The result was that when Henry reappeared, Thomas broke his own rules as to how to handle him. When he ought to have remained silent or even simply groveled as Pope Alexander had urged, mindful that the Angevin king should always be approached "with the greatest restraint and the avoidance of too much talk," he became increasingly garrulous and condescending, "tossing words backward and forward" (as he afterward conceded). At a moment when he should simply have trusted to Henry's promises of goodwill without troubling himself too much about the behavior of the king's cronies, he began worrying whether men such as John of Oxford, Geoffrey Ridel, or Ranulf de Broc, now (as he said) "made uneasy by the pricks of their depraved consciences," would actively subvert the reconciliation.

Worse still, he flatly refused to restore normal relations with Henry by moving back into his old lodgings at court, as the king wished, until his crossing back to England could be arranged, saying that first he must return to France to offer his thanks to King Louis and his other benefactors. Such reticence courted skepticism about his true intentions, and sure enough the slippery Arnulf of Lisieux stepped forward as if on cue. He proposed "very cunningly and urgently" that since Henry had reconciled himself to the archbishop and his companions, Thomas should do the same to all those courtiers whom he had previously either excommunicated or denounced as evil counselors. It was the end of a long day, and Becket fell into the trap, answering that the two cases were not alike. Whereas the exiles had been deprived of their incomes and wrongfully persecuted to their great loss, he said, the king's counselors had acted of their own free will. In any case, some of these excommunications were the pope's, not his own, and not everyone he had censured had been excommunicated. "Consequently," he insisted, "the logic of law and equity forbids that there should be the same judgment for persons and cases so dissimilar."

It was surely a disastrous mistake. As it appeared to Henry's supporters, Becket had been far from magnanimous when presented with an opportunity to forgive and forget. He seemed to be quibbling over the small print of the peace agreement like a pettifogging lawyer, acting in less good faith than Henry. In fact, the true underlying source of his extreme caution was his sheer sense of incredulity and disbelief that a peace settlement could have been this easy, coupled with his growing sense of unease in the absence of any signals from those around the king that Henry would honor his word.

The result was that Geoffrey Ridel, whom Becket had nicknamed the "arch-devil," cried out, "If he hates me, I'll hate him; but if he wants to love me, I'll love him." An ugly scene started to develop, requiring Henry to intervene to calm things down. Drawing Thomas quietly aside, he begged him not to pay heed to such backbiting, which he should dismiss as bait. The king then declared the interview over, cleverly asking Becket for his blessing to avoid any further mention of a kiss, before mounting his horse and galloping home to the castle.

HENRY HAD SCARCELY put a foot wrong at Fréteval. Desperately in need of a peace settlement to avert the threat of interdicts on his lands, he had more than satisfied Alexander's representatives, committing himself to the idea of peace without binding himself to anything very specific other than that the sequestered Canterbury properties would be restored and allowing the exiles to return to Sainte-Colombe under the impression that they had won a glorious victory. Soon, they supposed, they would be on their journey home, and their lands and livings would be restored to them, with the prospect of at least partial compensation for their losses in the future. The clock, they believed, was to be turned back to where it had been when Becket was elected archbishop, and such shibboleths as the disputed ancestral customs declared at Clarendon and the antipapal ordinances were to be forgotten.

Unfortunately for them, Henry never saw it this way. In his eyes, he had been forced to make a tactical retreat under pressure from the pope—that was all. He would live to fight another day and had no intention of allowing the ancestral customs to be sidelined or rescinded. Rather than declaring that now, he simply had to wait for Becket to wrong-foot himself, for he understood his former chancellor well enough to know that as soon as he got the opportunity, he would take his revenge on the three delinquent bishops. And Henry was not mistaken, since directly after the interview at Fréteval, the archbishop's servant Gunther of Winchester set out for the papal curia to seek letters authorizing another round of excommunications. The new decrees would, furthermore, be obtained—catastrophically, if almost certainly not deliberately—under false colors. In his ignorance of what precisely had occurred at Westminster Abbey on June 14, and forced to act solely on the reports he had received from his anonymous informants, who may not themselves have been present, Thomas had apparently told Pope Alexander that at the ceremony, the junior King Henry, instead of swearing the traditional coronation oath with its promise to defend and protect the Holy Church of God and its liberties, had at the behest of the three delinquent bishops sworn to preserve the ancestral customs recorded in the chirograph at Clarendon, including those condemned by the pope. Although copies of Thomas's letters to the papal curia about the coronation have not survived, Alexander's response makes plain that Thomas had assured him that an oath "to preserve the evil customs" had been used.

The conference at Fréteval was followed by a lull. Within three weeks of leaving the castle, Henry fell seriously ill with malaria at La Motte, near Domfront. Staring death in the face, he made his will, broadly confirming the territorial dispositions he had made the previous year at Montmirail. The younger Henry was to inherit England, Normandy, Maine, and Anjou and was to become the guardian of his youngest brother, John. Richard, already invested as Count of Poitou and living there with his mother and her uncle, was to hold Aquitaine directly from King Louis. Geoffrey, who had received the homage of the barons of Brittany at Rennes in 1169, was to have that duchy on the same basis, not as his eldest brother's vassal as their father had originally planned.

Henry's fever was so grave, rumor had it that he had died. Recovering at the end of September, he made a pilgrimage to Rocamadour in the county of Quercy in fulfillment of a vow he had taken on his sickbed. Climbing the steep steps carved into the side of the gorge above the river Alzou, a tributary of the Dordogne, to the spectacular shrine of the Virgin Mary on its ledge halfway up the cliff face, he was repeating a visit he had made in 1159 on the way to his campaign in Toulouse, when he had prayed for success in battle. By October 1, he was back with his barons at Tours. Meanwhile, the special legates were awaiting Pope Alexander's reactions to the peace settlement, while Henry's courtiers, with Geoffrey Ridel in the vanguard, were busily colluding with their friends and counterparts in England, wondering how best they might obstruct the return of the sequestered Canterbury properties to the archbishop's nominees.

After visiting King Louis in Paris and preaching a sermon on the theme of peace at the abbey of Saint-Victor on the left bank of the Seine, close to where he had sat at the feet of his masters as a student, Becket rejoined his fellow exiles at Sens. He quickly discovered that their mounting suspicions as to Henry's sincerity were well-founded, since at least one of the royal writs authorizing the return of the confiscated property to its rightful owners had been qualified by the proviso "saving the honor of my realm" (*salvo honore regni mei*).

Similar doubts were shared at the papal curia, where on first hearing the reports of the Fréteval conference brought by the archbishop's messengers, the much maligned but still supportive Cardinal Albert informed the exiles, "I thought that more had been given to you in appearance than in reality . . . [since] we know that an Ethiopian cannot easily change his skin nor a leopard change his spots." Would he be proved right, or would Henry's brush with death make him a newly reformed character?

Thomas was soon going to find out.

A king enthroned, probably Stephen, who was famous for sitting with crossed legs.

Prize falcons sitting on their perch in a niche.

Matilda, Stephen's rival for the throne, seated and holding up a charter.

Archbishop Theobald crowns Henry II.

A cardinal presiding over a busy church court.

Pontigny Abbey, south view.

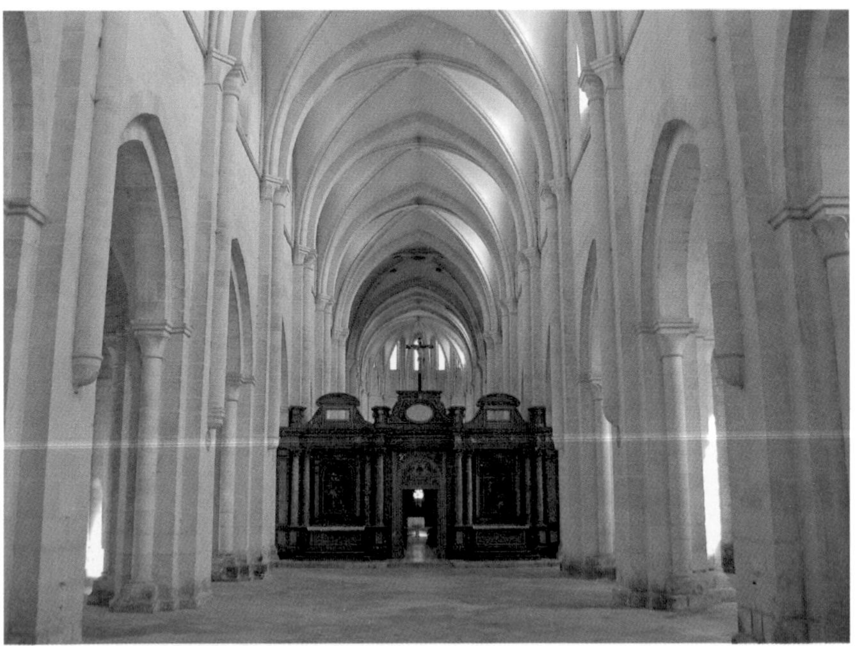

The nave at Pontigny Abbey.

Becket pronounces the Vézelay excommunications (left), and addresses Henry II and Louis VII at their peace conference at Montmirail, where he is reproached (right).

Becket with Henry II (center) and Louis VII at the peace conference at Montmirail, Sens Cathedral.

The younger Henry is crowned and anointed by Roger of Pont l'Évêque, assisted by Gilbert Foliot and Jocelin of Salisbury (left), and the elder Henry serves his son at the coronation banquet (right).

While making ready to sail home to England, Becket is warned by Milo, dean of Boulogne, that the coasts are closely guarded.

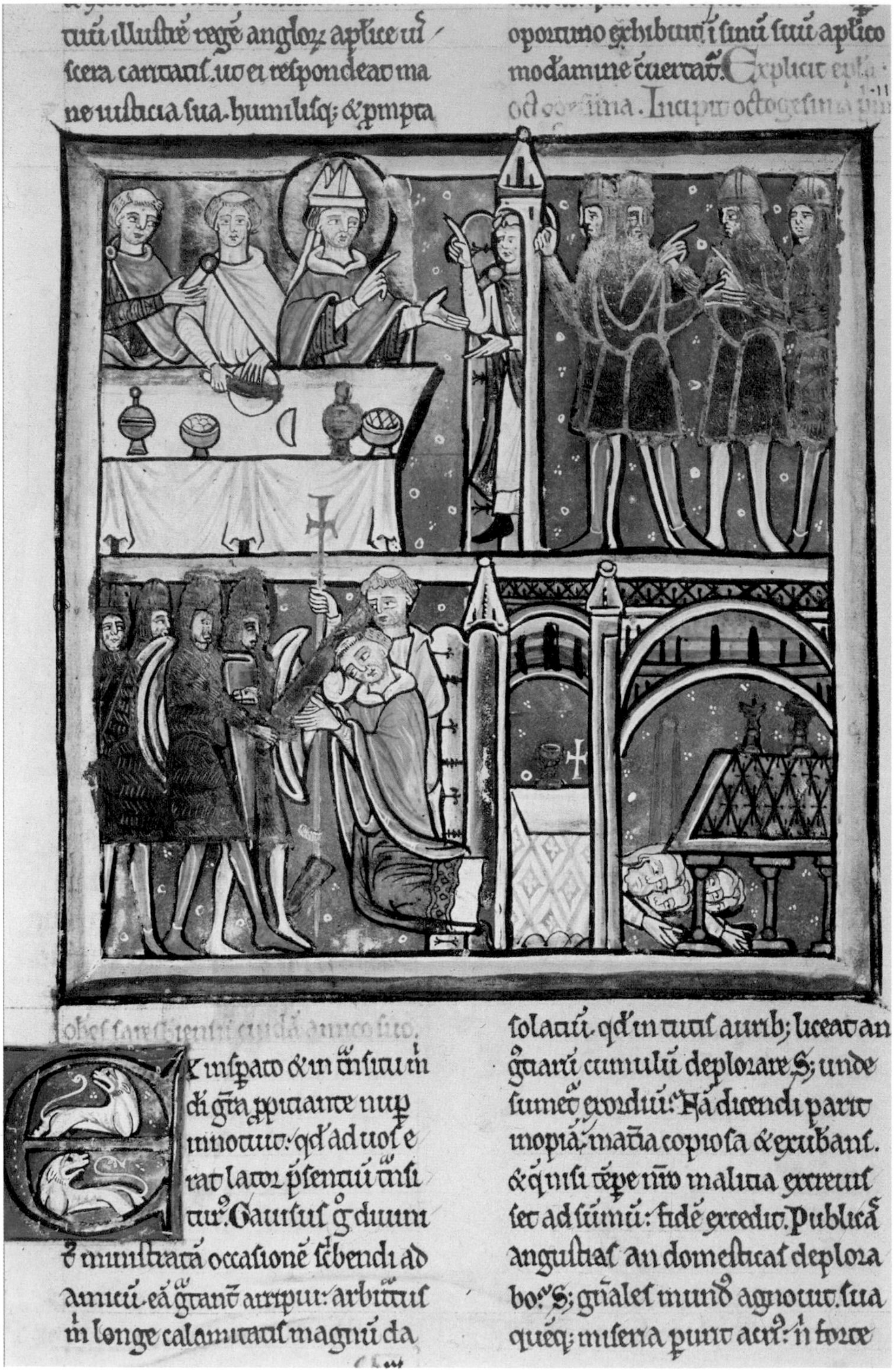

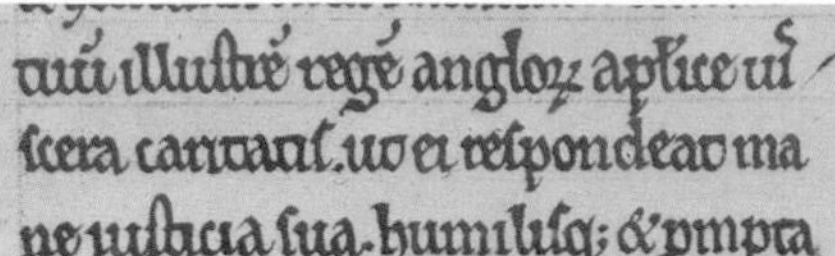

tuũ illustrẽ regẽ angloꝝ aplice ui
scera caritatis. ut ei respondeat ma
ne iusticia sua. humilisq; & pmpta

The oldest and most authentic image of Becket's murder, prefacing a copy of John of Salisbury's letter of early 1171 describing it. The arrival of the four knights is announced (above), and Reginald fitz Urse strikes the first blow (below).

The place where Becket was murdered as it appears today.

The burial place in the crypt.

Henry II's second penance at Canterbury, from a nineteenth-century engraving.

Scenes from the life of Thomas Becket, Sens Cathedral.

Miracles of healing at Becket's pre-1220 shrine, Canterbury Cathedral.

The shrine of St. Alban, giving a very basic idea of Becket's post-1220 shrine, St. Albans Cathedral.

26

RETURN TO CANTERBURY

A MERE FIVE MONTHS ELAPSED BETWEEN THE CONFERENCE at Fréteval and Becket's murder. After Henry had left Rocamadour and Thomas finished saying his farewells to his French hosts, the two men met in the Loire Valley to make ready for Thomas's return to Canterbury, beginning at Tours around October 12, 1170. For the first time in almost six years, Becket crossed the frontier into Angevin territory, but clearly all was not well. When he arrived at Tours, Henry treated him with undisguised contempt. There was no kiss of peace, the king did not visit him in his lodgings in the evening, and when they did get to talk, they quarreled over the lack of progress in restoring the Canterbury properties to the church.

The next morning, Thomas found that orders had been given for the court to move to Amboise, fifteen miles upstream. No one had bothered, or deigned, to tell him. He caught up with Henry at Montlouis, halfway between Tours and Amboise, but when it looked as if he might accompany the king to mass in the royal chapel, the order of service was hastily changed from the liturgy for the day to the liturgy for the dead, in which the prayer for peace is omitted and no kiss exchanged.

At Chaumont-sur-Loire, the atmosphere was more relaxed. Henry and Becket talked for a long time alone, again reinvigorating something of their old familiarity, agreeing that Thomas would leave Sens for the last time in mid-November. Henry would come to meet him at Rouen, where, after paying his debts and supplying him with all that was necessary for his journey, either he or Archbishop Rotrou would accompany him across the Channel.

The two men then bade each other farewell. Henry said, "Go in peace. I will follow you and will meet you in Rouen or in England as soon as I can."

"My lord," answered Thomas, "something tells me that I now take leave of you and that in this life you will see me no more."

"Do you think me a traitor?" retorted the king.

"Far be it from you, my lord," replied Becket. And on this they parted.

On the road back to Sainte-Colombe, Becket told Herbert of Bosham that Henry had also asked him, "Oh, why is it that you won't do what I want? Because for certain, if you would, I'd put everything into your hands." Reflecting ruefully on the meaning of these words, he told Herbert that they had reminded him of Satan's temptation of Christ: "All these things will I give you, if you will fall down and worship me."

Henry's next move was to issue a writ to his son, from Chinon, ordering that the exiles be reinstated in all the lands and livings they had held three months before leaving England. But what seemed to be a reconciliatory gesture had a sting in the tail. It did not include any of the lands pillaged from the church in King Stephen's reign, notably Saltwood Castle, now occupied by Ranulf de Broc. Thus, it was a recipe for conflict, and the fact that John of Oxford and Geoffrey Ridel appended their seals to this writ as witnesses shows that Henry was taking his advice from the "untamed beasts," men determined to hold on to their spoils if they could.

From England the news was worse. Increasingly menacing reports arrived from Herbert of Bosham and (later) John of Salisbury, whom Becket sent on ahead. "All the revenues," John says, "which could have accrued up to Christmas have been seized in the king's name." The bailiffs—with the de Brocs in charge—were stripping the Canterbury lands of assets; briefly reinstating the exiles' nominees to satisfy the letter, if not the spirit, of Henry's agreement; and evicting them again a few days later. John was indignant that a living of his own, worth 40 marks a year, had been withheld. If that were not enough, the delinquent bishops—Roger of Pont l'Évêque, Gilbert Foliot, and Jocelin of

Salisbury—fearing the archbishop's reprisals, were plotting to obstruct him in every possible way. Rumor had it that they planned to advise Henry to force Becket to observe the ancestral customs before he was even allowed to set foot on English shores.

Few in England believed that Henry would honor his promises. "I found everything," John laments, "in confusion, quite contrary to our hopes and the good reputation and fine promises of the king." He says that, far from feeling at home in his own country, "I was (as it were) in a sort of prison." At least he had been warmly welcomed at Canterbury, where the citizens regarded Becket as a hero. Frustratingly, John was unable to expand on this observation to explain why popular opinion had swung so decisively against Henry. He had at once to visit his dying mother at Exeter, whom he asked Thomas to remember in his prayers. Most likely the extortions and oppressions of the de Brocs were the cause. Seeking to clear as much profit in as short a time as possible from the archbishop's estates, they were looting his manor houses, hoarding his grain, chopping down his trees, and killing his livestock, claiming that they acted in Henry's name and with his full consent.

Herbert of Bosham, writing to similar effect, warned Becket to delay his homecoming. The de Brocs, he said, had become dangerously violent. He dared not mention the details in a letter, but he believed that before long their crimes would grow to include piracy. On hearing that Becket might soon be returning, they were patrolling the coasts and had already captured one of the archbishop's transport vessels on the high seas, looting his wine casks, massacring some of his crew, and throwing the rest into dungeons.

Such dispiriting firsthand intelligence did not deflect Thomas from his purpose. As late as the end of October, he was still striving steadfastly to make his reconciliation with the king work. To his great credit, his self-control in these extremely difficult weeks is remarkable. If he made mistakes, they were to continue to insist that every single yard of lost Canterbury land had to be restored to him and naïvely to imagine that if he could only drive a wedge between the king and the "untamed beasts"—talking to Henry as he had once done during the height of their intimacy and rebuilding their old mutual rapport—he would succeed, and everything would come right in the end.

It was in exactly this spirit that he now wrote to Pope Alexander urging moderation. Despite seeking revenge on the three bishops for their role in Prince Henry's coronation, he realized that timing would be critical. He needed, he told Alexander, the maximum flexibility. Most of all, and despite the coolness of his reception at Tours and Amboise, he wanted Henry to be given the benefit of the doubt. "We fear," he cautioned, "that a sharp word may inflame the tender ears of that very powerful man and impede the recently begun peace."

He also appealed to Henry in a similar vein, not courting martyrdom, but facing facts—voicing his credible fear that he might be thrown into prison or physically assaulted at the hands of ruffians like the de Brocs when he reached England. After first praising the king's efforts to grant the exiles peace and security, he complained of the snail-like progress in restoring their lands, blaming Ranulf de Broc, lately overheard boasting that Becket "shall not long rejoice in your peace" and threatening to murder him "before he can eat a whole loaf in England." "Fate," Thomas declared, "is drawing me, unhappy wretch that I am, to that afflicted church; by your license and grace I shall return to her, perhaps to die to prevent her destruction, unless your piety deigns swiftly to offer us some other comfort."

In his letter to the pope, Becket puts his finger on the root of the problem: Henry's desire was that his archbishop should obey him in all things. "Oh, why is it," he had said, "that you won't do what I want?" As Thomas explained the situation to Alexander, "He promises that if we wait and show him our earlier devotion, he will compensate us in such manner that no just cause of complaint will remain." What he wanted was for Becket to admit defeat, submit to his will, and promise to obey the ancestral customs—the inference screams from the page. Only then, and not until then, would he be truly reconciled to his former chancellor and throw his weight behind the peace settlement. This was the harsh reality, and no better instance of Becket's capacity for self-restraint, when it was really needed, can be found than when he now refrained from repeating his claim that Henry was a tyrant, instead biting his lip and praising him for his acts of "humanity and kindness to us." Not always did his heart get the better of his head.

Then in November, his hand was incalculably strengthened by the arrival of a bundle of letters from the papal curia. Pope Alexander—whose correspondence had to cross the Alps and who was still under the misapprehension that the younger King Henry had sworn an oath "to preserve the evil customs" at his coronation—had sent decrees ordering the immediate excommunication and suspension of the delinquent bishops. All Thomas had to do was deliver them. Such lesser fry as Geoffrey Ridel and his ilk, the pope left to Thomas to punish. Further decrees—some addressed to Becket, others to William of Sens and Archbishop Rotrou—reestablished the archbishop of Canterbury as resident papal legate for England (as in 1166, the terms covered all of England, with the exception of jurisdiction over Roger of Pont l'Évêque and the Diocese of York) and ordered fresh interdicts to be imposed on Henry's continental lands if the Fréteval agreement did not stick. Perhaps the most dangerous decree was one, issued from Segni on October 13, confirming Thomas's authority to excommunicate anyone he chose, apart from Henry, Eleanor, and their children.

This was the breakthrough for which Thomas had waited so long. This, not Henry's blandishments, was his fatal temptation, and with such an arsenal at his disposal, the risk was that his old impulsiveness would reassert itself. His theatrical instinct certainly did. When he rode out from Sainte-Colombe on his way to rendezvous with Henry at Rouen, he wore silk clothes and was accompanied by a detachment of one hundred horsemen lent to him by sympathetic French noblemen. But when he arrived at Rouen on the appointed day, Henry was nowhere to be found. Instead, John of Oxford, excommunicated at Vézelay and never in Becket's eyes absolved, was there to meet him and hand over a curt note explaining that the king had gone to deal with a skirmish between his vassals and King Louis in the Auvergne.

"How times change!" exclaimed Thomas with a withering glance at John. "Once it would have been the archbishop of Canterbury's job to provide you with a safe-conduct to England, and one considerably safer than you are offering him." To Archbishop Rotrou, who had kept the rendezvous out of politeness and in a purely personal capacity, he then rattled off an avalanche of questions. Why is the king not here in person? What has happened about the agreement we had? Will he not keep his word? What about the money I was promised? Have you received orders to accompany me to England?

"Not at all," Rotrou replied, only to the last. But since Thomas had brought his creditors with him and an embarrassing scene was fast developing as they were insisting on payment, Rotrou offered £300 from his own money to settle the debts.

ON NOVEMBER 24, 1170, after a few days' rest at Rouen, a distinctly crestfallen Becket rode with John of Oxford—now without a cavalry escort—toward the port of Wissant. There, while Thomas was strolling along the beach, studying the weather and the tide, Milo, dean of Boulogne, came to warn him that the English coasts were being closely watched. In a shabby intrigue with the three delinquent bishops, Ranulf de Broc and his men were scouring the horizon for his ship, intending to search his baggage and seize any papal decrees while threatening to cut off his head if he so much as dared to land. To make matters worse, the three bishops meant to collude with Henry in filling five vacant bishoprics without reference to the primate—a flagrant violation of Becket's rights—and were awaiting the arrival of a vessel to carry them over to Normandy.

Stung by such treachery, Becket decided to fire some of his weapons, sending a boy named Osbern to serve the papal decrees on the delinquent bishops. Bravely tracking them down at a church in Dover, the boy thrust their excommunications into their hands before escaping into the busy marketplace.

Thomas set sail for England on December 1, still with John of Oxford as his chaperone. Dropping anchor at Sandwich after a fast, smooth, easy crossing, he found Ranulf de Broc and a gang of armed thugs scurrying toward the quayside. Boarding his ship, they rummaged through his luggage, made violent threats until John of Oxford restrained them, and ordered him to rescind his sentences on the three bishops. He replied that the excommunications were not his but the pope's. The conditions of his appointment as a papal legate did not allow him to absolve Roger of Pont l'Évêque, but he would absolve Gilbert Foliot and Jocelin of Salisbury if they humbly sued for pardon and swore to submit themselves to Alexander's final judgment.

He then took the road for Canterbury, where all along the twelve-mile route he was received as a liberator and with a far greater acclaim than had ever awaited Henry. Clad in his silk robes again, he may also have been able to ride in style, since shortly after landing, he was reunited with three magnificent warhorses he had arranged to be transported from France as a gift for his former charge, the younger Henry.

As he left Sandwich and set out through the villages and hamlets of Kent, bells rang, organs sounded, psalms, hymns, and spiritual songs were sung, parishioners processed with their crosses before them, monks knelt in prayer. Such things partly reflected the usual protocol for a returning archbishop, but the de Brocs were now so unpopular for their extortions that Becket's reception was something far more spectacular. In defiance of the elder Henry's orders, vast crowds of commoners had turned out, young and old, tearing off their outer garments and throwing them into the road, clamoring for a blessing and hailing Thomas as "the father of the orphans and the judge of the widows." "Blessed is he who comes in the name of the Lord," many of them cried. Herbert of Bosham, an eyewitness, felt that he scarcely exaggerated when he ventured a comparison with Christ's entry into Jerusalem on Palm Sunday.

Arriving at Canterbury, Thomas found the city and cathedral bedecked as if for a major festival. William fitz Stephen, who returned to his old loyalty and position on hearing that Becket had landed, says that the citizens wore their best Sunday clothes, held a public banquet, and greeted their primate in a solemn procession. Organ music and the chanting of the Christ Church monks filled the cathedral, the archbishop's hall resounded with fanfares of trumpets, the citizens cheered. Much gratified by the manner of his reception but still extremely apprehensive for the future, Thomas preached a sermon to his monks in the cathedral chapter house, taking as his text "Here we have no abiding city, but we seek one to come."

The next day, Henry's officers appeared, demanding that the archbishop rescind the sentences on the delinquent bishops, which (they said) contravened the ancestral customs. He flatly refused, repeating the offer he had made on the previous day. The bishops then strode in, and after a further discussion, Gilbert and Jocelin came within a whisker of submitting until Roger of Pont l'Évêque overruled them, saying that they could do nothing without first consulting the king and boasting that he had more than enough money in his treasury at York to finance any number of appeals to the pope.

The three bishops did not sail for the elder Henry's court in Normandy without first stirring up more trouble. Seeking to cripple their hated rival forever, they sent their ally Geoffrey Ridel to the junior king with the slanderous, inflammatory message that Becket was plotting to depose him, for which the archbishop should be declared "a public enemy to the king and the kingdom." Following the spontaneous acclamation of the crowds in his favor, Thomas was to be smeared as an insurgent set on alienating the king from his people, even a rebel already raising a strong force of armed men for war.

The result was a national security alert. When a week later Thomas rode to London, the city of his birth, on the first stage of a visit to seek reconciliation with the junior Henry at Woodstock, he was ordered to return with his followers to Canterbury and forbidden to enter any more cities or towns. The aged Henry of Winchester, his consecrator and himself once a kingmaker, at whose palace at Southwark on the south bank of the Thames Becket lodged overnight, was powerless to assist him. Once again he had received a tumultuous welcome from a crowd more than three thousand strong, with bells ringing, organs playing, choirs chanting the canticle *Te Deum Laudamus* (*We Praise Thee, O God*), and processions of commoners streaming as far as three miles out of the city to meet him. Challenging the messenger, whose instructions he did not believe really came from the same fifteen-year-old Henry he had tutored in his own household and known so well, Thomas asked whether it was the young king's intention to snub him. "I have given you your orders," the messenger spat back evasively.

Unconvinced and utterly incredulous that the younger king should have denied him an audience in this coldhearted way, Thomas sent the abbot of St. Albans to make a personal appeal on his behalf to the teenager, who had now reached Windsor on his way to Winchester. But the abbot was forced to deal with intermediaries, and all he achieved was the restitution of the wine stolen earlier by the de Brocs. Seeking reliable information from a different source, Becket next sent his personal physician to Earl Reginald of Cornwall, the elder king's uncle, who had a fistula and had quietly sought his aid. Perhaps the earl was already worrying about his fate in the world to come and wanted to make his peace with the archbishop in this one. He was certainly eager to avoid bloodshed, since when the physician was suddenly recognized though in disguise, Reginald told him to flee for his life and warn Thomas that he and John of Salisbury were in grave danger of assassination. On discovering this news, John promptly burst into tears. Thomas was more sanguine, touching his neck with the palm of his hand and saying, "Here, here (*hic, hic*) is where the knaves will get me."

Returning to Canterbury around December 18, three days before his fiftieth birthday, Becket found the de Brocs as firmly entrenched as ever at Saltwood Castle, with the city itself under a virtual siege from their armed gangs, who guarded the gateways and stationed themselves at key positions around the old Roman walls and along all the nearby roads. Terrorizing the entire neighborhood with their murderous threats like a bunch of mafiosi, they had now turned to robbing the townspeople who supplied the archbishop's provisions and to poaching his deer, kidnapping his dogs, and ambushing and beating his servants. At the instigation of the apostate Cistercian monk Robert de Broc, one of their kinsmen cut off the tail of one of Thomas's packhorses with an ax to vaunt their cruelty.

Christmas Day fell on a Friday in 1170, and Thomas waited until then, choosing not to retaliate until he knew that his cathedral would be packed. After celebrating high mass, he mounted the steps into the pulpit. Preaching a sermon in which he bravely told his audience that he had returned from exile for no other reason than to lift the yoke of servitude from their necks or to suffer death among them, he added that "they already had one archbishop who was a martyr, St. Alphege, and that it was possible that they would shortly have another."* His text was the passage in the Vulgate that reads, "Peace on earth toward men of

* St. Alphege had been murdered by drunken Danes in 1012 for defending the property of the church of Canterbury and refusing to plunder his tenants to pay a ransom.

goodwill." Far from being a promise of universal concord, as is suggested by the later translation in the King James Version, Becket interpreted the text to mean that peace would be limited to men of goodwill, allowing retribution to be unleashed against those, like the de Brocs and their henchmen, who continued to disobey God and the church.

After reciting the customary prayers for the pope and the king, Thomas excommunicated by name all those continuing to occupy the Canterbury lands unlawfully or committing violent acts, with a particular condemnation of Robert de Broc. He had previously warned them of his intentions and urged them to repent, but Robert, for one, had merely laughed in his face and said that if he was to be excommunicated, he would behave like an excommunicate.

After celebrating high mass again the next day, Thomas dispatched Herbert of Bosham and Alexander Llewelyn on a mission to France to inform King Louis of his belief that the Fréteval agreement had failed. In floods of tears as they received their final blessing, his two most loyal and devoted servants protested in vain that the archbishop only wanted them out of the way so that they would not get killed if someone decided to assassinate him. Next, Becket sent a chaplain and another of his clerks on a seemingly routine pastoral mission. But in their leather letter pouch, they carried a short, poignant note for William of Norwich, who—for all his weakness at the Councils of Clarendon and Northampton—had stood by Thomas during his years in exile, one of the few sympathetic bishops daring to dissociate himself publicly from Henry's misdeeds.

"Farewell for ever" (*Semper valete*), said Thomas to this old man who had expressed a heartfelt wish to see him again before he died. They would be the last words he ever wrote.

ON LANDING AT BARFLEUR, the three delinquent bishops had sent copies of their letters of excommunication on ahead to the elder King Henry, which caused him to bang his fists together and, white with fury, storm upstairs to his bedchamber. Arriving at Bayeux on or about December 21, they found him relaxing with his courtiers after agreeing to a truce in the Auvergne. Quickly obtaining an audience, they told their version of the story, making it appear that Becket, by his sentences, had challenged the validity of the junior king's coronation, thus setting out on a course of sedition and revolt with the intention of deposing him and "careering about the kingdom at the head of a strong force of armed men."

Although it was a pack of lies from start to finish, Henry was angry enough to find the tale convincing. "By God's eyes," he swore, "then I'll be next." He simply could not see that the issue for Becket had never been the coronation itself, but the usurpation of his ancient right as primate to perform the ceremony, a right confirmed by the pope. In Henry's mind, the archbishop was now threatening the future of his dynasty.

"Take counsel from your barons and knights," Roger of Pont l'Évêque advised. "It is not for us to say what should be done." Such phony reticence did not, however, stop another of them, probably Gilbert Foliot, from insinuating, "My lord, while Thomas lives, you will have neither peace nor quiet, nor see good days."

Henry kept his Christmas court at Bur-le-Roi, where either that day or, more likely, the next, he convened a great council of barons and prelates almost identical to that which had accused Becket of embezzlement and false accounting at Northampton Castle in 1164. Such was Henry's justice—as first seen in revealing depth in the Battle Abbey case—he had no compunction about trying Becket for his life and liberty in his absence, and without even sending him a formal writ of summons commanding him to attend. Henry presided in court himself, and although the sources are meager, vivid reports by Guernes of Pont-Sainte-Maxence and William fitz Stephen suggest that after denouncing Becket as an "evil man" and a "dangerous enemy" whom he had nurtured and rewarded as his chancellor, only to see Thomas betray him as archbishop, the king leveled a specific charge of treason, saying that Thomas had declared war on him in defiance of the peace terms agreed to at Fréteval and with the malicious intent of depriving the younger Henry of his crown. And in a further litany of charges sent to the pope, Arnulf of Lisieux condemned Becket as the aggressor, who had damaged the church by not tempering his excess of zeal to suit the times and breached his duty as a good pastor by not first allowing those about to be excommunicated enough time to repent.

No sooner had Henry finished speaking than Robert de Breteuil, son of Robert de Beaumont and the new Earl of Leicester, a leading supporter of the junior Henry, led the attack on Becket, calling him a dangerous man who should be outlawed. The old Ingelram de Bohun, Jocelin of Salisbury's uncle, echoed his words, saying, "The only way to deal with such a man is to hang him on a gibbet." A Breton lord, William Malvoisin, spoke next. "Once," he recalled, "as I was returning from Jerusalem, I passed through Rome, and while I was there, I asked my host about, among other things, the popes, and was told that a certain pope had been killed for his insolence and intolerable impudence" (possibly Lucius II, who had been felled with a stone in 1145 while leading an assault on the Capitol in an attempt to suppress a popular revolt). That, it seems, was the way to deal with troublesome priests.

Swiftly concluding the debate, Henry gave his decision, which was to send William de Mandeville, Earl of Essex, and Richard de Humez immediately across the Channel with instructions to capture Thomas with a force of knights, perhaps with the intention of holding him under house arrest, but more likely throwing him into prison.

Perhaps during these deliberations, perhaps a day or so earlier (the sources disagree or are ambiguous), Henry let slip the fatal words that led directly to Becket's murder. Although recorded in variant versions, their force is the same. Edward Grim reports him as shouting, "What miserable drones and traitors have I nourished and promoted in my realm, who let their lord be treated with such shameful contempt by a lowborn clerk!" Guernes says that he cried out, "A man who has eaten my bread, who came to my court poor and I have raised him high—now he draws up his heel to kick me in the teeth! He has shamed my kin, shamed my realm. The grief goes to my heart, and no one has avenged me!" The chronicler Gervase of Canterbury says that he bellowed, "How many cowardly, useless drones have I nourished that not even a single one is willing to avenge me of the wrongs I have suffered!"

The most famous and compelling rendition—"Who will rid me of this turbulent priest?"—is apocryphal. Generally assumed to have originated with Lord Lyttelton in his *History of the Life of King Henry the Second,* begun in 1767, these words were first used by Thomas Mortimer in the opening volume of his *New History of England,* published three years earlier. Inaccurate and misleading as a translation of the Latin sources, this variant also misses the crucial point that—true to form—Henry's grudge was as much rooted in his view of his archbishop's ingratitude and presumption as of his alleged treachery. As he had said many times before, he regarded Thomas as "lowborn," "the son of one of my villeins." The social slur is integral to the offense. He also believed that it was only the cowardice of his own courtiers—their cowering reluctance to defy the church—that was stopping him from silencing Becket.

Henry's latest tantrum closely resembled an earlier one at Chinon in May 1166, when he had cried out that his barons were all traitors "who had neither the zeal nor the courage to rid him of a single man." To those who did not know him well, such outbursts could easily be taken literally. Barons more familiar with his habits, like those present at Chinon, knew differently. For all their apparent incitement to murder, these were rages more like the one at Caen in 1166, when in his fulminations against Richard de Humez, Henry had torn off his hat, hurled his cloak and clothes into a distant corner of the room, and pulled the silk covering off his bed before groveling on the floor and eating straw. In such a moment of extreme fury, he could become sufficiently uncontrolled or irrational as to lose momentarily all psychological balance. He would soon pull himself round and think better of it, and yet it is easy to see how some of his lesser flunkies might have taken his words at face value.

It was essentially just bad luck that this time there were within earshot four of Henry's least important household knights, men thus far merely on the fringes of intimacy with the king but with ambitions to rise high and fast in his favor. Taking his latest outburst literally, they resolved to prove their valor by setting out on an enterprise of their own, seeking to ensure that their king was indeed avenged and themselves suitably rewarded. Even Henry afterward admitted this, conceding that it was undoubtedly "for" him, if not "by" him, that Thomas was murdered by these four knights.

Reginald fitz Urse, William de Tracy, Richard Brito, and Hugh de Morville were all prominent landowners in the southwestern shires of England. All had become royal servants, but at least three had had some sort of previous relationship with Becket. If fitz Stephen is to be believed, Reginald, Hugh, and William had each done homage to Thomas as chancellor and sworn a mutual pact, saving only their liege loyalty to Henry. The same three too, whether personally or through their fathers, had been closely bound to King Stephen and so had been threatened after Henry's accession—perhaps intriguingly by Becket—with the forfeiture of property that they had pillaged during the civil war. Since Richard Brito, a younger son and the least socially exalted of the four, was a satellite of either fitz Urse or de Tracy, it is clear that this group had not come together entirely by accident. But how far any of their earlier encounters with Becket now inspired them to commit murder will never be known. Their backstories are far too murky and obscure.

The four knights slipped out of Bur-le-Roi secretly on the evening of December 26 as soon as the great council had ended. Traveling independently at high speed and sailing from different ports, they found the wind and tide in their favor and reached Saltwood Castle within two days. There they rested overnight before mustering a large force of knights and armed men with the willing assistance of the de Brocs. Riding to Canterbury, they and a small detachment of about a dozen men made their way quietly and unobtrusively through the main gateway of the archbishop's palace into the courtyard, while others scoured the city, ordering the citizens to take up arms in the king's name and to accompany them to the palace. When the frightened citizens refused to cooperate, the de Brocs ordered a curfew, instructing everyone "to stay indoors and keep the peace, no matter what they might see or hear." The de Brocs then stationed their crack troops in the house of a man called Gilbert opposite the gateway to the archbishop's palace. They positioned the rest of their forces around the walls and especially at the exits of the city to ensure that no attempt could be made to launch a rescue bid—or if there was one, that no way of escape could be found from the city into the countryside and on toward the coast.

So it was that shortly before three o'clock on the afternoon of Tuesday, December 29, the scene would be set for one of the most infamous events of the Middle Ages. It is not absolutely certain that all four of the knights planned to kill Becket when they first arrived, unarmed and fortified by drink, at the door of his great hall after leaving their swords in the courtyard. Edward Grim, for one, says that at first they intended simply to capture Thomas and throw him in prison. But Grim contradicts himself, agreeing with Roger of Pontigny that at least one of the knights boasted afterward that far from waiting until they had returned to the courtyard for their swords and bludgeoned their way into the cathedral, they would have killed Thomas with the haft of his own processional cross before leaving his great hall, if only they could have contrived to be alone with him for long enough.

Impetuous, warlike men, reckless of bloodshed and with a burning desire to prove themselves in the eyes of the king and win the highest of rewards, the four knights had ridden into Canterbury with violence on their minds. They were to leave—as de Tracy would afterward confess and Herbert of Bosham record—spattered with blood and quaking with sheer, stark terror, afraid at every step that the earth was about to open up before them and devour their bodies alive.

27

MURDER IN THE CATHEDRAL

SWIFTLY DISMOUNTING FROM THEIR HORSES IN THE COURTyard, for soon it would be dusk, leaving their chain mail and weapons stacked up beneath a great mulberry tree, the four knights strode into the archbishop's great hall, where the members of Becket's household were finishing dinner and the plates being cleared away. They demanded to talk to the archbishop immediately.

Becket deliberately kept them waiting. When at last he arrived to greet them, all save Reginald fitz Urse, a natural bully, were tongue-tied. The verbal confrontation is described by at least five eyewitnesses, all monks or clerks who were present throughout. Their reports, written independently at different times and quoting what they claimed to be the exact words spoken, concur remarkably and read so vividly and journalistically, though set down originally in Latin, that they might have been compiled yesterday.

"God help you," began fitz Urse, making himself spokesman for the four. "We have brought you a message from the king. Will you hear it in public or in private?"

"Whichever you choose," replied Thomas.

Hastily putting aside their plates, the monks and clerks began slipping away. Thomas recalled them, correctly guessing that if he was left alone with these potential assassins, they could easily kill him on the spot with their bare hands.

John of Salisbury interjected, "My lord, let us discuss this in private."

But Thomas knew better. "It would serve no good purpose," he answered firmly. "Such things should not be spoken in private nor in the chamber, but in public."

"When the king made peace with you," fitz Urse resumed accusingly, "he sent you back to Canterbury as you requested, but you—in contrary fashion, adding insult to injury—have broken the peace and in your obstinate pride have excommunicated those at whose hands the king's son was crowned and anointed, from which it is all too clear that your intention would be to depose the king's son and take away his crown if you had the power."

"Never was it my wish as God is my witness," said Thomas, "to disinherit my lord the king's son or to diminish his power. Even now I am ready to satisfy my lord wherever he pleases, if in anything I have done amiss; but he has forbidden me with threats to enter any of his cities and towns. In any case, it was not by me but by the lord pope that the bishops were excommunicated."

"You were behind it," snarled fitz Urse.

Thomas remained calm. "I do not deny that it was done through me, but the sentence itself was given by my superior and is beyond my power to change, and it is certainly beyond my power to absolve the archbishop of York as he is outside of my jurisdiction. I made an offer to the bishops of London and Salisbury for their absolution if they humbly sued for pardon and agreed to accept the verdict of the pope, but they rejected it."

"The king's orders are that you and yours must depart this realm with all your men: From this day forth there can never be peace with you, for you have broken the peace."

"Stop threatening me, Reginald. I put my trust in the king of Heaven and from this day forward I refuse to leave my church. Once I fled like a timid priest. Now I have returned to my church in the counsel and obedience of the lord pope. I have not come back to flee again. Anyone who wants me can find me here. You know that the lord king, on St. Mary Magdalene's day at Fréteval, admitted me again to his peace and favor and sent me back to England with a letter of safe-conduct? Some of you I know were present there, and it seemed to me that you were pleased at the event."

"From whom, then," countered Reginald, "do you hold your archbishopric?"

"My spiritual authority," answered Thomas, "I hold from God and the lord pope, my temporalities and material possessions from the lord king."

"Do you not recognize that you hold everything from the king?"

"By no means; we must render to Caesar the things that are Caesar's and to God the things that are God's."

"But I'm telling you," said Reginald, grinding his teeth, "what the king says. You've been rash enough to excommunicate his officers when you ought to have shown respect to the king's majesty and submitted your vengeance to his judgment."

Thomas, bridling and pausing for breath, drew himself up to his full height. "In vain you threaten me. If all the swords in England were aimed at my head, your threats could not dislodge me from my observance of God's justice and my obedience to the lord pope. I tell you I shall strike at anyone who violates the right of the pope or Christ's church. I will not spare him, nor will I delay to impose ecclesiastical sentences upon him."

The knights stepped forward, jostling him and threatening, "You've risked your head by saying that."

"Are you then come to slay me? If so, I shall commit myself and my cause to the great Judge of all mankind. I am not moved by threats, nor are your swords more ready to strike than is my soul for martyrdom. Find someone else to frighten—you will find me steadfast in the battle of the Lord."

"We are King's men," growled fitz Urse. And turning to the monks and clerks, he cried out, "In the king's name, we command you, both clerks and monks, to seize and hold that man, lest he flee before the king can take full justice on his body."

Storming out, they took two of the archbishop's servants as hostages as they left, provoking Becket to pursue them as far as the door, angrily demanding that they release his men. Contemptuously, they took no notice.

Once outside, at a signal from one of the knights, the crack troops stationed in the house opposite the gateway to the archbishop's palace charged into the courtyard, crying, "King's men, King's men!" Once they were inside, the great gate was slammed and bolted behind them, and Simon de Croil, a tenant of the neighboring abbey of St. Augustine's, was put on guard in the porter's lodge with orders to prevent anyone from entering or leaving. Gathering a handful of their retainers, the four knights then returned to the mulberry tree to collect their swords and chain mail, arming themselves in the porch of the archbishop's great hall.

Thomas, meanwhile, had returned to his clerks, reassuring them and telling them not to be afraid. Some were utterly terrified; others believed there was no undue cause for alarm. "The knights," they said, "were drunk when they arrived. It was the drink speaking, and we have the assurance of the king's peace."

John of Salisbury, who believed that Becket could have shown more tact toward the four knights, took the lead in trying to calm things down, talking candidly to his friend as he had done so many times before during the past twenty-five years.

"Look, Thomas. You're doing what you always do. You act and speak on impulse, saying just what you like, never asking anyone's advice. What need was there in a man of your rank to inflame and exasperate those butchers still further? Would it not have been better to have taken our advice and given them a softer answer?"

His intervention has always been taken by Becket's biographers to support the notion of Thomas as incorrigibly reckless and impetuous. Impulsive and a risk taker he often could be, but on this occasion nothing would have been different whatever he had said to the angry knights. John—ever prudent; a lover of life, his friends, his books, and a bottle of wine; and at fifty-three only three years older than Thomas and too young to die—lived mainly in a world of scholars and of the mind and was terrified at the prospect of violence. For all his fine talk in his *Policraticus* and elsewhere, he was no more willing to stand up to the king and the "untamed beasts" than Becket's old Paris master Robert of Melun had been. Only when Henry had insisted in 1166 that, as the price of his return to favor, John should swear an oath to observe the ancestral customs had he reluctantly accepted that in all good conscience, he had to stand his ground. Otherwise, his philosophy (as he had more than once declared) was to accept what Pope Alexander and Thomas had accepted and to reject what they had rejected.

Becket, who as chancellor at the council of war outside the gates of Toulouse had discovered to his cost what angry knights could be like, was in no mood for a lecture on philosophy, cutting the discussion short. "My counsel is now all taken," he said. "I know well enough what I ought to do."

"Pray God that it may turn out well," said John.

"May God's will be done," Thomas replied.

NO SOONER WERE these words uttered than a terrible noise was heard outside. The knights were back, and this time their followers were with them. Clad in full armor, carrying swords, axes, and hatchets, they tried the door between the porch and the archbishop's hall, only to find it locked and barricaded against them by Becket's servants. Frustrated in their first attempt, they hurriedly retraced their steps into the courtyard to search for a back way in. They were lucky, because one of their number was Robert de Broc, the royal sequestrator who had occupied the archbishop's palace for the past six years and so knew all its entrances and secret passages. Following him, they scrambled along a side path and through some bushes into an orchard, where a set of stone steps led up to an oriel window on the opposite side of the building.

There they were in luck again, for workmen repairing the steps had finished for the day, leaving their tools and a ladder behind. Clambering up the ladder, the knights smashed open the wooden shutters of the window and jumped inside the hall, unbolting the door to admit their men waiting outside.

The monks, many of whom now stood around Thomas so as to shield him, urged him to take sanctuary inside his cathedral.

"No," he answered. "Far be it from me. Most monks are too easily intimidated. Do not be afraid."

The bell then rang for vespers, which Thomas had promised to attend. He rose, and instantly the monks tried to drag him toward a door, at the opposite end of the hall from the main entrance, that led into a passage directly linked to the cloister. But he resisted their efforts until his processional cross was borne before him. Since his faithful cross-bearer, Alexander Llewelyn, had already left for France with Herbert of Bosham, it was carried by a junior clerk named Henry of Auxerre.

The monks reached the connecting door, only to discover that the bolt was stuck. All hope of escape seemed lost until one of them, rushing forward, quickly said a prayer and pulled on the bolt, which slid back "as if in liquid glue." Hurrying Thomas around the freezing cloister, a group of monks pushed him through a door leading into the north transept of the cathedral, slamming it shut before everyone was inside.

Thomas ordered them to reopen the door. "The church," he said sternly, "is a house of prayer and is not to be made into a fortress."

It was now dark, and the monks whose turn it was to say vespers were chanting in the choir. The only light came from their candles and from the oil lamps above the altars in the adjacent chapels. Seeing Thomas stride into the cathedral, the monks ceased vespers and ran to meet him, rejoicing that he was alive and unharmed, since rumor had it that he had already been arrested or was dead.

Becket started to walk up the steps toward the high altar in the choir. He had already mounted four steps when fitz Urse burst through the cloister door, still in full armor and brandishing his sword. "Where is Thomas Becket, traitor to the king and the kingdom?" he shouted. It was a deliberate use of the archbishop's lowborn surname—an insult designed to remind him that he was very much the social inferior of his assailants. Within a few seconds, the other knights were behind him, their swords drawn, followed by their retainers and friends. Pandemonium broke out inside the cathedral, as all those who had been at vespers gasped in horror at the armed gang.

Greeted by a stunned silence, fitz Urse cried out again, "Where is the archbishop?"

"Here I am. What do you want from me?" answered Thomas. "I am no traitor to the king, but a priest." He now stood by the east wall of the transept, encircled by his clerks and monks, beside a pillar of the arcading. He might so easily have fled or hidden himself in the dark and winding passages of the crypt below, or climbed a spiral staircase behind a concealed door nearby leading to the vaulted chambers in the cathedral's roof, but he refused.

One of the assassins shouted, "Absolve and restore to communion those whom you have excommunicated."

"I will not absolve them until they have repented and made satisfaction," he replied.

"Then you will die now and receive your just deserts."

"And I am ready to die for my Lord, so that in my blood the church may obtain peace and liberty. But I forbid you in the name of God Almighty and on pain of excommunication to harm any of my men, whether clerk or lay."

Then the knights rushed at him, and with bloodshed plainly imminent, three of his more fearful companions—John of Salisbury, Benedict of Peterborough, and William of Canterbury—fled to hide under altars or in the crypt down a small flight of stairs, out of sight but still within earshot. Only Robert of Merton, Edward Grim, and William fitz Stephen stood beside him to the last.

When the other knights attempted to bundle Thomas onto the shoulders of William de Tracy so that they could deal with him outside, he threw his arms around the adjacent pillar, holding on with all his strength, so that they could not dislodge him. Fitz Urse was the first to use his sword, taunting the trapped archbishop by flicking his fur cap off his head with the tip, then striking him with the flat side of the weapon, saying, "Fly, you are a dead man."

"Unhand me, Reginald," said Thomas. "You are my sworn vassal. You know well the bond existing between us. You and your accomplices are acting like madmen."

These words, usually thought impossible to explain, make perfect sense in the light of fitz Stephen's observation that fitz Urse, de Morville, and de Tracy had sworn homage to Becket as chancellor, saving only their liege loyalty to the king. In reply, these three knights cried out their defiance, declaring that now they were the king's men, not his, and fitz Urse grabbed at the archbishop's cloak.

"Unhand me, Reginald, you pimp," shouted Thomas, still enough of an athlete to shove him away with such force that he keeled over backward. "I will not leave this church. If you wish to kill me, you must kill me here."

Whether Becket called fitz Urse a "pimp" as something more than a general insult is hard to unpick. A credible reason for using this term might be that his position at Henry's court was that of an under-marshal, an assistant to his friend and coconspirator Ranulf de Broc, the king's crony and official whoremaster.

"Strike, strike," shouted a furious fitz Urse to his companions. Thomas, realizing the moment had come, bent forward, covering his eyes with his hands and saying, "To God and St. Mary and the saints who protect and defend this cathedral, and to the blessed St. Denis and St. Alphege, I commend myself and the church's cause."

William de Tracy lunged forward, aiming a blow with his sword that glanced off the top of Becket's cranium and cut through his clothing to the shoulder bone. Edward Grim, who stood his ground and was closest to Thomas, instinctively threw out one of his arms to shield him and was grievously wounded, his arm almost severed.

With blood streaming down his face from his head, Thomas continued to pray: "Into thy hands, O Lord, I commend my spirit." As he knelt down, clasping and stretching out his hands to God, de Tracy slashed again, aiming at his head, causing him to fall prostrate beside an altar dedicated to St. Benedict, his arms still outstretched.

While he lay there in agony, murmuring, "For the name of Jesus and the protection of the church I am ready to embrace death," Richard Brito smote his skull with such force that he lopped off the whole upper portion of his head, causing sparks to flash as his sword struck the paving stones below and shattered into shards. "Take that," he screamed, "for love of my lord, William, the king's brother!" William, always one of Henry's favorites, had, of course, supposedly pined to death in 1164 as the direct result of Becket's refusal to license his marriage to the widowed Isabel de Warenne. These knights were certainly settling some old scores.

Hugh de Morville, the fourth assassin, had been holding back the onlookers and did not touch Thomas, but one of his flunkies, Hugh of Horsea, a renegade clerk known as "Mauclerk" for his evil ways, delivered the coup de grâce, putting his foot on the archbishop's neck to hold it still and, with the point of his sword, scraping out the brains from the hollow of his skull and smearing them, mixed with blood and bone fragments, over the paving stones. "This one won't get up again," he shouted.

The knights then hurried out of the cathedral and went back inside the archbishop's palace, where they ransacked Becket's chests and traveling coffers, stripping them of their gold and silver plate and cash. Then they mounted their horses and returned to Saltwood Castle, leaving the de Brocs and their men to loot anything else of value. They stole everything from clothes, furniture, rings, ornaments, vellum books, and jeweled vestments to the horses and harness from the stables, dividing the spoils among themselves.

WHEN AT LAST the looters had gone, torches were fetched, and the monks and clerks, with a crowd of weeping citizens, thronged around the murdered archbishop. Even while his body lay cold on the paving stones, some of these onlookers, aware that a truly awesome event had occurred, cut off pieces of their clothing and dipped them in his blood for use as relics. Some daubed their eyes with his blood, perhaps hoping that their defective sight might be cured. Others brought tiny bottles and made off with as much blood as they could, either to keep or to sell. The paralyzed wife of one of these souvenir hunters, when he returned home, asked to be washed in water mixed with drops of the blood. No sooner was her bath completed, says fitz Stephen, than she was miraculously cured. And within a week, a local woman named Brithiva had recovered her sight through the application of a bloodstained piece of cloth, another woman married to a Sussex knight had been cured of blindness, and a Berkshire knight had been cured of rheumatism in his left arm.

At last the monks succeeded in clearing the cathedral of the crowd. The remaining blood and brains, already beginning to coagulate and turn black, were carefully collected and put into a silver basin by a monk called Ernold, to become a precious treasure in later years. Becket's pallium and vestments, stained with blood, were—"for the sake of charity and his soul"—given to the poor, who immediately sold them for what they would fetch.

After his shattered skull had been bound with a white linen cloth, the archbishop's body was placed on a bier, carried through the choir, and laid before the high altar. Robert of Merton then said silent prayers, before thrusting his hand beneath Thomas's outer garments to reveal a hair shirt. Probably first put on while Becket was in sanctuary at the abbey of Pontigny and now teeming with lice, it caused a sensation among the monks, who had never been privy to this final secret, making many of them believe that they had seriously misjudged their spiritual leader.

The next day, Robert de Broc reappeared with another gang of thugs, threatening to drag Becket's corpse behind horses to the gallows and hang it as a traitor's, or else tear it apart and throw the pieces into a swamp, unless the monks disposed of it speedily. Fearful of a second act of sacrilege, the monks made haste to bury it. There was no time either to wash the body or to embalm it according to the usual custom for a deceased archbishop. Instead, after removing what still remained of his clothing—apart from his shoes, hair shirt, and the monastic underclothes that he had also begun to wear at Pontigny—they dressed him as best they could in the vestments he had worn on the day of his consecration, all of which he had ordered to be kept ready for his return. Reverently, they laid his chalice, ring, gloves, sandals, and pastoral staff upon the corpse. The burial rites were said by the monks, but because the cathedral had been desecrated by bloodshed, no mass was held. Once the service was over, the body was interred in a stone coffin in the crypt, facing two altars built into the east wall—one dedicated to St. John the Baptist, the other to St. Augustine—directly beneath the high altar where Thomas had celebrated his first mass.

Finally, a small group of monks—fitz Stephen says they were led by the same Ernold who had scooped up the last of the archbishop's blood and brains—returned to the north transept to put benches over the spot where Becket had been murdered, to mark it out and prevent it from being trampled on by the feet of visitors. That place can still be seen, a site of pilgrimage scarcely altered after almost nine hundred years.

28
AFTERMATH

THE NEWS OF BECKET'S ASSASSINATION SENT SHOCK WAVES throughout Europe, and at the speed that the fastest of couriers could ride. "Where shall I begin?" asked John of Salisbury in a vivid and detailed narrative of the terrifying events he had seen and heard with his own eyes and ears in the cathedral, a document he circulated in multiple copies among his friends. "For every aspect of the archbishop's death-agony conspires to glorify the dying man forever, to reveal the depravity of his assailants and brand them eternally with shame."

Accusing the three delinquent bishops, and especially Roger of Pont l'Évêque, of maliciously inciting Henry to order the murder, John was already predicting that the site where Becket had been martyred would become a notable place of pilgrimage. The palsied would be cured there, the blind would receive their sight, the deaf would hear, the dumb speak, the lame walk, those with fevers be restored to health, lepers would be cleansed, devils be cast out.

Roger of Pont l'Évêque instantly retaliated, accusing John of lying, but since rumor already had it that Roger was the main instigator of the story that Becket was "plotting" to depose the younger king, on the strength of which he had advised the elder Henry to summon the great council that had tried the archbishop for treason in his absence, the moral high ground was John's. Moreover, Roger, a fortnight before the murder in a round-robin to his own subordinates, had accused Becket in writing of behaving with Pharaoh's pride, so he had only himself to blame when John took his revenge by circulating copies of this incriminating document even as its author was trying to suppress it, also making public the sordid details of Roger's moral shortcomings as a sodomite and pedophile. Mud sticks, and John would ensure that Roger was pelted with bucketfuls.

Henry was at Argentan when the news reached him around January 1. Arnulf of Lisieux, in a letter to Pope Alexander, described the near panic triggered by its arrival. "At the first words of the messenger," he began, "the king burst into loud lamentation and exchanged his royal robes for sackcloth and ashes. Mourning more, it seemed, for a friend than for a subject, at times he fell into a stupor, after which he would again utter groans and cries louder and more bitter than before." For three days, he remained shut in his bedchamber, neither eating nor admitting visitors. He was only too aware that his taunts had inspired the four knights to commit their terrible crime; he also knew that his enemies would charge him with complicity in it. But Arnulf's attempts to paint Henry in the colors of deep mourning for the assassination of an old friend were overblown. Horrified at the enormity of the deed and its consequences for his reputation, Henry assuredly was; troubled in his conscience he was not.

In fact, he at first seems to have believed that he could brazen it out, for it would take six weeks at the least for someone to carry the news to Pope Alexander, now settled comfortably at Frascati in the Campagna. Believing that his own courier could get there first, Henry tried to exculpate himself, composing a shameless letter to the pope spinning the tale that Becket had not returned to England in a spirit of peace and reconciliation as he had promised at Fréteval, but with fire and the sword, stirring sedition, excommunicating royal servants right and left, and "behaving so impudently that he made some powerful enemies, who had fallen upon him and murdered him." In short, the blame was Becket's alone.

Yet Henry's defiant approach, devoid of surprise at the assassination and with barely expressed grief, was a grave error. So angry and distressed would Alexander become that for eight days he would refuse to discuss the affair even with his own cardinals. In any case, Alexander Llewelyn, sent posthaste by Herbert of Bosham from Paris, made the journey to Frascati in record time, so that even when the fastest of the king's envoys galloped into the courtyard of the papal villa on March 3, they discovered that the pope had already given orders that no Englishman should be granted an audience under any circumstances, and by the time the slowest arrived on March 20, the eve of Palm Sunday, there was still little hope of access being granted imminently.

As Maundy Thursday approached, on which day the king's envoys feared that the pope intended to excommunicate Henry and place all his territories under a general interdict, they dramatically reversed their tactics and humbly offered, through the mediation of those cardinals most susceptible to bribery, to swear an oath on Henry's behalf that he would submit unconditionally to the pope's future judgment. According to a report from one of these diplomats, they "no longer denied that the king had given cause for the murder by uttering the words which had given the murderers their excuse for killing the archbishop." So when Maundy Thursday arrived, somewhat mollified and doubtless more than a little relieved—since when confronted by so stark a choice, he was no more anxious than Becket had been to punish the Angevin king—Alexander excommunicated only the murderers and all their aiders and abettors, content once more to await future developments.

Meanwhile, William of Sens, the papal legate for France, had seized the initiative. "Of all the crimes we have ever read or heard of," he railed in a letter to the curia, "this murder easily takes top place, exceeding all the tyranny of Nero, the perfidy of Julian [i.e., Julian the Apostate, a fourth-century Roman emperor who renounced Christianity and reinstated the pagan cults], and even the sacrilegious treachery of Judas." Reviling Henry as "that enemy to the angels and the whole body of Christ," William used the powers granted to him by his existing papal commissions to reimpose a general interdict on Henry's continental lands and begged the pope to approve it, "that God's honor and yours may be preserved."

Hearing of this sentence a few days after Easter, Alexander confirmed both it and the excommunications that Becket had imposed on the three delinquent bishops before he died. He forbade Henry to enter a church or to hear mass until new legates could arrive in Normandy to hear his confession and absolve him, but Alexander stopped short of excommunicating him. As to the three bishops, he ruled that the two lesser offenders, Gilbert Foliot and Jocelin of Salisbury, could be conditionally absolved if they swore on the Gospels that never "by letter, word, or deed" had they incited the king to violence against his archbishop. Only Roger of Pont l'Évêque was more harshly treated. To secure his absolution, he had to wait another eighteen months and employ one of the most distinguished lawyers in Christendom, the same Master Vacarius whom Theobald had invited to England and who was now settled at York. But none of their careers could survive the damage to their reputations caused by Becket's murder.

Sent as papal representatives to Normandy to absolve Henry were Cardinals Albert de Morra, Becket's old law teacher from Bologna, and Theodwin of San Vitale, both fair-minded churchmen of excellent repute. To their surprise and dismay, Henry seemed unconcerned whether they absolved him or not, nor did he mean to hang around in Normandy, for even as he approached the age of forty, he could neither rest nor settle in one place. Barely had the cardinals set out across the Alps than he took ship at Milford Haven in south Wales. Destined for Ireland with a large army, he was determined to subject the native Irish kings to the authority of the English Crown on the death of his old ally Dermot MacMurrough, king of Leinster.

Summoned by the papal envoys to return to Normandy in February 1172, he used such familiar excuses as the long distance, bad weather, and the uncertain perils of the Irish Sea to delay his departure until his campaign was all but completed and the Irish kings (or most of them) had come to offer him their fealty. When at last he met the envoys in May, initially at the Cistercian monastery of Savigny, he stormed out after refusing to submit to their unconditional judgment, despite his earlier promises to obey them. If he was to be forced to submit to the church, he said, he expected to be told first exactly how, where, and on what terms. But when he had cooled down, a settlement was reached in only two days. A ceremony of absolution would take place on May 21 outside the cathedral of Avranches, with a second performance at Caen on May 30. This was to be ratified by the publication of an official "charter of reconciliation for the death of the blessed Thomas," which was to be sealed by Henry and the papal envoys, with copies sent to the papal curia and to some (if perhaps not all) of the primates in Europe to ensure maximum publicity.

After Henry had knelt before the pope's representatives in front of the cathedral of Avranches, they absolved him and led him inside. It was a rare capitulation on his part, and the reason is simple. He had no choice. Despite this, he insisted on maintaining his royal dignity, refusing to observe many of the customary rituals used on these occasions, such as walking from the gates of the city to the cathedral in penitential garb or taking off his shoes, nor was he scourged by monks.

Like the delinquent bishops, he first had to exonerate himself from complicity in the murder by swearing a solemn oath with his hands on the Gospels, declaring that he had "neither ordered nor willed" Becket's death, adding spontaneously for the benefit of his listeners (and possibly said in a backhanded way) that "he grieved more for it . . . than for the death of his own father or mother." But as the papal envoys had insisted, he confessed that he had himself been the principal cause of the murder: not that he had expressly ordered it (as an eyewitness reports his words), "but that his friends and retainers, seeing his angry face and his burning eyes . . . made ready, without his knowledge, to avenge his wrongs."

Henry's reconciliation to the church did not come without strings. He had to promise first to allow all future appeals from the church courts to the papal curia without license or other restrictions. "They will," he promised, "be permitted freely and in good faith, without fraud or trickery." Only if it could be proved at the outset that an appeal was malicious could he ask the appellants to give security "that they will seek no wrong to me or disgrace to my kingdom." He then agreed to "abrogate utterly the customs that were introduced against the churches of my land during my time." Although inevitably he continued to pretend that no such "novel" customs existed—"I reckon them to be few or none," he said afterward—the church would force him to back down over criminous clerks as well as appeals to the pope. Once again, he simply had no choice.

Subsequent clauses of the official "charter of reconciliation" required him to make full restitution to the church of Canterbury and to the exiles, restoring everything that they had possessed a full year before Becket had gone into exile, not merely three months before as he had previously offered. He was to grant an amnesty to all the returning exiles and was to perform certain acts of prayer and fasting, which were kept confidential to spare his honor. He was to maintain a contingent of two hundred knights for the defense of Jerusalem for a year, the costs to be assessed by the Knights Templar, and to take the cross himself by the following Christmas, departing for the East by the summer of 1173 at the latest and staying there for at least three years unless excused by the pope. Lastly (and something he always wanted to forget), he swore an oath of allegiance to "Pope Alexander and his Catholic successors." According to the "charter of reconciliation," it said, "you have sworn that you will not withdraw from the lord pope Alexander and his Catholic successors as long as they regard you as a Christian and Catholic king like your forebears."

During the repeat ceremony at Caen, the junior King Henry was brought center stage and compelled to accept terms similar to his father's, swearing oaths denying his culpability in Becket's murder and to Pope Alexander and his successors, and promising to allow appeals to the pope, to abrogate the offending "customs," and to make restitution of church property. Possibly he also did the same at Avranches—for it appears that the intention was always to bring him over from England in time—but the exact date of his arrival is uncertain. The ceremony at Caen may have been conducted chiefly to ensure that he too was securely bound into the settlement. The pope did not want the hard-wrung agreements to lapse when the younger king took over.

Herbert of Bosham later claimed that some of the offending practices would still be observed regardless of Henry's oaths. But while the precise boundaries between the jurisdictions of church and state would continue to be disputed on an almost infinite number of points of detail until the Tudor Reformation, the concessions won from Henry meant that Becket (and Pope Alexander) had finally gained their main aim. If Henry's project had all along been to cut off the English church from the incursions of papal authority and canon law by creating a regional church under royal control, enclosed within the ring fence of the coast and with himself as the final court of appeal, he had failed abysmally.

Henry was also forced to make good on the amnesty he had granted, even allowing Becket's relatives to return home. The dead archbishop's eldest sister, Agnes, and her family recovered their land and position in London, and in 1173 Henry grudgingly made Mary, Thomas's youngest sister, abbess of the great nunnery of Barking in Essex. A year later, he granted their sister Rose a pardon and provided her and her two sons with an annuity of 10 marks as alms. And in 1179, he allowed the Christ Church monks to present Agnes's son, John, to the vicarage of Halstow in east Kent and his cousin John, Rose's son, to the living of St. Mary Bothaw, a parish tucked away in a narrow lane within a stone's throw of the family's old house in Cheapside, London. Becket would surely have appreciated that very much.

SUCH CONCESSIONS ASIDE, the idea that Henry was ever truly penitent is romantic and absurd. When Bishop Hamo of Saint-Pol-de-Léon, one of his sworn vassals, was assassinated in Brittany in January 1171 at the behest of his elder brother Guihomar, Henry would take strong and speedy reprisals—but only because it suited him to do so. Marching into Brittany, he annexed the most important of Guihomar's castles and destroyed the rest. The Norman chronicler Robert of Torigni cheekily makes no direct reference to Becket's murder in his annal for 1170, reporting Hamo's in its place and only later inserting verses referring to Thomas in the margin of his manuscript.

But if Henry hunted down Hamo's killers, he did very little to Becket's, at least at first. After sharing out their spoils at Saltwood, the four knights retired to one of Hugh de Morville's castles at Knaresborough in Yorkshire, where they hunted with impunity in the royal forests and were entertained by sheriffs and royal constables. Only after Pope Alexander excommunicated them did the consequences of their terrible deed begin to catch up with them. William de Tracy showed some remorse by confessing his sins to Bartholomew of Exeter, his local bishop. He then went to Rome to seek absolution, stopping briefly at Henry's court at Argentan, where the king urged all four knights to seek penance from the pope.

Of course, advising the knights to obtain absolution from the church in no way prevented Henry from severely punishing them himself had he wanted to. He did not. When prominent churchmen advised him to act, he simply ignored their advice or made feeble excuses. Such was his warped sense of justice, he took the view that if Becket and the church had chosen to claim jurisdiction over criminous clerks, it was up to the church to punish criminous laymen who had murdered or injured priests—they could not have it both ways.

Or at least that was his view until it suited him to think differently about it, for almost exactly as John of Salisbury had predicted, a cult grew up around the tomb of the murdered archbishop with breathtaking speed. The cathedral was reopened to visitors during Easter week in 1171, and on December 21, Becket's birthday and a week before the first anniversary of his murder, services there resumed when, in response to eager public demand, the monks—unwillingly at first—opened the crypt where the dead archbishop's body was interred. No sooner had they done so than miracles began to occur.

Stemming initially from the hero's welcome accorded to Becket on his return from exile, the popularity of his cult came to focus on the blood and brains that Ernold the monk had scooped up from the paving stones. Even when diluted heavily with water, they were said to perform legendary acts of healing, requiring the secondment of one, then two of the Christ Church monks as full-time guardians of the shrine.

Soon operating on a fully commercial basis, the shrine quickly built up a lively trade in what turned out to be an inexhaustible supply of watered-down blood known as "the water of Canterbury," a liquid said to be so potent, it was able to perform up to as many as ten cures a day. Sold first in small wooden boxes lined with wax, the liquid leaked out so easily that the boxes were soon replaced by small phials molded out of tin or lead, which could be worn loosely around the purchaser's neck on a chain or piece of twine.

To match the pilgrims' rising expectations, the monks boxed in the original plain stone coffin by covering it with a heavy marble slab and surrounding it with marble side walls, all held together with iron rivets and sealed with lead, to create an elaborate tomb monument. Holes were carefully positioned in the sides of the tomb, allowing pilgrims to insert their heads and kiss the coffin before they purchased their souvenirs, a move that could occasionally backfire, as when a man called Edward, from Selling in Kent, managed to slither his whole body inside the monument and lie with his head next to the martyr's feet and his feet next to the head. The monks feared they would have to dismantle the entire edifice to get him out, but fortunately he managed to wriggle free.

Naturally, given the cash cow that had so unexpectedly come their way, the monks petitioned Pope Alexander to canonize Thomas as a saint, which he swiftly did, issuing the necessary decree at Segni on Ash Wednesday 1173. After that, the shrine's fame was unstoppable. At first it had attracted chiefly paupers and priests, rather than the affluent. This began to change in 1172, when the junior King Henry visited the tomb in an attempt to show he was his own man, deliberately seeking to score points off his father by marketing himself as a defender of the liberties of the church. His visit became his cue to quarrel with his father. Crowning his eldest son in his own lifetime would turn out to be one of the worst decisions of the elder Henry's reign. Tall, blond, and charming, the younger man was also vain, idle, and a spendthrift. His father had unwisely encouraged his regal aspirations, giving him his own royal seal and the title "Henricus Rex" and even sometimes waiting on him at dinner, serving his food and wine, but denying him power, leaving him smoldering with discontent and resentment.

After his eighteenth-birthday celebrations in 1173, the younger Henry demanded to control the lands and revenues settled on him at Fréteval. When his father refused, he countered that it was his father-in-law, King Louis, who had suggested it. The youth was playing with fire. Quickly escalating into a threatening revolt, the clash drew in Eleanor, her younger sons Richard and Geoffrey, and a significant proportion of the baronage, all of whom sided with the junior Henry. This triggered a civil war joined by King Louis, the king of Scots, and Count Philip of Flanders, who circled the scene like vultures hoping to dismember the Angevin empire and divide it among themselves.

By the beginning of July 1174, Count Philip had been defeated on the battlefield, but with Normandy under siege from the French; with Aquitaine, Anjou, Maine, and Brittany still in turmoil; and with much of northern England, the Midlands, and East Anglia ravaged by revolt or invasion, the elder Henry landed at Southampton and ordered his courtiers to prepare to ride to Canterbury. Struggling to fight on multiple fronts, he found that he needed the charismatic power that could come only from his association with a canonized saint, and St. Edward the Confessor was not good enough. Since he could not compete with the newly emerging Becket cult, Henry knew he would now have to join it.

On Friday, July 12, after dismounting at a leper hospital two miles outside the city, he put on penitential clothes beneath his cloak—a woolen smock, says Gervase of Canterbury; a green smock over a hair shirt, says Guernes of Pont-Sainte-Maxence—and set out on foot for the chapel of St. Dunstan immediately outside the walls, where he took off his shoes and walked barefoot to the cathedral. There, in the presence of his dumbfounded courtiers and the monks, he knelt before the tomb in the crypt and repeated his earlier confession that his "incautious words" had been the principal cause of Becket's murder. Then, after placing 4 marks of pure gold and a silk covering on the tomb, while pledging to endow the cathedral with enough land to pay for candles or oil lamps to illuminate the shrine in perpetuity, he removed his cloak, leaned forward, and placed his head inside one of the holes in the marble walls. He was then lightly scourged (probably with rods of birch or elm bound together in a bundle), receiving five strokes each from the bishops present and three from each of a hundred or so Christ Church monks. Afterward, he stayed motionless in prayer and fasting before the tomb, keeping vigil until Saturday morning, when he attended mass and joined in a conducted tour of the many side altars, tombs, and other relics kept in the cathedral.

With so many strokes delivered, Henry's scourging cannot have been severe and was more symbolic than real. The public humiliation was, however, the same, which for a royal penitent was the true penalty. And the dividends were immediate, for miracles, as it now seemed to all the world, could really happen at the shrine of St. Thomas Becket. On this same Saturday, perhaps even while Henry was still in the cathedral, the unlucky king of Scots was ambushed in a meadow near Alnwick Castle, Northumberland, in the early morning mist and captured, an event triggering the collapse of the revolt in England. On the Continent, it took

Henry until the end of August to regain control, but he comfortably managed it with the aid of a large force of mercenaries, obliging King Louis to sue for peace.

After that, it would be only a matter of time before his unruly sons fell into line, although they would continue to stir up trouble for him until the younger Henry died from dysentery in 1183, when yet another succession crisis propelled his surviving children into a rebellion against their father and a war against one another, allowing him no peace until his death in 1189 at the age of fifty-six. He never forgave Eleanor, whom his forces had intercepted in 1173 as she attempted to flee to join the rebels, disguised as a man. Blaming her more than their sons for instigating the civil war, he set about airbrushing her out of history, taking as his mistress Rosamond Clifford, for whom, if the colorful fourteenth-century chronicler Ralph Higden is to be believed, he built a luxurious villa and pleasure garden at Woodstock designed around a spring from which the water ran through a series of rectangular pools surrounded by cloistered courts. By early 1174, Eleanor was back in England, taken under close guard to Salisbury, where she was imprisoned, if in modest luxury, for more than ten years. The fact that Henry could do this to his wife meant that, psychologically, it would have been well within his capabilities to have done the same to Becket had his own agents reached Canterbury (as he had originally planned) to seize Thomas before he could be killed by the four knights.

The one genuine shift in Henry's attitude after his reconciliation to the church was that toward the four knights themselves. Whereas earlier he had left it to Pope Alexander to punish them, now he sought them out himself in subtle, increasingly punitive ways. When William de Tracy returned home from the papal curia to settle his affairs after receiving a sentence of fourteen years in exile in the Holy Land, he found portions of his Devon estates and other lands he held in Maine to be mysteriously forfeited to the Crown. Taking the hint, he made his way to Sicily to find a passage to the East. Hugh de Morville would be next at the papal curia, followed by Reginald fitz Urse and Richard Brito. According to one of the Canterbury monks, Henry had ordered them to lie low in Scotland, but if they did go there, they were quickly expelled on pain of hanging. Their infamy ensured that without Henry's protection, there was nowhere for them to seek asylum.

By the eighteenth century, a Jesuit scholar could report that all four knights ended their days as hermits in Flanders, while in Devon and Gloucestershire rumor had it that William de Tracy's ghost haunted the land. As late as 1986, an eminent medievalist claimed that Hugh de Morville died in his bed in 1202 at Burgh by Sands in Cumberland after marrying a rich widow. All such tales are false. The four knights had arrived in the Holy Land by Easter 1173, where, reports the Italian chronicler Romuald of Salerno, they visited Jerusalem barefoot and in hair shirts, giving alms to the Templars and the Lazarites for distribution to the poor. Before Romuald wrote his account in about 1182, all four had died in the East, probably at a place known as the Black Mountain near Antioch, where "they had spent out their lives in fasting, vigils, prayers and lamentations." As their extraordinary notoriety required, they were buried before the gate of the Temple in Jerusalem as an example to others. Sometime in 1190 or 1191, the chronicler Roger of Howden visited their graves and recorded their epitaph, carved in stone: "Here lie those wretches who martyred the Blessed Thomas, archbishop of Canterbury," words still perhaps legible when the city walls were rebuilt by the Ottoman Turks on the orders of Suleiman the Magnificent between 1537 and 1541.

For the chroniclers as much as for Becket's early biographers, it was an edifying and suitable end.

29
MARTYR

ON LEARNING OF THE FOUR KNIGHTS' DEATHS, HENRY DISrupted their children's rights of inheritance, either by diverting their property elsewhere or by forcing the unfortunate heirs to make generous gifts to religious houses. His conscience could so easily be appeased by the sacrifices of others, for despite his defeat on the central issues contested by Becket, he still did not see himself as in any way morally culpable for Thomas's bloody end. Nor did he ever fulfill his promise to take the cross and to equip two hundred knights for the defense of Jerusalem for a year. A notorious perjurer from early in his reign, he was not about to let a little matter of murder change the habits of a lifetime. Instead, he struck a deal with the pope allowing him to defer his crusade in exchange for other acts of piety, including reendowing or enlarging religious houses such as Waltham Abbey in Essex and Amesbury Priory in Wiltshire. Taking the opportunity offered by his wife's disgrace to appease his conscience at minimal cost to himself, he paid for his gifts with lands that had previously formed part of Eleanor's English estates.

Expiation, for Henry, was a commodity to be bought and sold rather than felt or earned. He did send annual remittances, ostensibly for the crusaders, to the Templars and Hospitallers in Jerusalem at the rate of 2,000 silver marks a year, earning him the sobriquet "Chief Benefactor of the Holy Land," but he refused to allow this money to be spent. Over fifteen years, it accumulated to a total of 30,000 marks, worth roughly

£11 million today. Shortly before his death, envoys from the East were still desperately pleading with him to unfreeze it, and only after the catastrophe of the fall of Jerusalem to the victorious Saladin in 1187 could he be persuaded to unlock it, by which time it was too late to be of much use.

This was typical of Henry, who professed himself to be a "tester of character" but in reality always tried to bribe, bargain, or bully to obtain what he wanted. Beginning by exploiting the papal schism to bend Pope Alexander to his will, he ended up trying to create a regional church under royal, and therefore his personal, control. Hardly ever would he offer a reasoned defense of his actions, even when, as in the case of criminous clerks, he believed that he had one. Preferring instead to dictate his demands and force matters quickly to a head, he would fall back on devious means, such as the trumped-up charges of embezzlement and treason leveled against Becket.

Promising future favors was his classic technique. "Oh, why is it that you won't do what I want?" he had asked Thomas in their conversations after the peace conference at Fréteval. "Because for certain, if you would, I'd put everything into your hands." Weasel words and promises to obey the pope's future judgment were other favorite tricks, knowing that Alexander had more than enough of his own problems and that distance alone would force him to send envoys whom Henry could hope to bribe, intimidate, or stonewall.

As Thomas had discovered the hard way, only by standing up to such intimidation could a royal minister keep his credibility or get anything useful done. "If he senses that he can corrupt you by promises or frighten you by threats so that he can obtain something against your honor and some security for himself in the matter, from that moment your authority with him will utterly vanish, and you will become contemptible, a mockery and a laughingstock to him." Or as John of Salisbury warned, "The king of England puts forward much on his own behalf, and much against you, so as to influence weak and wavering minds in his customary fashion, first by threats, then by promises, then by all sorts of wheeling and dealing." Anything involving a tactical retreat or climbdown on Henry's part had to appear to come from him alone. Cutting to the pith of his psychology, Arnulf of Lisieux advised, "Whatever does not yield to him, he considers unlawful. . . . Whatever he does should appear to have proceeded from his will rather than from weakness."

Henry's hatred for Becket sprang logically and psychologically from the affection he had once held for him, but their relationship had always been unequal, and even at its most intense moments it had required the king to set aside some of his strongest social prejudices. He would routinely reproach Becket for his ingratitude. "Are you not the son of one of my villeins?" he would ask. "How comes it that so many benefits, so many proofs of my love for you, well known to all, have so been erased from your mind, that you are now not only ungrateful, but obstruct me in everything?"

For his attack on the church's claims of immunity from secular jurisdiction, Anglo-American lawyers and constitutional historians in the nineteenth century would put on rose-tinted spectacles and reinvent Henry as a legal reformer *avant la lettre,* a pioneer of fair trials and equality before the law who paved the way for some of the most important clauses later incorporated into Magna Carta and the U.S. Constitution and Bill of Rights. In reality, however, his actions showed that the rights of the accused could always be overridden by political considerations and the king's will. Far from remodeling the legal system and the courts in the interests of justice and the common good, Henry sought to strengthen his own power. And far from being a pioneer of "equitable" or "impartial" justice, he happily presided over his own court in the Battle Abbey case and at Becket's trial for embezzlement and false accounting at Northampton, acting simultaneously as chief counsel for the prosecution, judge, and jury. In response, Thomas would prove that a middle-class Londoner could transcend his social origins and challenge a ruler who he believed was degenerating into a tyrant, but it would cost him his life. Thomas More would take a similar path in Henry VIII's reign, and it may be no coincidence that More's working library contained many of the same books as Becket's.

HENRY'S SURROGATE FOR remorse was brazenly to associate himself with Becket's cult, making it a vital prop of his image of himself as a divine-right ruler and replacing his earlier championing of St. Edward the Confessor with it. Nine or ten more times would he take the pilgrim road to Canterbury—twice with Count Philip of Flanders and once with King Louis, who made offerings of a cup of gold and a ruby the size of a hen's egg called the "regal of France"—routinely visiting Thomas's tomb on returning from the Continent, except in early 1188, when the cathedral was closed to visitors. Following his example, Edward I would kneel before Becket's shrine in 1286 and 1287. Henry IV and his uncle Edward the Black Prince would build their own funeral monuments on either side of it. Henry VI would be anointed at his coronation with the sacred oil of St. Thomas, while Edward IV's sister, Margaret of York, would make at least two pilgrimages to the shrine. Henry VIII and Katherine of Aragon would come in 1520, when they showed off the cathedral's treasures to Katherine's nephew, the emperor Charles V. And on Henry VIII's return from Calais two months later, he came again to make a further offering.

Long before then, the tomb had become a highly elaborate and costly affair. Building a new and splendid sepulchral monument at Canterbury was a condition buried in the small print of Pope Alexander's canonization decree, but the work was considerably delayed by a disastrous fire on September 5, 1174, caused by sparks from a house fire in front of the main cathedral gate. The fire barely touched the nave or crypt of the church but set the roof of the choir ablaze, leaving only the outer walls standing and the rest a pile of smoking rubble. After an international competition to appoint an architect, William of Sens (no relation to the archbishop and papal legate for France by the same name), famous for his work at Sens Cathedral, was given the commission. Work on rebuilding the choir began in September 1175, and plans for a large polygonal rotunda to house the new shrine were approved before Holy Week 1177, when Henry returned to Canterbury to renew the Christ Church charters. If the design for this rotunda had ever been realized, it would have created a funerary monument of a type unrivaled in the Romanesque or Gothic world, modeled on the circular Church of the Holy Sepulchre in Jerusalem and on a scale that (in England) would be attempted only by the Knights Templar at their new London headquarters.

All was going well until just after the solar eclipse on September 13, 1178, when the scaffolding from which the unlucky architect was supervising the construction of the vault over the crossing of the new choir collapsed, pitching him fifty-five feet to the ground. While he lived to tell the tale, his injuries were so severe that he was obliged to resign his commission and retire to France. "William the Englishman" was appointed to succeed him, and with the change of architect came a radical rethinking of the plans. The shrine was now to be situated in a magnificent new chapel positioned on an elevated platform behind the high altar in the retrochoir and with a considerably raised roof, allowing the space between the structural pillars around the sides to be filled with glorious stained-glass windows depicting the life and miracles of the saint.

Progress, however, would be slow. Lack of money halted the work in 1183, and although the central section of the new chapel and its roof were largely finished in the building season of 1184, it was not until three o'clock on the afternoon of Tuesday, July 7, 1220—fifty years after the murder—that the bones of St. Thomas would be carried in solemn procession, in an iron-covered box secured by padlocks, from his tomb in the crypt to their new place of honor. Besides a papal legate, the archbishop of Rheims, bishops and abbots, barons and knights, and a vast throng of priests and laypeople, the young Henry III, grandson of the king who had made Thomas his archbishop, was in the crowd. At just twelve years old, he was too short and delicate to help carry the heavy box on his shoulders with the other luminaries.

Consisting of an elevated marble base decorated with openwork quatrefoils, on which lay an effigy of the saint on a slab, the new shrine was surmounted by thin columns the height of a man. These columns framed open arches, four bays long and two wide, and were crowned by a sculpted cornice on which a wooden feretory (reliquary chest) rested, placed high to deter thieves. A fine mosaic pavement led up to the structure; to the side was an altar offering a sacred space for pilgrims to pray and make their offerings. Plated all over with the purest gold, the sides of the feretory were studded with golden baubles, pearls, and precious jewels; its gabled roof was embossed with golden quatrefoils set in a diaper pattern. As pilgrims offered their votive gifts, they would be attached directly to the surface or onto the crest of the feretory by waiting goldsmiths. According to Erasmus of Rotterdam, who visited the shrine with his friend John Colet, dean of St. Paul's, in or around 1512, "Every part glistened, shone, and sparkled with very rare and very large jewels, some of them bigger than a goose's egg."

What was rarely possible was for pilgrims to be allowed to see the lid of the feretory raised so that they could look inside and view the saint's bones in the iron box. Only by mounting a ladder could that be accomplished, and this was seldom if ever allowed. Even the feretory itself could be covered over to protect it. If Erasmus's information is accurate, it was only when a protective covering, or canopy, was raised on a pulley attached to the roof of the cathedral that the feretory was revealed to pilgrims in all its glory.

Skillfully overseen by the guardians of the shrine, the Becket legend soon came to offer something for everyone. So prodigiously successful, so fabulously wealthy would his cult become that it quickly rivaled then overtook such renowned centers of pilgrimage as Santiago de Compostela, Assisi, Chartres, and Rocamadour, inspiring Chaucer's *Canterbury Tales* and creating a highly lucrative tourist and hospitality trade all along the road from London to Canterbury. The "Book of Miracles" begun by the first guardian of the shrine, Benedict of Peterborough, and faithfully continued by his successors reports St. Thomas showing special favor to fine courtiers, knights, merchants, and their families, curing their piles, diarrhea, and stomach ulcers and restoring their lost falcons, fugitive servants, or stolen rings. But since a majority of pilgrims were women, priests, and commoners, it also records innumerable cases of safe delivery in childbirth; poor folk cured of blindness, palsy, dropsy, and leprosy; and even instances of babies being brought back from the dead.

As the story was retold in the *Golden Legend,* a thirteenth-century compendium of saints' lives turned into an instant bestseller by William Caxton after the invention of printing, Becket was a Londoner of humble origins who had achieved fame and fortune partly by working hard at school. When the king made him his chancellor, he "had great rule and the land stood in prosperity, and St. Thomas stood so greatly in the king's favor that he was content with all that he did." A Damascene conversion followed his appointment as archbishop. "He became a holy man suddenly changed into a new man doing great penance as in wearing a hair shirt with knots." But Lucifer stepped in, casting his evil spell and sowing hatred and discord, so that the king's relationship with his truest and most honest counselor was doomed.

When (according to Caxton's version of the famous outburst) Henry said in his fury, "If only I had men in my land that loved me, they would not suffer such a traitor in my land alive," the murder became a foregone conclusion, its most gruesome details spelled out in exactly the way they would be today in a tabloid newspaper. So too were the supposedly miraculous powers of the saint even in his lifetime. For instance, fleeing to the papal curia at Sens from Northampton in 1164, Thomas—arriving late in the afternoon of a fast day after the market was closed—was unable to buy fish for his dinner. He ate roast capon instead, causing a horrified cardinal to pick up a leg of the offending fowl in his handkerchief to show to Pope Alexander, whereupon it instantly changed into carp. Again, immediately after Thomas preached his Christmas Day sermon in the cathedral four days before his murder, Henry reached out to take some bread at dinner, only to discover that the loaf turned moldy in his hands.

A FEW YEARS after Becket's murder, Peter of Celle, who had once brutally snubbed him when shortly after his consecration as archbishop he had asked to be Peter's pen friend, wrote to John of Salisbury reminding him of jests they had shared over a bottle of wine on some of the long winter nights at his monastery at Rheims while John was in exile. How on earth, he remembered asking, could a big enough tomb monument be found for a man like that? Now, he mused wryly, the joke was on them: "God has turned the tables and made it all come true. What we laughed about has actually happened in real life!"

To an old friend like John of Salisbury, who had known Thomas from his earliest days in Theobald's household and still had the bruises to show for it, his journey had been incredible. Believing, as a Londoner born and bred, in the values of meritocracy despite his lowly origins as the son of Norman settlers and in spite of modest academic achievements, Becket had risen to a position where he was able to shake the power of one of the strongest rulers in Christendom and prove to his fellow Englishmen that the values he embraced could be defended, albeit at the price of his own life. Even a pope to whom Thomas had often seemed an embarrassing nuisance had, swept away on a tide of emotion following his bloody assassination, canonized him with almost indecent haste.

Commentators as cosmopolitan and astute as John of Salisbury and Peter of Celle knew from their wide experience of the church and its politics that Becket had become a saint less for his own merits than on account of the blows of the four knights. Others whose viewpoints were more parochial, coming primarily from within his own household—including Herbert of Bosham, Alexander Llewelyn, and William fitz Stephen—despite their occasional sharp differences over the wisdom of the uncompromising nature of their leader's positions, would have thought differently about it, arguing that by the time of his Christmas Day sermon, he had earned a special place in heaven regardless of what was to come.

As prickly as he was smooth and once compared to a man with the habits of a hedgehog, Becket could sometimes act impulsively, as John of Salisbury several times complained. His sudden decision in the autumn of 1162 to resign the chancellorship smacked of a certain intellectual arrogance. He assumed that everyone shared his values and had the same ardor in pursuing them. And yet John's criticisms should not always be taken at face value. He was himself the source of many of Becket's ideas and yet was himself unwilling to suffer poverty or physical hardship for his friend's beliefs, which is why he had all along chosen to take sanctuary at the abbey of Saint-Rémi at Rheims with his friend Peter, and not to join Herbert and the rest of the exiles in the harsher regime of Pontigny or even at Sainte-Colombe after the lease on his lodgings in Paris had expired. In John's opinion, Thomas could, and probably should, have settled with the king at any one of three moments: shortly after he fled into exile and persuaded the pope to condemn the offending "customs" as "obnoxious"; at Montmirail when instead of accepting the terms he had previously agreed on with the papal mediators, the ascetic, rebel's instinct in him kicked in and at the last moment he added the forbidden words "saving God's honor"; and at Montmartre, when after an agreement had been reached, he appeared to spoil it by demanding the kiss of peace as his security for Henry's compliance.

In Thomas's defense, Pope Alexander had given him a counsel of perfection. "Humble yourself before the king as far as it can be done," was the gist of this advice, "but do not agree to anything which leads to the diminution of your office and the church's liberty." When read in the context of Henry's weasel words and slippery tactics, this advice gave Thomas the superhuman task of figuring out how to meet the expectations of both these principals to whom he owed allegiance. If Henry broke his oaths so freely, why would he honor a peace treaty? How was the lack of trust between them to be overcome? These were questions with which King Louis and a parade of papal envoys had already wrestled in vain. In fact, the argument about the kiss sprang from the pope's earlier warning that Becket should *not* attempt to provoke Henry further by demanding an oath as a guarantee of an agreement, but instead content himself *merely* with a kiss of peace.

The vexed, perennial problem of trust in Henry's promises would come to haunt the final settlement at Fréteval. With a verbal agreement in hand, Thomas—beguiled and elated by the brief illusion of a revival of his old familiarity with the king—became overconfident, forgetting his own rules about how to handle Henry. His insistence on exacting vengeance on his hated rivals, the delinquent bishops, would be his Achilles' heel, as Henry—judging by his observations on this very topic at the time—may have predicted. The archbishop's repeated protestations that he would not return to Canterbury until every single yard of sequestered ground had been restored to him turned out to be extremely foolish, since he had to eat his words and return anyway. After the murder, Arnulf of Lisieux wrote to the pope criticizing Becket for his spitefulness, saying it had tarnished his martyr's crown. But the pressure on him—not least from Pope Alexander—should not be underestimated. Becket had never coped well with stress, as his debilitating attack of colitis at the Council of Northampton showed, and he had very few people on his side whom he could really trust.

Peter of Celle thought he had the measure of his man when he criticized Becket's love of grand gestures and desire to prove himself. Thomas, socially, always had a mountain to climb. It is hardly surprising that he felt himself a newcomer and an outsider trying to become an insider, when the gulf between a middle-class Londoner and the king was unbridgeable, their relationship always unequal. And Becket had long known it. According to John of Salisbury, for all his apparent ruthlessness, he had always had a divided consciousness, aware that the day would come when he could no longer go on vacillating between self-assertion and dishonest compliance. "He was every day forced," John says, "to contend as much against the king himself as against his enemies and to evade innumerable crafts and deceits."

Despite being frequently castigated by his modern biographers as an "actor-saint" who had to "out-bishop" his fellow bishops and unnecessarily dramatize situations, Thomas was surely correct to claim that it was impossible for him to assent to customs that were in several instances novelties, twice condemned as "obnoxious" by the pope. Such customs, he knew, would quickly be taken for established norms if he did not take a lead. In particular, Henry's attempts to prohibit appeals to the pope would have done more than any of his other measures toward creating a self-contained, regional church under royal control. Becket's darkest hour was at the Council of Clarendon, when he cut the ground from under the feet of his colleagues and promised to "keep the customs of the realm in all good faith," only to rescind his pledge when Henry produced a text of these customs in writing. Undoubtedly, he had been too trusting. It simply had not occurred to him to insist that the customs be declared in full before he promised to observe them. But there again, he had been cruelly tricked by a duplicitous Henry into believing that a simple verbal assent would suffice, and that once it had been given and the king's honor satisfied, the matter would never be spoken of again.

WHETHER THOMAS REALLY was a saint and martyr is a question that has been fruitlessly debated for centuries. As the sword blows rained down on his head in the cathedral, he appealed to the Virgin Mary; to St. Denis, the patron saint of France; and to St. Alphege, the archbishop murdered by drunken Danes for defending the property of the church of Canterbury. That final entreaty, reliably reported, suggests that it was less doctrinal orthodoxy or the liberties of the church as a whole for which he believed he was about to be killed, than for defending his own beloved church and its privileges—chiefly the cathedral and monastic chapter's property rights and the primate's right to preside at the coronation ceremony.

Both St. Augustine and St. Cyprian had stressed that it was the validity of the cause for which a victim died, not the violence or sacrifice he or she had suffered along the way, that made a true martyr. "Willing" or "eager" martyrs offering themselves for sacrifice were suspect, even if St. Ignatius of Antioch had taken an opposing view, not condemning, indeed encouraging, "eager" martyrdom. The church fathers discussing the topic all agreed that martyrs should show confidence, fortitude, and constancy. The greatest danger was fear or despair, since anyone dying in despair could not be a martyr. Underlying all of the early biographies is the controlling idea that Becket, foreseeing his death, went willingly and knowingly to it. An enduring trait of hagiography as a genre, this muddies the waters, making it impossible to assess realistically where "confidence," "fortitude," and "constancy" end and "eagerness" begins, but the multiple reports of his Christmas Day sermon suggest that, by then at the very latest, he understood and accepted his fate. Whether this made him "eager" to die is a question that will continue to trouble his admirers for as long as his name is known.

More relevant today is the broader criticism that he sought martyrdom out of "obstinacy" or spiritual pride. In *Murder in the Cathedral*, a so-called pageant play written for the Canterbury Festival and first staged there in 1935, T. S. Eliot, well-versed in this conundrum, scripts a temptation scene in which Thomas is urged to think of glory after death. By making the ultimate sacrifice, he can rule from the grave as a saint and martyr. One of his tempters even conjures up a vision of a glittering, jewel-encrusted shrine, before which lines of pilgrims stand in awe, kneel in prayer, or creep in penance, thinking of the miracles he will be able to perform for them from his place in heaven. Thomas seems to see this delusion of the devil for what it is: a dream to damnation. And yet, in the cathedral, as the assassins approach the cloister door, shouting and brandishing their swords, he orders the monks who have slammed it behind them and bolted it for safety to reopen it. Eliot offers his audience an opportunity to go for the jugular, giving the fourth knight, Richard Brito, a concluding speech in which he claims the murdered archbishop's egotism is proved by his decision to reopen the door and invite his fate, rather than keeping it shut and escaping until the fury of the murderers has abated.

With such facts before them, says Brito, the only possible verdict of the audience can be one of suicide while of unsound mind. That line of argument had its defenders even in the Middle Ages, and at the time of Henry VIII's break with Rome, another pope, Paul III, wrestling with the threat of schism from a second Henry and poised to excommunicate him, declared to another king of France that John Fisher, bishop of Rochester—whom the king had executed in 1535 for opposing his claim to be the Supreme Head of the Church in England—had been a "true" saint and martyr, giving his life for the truth of the universal church, unlike Becket, who had thrown his life away in a petty squabble over the assets and privileges of Canterbury.

But when he made this pronouncement, the pope was applying an anachronistic scale of values. When the question of St. Alphege's claim to sanctity had first been put, in William Rufus's reign, to Archbishop Anselm, the reply had been, "He died for the freedom and the salvation of his fellow men. Nobody has greater charity than he who gives his life for his friends: For innocence, even when no struggle has taken place, makes a martyr." Despite the fact that Alphege died solely for the rights and material possessions of the church of Canterbury, his martyrdom was considered to have had universal significance; it belonged to the divine plan of salvation, and it is no surprise, then, to discover that the early biographers would apply exactly the same rule of thumb to Becket.

Nor did Peter of Celle, for all his earlier skepticism, have any remaining doubts. "Our mourning is turned to joy!" he exclaimed shortly after the murder, this time in a letter to another old friend, Bartholomew of Exeter. "Who," he asked, "will give me wings like a dove that I may fly and visit the tomb of the precious martyr St. Thomas?" And with Peter and his circle of celebrity correspondents joining Becket's fan club, his cult would flourish as rapidly on the Continent as in England itself, stretching within fifty years from Paris to Cracow, Barcelona to Reykjavík and Hólmr, his story represented in wall paintings and altarpieces all over Europe, his miracles reported not just in Latin and French but also in Polish, Catalan, and Icelandic.

Ironically, it would be the phenomenal success of the new Becket shrine that led to the corruption of the Christ Church monks by their newfound wealth, until the moment when Henry VIII would quarrel with the pope and decide to avenge his royal predecessor and namesake. In September 1538, the shrine would be demolished and its rich treasures despoiled, carried off in two large chests "such as six or eight men could but convey out of the church." Henry had the ruby known as the "regal of France" made into a thumb ring. Becket was declared a traitor: His bones would be ignominiously burned. Iconoclasts would obliterate his image with hammers, knives, or whitewash in cathedrals and parish churches all over England, smashing many of the stained-glass windows containing the stories of his miracles. Even his very name would be carefully excised from missals, Psalters, and the calendar of saints. Only with the aid of ultraviolet light is it possible now to read the inscription on the flyleaf of the presentation copy of John of Salisbury's *Policraticus* sent, with its verse dedication, to Thomas in 1159, saying that the book had once belonged to him.

With "St. Thomas Becket" downgraded to plain "Bishop Becket, sometime archbishop of Canterbury," the layered story of his relationship with the earlier Henry would be turned into a Punch-and-Judy show to match the tabloid newspeak of religious sectarianism. For "notwithstanding the said canonization," thundered Henry VIII, ensuring no mistakes were made by vetting this proclamation personally, "there appeareth nothing in his life and exterior conversation whereby he should be called a saint, but rather esteemed to have been a rebel and traitor to his prince."

Only a monarch, not unlike the earlier Henry, set on building a regional church under tight royal control, ring-fenced by the coast as an integral part of a centralized state controlled by himself, could have spoken that way. Becket was far from saintly or infallible as a human being, and he made many enemies and mistakes along the way. Peter of Celle was right that his major defects were his ambition and fondness for mingling with the great and the good, but his moral unease as royal chancellor, combined with his dogged resilience and fortitude as archbishop, would win him the dedicated loyalty (and even the affectionate mockery) of many honorable, rational men. As the distinguished Oxford scholar Henry Mayr-Harting wrote in *The Times* in June 1996, for that he must have been a truly charismatic man; otherwise he could hardly have retained their loyalties for so long and at such a punitive cost to their careers.

As the young knight with the prize gyrfalcon had instantly guessed when he passed Thomas on the road to Saint-Omer, "Either that's the archbishop of Canterbury or his double!"

ACKNOWLEDGMENTS

Researching and writing the life of Thomas Becket have been a thoroughly invigorating experience, fulfilling another of my long-standing ambitions. I first glimpsed the main elements of Becket's story at Cambridge from two exemplary scholars and inspiring teachers, the late Professor Christopher Cheney and the late Professor Walter Ullmann. Despite specializing mainly in the Tudor period, I've always retained a fascination for the twelfth century, above all for its extraordinary galaxy of larger-than-life characters. As with my biographies of Mary Queen of Scots and of Thomas More and his eldest daughter, Margaret, I've tried to sweep away the cobwebs, dismantle the legends, and use the original sources to conjure back to life a highly controversial figure who helped to change the course of history and who has divided opinion ever since.

As the vast majority of the contemporary records and firsthand accounts are in Latin or Old French, I must express my deep gratitude and sense of obligation to several generations of my predecessors, as well as to my old schoolteachers, who taught me enough Latin and French to make a start. My greatest debts are to Professor Anne Duggan, the editor of the definitive two-volume *Correspondence of Thomas Becket, Archbishop of Canterbury,* and to Professor Christopher Brooke and his fellow editors of the magisterial two-volume edition of *The Letters of John of Salisbury,* as well as to the Oxford University Press, which has published these volumes. They constitute landmark works of scholarship, and although the vast majority of these letters are available in Latin and often in translation elsewhere, the Oxford texts have become the indispensable companion to Becket studies. The availability of several new electronic search aids has given me an advantage over earlier biographers, although the texts of the primary sources still have to be read in full and in context, and many texts, even where digitized, are not yet fully searchable.

I gladly acknowledge the generosity and kindness of many archivists and librarians who have helped to smooth my path, chiefly at the British Library;

the Parker Library at Corpus Christi College, Cambridge; the Wren Library at Trinity College, Cambridge; the Fellows' Library at Clare College, Cambridge; the Bodleian Library; Cambridge University Library; the Bibliothèque Nationale de France; the National Archives at Kew; and especially the London Library. I am most grateful to Dr. Suzanne Paul and Ms. Gill Cannell, the sub-librarians at the Parker Library, who found me a space and later provided high-resolution digital images at an unusually busy time. The genealogical table and maps were drawn and digitized by Richard Guy of Orang-Utan Productions from my rough drafts.

I've nothing but thanks and admiration for Peter Robinson and Gráinne Fox, my agents in London and New York, for their constant encouragement and for giving helpful advice on the manuscript. I owe an immense debt to Venetia Butterfield and her assistant, Will Hammond, my editors at Viking; and to Jonathan Jao, my editor at Random House, for their unstinting support. Their detailed and exacting comments on my first complete draft were expertly pitched, challenging and encouraging me to produce my very best work. I express heartfelt thanks to my students at Cambridge, especially those from Clare College and Gonville and Caius College, whose supervisions on the Tudors unaccountably strayed on several occasions into aspects of the Becket story. Emma Guy regularly checked on her father's progress, urging me not to forget that other aspects of life existed apart from "the book," as did David and Frances Waters, whose vigilance in keeping me abreast of the imminence of booking dates ensured I got my opera tickets.

Julia, ever patient with a spouse obsessed by his current writing project, has uncomplainingly survived the past three years, this time living with Thomas Becket as if his struggle with Henry II was happening in our home, reading drafts of the whole book several times, discussing them over mugs of tea at two and three o'clock in the morning, and taking time out from her own double biography of Katherine of Aragon and her sister Juana of Castile to advise on research or writing problems. I am unable adequately to repay her love. Our rescue cats—Susie, Tippy, and Sherry—as usual tried hard to give this book their own special imprint, but Oscar, my brother-in-law's Shih Tzu, was more persuasive in getting me away from my desk.

London
September 12, 2011

APPENDIX A
AN EARLY BECKET BIOGRAPHERS' WHO'S WHO

A remarkably rich body of firsthand source materials in the form of early Latin "lives" of Thomas Becket, together with one in Old French verse, allows the biographer to reconstruct his life with exceptional accuracy, even though the hagiographic bias of some of this material renders it partially unreliable. All these early biographies were begun within four years of Becket's murder in 1170 and completed within seven years, with the exception of Herbert of Bosham's, which was finished between 1184 and 1186. Many of the names that follow will appear not just as commentators but as characters within the action itself. These authors were Becket's contemporaries, many of whom knew him personally. This section is intended as a handy means of reference, allowing readers to identify them and place them in their historical settings.

Alan of Tewkesbury, an Englishman who became a canon of Benevento and subsequently a monk and prior of Christ Church Canterbury and abbot of Tewkesbury, is the compiler of the "master" manuscript of Becket's letters, put together between around 1174–76 and 1180–84 from a variety of earlier collections, including John of Salisbury's. To enhance his work and encourage its circulation, he prefaced it with a brief "life" that built on and expanded an earlier prologue written by John to introduce his own letter collection. Although his coverage is distinctly patchy and presumably designed to fill gaps in the story not covered by the letters, Alan provides some invaluable details unknown to the other early biographers, much of them in the form of reported speech. He may have owed some of his information to Master Lombard of Piacenza, Becket's canon law tutor at Pontigny.

"Anonymous I" (probably Roger of Pontigny) finished writing Becket's "life" in about 1176–77. A monk of the Cistercian abbey of Pontigny, near

Sens and Auxerre in northern Burgundy, where Becket stayed for the first two years of his exile, he was identified in the nineteenth century as the author of the more important of the two "anonymous" biographies, and this attribution, though still occasionally contested, is now widely accepted. The writer, known to have been a foreigner because of his peculiar handling of English terms and names, says that he ministered to the archbishop in his exile and was ordained a priest by him, which best fits Roger's career. And in a composite "life" of Becket compiled out of several of the early biographies by Thomas of Froimont, it is stated that a monk named Roger was deputed to assist Becket during his exile at Pontigny. While his approach is broadly hagiographic and derivative from Edward Grim and Guernes of Pont-Sainte-Maxence, he does report a number of incidents not recorded elsewhere.

"Anonymous II" is possibly someone born in London who may have had links to Gilbert Foliot, although he was later a Canterbury monk. The author claims, improbably, that he was a witness to the murder. His "life," completed in around 1172–73, consists largely of a chronological narrative and reflective passages but lacks descriptive details, often omitting the most basic facts. Its value lies in a number of the contemporary criticisms it reports of Thomas, which it attempts to refute—for instance, those leveled at the time of his promotion to the archbishopric.

Benedict of Peterborough compiled the first and what would eventually become the most influential collection of Becket's "miracles" in three books in about 1173–74, adding a fourth by 1179 at the earliest. In about 1174, he also wrote an account of the events of the murder to serve as an introduction to the first three books, which is preserved only in the form of extracts copied at a later date. One of the Christ Church monks, he is said to have been "among the archbishop's familiar friends, in especially familiar attendance on the day of his death," when he was present in the cathedral. Appointed prior of Christ Church in 1175 and abbot of Peterborough two years later, he was the first guardian of Becket's shrine and went on to found a chapel of St. Thomas beside the gate to the monastic precinct at Peterborough, digging up and taking with him the bloodstained paving stones from the place of the martyrdom at Canterbury to use as altars.

Edward Grim completed writing Becket's "life" in around 1171–72. Said to have been born in Cambridge, he was never a member of the archbishop's household or a monk of Christ Church. He was a visitor to Canterbury, who happened to find himself at vespers in the cathedral on the day Becket was murdered. As the displaced rector of Saltwood in Kent, probably ousted after

April 1163, when the king seized the honor of Saltwood, he would have seen and heard the archbishop in action. Only recently returned from Normandy when Becket was killed, he was one of the closest to Thomas in the cathedral, when his arm was almost severed in a heroic attempt to deflect the knights' blows aimed at the archbishop. His "life," unashamedly hagiographic in tone, was one of the earliest to be written. Since he had witnessed only the end of Thomas's life, he must have depended on others for substantial portions of his information. Despite this, his material would be appropriated by several of the other early biographers.

Guernes of Pont-Sainte-Maxence, a clerk born in Pont-Sainte-Maxence in Picardy, describes himself as a traveling poet and wrote a "life" in Old French verse. Completed in about 1174, it is not only among the earliest but also the one most reliant on oral testimony. Although he never met Becket, he claims to have seen Thomas several times when the latter, as chancellor, rode out against the French. Guernes also visited Canterbury, where he interviewed everyone he could find who had known the archbishop. He sought out Becket's sister Mary and a servant who had fled with him into exile, a man named Brown. Despite striving to stick to the facts and his own knowledge, he drew extensively on the work of Edward Grim and William of Canterbury. He also consulted William fitz Stephen and Benedict of Peterborough. As he pursued his research, he was prepared to alter or correct what he had written earlier in the light of new testimony: "I know," he explains, "how to bear the burden of crossing out and writing it again." The extant version is his second attempt. An earlier version, which it has been suggested drew even more extensively on Edward Grim, does not survive.

Herbert of Bosham wrote by far the longest of the early "lives" at around eighty thousand words, completed in 1184–86. Another of Becket's clerks as chancellor, he afterward became his divinity tutor and one of his leading advisers as archbishop. He was Becket's close friend and confidant, and alongside John of Salisbury he had a powerful influence on Thomas's intellectual development. An eyewitness to all the major encounters of Thomas's archiepiscopate, he is the only one of the early biographers to have remained at the archbishop's side throughout his exile, apart from a brief excursion to Auxerre while Thomas remained at Pontigny. To his everlasting regret, he was sent away by Becket on a mission to France in 1170 and so missed the murder. A zealot who allowed his tongue and his pen to run away with him, he sat at Becket's feet during the Council of Northampton in 1164 and rashly advised him to excommunicate his enemies. At the failed peace talks at Montmirail in Maine in 1169, he whispered something into the archbishop's ear at a critical moment, with disastrous results. A theologian of distinction in his own right, he had been a student of the famous Peter Lombard and a master in theology in the "schools" in Paris before Becket recruited him. Tall and handsome, and known to be a smart dresser, he was a colorful character who relished a fight, a gifted writer, an original thinker, and a brilliant Hebraist. Gaining his understanding of Becket's psychology and vision of the world earlier than anyone except John of Salisbury, he tried to write historically, attempting (as he says) to explain "not just the archbishop's deeds, but the reasons for them; not just what was done, but the mind of the doer." Despite an obvious hagiographic bias, much of his writing, in particular his description of Becket's first year as archbishop, is commendably honest.

John of Salisbury wrote in two stages, first composing a vignette of Becket in the form of a letter addressed early in 1171 to their mutual friend John of Canterbury, bishop of Poitiers, that was widely distributed, and subsequently a brief "life" begun a year or two later in the shape of the preface to a collection of the archbishop's correspondence that was later reworked by Alan of Tewkesbury. A brilliant classicist and philosopher, John was one of Becket's fellow clerks in Archbishop Theobald's household and, alongside Herbert of Bosham, a powerful influence on his intellectual development as archbishop, even if he chose not to stay in Thomas's entourage in exile and aided him from a distance. Present in the cathedral when Thomas was murdered, he wrote the earliest eyewitness account and comes the closest of any external observer to capturing Becket's true character and psychology. One of the most important actors in the drama in his own right, John ranks with Peter Abelard (at whose feet he once sat) as one of the sharpest, most dazzling minds of the age. Blessed with a large and well-developed network of friends—men like the highly influential Peter of Celle, abbot of Saint-Rémi at Rheims, whom he had first met as a fellow student in the "schools" in Paris while studying the liberal arts—he was able to pump them for information or recruit them to Becket's cause. Hagiography in its purest form never suited John's talents, and neither did sycophancy; he is a perfect foil in attempting to understand the values Becket stood for and what he really sought to achieve.

John also helps to capture the political atmosphere at Henry II's court while Becket was chancellor. In 1159, he dedicated his *Policraticus* (*The Statesman*), a treatise on statecraft and politics, to Thomas, even inserting a verse dedication of 306 lines (sometimes known as the *Entheticus Minor*) into the presentation copy he sent to Becket as he was camped with Henry's army outside the walls of Toulouse. This manuscript still survives in its original binding in the Parker Library at Corpus Christi College, Cambridge (MS 46). And long before Becket was made archbishop, John began a longer verse satire, the *Entheticus de Dogmate Philosophorum* (*An Abstract of Wise Men's Doctrine*), amounting to 1,852 lines in the form in which it survives. An advice book considering the nature of true wisdom and ideal philosophy, the *Entheticus* is a mine of information about the values, vices, and corruption of the "untamed beasts" at the courts of King Stephen and the younger Henry II, complete with thinly disguised, lacerating vignettes of real-life individuals.

Robert of Cricklade, prior of St. Frideswide's Oxford, had Saxon ancestry and came originally from Cricklade in Wiltshire. An Augustinian canon at Cirencester Abbey before moving to St. Frideswide's, he was a biblical scholar of some distinction, but his main claim to fame is the lost "life and miracles" of St. Thomas that he completed in about 1173–74 after his bad leg acquired on a pilgrimage to Sicily was providentially cured following a visit to Becket's tomb in 1171. Beyond this he had no direct connection to Becket and was not a member of the closed Canterbury coterie, making his opinions more skeptical and independent-minded than most. Fragments from his work can be reconstructed, since in about 1200 it was translated into Old Norse and subsequently formed an important source for the "life" of Becket known as the "Thomas Saga Erkibyskups." These fragments have been brilliantly traced and pieced together by Dr. Margaret Orme.

"Thomas Saga Erkibyskups." Written in Icelandic and known for certain to exist in 1258, the "Thomas Saga" survives in its fullest and most developed form only in a version compiled in about 1320–50. It was put together over many years from a diverse mixture of Norwegian and Latin sources, including the writings of John of Salisbury and Benedict of Peterborough, and much of its original backbone seems to have been the "life and miracles" compiled by Robert of Cricklade, which was translated into Old Norse in about 1200.

William fitz Stephen finished writing Becket's "life" in around 1173–74. As his fellow Londoner, clerk, and friend; a subdeacon in his chapel; and a draftsman and advocate in his court, he had close and frequent contact with Becket over many years and tells us more than anyone else about his career as chancellor. Unlike most of the other biographers except Roger of Pontigny, he did not belong to a select and inward-looking Canterbury coterie. Much of his material is unique, and it seems that, apart from consulting the archives of Gilbert Foliot in order to refute his attacks on Thomas, he wrote from memory. Since he knew more than anyone else about Becket's career as chancellor, it is likely that he entered Becket's service before Thomas's embassy to Paris in 1158, which he describes with lingering delight. In 1164, he was Becket's legal spokesman at the Council of Northampton. Despite reconciling himself to Henry when Thomas went into exile, with the result that his account of Becket's experiences at Pontigny and Sainte-Colombe is thin, he visited the archbishop at least once in France before rejoining him late in 1170. Returning with the exiles to Canterbury, he was one of those closest to Thomas in the cathedral when the archbishop was murdered. For all the verve and elegance of his writing, he can sometimes appear partisan, giving Thomas the benefit of the doubt and justifying his opinions whether right or wrong. But his eye for color and fine detail is unrivaled, and he offers some of the most informative and evocative scenes of all the early "lives." No other writer mentions him, and no evidence can be found to substantiate the claim that he may be the William fitz Stephen who served as sheriff of Gloucester and an itinerant justice between 1171 and 1188.

William of Canterbury began compiling an important collection of Becket's "miracles" in about 1172 and finished the first five books by around 1175, with a sixth book added in 1178 or 1179. One of the monks of Christ Church Canterbury, he had been ordained a deacon by Becket and was present in the cathedral when he was killed. Later attached to the shrine, he was given the task of receiving pilgrims and listening to their stories, assisting Benedict of Peterborough, the first official guardian of the shrine. He also wrote a "life" of Becket, completed in about 1174 and divided into two sections, the first covering events up to Thomas's return to Canterbury and the second describing the events of December 1170 in depth.

APPENDIX B

NOTE ON PRIMARY SOURCES

The primary sources are rich and varied: contemporary histories and chronicles, early Latin "lives" of Becket, his correspondence (not least some 230 letters he wrote himself or worked up from first drafts submitted by his clerks, some being rough drafts of letters never sent with glimpses of his interior world), the letters of John of Salisbury (some 300), the panegyrics of friends, the invectives of enemies such as Gilbert Foliot, Roger of Pont l'Évêque, or Jocelin of Salisbury, whom Becket excommunicated and who would stop at nothing in their efforts to silence or depose him.

Of the chroniclers, several describe the events of the twelfth century in depth. All wrote in Latin; none wrote in English, and the Anglo-Saxon Chronicle breaks off at Henry II's accession. Valuing chronology and factual accuracy more than the contemporary biographers, the chroniclers set the scene and establish a story structure. They can indulge in manufactured speeches and drama, and for much of the time seek to ferret out information that those in authority were trying to keep secret. But despite sometimes resembling tabloid journalists more than historians, they rarely invent information for the sake of it. "A rich, disorderly profusion" is characteristic of their work; otherwise their tone is investigative, seeking to do justice to the evidence, teasing out the motives and actions of king and archbishop, but not scrupling to criticize both. The main limitation of these narrators is that they were chiefly interested in men of power and have little time for women. They could not completely ignore Eleanor of Aquitaine, but their "discoveries" about her alleged transgressions were more interesting to them than seeking out the extent of her true role in politics and patronage and her relationship to her husband and Thomas Becket, and they write about her actions in the light of their own stereotyped assumptions concerning the role of royal women.

Up to the middle of Stephen's reign, the most useful background narratives are by Orderic Vitalis, a monk at Saint-Évroult in Normandy and a keen student of the classics, who was of mixed Anglo-French parentage, and William of Malmesbury, an omnivorous reader and a gifted historical scholar of Anglo-Norman parentage, who traveled widely in England but spent his entire career at Malmesbury Abbey in Wiltshire. The anarchy of Stephen's reign is evocatively covered by the author of the so-called *Gesta Stephani* and by Henry of Huntingdon, the most important Anglo-Norman historian to emerge from the parochial clergy. Both these writers share the critical and analytical skills of Orderic Vitalis, and neither stints on detail. For this and the later period, Robert of Torigni, a monk and later prior of Bec Abbey, who became abbot of Mont-Saint-Michel in 1154, adds essential chronological and factual information, especially on Norman history and politics, including summaries of key diplomatic documents. Personally acquainted with the most important figures, he met Henry II and Eleanor of Aquitaine at least twice. As a partisan royalist, however, he rarely mentions Becket's quarrel with the king.

The fullest and most sophisticated of the contemporary chroniclers of Henry II's reign is Ralph of Diss, a canon of St. Paul's in London. Although writing when Becket was already a canonized saint, he had been collecting his materials for many years. Based in London, he had good connections with the royal court, although he never held an official position there. A methodical compiler of facts illustrated by abridged versions of important letters and documents, he gives a vivid, commendably balanced narrative divided into sections, with marginal symbols (such as a crown or a bishop's staff) to distinguish different topics, and quotes extensively from documents. Henry was something of a hero in his eyes. Even so, Ralph remains a fair and honest rapporteur, including several important scenes in his work that the early biographers omitted.

Roger of Howden, William of Newburgh, and Gervase of Canterbury were younger men, whose writings draw freely on the early "lives" but correct their omissions and inventions. Howden, an absentee parson born in the East Riding of Yorkshire, is rightly regarded as one of the finest chroniclers of Henry II's reign. He wrote two overlapping chronicles from the time of Bede to 1201, both admittedly fairly derivative before Christmas 1169, that are invaluable despite lacking color and a sense of perspective. He was himself a clerk in royal service and so regularly includes full, unexpurgated versions of documents or gives coherent summaries based on written information and materials supplied to him by others, including letters by Becket, Pope Alexander III, and Gilbert Foliot. Writing from within the inner circles of government by the time of the climax of the Becket dispute, he offers a useful corrective to the views of the monastic chroniclers.

William of Newburgh, an Augustinian canon born in Bridlington, begins his story in 1066 and ends in 1198. A man with an encyclopedic knowledge of

Norman and continental politics, he brings a sense of distance to his narrative, as he did not begin writing until the 1190s. One of the most critically attuned of the monastic chroniclers, he stands above the crowd. When discussing the Becket conflict, he considers neither side to be wholly free from blame, criticizing Henry for his bullying and intimidation, and the bishops for being keener to defend the church's privileges and immunities than to correct its vices.

More derivative is Gervase of Canterbury's chronicle, but since he and his brother, another Thomas, were both Christ Church monks, they had known Becket personally and seen him in action as archbishop despite being his juniors by more than twenty years. Though borrowing extensively from other writers, Gervase adds his own independent sources into the mix and for a number of key topics appears to have had access to unique information. Professed as a monk by Becket himself in 1163, he was very much a Canterbury insider. Besides attending the murdered archbishop's funeral, he observed the destruction of the cathedral choir by fire in 1174 and describes it in some depth.

The chief Latin "lives" are by William fitz Stephen, Herbert of Bosham, John of Salisbury, "Anonymous I" (probably Roger of Pontigny), and Edward Grim. Almost as important, though in some instances partly derivative, are the works by Alan of Tewkesbury, "Anonymous II" (possibly someone born in London, although he was later a Canterbury monk), William of Canterbury, Benedict of Peterborough, and Guernes of Pont-Sainte-Maxence, the last of whom wrote in Old French verse. All were Becket's contemporaries, most of them known to him personally. Another "life" by Robert of Cricklade, prior of St. Frideswide's Oxford, whose lingering illness contracted after a pilgrimage to Sicily was providentially cured after a visit to Becket's shrine in 1171, no longer survives. Fragments from it can, however, be reconstructed, since in about 1200 it was translated into Old Norse and forms an important source for the biography of Becket known as the "Thomas Saga Erkibyskups," written in Icelandic and compiled from a mixture of Norwegian and Latin sources. These fragments, valuable for the years before Becket became archbishop, show that had it survived, Robert's "life" would have contained unique material. A brief supplementary Latin work by an anonymous author, "A Summary of the Dispute Between the King and Thomas," gives a firsthand account of the earlier stages of the quarrel, thus complementing the "lives," notably the events of the Council of Westminster in October 1163.

Since these "lives" can sometimes be little more than elaborate exercises in hagiography, they should be approached with appropriate caution. Whatever Becket's contemporaries may have thought about him while he was alive, after his gruesome murder they had to change their tune. And when the pope canonized him as a saint, they had to work with the assumption that his entire life had been part of a journey toward martyrdom, making irresistible the temptation to reconsider the whole of his life in the light of its unexpected ending. Although mostly completed within seven years of the murder, all these "lives" are retrospective, meaning that with the exception of John of Salisbury's earliest account in his letter to John of Canterbury, written early in 1171, they are constructed to explain, and justify, Becket's "martyrdom," so legitimizing his canonization by the pope. A sharp distinction should be drawn between the sources written before the murder and those written after, because anything written after that shocking event would have been automatically influenced by it.

Becket's own letters, which survive in profusion from the time he was archbishop, and the voluminous writings of his friend John of Salisbury, notably his letters, provide the essential correctives. They, unlike the "lives," are strictly contemporary sources. John's letters, which are especially informative for the final years of Theobald's life and the diplomacy of the years 1163–67, are also wonderful repositories of the latest gossip. John knew everyone and everything, providing his wide circle of friends with news and information not just concerning Becket, but about events all over Europe and as far afield as Sicily and the Middle East. By comparison, Alan of Tewkesbury's main claim to fame is his "master" manuscript of Becket's letters, surviving in the form of a dossier compiled between 1174–76 and 1180–84 from the disorderly residue of Becket's scriptorium in exile and from a variety of earlier important collections, including that begun by John of Salisbury, which Alan took over.

Considered in their original contexts, Becket's letters are accurate, informative, and durable. Assembled originally by different hands for different purposes, they provide a more varied and reliable view of his position during the quarrel with the king than that given by any of the early biographers. Until very recently, they were abominably edited, being ill arranged, misdated, and sloppily translated from the Latin, and for those reasons insufficiently used. Now expertly dated and translated in a masterly two-volume work of scholarship by Anne Duggan published in 2000 (which inexplicably omits the dozen or so of his letters written while he was still the king's chancellor—those must still be trawled from the original Latin), the letters open up a whole new area. True, they are unbalanced chronologically—the vast majority come from the years of Becket's exile in France, especially the final phase of the conflict with Henry after 1165, which was largely conducted as a war of letters—but they include frequent reflections on his earlier career, and there is more than enough for us to hear his own voice clearly and authentically.

Full of information, the letters, especially those that are private and intimate, help us to get inside Becket's head, revealing his hopes and fears, his likes and dislikes, his genuine, practical, living faith and vision of the world, as well as his better-known talent for vivid, fiery oratory and theatrical scenes. Under

Herbert of Bosham's guidance, he came to regard the scriptures as oracles, appears to have known them inside out, and quotes them constantly. Under the extreme pressure of the quarrel, he identified his cause with that of Christ against the Jews and Romans. "Tell me," he wrote to the English clergy in 1166, "have you forgotten what was done to me and God's church when I was still in England? What was done after I fled, what is still being done? Especially what was done at Northampton, when Christ was again being judged in my person before the judgment seat of the king? Where was the authority found for that? Doesn't such a scandal make you blush?" As Duggan remarks, the letters carry the reader into the heart of the controversy, revealing the unfolding of the crisis and the dark uncertainty in which Becket and his fellow exiles lived from day to day. Most of all, they restore to Becket—a man too easily dismissed as a hypocrite, a pretender, or an "actor-saint"—his values and his human face. If we are ever to recapture his true character and psychology, the letters must be collated against the often harsher opinions of the chroniclers, while taking into account the impression of his mindset that a fortuitous survival of the inventory of books that he owned and was studying in exile makes possible. A few of his own copies of these books, some even in their original vellum bindings, can still be traced in Cambridge libraries.

Other letter collections, such as those of Peter of Celle and his circle of famous correspondents, help us to sketch the wider picture. It is clear that throughout his years in exile and with the invaluable assistance of John of Salisbury as his intermediary, Becket used the abbot's own extensive network of pen friends as a channel through which he could publicize his ideals and intentions, enabling him to fight the propaganda war and paint Henry in the colors of a tyrant.

NOTES AND REFERENCES

Abbreviations

In citing manuscripts or printed materials, the following abbreviations are used.

Actes	*Recueil des Actes de Henri II, Roi d'Angleterre et Duc de Normandie, Concernant les Provinces Françaises et les Affaires de France,* ed. L. Delisle and E. Berger (3 vols. and introduction, Paris, 1909–27).
ALCD	M. R. James, *The Ancient Libraries of Canterbury and Dover* (Cambridge, 1905).
Barlow	F. Barlow, *Thomas Becket* (Berkeley and Los Angeles, 1986).
BL	British Library, London.
CCCC	Corpus Christi College, Cambridge.
Chronicles	*Chronicles of the Reigns of Stephen, Henry II and Richard I,* ed. R. Howlett (4 vols., London, 1884–89).
CTB	*The Correspondence of Thomas Becket, Archbishop of Canterbury, 1162–1170,* ed. A. J. Duggan (2 vols., Oxford, 2000).
CUL	Cambridge University Library.
DSCDR	*Dialogus de Scaccario: The Dialogue of the Exchequer,* ed. E. Amt, and *Constitutio Domus Regis: Disposition of the Royal Household,* ed. S. D. Church (Oxford, 2007).
Duggan	A. J. Duggan, *Thomas Becket* (London, 2004).

EHD	*English Historical Documents,* vol. II: *1042–1189,* ed. D. C. Douglas and G. W. Greenaway (2nd ed., London, 1981).
EHR	*English Historical Review.*
Eyton	R. W. Eyton, *Court, Household and Itinerary of King Henry II* (London, 1878).
Foedera	*Foedera, Conventiones, Litterae et Cuiuscunque Generis Acta Publica inter Reges Angliae et Alios Quosuis Imperatores, Reges, Pontifices, Principes vel Communitates,* vol. I, part I, ed. T. Rymer (London, 1816).
GC	Gervase of Canterbury, "Cronica Gervasii," in *HASD,* cols. 1338–1628.
GH	Gervase of Canterbury, "The History of the Archbishops of Canterbury," in *The Church Historians of England,* vol. V, part I, ed. J. Stevenson (London, 1858), pp. 293–348.
Greenaway	*The Life and Death of Thomas Becket, Chancellor of England and Archbishop of Canterbury . . . with Additions from Other Contemporary Sources,* ed. G. W. Greenaway (London, 1961).
GS	*Gesta Stephani, Regis Anglorum et Ducis Normannorum,* ed. R.H.C. Davis and K. R. Potter (Oxford, 1976).
Guernes	*La Vie de Saint Thomas Le Martyr, Archévêque de Canterbury,* ed. C. Hippeau (Paris, 1859).
HASD	*Historiae Anglicanae Scriptores Decem,* ed. R. Twysden (London, 1652).
Henry II	*Henry II: New Interpretations,* ed. C. Harper-Bill and N. Vincent (Woodbridge, U.K., 2007).
HH	*The Chronicle of Henry of Huntingdon,* ed. Thomas Forester (London, 1853), pp. 1–297.
HP	*The "Historia Pontificalis" of John of Salisbury,* ed. M. Chibnall (2nd ed., Oxford, 1986).
Knowles	D. Knowles, *Thomas Becket* (London, 1970).
Laarhoven	*John of Salisbury's Entheticus Maior and Minor,* ed. J. van Laarhoven (3 vols., Leiden, 1987).
LJS	*The Letters of John of Salisbury,* ed. W. J. Millor, H. E. Butler, and C.N.L. Brooke (2 vols., Oxford, 1979–86).

LPC	*The Letters of Peter of Celle,* ed. J. Haseldine (Oxford, 2001).
Lyttelton	George, Lord Lyttelton, *The History of the Life of King Henry the Second* (5 vols., new ed., London, 1777).
Map	Walter Map, *De Nugis Curialium: Courtiers' Trifles,* ed. M. R. James (Oxford, 1983).
MS	Manuscript.
MTB	*Materials for the History of Thomas Becket,* ed. J. C. Robertson and J. B. Sheppard, Rolls Series (7 vols., London, 1875–85).
ODNB	*The New Oxford Dictionary of National Biography,* ed. C. Matthew and B. Harrison (60 vols., Oxford, 2004), http://www.oxforddnb.com/public/index.html.
OV	*The Ecclesiastical History of England and Normandy by Ordericus Vitalis,* ed. T. Forester (4 vols., London, 1853–56).
PJS 1	John of Salisbury, *Policraticus,* ed. C. J. Nederman (Cambridge, 1990).
PJS 2	John of Salisbury, *Frivolities of Courtiers and Footprints of Philosophers* [translation of the first, second, and third books, and selections from the seventh and eighth books of the *Policraticus*], ed. J. B. Pike (New York, 1972).
PL	*Patrologia Latina,* ed. J.-P. Migne (221 vols., Paris, 1844–64).
Radford	L. B. Radford, *Thomas of London Before His Consecration* (Cambridge, 1894).
RC	"A Reconstruction of Robert of Cricklade's *Vita et Miracula S. Thomae Cantuariensis,*" ed. M. Orme, *Annalecta Bollandiana* 84 (1966), pp. 379–98.
RD	Ralph of Diss, "Ymagines Historiarum," in *HASD,* cols. 525–710.
RH	*Chronica Magistri Rogeri de Houedene* [*The Chronicle of Roger of Howden*], ed. W. Stubbs (2 vols., London, 1868).
RM	Robert de Monte, "The Chronicles of Robert de Monte," in *The Church Historians of England,* vol. IV, part II, ed. J. Stevenson (London, 1856), pp. 675–813.

RN	*The Chronicles of Ralph Niger,* ed. R. Anstruther, Caxton Society (London, 1851).
SC	*Select Charters and Other Illustrations of English Constitutional History,* ed. W. Stubbs (9th ed., Oxford, 1962).
Staunton	*The Lives of Thomas Becket,* ed. Michael Staunton (Manchester, 2001).
TCC	Trinity College, Cambridge.
TRHS	*Transactions of the Royal Historical Society.*
TSE	*Thomas Saga Erkibyskups: A Life of Archbishop Thomas Becket in Icelandic, with English Notes and Translation,* ed. E. Magnusson (2 vols., London, 1875–83).
WM	*William of Malmesbury's Chronicle of the Kings of England,* ed. J. A. Giles (London, 1847).
WN	William of Newburgh, "The History of William of Newburgh," in *The Church Historians of England,* vol. IV, part II, ed. J. Stevenson (London, 1856), pp. 397–672.

Note on Dates

In giving dates, the Old Style has been retained, but the calendar year has sometimes been amended so that it begins, as now, on January 1 and not on Christmas Day, as was the custom until about 1150, although at Canterbury the older rule prevailed for many years after that time. In respect to more recent dates, the practice of reckoning the year from Lady Day (the feast of the Annunciation, March 25) came into fashion after about 1150 and was the norm in France, Spain, and Italy until 1582; in Scotland until 1600; and in England, Wales, and Ireland until 1752. In respect to these dates too, I have taken the calendar year as beginning on January 1.

Transcription of Primary Documents

The spelling and orthography of primary sources in quotations are always given in modernized form. Modern punctuation and capitalization are provided where there is none in the original document.

Translation from Latin Writings

In citing translations of Latin writings, I have occasionally substituted my own modified translation where it better matches the sense of the original, avoids an anachronism, or is more colloquial.

Prologue

No fewer than seven accounts of the events of November 25, 1120, and their aftermath survive, but only two appear to be based on firsthand information, those of Orderic Vitalis and William of Malmesbury: OV, IV, pp. 32–42; WM, pp. 454–57. The accounts differ in some of the smaller details, for example the exact phase of the moon and whether it was the king who took the decision to choose the *White Ship* or Prince William. Henry of Huntingdon's brief account is from HH, pp. 248–49. Other accounts by Simeon of Durham, Eadmer, Hugh the Chanter, and Robert of Torigni are too fragmentary to be of much use. The most useful modern account of the wreck is T. Brett-Jones, "The *White Ship* Disaster: An Investigation into the Circumstances of the Loss," *The Historian* 64 (1999), pp. 23–26.

1 | ANCESTRY

"Lux Londoniarum" is from CUL, MS Ff.VI.8. A conflict exists over the year of Becket's birth among different biographers and the unanimous liturgical tradition. An exhaustive analysis of this problem by Professor Frank Barlow has concluded that 1120 "has no persuasive rival" as the correct date; see Barlow, p. 281. Information on the family's house and its dimensions is from "St. Mary Colechurch 105/18," in D. J. Keene and Vanessa Harding, *Historical Gazetteer of London Before the Great Fire* (London, 1987), pp. 490–517; A. J. Forey, "The Military Order of St. Thomas of Acre," *EHR* 92 (1977), pp. 481–503; J. Watney, *Some Account of the Hospital of St. Thomas of Acon in the Cheap, London, and of the Mercers' Company* (2nd ed., London, 1906), pp. 10–11. See also A. Quiney, "Hall or Chamber? That Is the Question. The Use of Rooms in Post-Conquest Houses," *Architectural History* 42 (1999), pp. 24–46. Most of what we know about Becket's parents is from *MTB*, II, pp. 356–59; Staunton, pp. 40–42; Barlow, pp. 10–15; Radford, pp. 1–9. Information about the Beckets' ancestry is from William fitz Stephen and "Anonymous II" (both natives of London): *MTB*, III, pp. 14–15; *MTB*, IV, p. 81; Greenaway, pp. 35–37. The legend of the Saracen princess is from *MTB*, II, pp. 451–58; *HASD*, cols. 1052–55. Edward Grim's account of Matilda Becket's visions is from *MTB*, II, pp. 356–58. Becket's defense of his middle-class ancestry is from *CTB*, I, pp. 403–5, 431–33. The social organization, government, and civic institutions of London are from C. M. Barron, *London in the Later Middle Ages: Government and People, 1200–1500* (Oxford, 2004); J. McEwan, "Medieval London: The Development of a Civic Political Community, c. 1100–1300" (University of London, Ph.D. thesis, 2007). Background on privileges and charters to the Londoners is from *EHD*, pp. 1011–17; J.S.P. Tatlock, "The Date of Henry I's Charter to London," *Speculum* 11 (1936), pp. 461–69; J. A. Green, *Henry I: King of England and Duke of Normandy* (Cambridge, 2009), pp. 249–51, 298–301. Background on buildings, social customs, and everyday life is from R. Bartlett, *England Under the Norman and Angevin Kings, 1075–1225* (Oxford, 2000); L. F. Salzman, *English Life in the Middle Ages* (Oxford, 1926); K. Norgate, *England Under the Angevin Kings* (2 vols., London, 1887). Gilbert Becket's chapel in St. Paul's Churchyard is from *Stow's Survey of London*, ed. H. B. Wheatley (London, 1956), p. 293.

2 | UPBRINGING

Thomas's childhood is discussed in Barlow, pp. 11–19; Radford, pp. 1–11. Background on language and ethnicity is from J. Green, *The Government of England Under Henry I*, pp. 11, 155–57; Green, *Henry I*, p. 317; H. M. Thomas, *The English and the Normans: Ethnic Hostility, Assimilation and Identity, 1066–c. 1220* (Oxford, 2003). Accounts of Becket's early education are from *MTB*, III, pp. 4–5, 14–15; *TSE*, I, pp. 19–21; Radford, pp. 13–16; Barlow, pp.17–18; Duggan, pp. 9–11. The *Ars Minor* of Aelius Donatus is from the edition printed by Wynkyn de Worde (London, 1496?). Background is from N. Orme, "Children and Literature in Medieval England," *Medium Aevum* 68 (1999), pp. 218–46; N. Orme, "Children and the Church in Medieval England," *Journal of Ecclesiastical History* 45 (1994), pp. 563–87; N. Orme, "For Richer for Poorer? Free Education in England, c. 1380–1530," *Journal of the History of Childhood and Youth* 1 (2008), pp. 169–87. Thomas's later summons to Robert of Merton is from *MTB*, III, p. 147. Sources for writing and dictation, including the comments of Orderic Vitalis, are from M. T. Clancy, *From Memory to Written Record: England, 1066–1307* (Cambridge, Mass., 1979), pp. 88–103. William fitz Stephen's graphic description of London—its sports and recreations, food, and amenities—is from *MTB*, III, 2–13; S. Pegge, *Fitz Stephen's Description of the City of London . . . with a Necessary Commentary* (London, 1772). Becket's digestive ailment is from D. Knowles, *The Episcopal Colleagues of Thomas Becket* (Cambridge, 1951), pp. 167–68; Barlow, p. 25; see also notes to chapter 12. The career of Richer de l'Aigle is from K. Thompson, "The Lords of Laigle: Ambition and Insecurity on the Borders of Normandy," *Anglo-Norman Studies* 18 (1995), pp. 177–99; Radford, pp. 16–18; Green, *Henry I*, pp. 142, 149–50, 154; OV, III, pp. 472–73. Becket's accident at the millstream is from *MTB*, II, pp. 360–61 (Edward Grim's version); *MTB*, IV, pp. 6–7 (Roger of Pontigny's version); Staunton, pp. 43–44; Radford, pp. 16–18. Robert of Cricklade's more cynical account of Becket's encounter with Richer de l'Aigle is from *TSE*, I, pp. 31–33; RC, pp. 384–85; Radford, p. 17, n. 3.

3 | POLITICS

Information on Henry I's character and achievements is from OV, III, pp. 267–72, 386; OV, IV, pp. 148–54; WM, pp. 331–33, 424–89; HH, pp. 240–60; *PJS 1*, p. 118. See also Green, *Henry I;* C. Warren Hollister, *Henry I* (New Haven and London, 2001); Green, *Government of England Under Henry I;* C. Warren Hollister, "Royal Acts of Mutilation: The Case Against Henry I," *Albion* 10 (1978), pp. 330–40; W. L. Warren, *Henry II* (2nd ed., London, 2000). Background on Henry I's court is from C. Warren Hollister, "Courtly Culture and Courtly Style in the Anglo-Norman World," *Albion* 20 (1988), pp. 1–17. Henry's movements are from W. Farrer, "An Outline Itinerary of King Henry the First," *EHR* 34 (1919), pp. 303–82, 505–79. His judicial role is from P. Wormald, *Lawyers and the State: The Varieties of Legal History,* Selden Society (London, 2006), especially pp. 6–7. The Norman political and military background is from D. Douglas, *William the Conqueror: The Norman Impact upon England* (London, 1966); D. Bates, *William the Conqueror* (London, 2004); F. Barlow, *William Rufus* (London, 1983); C. W. David, *Robert Curthose, Duke of Normandy* (Cambridge, Mass., 1920); J. A. Green, "Robert Curthose Reassessed," *Anglo-Norman Studies* 22 (1999), pp. 95–116; A. L. Poole, *From Domesday Book to Magna Carta, 1087–1216* (2nd ed., Oxford, 1964). The Conqueror's writ of 1072 is from *EHD,* pp. 647–48. Information on naval history and ship construction is from N.A.M. Rodger, *The Safeguard of the Sea: A Naval History of Britain,* vol. I: *660–1649* (London, 1997).

4 | PARIS

The background to Stephen's reign and Matilda's bid for the throne is from R.H.C. Davis, *King Stephen, 1135–1154* (3rd ed., London, 1990); M. Chibnall, *The Empress Matilda: Queen Consort, Queen Mother and Lady of the English* (Oxford, 1991). The account of Stephen's landing and coronation is from *GS,* pp. 2–7. John of Salisbury's account of Stephen's perjury is from *HP,* p. 83. The coronation charter is from *SC,* p. 142. The Oxford charter is from *SC,* pp. 143–44. Peter of Celle's warning of the temptations of Paris is from *LPC,* pp. 657–59; John of Salisbury's account of its delights is from *CTB,* I, p. 69. The description of the city and the schools is from S. C. Ferruolo, *The Origins of the University: The Schools of Paris and Their Critics, 1100–1215* (Stanford, Calif., 1985); Amy Kelly, *Eleanor of Aquitaine and the Four Kings* (Cambridge, Mass., 1950); S. Roux, *Paris in the Middle Ages* (Philadelphia, 2003). R. L. Poole, "The Masters of the Schools of Paris and Chartres in John of Salisbury's Time," *EHR* 64 (1920), pp. 321–42, is dated but still useful. The most important accounts of Thomas's studies and his mother's death are those of William of Canterbury, John of Salisbury, William fitz Stephen, Roger of Pontigny, Herbert of Bosham, Edward Grim, and the Icelandic "Thomas Saga Erkibyskups," which is based in part on the lost "life" of Robert of Cricklade: *MTB,* I, pp. 3–4; *MTB,* II, pp. 302–3, 359–60; *MTB,* III, pp. 14–15, 163–66; *MTB,* IV, pp. 5–8; *TSE,* I, pp. 21–23; Staunton, pp. 42–43. Further information is from Radford, pp. 18–23; Duggan, pp. 10–12; Barlow, pp. 20–23. The accounts of the teaching of Hugh of Saint-Victor, Robert of Melun, and Robert Pullen are from Ferruolo, *Origins of the University,* pp. 22–26, 27–44, 64–65, 227; Beryl Smalley, *The Becket Conflict and the Schools* (Oxford, 1973), pp.

28–30, 39–58; F. Courtney, *Cardinal Robert Pullen: An English Theologian of the Twelfth Century* (Rome, 1954). I follow Radford (p. 23) in believing that Becket's mother's death preceded his father's and that his father had sustained a series of losses through fires. Edward Grim places these losses before the mother's death. He also thought both Becket's parents died at more or less the same time, but as he did not meet Becket until shortly before the murder, his chronology is likely to be confused: *MTB,* II, p. 359. The opinions of William of Canterbury and Herbert of Bosham as to why Becket abandoned his studies are from *MTB,* I, pp. 3–4; *MTB,* III, pp. 163–64. John of Salisbury's comments about Becket's "rakish pursuits" and chastity are from *MTB,* II, p. 303. William of Canterbury makes a similar remark but places it later in the story, after Becket's appointment as chancellor: *MTB,* I, pp. 5–6. The satirical verse is from Ferruolo, *Origins of the University,* p. 129.

5 | A FRESH START

Becket's employment with Osbert Huitdeniers is from Radford, pp. 23–26; Barlow, pp. 27–28. Information on Matilda's invasion and the events following the battle of Lincoln is from Davis, *King Stephen,* pp. 34–51; Norgate, *England Under the Angevin Kings,* I, pp. 308–44. The background to the anarchy is from H.W.C. Davis, "The Anarchy of Stephen's Reign," *EHR* 18 (1903), pp. 630–41; E. King, "The Anarchy of Stephen's Reign," *TRHS* 34 (1984), pp. 133–53; E. J. Kealey, "King Stephen: Government and Anarchy," *Albion* 6 (1974), pp. 201–17. The archbishop of Rouen's letter to the Londoners is from Davis, *King Stephen,* p. 55. Matilda's arbitrary levy and berating of the citizens are from *GS,* pp. 122–24. The Peterborough chronicler's description of the anarchy is from *EHD,* pp. 210–11 (where the account is placed in the wrong year). That from the *Gesta Stephani* is from *GS,* pp. 91–221. Becket's letter to Bishop Roger of Worcester is from *CTB,* II, pp. 1219–25. His entry into Theobald's household is from *MTB,* II, pp. 303–4, 361–63; *MTB,* III, pp. 15–17, 167–72; *MTB,* IV, pp. 9–12; A. Saltman, *Theobald, Archbishop of Canterbury* (London, 1956), pp. 3–55, 165–77; Radford, pp. 27–56; Barlow, pp. 28–40. John of Salisbury's role is from Saltman, *Theobald*, pp. 169–75. The fragment from Robert of Cricklade's lost chronicle is from *TSE,* I, p. 37; RC, p. 385. The pact with Roger of Pont l'Évêque and John of Canterbury is from *MTB,* I, p. 4. Information about Thomas's double rustication and reinstatement is from *MTB,* III, p. 16. Background on the archiepiscopal estates and on the movements and staffing of Theobald's household is from F.R.H. Du Boulay, *The Lordship of Canterbury* (New York, 1966), pp. 237–39, 251–64.

6 | APPRENTICE

William fitz Stephen's account is from *MTB,* III, pp. 16–17; Edward Grim's is from *MTB,* II, p. 361. Background on Roman and canon law is from J. A. Brundage, *Medieval Canon Law* (London, 1995); D. Luscombe and J. Riley-Smith, *The New Cambridge Medieval History of Europe,* vol. IV, part I (Cambridge, 2004), pp. 368–460; *Select Cases from the Ecclesiastical Courts of the Province of Canterbury, c. 1200–1301,* ed. N. Adams and C. Donahue, Selden Society (London, 1981), intro. pp. 6–12. Becket's studies at Bologna and Auxerre are from *MTB,* II, p. 304; *MTB,* III, p. 17. For Albert de Morra as his possible master at Bologna, see *Henry II,* p. 175, n. 2. Theobald's support for the study of Roman and canon law is from Saltman, *Theobald,* pp. 166, 175–77. Roger of Pont l'Évêque's nickname for Thomas is from *MTB,* IV, p. 10; Radford, p. 30. The rumors and superstitions are from Davis, *King Stephen,* pp. 86–87; *The Life of Christina of Markyate: A Twelfth-Century Recluse,* ed. C. H. Talbot (London, 1959), p. 185; H. Mayr-Harting, "Functions of a Twelfth-Century Recluse," *History* 60 (1975), pp. 337–52; Thomas, *The English and the Normans,* pp. 200–235. The events of the civil war are from Davis, *King Stephen,* pp. 75–107. Theobald's visit to Paris is from Saltman, *Theobald,* pp. 23–24; his relationship with Bishop Henry of Winchester and earlier popes is from ibid., pp. 7–22. Henry of Anjou's decision to retain Devizes is from King, "The Anarchy of Stephen's Reign," p. 140. John of Salisbury's account of Theobald's flight and the events of the Council of Rheims is from *HP,* pp. 6–52; see also Saltman, *Theobald,* pp. 25–30; Radford, pp. 42–44. Events after Theobald's return are from *HP,* pp. 49–52, 78–79; Davis, *King Stephen,* pp. 101–3. Becket's letter to Cardinal Boso is from *CTB,* I, pp. 719–21. The reports of his visits to Rome are from *MTB,* II, pp. 303–4; *MTB,* III, p. 16. The account of his role in securing Theobald's papal legacy is from GH, p. 325, where the date is wrong. The correct year is established by Radford, pp. 39–41; Saltman, *Theobald,* pp. 30–33. The Murdac affair is from John of Salisbury, *HP,* p. 83. The subsequent mission of Roger of Pont l'Évêque is from *CTB,* I, pp. 720–21, where the editor notes that it was indeed he who had acted for Stephen; Radford, pp. 50–51. See also Davis, *King Stephen,* pp. 97–99, 102–3, 114; Saltman, *Theobald,* pp. 36–37. Gervase of Canterbury's account of Becket's diplomatic interventions is from GC, cols. 1371–72; GH, pp. 325–29. Becket's letter citing the opinion of Cardinal Gregory is from *CTB,* I, pp. 777–87. Stephen's further efforts to bully Theobald are from HH, pp. 288–89; John of Salisbury, *HP,* p. 83; Saltman, *Theobald,* pp. 37–39; Radford, pp. 45–52; Davis, *King Stephen,* pp. 113–14. The story from the anonymous "Life of Theobald" repeated in the chronicle of Bec Abbey is from *PL,* vol. 150, cols. 733–34.

7 | INTO THE LIMELIGHT

The early biographers all describe Becket's ecclesiastical preferments: *MTB,* I, pp. 4–5; *MTB,* II, pp. 303–4; *MTB,* III, pp. 17, 168; *MTB,* IV, pp. 10–11. See also Radford, pp. 52–56; Barlow, pp. 36–38; Saltman, *Theobald,* pp. 167–69. Thomas's own account showing that he did not go unrewarded by Theobald is from *CTB,* I, pp. 431–33. The political events of the closing years of Stephen's reign are from HH, pp. 290–96; GC, cols. 1369–75; *GS,* pp. 238–40; RH, I, pp. 213–14; Lyttelton, II, pp. 187–277; Davis, *King Stephen,* pp. 111–24; Warren, *Henry II,* pp. 42–53. The divorce of Eleanor of Aquitaine is from *HP,* pp. 52–53; WN, pp. 441–42; E. R. Labande, *Pour Une Image Véridique d'Aliénor d'Aquitaine* (2nd ed., Poitiers, 2005), pp. 64–67. Information on Aquitaine and Eleanor's ducal forebears is from J. Martindale, *Status, Authority and Regional Power: Aquitaine and France, 9th to 12th Centuries* (Aldershot, 1997), no. X, pp. 87–116; no. XI, pp. 17–50. The alleged affair between Eleanor and Geoffrey of Anjou is from Map, pp. 475–77. Robert of Torigni's account of Eustace's attack on Normandy is from *Chronicles,* IV, pp. 164–71. The peace negotiations at Wallingford and Winchester are from HH, pp. 294–95; *Chronicles,* IV, pp. 171–77; Saltman, *Theobald,* pp. 39–41.Theobald's description of Becket as his "first and only counselor" is from *LJS,* I, p. 198. Becket's recollection of the hardships endured by Theobald is from *CTB,* II, p. 1267. His complaint to the pope about Henry's oath breaking is from *CTB,* I, p. 781; that to Cardinal Hubald is from *CTB,* II, p. 1017. Background to the Devizes affair is from Saltman, *Theobald,* pp. 40, 465–66; King, "The Anarchy of Stephen's Reign," p. 140. Essential background on the peace treaty and Henry's accession is from E. King, "The Accession of Henry II," in *Henry II,* pp. 24–46. The details of the Westminster charter are from *Foedera,* I, p. 18; *EHD,* pp. 436–38. The reconstruction of the fragments of Robert of Cricklade's lost biography is from RC, p. 385. The chroniclers' accounts of Eustace's death are from GC, col. 1374; HH, p. 293. William of Canterbury's and Roger of Pontigny's comments on Becket's promotion as archdeacon of Canterbury are from *MTB,* I, p. 4; *MTB,* IV, pp. 10–11. Gervase of Canterbury's report of Stephen's death and of Thomas's appointment as chancellor at the very beginning of Henry II's reign is from GC, cols. 1376–77.

8 | ARRIVAL AT COURT

Becket's arrival at court, where he witnessed charters in mid-January 1155, is from Eyton, pp. 3–5. The inner politics of his promotion are from *MTB,* III, pp. 17–18; *MTB,* IV, pp. 11–12; Staunton, pp. 47–48; Radford, pp. 57–61. Theobald's later advice to Henry against the predatory barons is from *LJS,* I, p. 220. Robert of Cricklade's interpretation is from RC, pp. 385–86; *TSE,* I, pp. 47, 57. Information on Theobald's motives and values is from C.N.L. Brooke, "Adrian IV and John of Salisbury," in *Adrian IV, the English Pope, 1154–1159: Studies and Texts,* ed.

B. Bolton and A. J. Duggan (Aldershot, 2003), pp. 8–9; Saltman, *Theobald,* pp. 41–55, 153–64; K. J. Stringer, *The Reign of King Stephen* (London, 1993), pp. 61–72. Becket's physical characteristics are from *MTB,* I, p. 3; *MTB,* III, pp. 17, 229, 327; *MTB,* IV, p. 84; *TSE,* I, p. 29. William fitz Stephen's classic description of Henry II and Becket's familiarity is from *MTB,* III, pp. 17–26; Staunton, pp. 48–53, 58–59. Henry's character and description are from *EHD,* pp. 409–20; Map, pp. 471–501; Peter of Blois, Epistolae 14, 41, 66, and 75, in *PL,* vol. 207, cols. 42–51, 121–22, 195–210, 229–31; RN, p. 169; *MTB,* III, p. 43; *MTB,* VII, pp. 570–76. Background on Henry's court is from N. Vincent, "The Court of Henry II," in *Henry II,* pp. 278–334. The letter to Becket about the constable of Normandy is from *CTB,* I, pp. 541–49. The affair of Northumbria is from Warren, *Henry II,* pp. 68–69. Information on Eleanor of Aquitaine is from Martindale, *Status, Authority and Regional Power,* no. XI, pp. 17–50; N. Vincent, "Patronage, Politics and Piety in the Charters of Eleanor of Aquitaine," in *Plantagenêts et Capétiens: Confrontations et Héritages,* ed. M. Aurell and N. Tonnerre (Turnhout, 2006), pp. 17–60; E.A.R. Brown, "Eleanor of Aquitaine Reconsidered," in *Eleanor of Aquitaine: Lord and Lady,* ed. B. Wheeler and J. C. Parsons (London, 2003), pp. 1–54; E.A.R. Brown, "Eleanor of Aquitaine: Parent, Queen, and Duchess," in *Eleanor of Aquitaine: Parent and Politician,* ed. W. W. Kibler (Austin, Tex., 1976), pp. 9–34; F. McMinn Chambers, "Some Legends Concerning Eleanor of Aquitaine," *Speculum* 16 (1941), pp. 459–68. Theobald's report of her frustration with the bishop of Worcester is from *LJS,* I, pp. 151–52. Arnulf of Lisieux's letter is from *The Letters of Arnulf of Lisieux,* ed. F. Barlow, Camden Society, 3rd ser., 61 (London, 1939), pp. 13–14. His character is from ibid., pp. xi–xxv.

9 | ROYAL MINISTER

John of Salisbury's report of Henry II's new vision of the monarchy is from *LJS,* II, p. 581. The report of Gervase of Canterbury is from GC, col. 1377. Henry's policy on the restoration of law and order is from E. Amt, *The Accession of Henry II in England: Royal Government Restored, 1149–1159* (Woodbridge, U.K., 1993), pp. 21–26; G. J. White, *Restoration and Reform, 1153–1165: Recovery from Civil War in England* (Cambridge, 2000), pp. 104–12; Warren, *Henry II,* pp. 59–63. The confiscation of the castles is from GC, cols. 1377–78; WN, pp. 445–46. Bishop Henry of Winchester's fascination with Domesday Book is from *DSCDR,* pp. 97–99. Information on Henry's and Becket's movements in England, Normandy, Anjou, and Aquitaine, including a chronology of the charters and confirmations to lands issued during these years, is from Eyton, pp. 2–57. The rebellion of Geoffrey of Anjou and its aftermath is from GC, cols. 1378, 1380–81; WN, pp. 450–51; Radford, pp. 78–80; Warren, *Henry II,* pp. 64–66, 71–77; Barlow, pp. 54–55. An invaluable account by Robert of Torigni is from *Chronicles,* IV, pp. 186–97. Scutage is from F. Stenton, *The First Century of English Feudalism* (2nd ed., Oxford, 1961), pp. 177–91; Radford, p. 157; Barlow, p. 59. Theobald's petition for exemption is from *LJS,* I, pp. 21–22. Henry's diplomacy with Louis in February 1156 is from *Chronicles,* IV, p. 186; RH, I, p. 215. Eleanor of Aquitaine's movements are from Eyton, pp. 6, 18, 24, 30–31, 40–43, 49–52, 55. Becket's diplomatic receptions are from *MTB,* III, p. 26; Radford, pp. 76–77. The embassy of the king of Valencia is from RM, p. 758. Becket's return to England with Eleanor is from *LJS,* I, p. 51. William fitz Stephen's unique account of Becket's embassy to France is from *MTB,* III, pp. 29–33; Greenaway, pp. 45–47; Staunton, pp. 55–56. See also Radford, pp. 80–84; Warren, *Henry II,* pp. 71–72; Barlow, pp. 55–57; Norgate, *England Under the Angevin Kings,* I, pp. 445–48. Although Herbert of Bosham refers to the marriage treaty, he has in fact confused its terms with those reached by a later treaty of 1160 following the Toulouse campaign: *MTB,* III, p. 175; Radford, pp. 83–84, 93–94. The capture of Guy of Laval is from *MTB,* III, p. 33; Radford, p. 83; Barlow, p. 57. Henry's confirmation as the hereditary high steward of France and the intervention in Brittany is from GC, cols. 1380–81; WN, p. 451; *Chronicles,* IV, pp. 196–97; Warren, *Henry II,* pp. 72–77; Norgate, *England Under the Angevin Kings,* I, pp. 449–53; J. Everard, *Brittany and the Angevins: Province and Empire, 1158–1203* (Cambridge, 2000), p. 34. Henry's diplomacy with Louis VII after his brother's death is from GC, col. 1380; *Chronicles,* IV, pp. 197–99; RD, col. 531; Radford, pp. 84–87; Warren, *Henry II,* pp. 72–77. Gervase of Canterbury's comment on the miraculous signals of the Anglo-French amity is from GC, col. 1380.

10 | BUREAUCRAT AND JUDGE

The summary of Becket's administrative duties is from *DSCDR,* pp. xx–xxv, xliv–xlviii, li–lv, 28–31, 197–99; *MTB,* III, pp. 18–19; Radford, pp. 68, 123–32; Barlow, pp. 42–43. The size of the scriptorium and the recruitment of clerks is from Kealey, "King Stephen: Government and Anarchy," pp. 204–11 and n. 8; T.A.M. Bishop, *Scriptores Regis* (Oxford, 1960), pp. 1–30; *MTB,* III, p. 29; *DSCDR,* pp. li–lv; M. T. Clanchy, *From Memory to Written Record: England, 1066–1307* (Cambridge, Mass., 1979), pp. 41–46. The refurbishment of the palace of Westminster is from *MTB,* III, pp. 19–20 (wrongly annotated by the editor as the Tower of London). Becket's duties in the Exchequer are from the account in *DSCDR,* pp. xx–xxv, lii–lv, and nn. 66, 73; Radford, pp. 123–33. John of Salisbury's observation on Robert de Beaumont's high view of kingship is from *PJS 1,* p. 137. Background on royal justice is from D. M. Stenton, *English Justice Between the Norman Conquest and the Great Charter, 1066–1215* (London, 1965), pp. 22–87; S. F. Pollock and F. W. Maitland, *The History of English Law Before the Time of Edward I* (2 vols., 2nd ed., Cambridge, 1968), I, pp. 108–73. Becket's role as a circuit judge is from Radford, pp. 111–15. Useful correctives to the usual whiggish interpretations of Angevin justice are Wormald, *Lawyers and the State;* R. V. Turner, "The Reputation of Royal Judges Under the Angevin Kings," *Albion* 11 (1979), pp. 301–16. Becket's attitude toward justice is from *MTB,* III, pp. 22–26; RC, p. 386; Staunton, pp. 51–52; *English Lawsuits from William I to Richard II,* ed. R. C. van Caenegem, Selden Society (London, 1991), p. 361. The Battle Abbey case is from *The Chronicle of Battle Abbey,* ed. E. Searle (Oxford, 1980), pp. 176–215; *English Lawsuits,* ed. van Caenegem, pp. 310–23; Saltman, *Theobald,* pp. 91–92, 243; Radford, pp. 105–11; E. Searle, "Battle Abbey and Exemption: The Forged Charters," *EHR* 83 (1968), pp. 449–80; *CTB,* II, pp. 1394–95. Hilary of Chichester's character is from H. Mayr-Harting, "Hilary, Bishop of Chichester (1147–1169) and Henry II," *EHR* 78 (1963), pp. 209–24. Professor Nicholas Vincent's brilliant exposé of the Battle Abbey chronicler is from his article "King Henry II and the Monks of Battle: The Battle Chronicle Unmasked," in *Belief and Culture in the Middle Ages: Studies Presented to Henry Mayr-Harting,* ed. R. Gameson and H. Leyser (Oxford, 2001), pp. 264–85. Becket's letter to the pope referring to the case in 1168 is from *CTB,* I, p. 782.

11 | WARRIOR

An invaluable introduction to Becket's military role is J. D. Hosler, "The Brief Military Career of Thomas Becket," *Haskins Journal* 15 (2006), pp. 88–100. John of Salisbury's report of Becket's resort to soothsayers is from *PJS 2,* pp. 127–28, Edward Grim's critique of Becket's penchant for warfare is from *MTB,* II, p. 365; Radford, p. 92. John of Salisbury's critique of hunting is from *PJS 2,* pp. 13–26. Henry's and Becket's movements are from Eyton, pp. 27–52. Background on the campaign in north Wales is from J. D. Hosler, "Henry II's Military Campaigns in Wales, 1157 and 1165," *Journal of Medieval Military History* 2 (2004), pp. 53–72; Warren, *Henry II,* pp. 69–71, 161–63. Gervase of Canterbury's account is from GC, col. 1380. William of Newburgh's description of the Welsh ambush and Henry of Essex's cowardice is from WN, pp. 447–48. Information on the Welsh vernacular chronicles is from Hosler, "Brief Military Career," pp. 91–92. Eleanor's role in pressing for the campaign in Aquitaine is from Brown, "Eleanor of Aquitaine Reconsidered," p. 12. The Aquitaine campaign itself is from *MTB,* III, pp. 33–34; Staunton, p. 57. Other details are from WN, pp. 454–59; RD, col. 531; GC, col. 1381; L. Combarieu and F. Cangardel, *Histoire Générale de la Province de Quercy* (2 vols., Cahors, 1884), II, pp. 68–72; J. Raynal, *Histoire de la Ville de Toulouse avec Une Notice des Hommes Illustrés* (Toulouse, 1759), pp. 59–60; M.J.M. Cayla and P. Paviot, *Histoire de la Ville de Toulouse depuis sa Fondation jusqu'à Nos Jours* (Toulouse, 1839), pp. 288–93. The loans from Henry and the Jews are from *MTB,* III, pp. 53–54. Information on the Vexin campaign and its aftermath is from *MTB,* III, pp. 34–35; RD, col. 532; *Actes,* I, pp. 251–53. Louis VII's anger is from WN, p. 477. See also Radford, pp. 87–94. The events surrounding Prince Henry's marriage to the infant Margaret are from L. Diggelmann, "Marriage as Tactical Response: Henry II and the Royal Wedding of 1160," *EHR* 119 (2004), pp. 954–64. Henry's decision to place his son and heir in Becket's household is from *MTB*, III, pp. 176–77. See also Greenaway, p. 43.

12 | A SOLITARY MAN

William fitz Stephen's stereotype is from *MTB*, III, pp. 17–26; Staunton, pp. 48–53, 58–59. Other verdicts on his relationship with Henry are from *MTB*, I, pp. 5–7 (William of Canterbury); *MTB*, II, pp. 304–9 (John of Salisbury); *MTB*, II, pp. 363–65 (Edward Grim); *MTB*, III, pp. 226–29 (Herbert of Bosham); *MTB*, IV, pp. 11–14 (Roger of Pontigny); RC, p. 387 (Robert of Cricklade). See also *TSE*, I, pp. 48–49; Radford, pp. 48–59. The parable of the beggar is from *MTB*, III, pp. 24–25; Staunton, pp. 52–53. The idea of the "charming joke" is from C. S. Jaeger, *The Envy of Angels: Cathedral Schools and Social Ideas in Medieval Europe, 950–1200* (Philadelphia, 1994), pp. 299–301. Arnulf of Lisieux's reflections on Becket's chancellorship are from *CTB*, I, pp. 184–85. Becket's own candid assessment is from *CTB*, II, p. 1167. Background on John of Salisbury is from A. Duggan, "John of Salisbury and Thomas Becket," in *The World of John of Salisbury*, ed. M. Wilks (Oxford, 1984), pp. 427–38. John's account of Henry and Becket's relationship while Thomas was chancellor is from *MTB*, II, pp. 304–5; Staunton, p. 53. The best modern edition of the *Entheticus de Dogmate Philosophorum* is Laarhoven, I, pp. 104–227, especially paras. 85–96. Notes and commentary are from ibid., I, pp. 14–64; ibid., II, pp. 253–424; R. Thomson, "What Is the *Entheticus*?" in *World of John of Salisbury*, ed. Wilks, pp. 287–301. For the identification of the characters, see also C. Petersen, *Johannis Saresberiensis Entheticus de Dogmate Philosophorum* (Hamburg, 1843), pp. 113–20. See also *PJS 2*, pp. 123–212. John's swipe at Henry's circus tricks is from Laarhoven, I, p. 200, para. 95. William of Canterbury's echo of John's verdict is from *MTB*, I, p. 5. Historical background for "Hyrcanus" is from L. H. Schiffman, *Texts and Traditions: A Source Reader for the Study of the Second Temple and Rabbinic Judaism* (Hoboken, N.J., 1998), pp. 187–506; J. C. Vanderkam, *An Introduction to Early Judaism* (Cambridge, 2001), pp. 30–33. The Battle Abbey chronicler's account of the faction around Richard de Lucy is from *Chronicle of Battle Abbey*, ed. Searle, pp. 160–61. John of Salisbury's dedication to Becket in his presentation of the *Policraticus* (usually known as the *Entheticus in Policraticum*) is from CCCC, MS 46, fos. i–ii^{v}; Laarhoven, I, pp. 230–49, especially paras. 1–5. Becket as a "trifler in the court" is from *LJS*, II, pp. 245–47. Shrewd comments on the inequality of Henry and Thomas's friendship are offered by E. Türk, *Nugae Curialium: Le Règne d'Henri Deux Plantegenêt (1154–1189) et l'Éthique Politique* (Geneva, 1977), pp. 14–16. Becket's abstemiousness and dietary concerns are from Barlow, pp. 24–25. His medical condition is discussed by Knowles,

Episcopal Colleagues, pp. 167–68 (in relation to his illness in 1164 at Northampton), where renal colic due to kidney stones is suggested. However, this is not a lifelong condition, and I agree with Professor Barlow that colitis, an inflammatory disease of the large intestine, is more likely. Herbert of Bosham (*MTB,* III, p. 300) simply calls Becket's illness "colic." A diagnosis of renal colic depends on fitz Stephen's use of the word "renes" (*MTB,* III, p. 56), which in classical Latin means "kidneys" but in ecclesiastical Latin means "loins" in general. Becket's piety and scourging are from *MTB,* III, p. 22; *TSE,* I, pp. 50–51; RC, p. 386; Staunton, p. 51; Radford, p. 231. The story told by Robert of Cricklade's kinsman is from *TSE,* I, pp. 51–53; RC, p. 386; Radford, pp. 231–32. Becket's chastity is from Guernes, pp. 11–12; *MTB,* I, p. 6; *MTB,* II, pp. 303, 365; *MTB,* III, p. 21; Staunton, pp. 50, 54–55; H. Vollrath, "Was Thomas Becket Chaste? Understanding Episodes in the Becket Lives," *Anglo-Norman Studies* 27 (2005), pp. 198–209. The case of Richard of Ambly is from *MTB,* III, p. 21; Staunton, p. 50; Radford, p. 230. The case of Henry's discarded mistress is from Guernes, pp. 12–13; Staunton, pp. 54–55. Corroborative versions are from *MTB,* I, p. 6; *TSE,* I, pp. 53–55. Edward Grim's qualification of Becket's chastity is from *MTB,* II, p. 365. Roger of Pontigny's report of the advice of his physicians is from *MTB,* IV, p. 14. John of Salisbury's take on Becket's chastity is from *MTB,* II, p. 303. In his review of Barlow's biography in *American Historical Review* 94 (1989), p. 422, Norman Cantor argues for a deep psychosexual tension between Henry and Thomas that made their final clash inevitable. Eleanor of Aquitaine's biographer Professor Amy Kelly believes their intimacy, whether homosexual or not, would be a contributory cause to the eventual breakdown of Henry's marriage. Becket as chancellor, she maintains, usurped Eleanor's influence over her husband, sidelining her and leading her to ostracize Thomas as a dangerous rival. See Kelly, *Eleanor of Aquitaine,* pp. 97–149. Professor Barlow is more cautious. While hinting that Theobald and Henry may both have found Thomas physically attractive, he finds no evidence for homosexuality. Becket's chastity, he argues, arose from an accidental convergence of stress, psychological repression, and a personal lack of warmth, combining to restrict his intimacy with either sex. See Barlow, p. 26. Useful background on sexuality and sexual crimes is from Bartlett, *England Under the Norman and Angevin Kings,* pp. 566–72; J. Boswell, *Christianity, Social Tolerance, and Homosexuality: Gay People in Western Europe* (Chicago, 1980), pp. 243–66; C. S. Jaeger, *Ennobling Love: In Search of a Lost Sensibility* (Philadelphia, 1999), pp. 1–58; D. F. Greenberg and M. H. Bystryn, "Christian Intolerance of Homosexuality," *American Journal of Sociology* 88 (1982), pp. 515–48; B. Holsinger and D. Townsend, "Ovidian Homoerotics in Twelfth-Century Paris," *GLQ: A Journal of Lesbian and Gay Studies* 8 (2002), pp. 389–409. John of Salisbury's exposé of Roger of Pont l'Évêque for sexual abuse, written on behalf of all Becket's clerks and in their name, is from *LJS,* II, pp. 742–49. Heroic efforts have been made to deny his authorship, but the piece was attributed to him in his lifetime by Alan of Tewkesbury. In any case, he was one of the clerks in whose name it was composed. The quarrel with Roger could not have been more vitriolic, since he had also been accused of inciting Henry II to murder Becket and of paying the expenses of the murderers. Roger's defense to the charges is from *LJS,* II, pp. 738–43.

13 | RENDER UNTO CAESAR

Information on scutage and the other levies for the Toulouse campaign is from Radford pp. 99–100, 156–59; Barlow, pp. 59–60; Saltman, *Theobald,* pp. 44–45. Gervase of Canterbury's estimate of the receipts is from GC, col. 1381. John of Salisbury's letter of 1166 discussing Becket's responsibility for taxing the church is from *LJS,* II, pp. 105–7. Becket's success in finding good candidates quickly for church appointments is from William fitz Stephen: *MTB,* III, p. 23; Staunton, pp. 51–52. Bartholomew of Exeter's case is from *LJS,* I, pp. 221–23, 240–44; Radford, pp. 171–72. John of Salisbury's praise for Becket's energy in church appointments is from *LJS,* I, p. 223. The nominations of Robert of Melun and Prior William are from *MTB,* III, p. 24; Radford, pp. 166–67. The marriage of Mary, abbess of Romsey, is from Saltman, *Theobald,* pp. 52–54; Radford, pp. 94–95. Herbert of Bosham's account of the case is from *MTB,* III, pp. 328–29; Robert of Torigni's is from *Chronicles,* IV, p. 207. Norgate claims in *England Under the Angevin Kings,* I, p. 469, that Henry had a papal license, which is not supported by the evidence. It would, in any case, have been difficult to obtain one during the papal schism. Henry's plans for Ireland are from *Chronicles,* IV, p. 186; Eyton, p. 12; A. J. Duggan, "Totus Christianus Caput: The Pope and the Princes," in *Adrian IV, the English Pope,* ed. Bolton and Duggan, pp. 143–46; Warren, *Henry II,* pp. 187–92; K. Norgate, "The Bull Laudabiliter," *EHR* 8 (1893), pp. 18–52. John of Salisbury's mission as Theobald's envoy, leading to his disgrace, is from Brooke, "Adrian IV and John of Salisbury," pp. 1–11; G. Constable, "The Alleged Disgrace of John of Salisbury in 1159," *EHR* 69 (1954), pp. 67–76; Radford, p. 169. John of Salisbury's own account of his troubles is from *LJS,* I, pp. 31–32, 33–34. His letter to Becket is from *MTB,* V, pp. 8–9; *LJS,* I, pp. 45–46. Another letter to Becket's secretary, Master Ernulf, is from *MTB,* V, p. 7; *LJS,* I, p. 44. John's account of the final outcome is from *LJS,* I, p. 48. Becket's and Eleanor's messages that Henry's wrath had abated are from *LJS,* I, p. 51. Eleanor's movements are from Eyton, p. 24. John's fear of a treason trial is from *LJS,* I, p. 50. The schism in the papacy is from Saltman, *Theobald,* pp. 45–52; Radford, pp. 167–68; Barlow, pp. 60–61. Theobald's letters to Henry about the papal decision are from *LJS,* I, pp. 190–92, 197–98, 201–2, 215–17. The church councils and Henry's extortions are from F. Barlow, "The English, Norman and French Councils Called to Deal with the Schism of 1159," *EHR* 51 (1936), pp.

264–68; Radford, p. 167. The canonization of Edward the Confessor is from Barlow, p. 61. The attack on the two Norman prelates is from *MTB*, III, pp. 27–28; Radford, pp. 167–68. Theobald's illness is from *LJS*, I, pp. 14, 215. His letter to Becket on "second aids" is from *LJS*, I, pp. 35–36; Radford, pp. 161–63. John of Salisbury's advice on the matter is from *LJS*, I, pp. 45–46. Theobald's last letters to Henry are from *LJS*, I, pp. 197–98, 199–200, 201–2, 203–4, 215–17, 218, 219–21. His last letter to Becket is from *LJS*, I, pp. 224–25. John of Salisbury's warning is from *LJS*, I, pp. 221–23. The versions of Theobald's will, and the codicil, are from *LJS*, I, pp. 245–48. His parting blessing and homily is from *LJS*, I, pp. 249–51. Background is from Radford, pp. 179–84; Saltman, *Theobald*, p. 54. The biblical quotation is from Matthew 6:24.

14 | ARCHBISHOP

Herbert of Bosham's account of the politics of Becket's nomination, election, and consecration as archbishop is from *MTB*, III, pp. 180–89; Edward Grim's is from *MTB*, II, pp. 365–68; John of Salisbury's is from *MTB*, II, pp. 305–6; William fitz Stephen's is from *MTB*, III, pp. 35–37; Roger of Pontigny's is from *MTB*, IV, pp. 14–19; William of Canterbury's is from *MTB*, I, pp. 6–10. Selected passages in translation can be found in Staunton, pp. 58–66; Greenaway, pp. 50–56. Invaluable modern accounts are from Radford, pp. 191–221; Barlow, pp. 64–73; Knowles, pp. 50–58. The chronicler Ralph of Diss provides a brief but factual description: RD, cols. 533–34. The version in the "Thomas Saga Erkibyskups" to which the "lost" Becket biography by Robert of Cricklade is closely related is from *TSE*, I, pp. 62–95; RC, p. 387. The first papal license empowering Roger of Pont l'Évêque to crown Prince Henry is from *MTB*, VI, pp. 206–7. It was revoked by the pope in 1166: *MTB*, V, p. 323. The second license allowing any bishop to perform the coronation does not survive, but the text can be inferred from the license to Roger. See A. Heslin, "The Coronation of the Young King in 1170," *Studies in Church History* 2 (1968), pp. 165–78. Becket's retrospective account to the pope of Henry's plans can be found in *CTB*, II, p. 1269. His reluctance to become primate is from *MTB*, I, pp. 7–8; *MTB*, III, pp. 25–26, 180–81; *MTB*, IV, pp. 85–88; *TSE*, I, pp. 64–65, 80–81. Henry's council of the barons in February 1162 at Rouen is from Eyton, p. 55. Henry of Pisa's interventions the following May are from *MTB*, I, p. 8; *MTB*, II, p. 306; *MTB*, IV, pp. 18, 86; *TSE*, I, p. 77; Eyton, p. 56. Background to the wrangle over precedence between Roger of Pont l'Évêque and Becket is from F. Makower, *The Constitutional History and Constitution of the Church of England* (London, 1895), pp. 281–93. The pope's confirmation of some of Roger's claims in 1162 is from *MTB*, V, pp. 21–22. See also *CTB*, I, pp. 41–43, 63–65. Herbert of Bosham's account of the general objections to Thomas is from *MTB*, III, pp. 182–84. The likely grounds of Gilbert Foliot's protest are worked out from *MTB*, IV, p. 85;

Guernes, p. 17; *CTB,* I, pp. 503–7. Fitz Stephen's quotation of Foliot's murmuring afterward is from *MTB,* III, p. 36. Foliot's career is from Smalley, *Becket Conflict and the Schools,* pp. 167–86; D. Knowles, *Saints and Scholars* (Cambridge, 1963), pp. 59–62; C.N.L. Brooke in *ODNB,* s.v. "Foliot, Gilbert." For the scandal of the boy abused by Roger of Pont l'Évêque, see notes to chapter 12. The case of the citizen of Scarborough is from *MTB,* III, pp. 43–45. Henry's decree at Falaise is from *Chronicles,* IV, p. 327. A valuable modern discussion of the York case is from R. C. van Caenegem, "Public Prosecution of Crime in Twelfth-Century England," in *Church and Government in the Middle Ages: Essays Presented to C. R. Cheney,* ed. C.N.L. Brooke, D. Luscombe, and D. Owen (Cambridge, 1976), pp. 41–76. Henry's subsequent attitude toward such cases is from *MTB,* IV, pp. 95–97. The fragment of the "lost" life of Becket describing the order of service at his consecration is from *MTB,* IV, pp. 154–57 (from BL, Lansdowne MS 398). Foliot's account of the "prognostic" chosen by Becket from the Vulgate edition of Matthew 21:19 is from *CTB,* I, pp. 505–7. Herbert of Bosham's account of the mission to collect the pallium is from *MTB,* III, p. 189. Fitz Stephen's reference to the pallium as the "yoke of Christ" is from *MTB,* III, p. 37. A putative account of the mission is from Guernes, pp. 24–25. Henry's and Becket's movements in 1161–62 are from Eyton, pp. 52–57.

15 | A BROKEN RELATIONSHIP

Arnulf of Lisieux's letter of congratulation is from *CTB,* I, p. 11. Becket's resignation as chancellor is from *MTB,* I, p. 12; Guernes, p. 29. His pungent letter to Bishop Henry of Winchester is from *CTB,* I, pp. 17–19. William fitz Stephen's account of Becket's project to recover all the lands and privileges that rightfully belonged to the church of Canterbury is from *MTB,* III, pp. 42–43. Herbert of Bosham's account is from *MTB,* III, pp. 250–52. See also RD, cols. 535–36; Staunton, pp. 70–72, Greenaway, pp. 59–60; Duggan, pp. 34–35. Becket's own reflections in 1169 are from *CTB,* II, pp. 1057–59. See also *CTB,* I, pp. 259–61; Du Boulay, *Lordship of Canterbury,* pp. 361, 366–67. Information on John the Marshal is from J. H. Round, *Geoffrey de Mandeville: A Study of the Anarchy* (London, 1892), pp. 82, 131, 171, 195, 409; D. Crouch, *William Marshal: Knighthood, War and Chivalry, 1147–1219* (London, 2002), pp. 12–23. Henry's and Becket's movements in the months before and after the king's return from Normandy are from Eyton, pp. 58–62. Herbert of Bosham's account of their reunion is from *MTB,* II, pp. 252–53. Ralph of Diss's version is from RD, col. 534. A London-based chronicler, he tells a different story. In his version, Becket was politely but less honorably received. "He was admitted to the kiss of peace," he says, "but not to the fullness of grace, as could clearly be seen when the king quickly turned his face away from him in front of everyone." The secret meeting between Henry and Pope Alexander at Déols is from *Pontificum Romanorum Vitae,* ed. I. M. Watterich (2 vols., Leipzig, 1862), I, p. 393; B. A. Lees, "The Letters of Queen Eleanor of Aquitaine to Pope Celestine III," *EHR* 21 (1906), pp. 92–93. Information on the Council of Tours is from R. Somerville, *Pope Alexander III and the Council of Tours* (Berkeley, Calif., 1977), pp. 1–67; Barlow, pp. 84–87. Herbert of Bosham's account of the council is from *MTB,* III, pp. 253–55. Stephen of Rouen's gibe against Becket is from *Chronicles,* II, p. 744. Gilbert Foliot's refusal of obedience to Becket is from *CTB,* I, pp. 29–31. The Council of Woodstock is from *MTB,* II, pp, 373–74; *MTB,* IV, pp. 23–24; Staunton, pp. 76–77; J. Green, "The Last Century of Danegeld," *EHR* 96 (1981), pp. 255–58. Becket's refusal of a license for William's marriage to Isabel de Warenne is from *Chronicles,* II, pp. 676–77; Norgate, *England Under the Angevin Kings,* II, p. 29; R. Foreville, *L'Église et la Royauté en Angleterre sous Henri II Plantagenêt, 1154–1189* (Saint-Dizier, 1943), pp. 242–43. For the feud it caused, see *MTB,* III, p. 142; Barlow, pp. 106, 236, 247. The sources are ambiguous as to the timing of this clash. It may have taken place shortly after Becket returned from the Council of Tours, or perhaps shortly before he left. William of Newburgh's report of the complaint of the judges on criminous clerks is from WN, p. 466. Essential background is from C. Duggan, "The Becket Dispute and Criminous Clerks," *Bulletin of the Institute of Historical Research* 35 (1962), pp. 1–28; Smalley, *Becket Conflict and the Schools,* pp. 122–33; Foreville, *L'Église et la Royauté*, pp. 136–51; Barlow, pp. 90–95; Duggan, pp. 46–58. For older interpretations, see F. W. Maitland, "Henry II and Criminous Clerks," *EHR* 26 (1892), pp. 224–34; H.W.C. Davis, *England Under the Normans and Angevins* (London, 1905), pp. 534–36. The early legal cases handled by Becket in which Henry showed an interest are from *MTB,* III, pp. 45–46, 264–65; *English Lawsuits,* ed. van Caenegem, pp. 404–5, 419–20. The case of Osbert of Bayeux is from *LJS,* I, pp. 26–27, 30, 42–43, 261–62. William of Canterbury gives the fullest references to the canonical authorities for the exemption of clerks from lay judgment: *MTB,* I, pp. 26–28.

16 | CONVERSION

For the idea of a Damascene conversion, see especially the account by "Anonymous II": *MTB,* IV, p. 19. Tennyson's adaptation is from his *Becket* (London, 1884), p. 29. The most accurate and discriminating source for Becket's altered lifestyle is Herbert of Bosham: *MTB,* III, pp. 198–238. John of Salisbury's version is from *MTB,* II, pp. 306–9. William of Canterbury's more florid account is from *MTB,* I, pp. 10–12; Edward Grim's is from *MTB,* II, pp. 368–71; William fitz Stephen's is from *MTB,* III, pp. 37–41; Roger of Pontigny's is from *MTB,* IV, pp. 19–22. See also Staunton, pp. 62–69; Greenaway, pp. 55–58; Barlow, pp. 74–83. An invaluable modern guide to the way the early biographers handle this material is M. Staunton, *Thomas Becket and His Biographers* (Woodbridge, U.K., 2006), pp. 82–96. Background on Herbert of Bosham as the new archbishop's divinity tutor is from Smalley, *Becket Conflict and the Schools,* pp. 35–36, 61–67. Herbert's own account is from *MTB,* III, pp. 204–5; Staunton, pp. 75–76. Becket's letters to Henry of Winchester and Gilbert Foliot are from *CTB,* I, pp. 16–19, 22–25. The early fourteenth-century inventory of his books is from *ALCD,* pp. 82–85. See also C.F.R. de Hamel, *Glossed Books of the Bible and the Origins of the Paris Booktrade* (Woodbridge, U.K., 1984), pp. 43–44, 90–91; Smalley, *Becket Conflict and the Schools,* pp. 135–37. Books can be identified from their descriptions as recorded by Prior Henry Eastry by using the cross-database search tool of the Brepolis electronic Library of Latin Texts, series A–B. Books possibly with Becket's marginal annotations are CCCC, MS 46; TCC, MSS B.3.29, B.3.12. See also notes to chapter 17. Becket's copy of Livy, recorded as a gift from John of Salisbury, is TCC, MS R.4.4. Books in which Eastry's inscription of Thomas's ownership can still be read on the flyleaf, despite the efforts of Henry VIII's commissioners to erase it, include CCCC, MS 46; TCC, MS B.16.17. John of Salisbury's vignette is from *LJS,* II, pp. 725–39. The annotations on the manuscript of Lactantius are from B. Ross, "*Audi Thoma . . . Henriciani Nota:* A French Scholar Appeals to Thomas Becket?," *EHR* 89 (1974), pp. 333–38. The identification of Peter of Celle as their author is from L. K. Barber, "MS Bodl. Canon Pat. Lat. 131 and a Lost Lactantius of John of Salisbury: Evidence in Search of a French Critic of Thomas Becket," *Albion* 22 (1990), pp. 21–37. Peter of Celle's letter to Becket is from ibid., p. 34; *LPC,* pp. 328–31. Modern scholars tend to follow Peter's critical line. Revisiting the puzzle in 1931, Zachary Brooke depicts Becket as an "actor-saint," even if his acting was only "unconscious," the result of adapting himself to whatever role presented itself. "The only explanation of him that seems to me to fit the facts at all," he writes, "is that he was one of those men who, exalting to the full the role they have to play, picture themselves as the perfect representatives of their office, visualizing a type and making themselves the living impersonation of it; actors playing a part, but unconscious actors." Frank Barlow goes further, claiming in 1986 that pride, the deadliest of the cardinal sins, is the key to Becket's character. Curiously, he links Becket's fondness for grand gestures to his modest social origins. "He had," he says (perhaps revealing his own prejudices in the process), "all the failings of a typical parvenu." See Z. N. Brooke, *The English Church and the Papacy: From the Conquest to the Reign of John* (Cambridge, 1931), pp. 191–214; Barlow, pp. 89, 270–75. For more balanced views acknowledging Becket's divided consciousness, see Knowles, pp. 54–55; Smalley, *Becket Conflict and the Schools,* pp. 113–16. John of Salisbury's viewpoint on criminous clerks is from Duggan, "The Becket Dispute and Criminous Clerks," pp. 17–18; *PSJ 1,* p. 205. See also Smalley, *Becket Conflict and the Schools,* pp. 124–25. John's theories of resistance to tyrants, too complex to summarize in full, are from *PSJ 1,* pp. 190–225. Wary of criticizing Henry directly as the quarrel with Becket gathered pace, he would instead tend to denounce surrogates, such as Roger II of Sicily, who had died in 1154, castigating him as a tyrant for his crude attempts "to reduce the church to slavery" by handling church elections like palace appointments, preventing papal legates from entering his kingdom, and anointing his son as his successor without consulting the pope. See *HP,* pp. 65–69. What appears to be Becket's system of marginal symbols, penciled into his presentation copy of John of Salisbury's *Policraticus,* is worked out from the original manuscript: CCCC, MS 46, fos. 157^{r-v}, 164^{v}, 165^{r-v}, 167^{r-v}, 168^{r-v}, 169^{r}, 172^{r-v}, 173^{r-v}, 174^{v}, 176^{v}, 177^{r}, 179^{r}, 180^{v}, 182^{r}. A number of separate marginal notes and marks in red chalk or crayon—e.g., at fos. 96^{r}, 168^{r}—are in a much later hand. Passages from John's *Metalogicon,* which follows in the same manuscript, marked with a small flag or banner include fos. 201^{v}, 202^{v}, 203^{v}, 209^{v}. The quotations from Becket's public pronouncement on Henry's tyranny are from the draft of his address to the papal curia at Sens in November 1164: *CTB,* I, pp. 143–49.

17 | THE CLASH

Becket's sermon is from *MTB,* IV, pp. 22–23. For Herbert of Bosham's account of similar views expressed by Becket at the Council of Westminster, see *MTB,* III, pp. 268–69. The historical and ideological background to the image of the "two swords" is from Smalley, *Becket Conflict and the Schools*, pp. 26–31. Becket's interpretation is from *MTB,* III, pp. 204–5; Staunton, pp. 75–76. His copy of the *Exhortation* of St. Bernard is from *ALCD,* p. 84. The quoted passage is from *PL,* vol. 182, cols. 463–64. The case of Philip de Broi is from *MTB,* I, pp. 12–13; *MTB,* II, pp. 374–76; *MTB,* III, pp. 45, 265–66; *MTB,* IV, pp. 24–25; *English Lawsuits,* ed. van Caenegem, pp. 405–11; RD, cols. 536–37; Staunton, p. 77. The excommunication of William of Eynsford is from *MTB,* III, p. 43; RD, col. 536; Staunton, pp. 78–79. Although the date of the Council of Westminster is contested, the case for it beginning on October 13 with the translation of the bones of Edward the Confessor, relying as it does on the testimony of Richard of Cirencester, a monk of Canterbury, is strong. See W. H. Hutton, *Thomas Becket: Archbishop of Canterbury* (London, 1910), p. 78 and n. 1; Barlow, p. 95 and n. 14. The events of the canonization and translation are from *MTB,* III, p. 261; F. Barlow, *Edward the Confessor* (Berkeley and Los Angeles, 1970), pp. 280–85. The legend of St. Wulfstan is from William of Malmesbury, *Saints' Lives,* ed. M. Winterbottom and R. M. Thomson (Oxford, 2002), p. xxxiii. Accounts of the Council of Westminster and its aftermath survive in several versions, not all of which agree. I have mainly followed those by Roger of Pontigny, from *MTB,* IV, pp. 25–27; Herbert of Bosham (who was present), from *MTB,* III, pp. 261–75 (although some of the material within these pages must relate to the Council of Clarendon); and that recorded in the paper titled "Summa Causae Inter Regem et Thomam," from *MTB,* IV, pp. 201–5. See also Staunton, pp.

79–83; Greenaway, pp. 62–64. The fullest and best version of Becket's and Henry's speeches at the council is the one that Robert of Cricklade obtained, which was afterward translated into Old Norse and incorporated into the Icelandic "Thomas Saga Erkibyskups," from *TSE*, I, pp. 147–57; RC, pp. 388–89. Herbert of Bosham's role in teaching Becket the implications of the Greek Septuagint text is from Smalley, *Becket Conflict and the Schools*, pp. 124–35. John of Salisbury's role is from Duggan, "The Becket Dispute and Criminous Clerks," pp. 17–18; *PSJ 1*, p. 205. The text itself is Nahum 1:9. Background on the bishops is from Knowles, *Episcopal Colleagues*, pp. 56–59. The interview at Northampton is from *MTB*, IV, pp. 27–29; Staunton, pp. 83–85; Greenaway, pp. 64–66. The role of Arnulf of Lisieux in building up a royalist party is from *MTB*, IV, pp. 29–30; RD, col. 536; Staunton, p. 85. See also Knowles, *Episcopal Colleagues*, pp. 59–60. Hilary of Chichester's visit to Teynham is from *MTB*, IV, pp. 30–31; Staunton, pp. 85–86. John of Salisbury's attack on the royalist bishops is from *LJS*, II, pp. 153–79. Becket's letters commissioning his envoys to the papal curia are from *CTB*, I, pp. 33–41. His letters to the pope are from *CTB*, I, pp. 31–33, 41–43. The letter of John of Canterbury to Becket is from *CTB*, I, pp. 43–47. Pope Alexander's letter to Becket is from *CTB*, I, pp. 49–51. His letter to Gilbert Foliot is from *MTB*, V, pp. 61–62. The mission of Philip, abbot of L'Aumône, is from *MTB*, IV, pp. 31–32; Staunton, pp. 86–87. The meeting at Woodstock is from *MTB*, III, p. 277; *MTB*, IV, pp. 32–33; Staunton, p. 87. Information on John of Salisbury's mission to France is from *LJS*, II, pp. 3–15. William fitz Stephen alleges that far from Becket sending John to France, it was Henry who exiled both him and John of Canterbury (who was sent to be bishop of Poitiers) in order to deprive Becket of their help and advice: *MTB*, III, p. 46. But this is not borne out by John's letter to Becket.

18 | CLARENDON

Information on the palace of Clarendon is from *The King's Works*, vol. II: *The Middle Ages*, ed. R. Allen Brown, H. M. Colvin, and A. J. Taylor (London, 1963), part I, pp. 910–18. The contemporary accounts of the council contain gaps and serious contradictions, which I have attempted to resolve. William fitz Stephen and Herbert of Bosham appear to have been eyewitnesses, but fitz Stephen seems to be in error when he says that Becket signed the ancestral customs. Apart from Herbert of Bosham, the most useful narratives are by John of Salisbury, Edward Grim, William of Canterbury, Guernes of Pont-Sainte-Maxence, and Roger of Pontigny. William's account is from *MTB*, I, pp. 18–24; Herbert's is from *MTB*, III, pp. 278–99; fitz Stephen's is from *MTB*, III, pp. 46–48; John of Salisbury's is from *MTB*, II, pp. 311–12; Edward Grim's is from *MTB*, II, pp. 379–83; Roger of Pontigny's is from *MTB*, IV, pp. 33–37. Guernes is unusually well-informed about this episode, and several of the biographers copy him:

Guernes, pp. 36–37. An invaluable corrective to the bias of these biographers is Gilbert Foliot's letter of 1166, *Multiplicem Nobis: CTB,* I, pp. 509–13. See also notes to chapter 23; Staunton, pp. 88–96; *EHD,* pp. 766–71; Greenaway, pp. 67–73. A text apparently derived in part from a transcript of one copy of the record of the council contained in the chirograph is from *MTB,* V, pp. 71–79. January 25 as the date on which the council convened is from RD, col. 536. Essential modern interpretations are Knowles, *Episcopal Colleagues,* pp. 60–65; Barlow, pp. 98–105; Smalley, *Becket Conflict and the Schools,* pp. 122–33; Duggan, "The Becket Dispute and Criminous Clerks," pp. 3–4, 24–25. Mary Cheney's attempt to argue that "Roger of Norwich" is a clerical error for Roger of Worcester rather than William of Norwich is unconvincing: M. G. Cheney, *Roger, Bishop of Worcester, 1164–1179* (Oxford, 1980), pp. 19–20. It could be that Henry of Winchester is the correct identification, but Knowles is more likely to be right that this is a slip by Herbert of Bosham and that William of Norwich was meant. The reaction of Becket's clerks to the events at Clarendon is from *MTB,* II, pp. 323–25; *MTB,* III, pp. 289–92. His rebuke on the road to Hilary of Chichester is from *MTB,* III, p. 292. His fasting and penances after his return to Canterbury are from *MTB,* I, p. 24; *MTB,* II, p. 325; *MTB,* III, p. 49. His repulse at Woodstock is from *MTB,* III, p. 49. His attempts to flee across the Channel and return to Canterbury are from *MTB,* I, p. 29; *MTB,* II, pp. 325–26, 389–90; *MTB,* III, pp. 49, 293; *MTB,* IV, p. 40; Guernes, pp. 49–50. See also Staunton, pp. 96–100; Greenaway, pp. 73–74. Pope Alexander's letters to Becket are from *CTB,* I, pp. 63–65, 78–89. See also *CTB,* I, pp. 40–43. John of Salisbury's letter is from *CTB,* I, pp. 88–95. Henry of Houghton's letter is from *CTB,* I, pp. 96–99. John of Canterbury's letters are from *CTB,* I, pp. 98–109, 127–33. Becket's letter to King Louis is from *CTB,* I, pp. 134–35. John the Marshal's case is from *MTB,* I, pp. 30–31; *MTB,* II, pp. 390–92; *MTB,* III, pp. 50–51, 295–96; *MTB,* IV, pp. 40–41. An invaluable chronology of events and the royal itinerary in 1164 is from Eyton, pp. 67–77.

19 | NORTHAMPTON

The best account of the case of John the Marshal is by M. G. Cheney, "The Litigation Between John Marshal and Archbishop Thomas Becket in 1164: A Pointer to the Origin of Novel Disseisin?," in *Law and Social Change in British History,* ed. John Guy and H. G. Beale (London, 1984), pp. 9–26. There are seven important contemporary accounts of the Council of Northampton, by William fitz Stephen, Herbert of Bosham, William of Canterbury, Alan of Tewkesbury, Edward Grim, Roger of Pontigny, and Guernes of Pont-Sainte-Maxence. Fitz Stephen's account is from *MTB,* III, pp. 49–68; Staunton, pp. 100–15; Greenaway, pp. 75–78, 79–89. Herbert's is from *MTB,* III, pp. 296–312; Greenaway, pp. 78–79. William's is from *MTB,* I, pp. 30–40. Alan's is from *MTB,* II, pp. 326–

34. Edward's is from *MTB,* II, pp. 390–98. Roger's is from *MTB,* IV, pp. 41–52. Guernes of Pont-Sainte-Maxence's is from Guernes, pp. 50–70. Translations of the most important of these sources are from *English Lawsuits,* ed. van Caenegem, pp. 423–57. Becket's illness is from *MTB,* I, p. 32; *MTB,* II, p. 392; *MTB,* III, pp. 56, 300–301; *MTB,* IV, p. 49. See also Knowles, *Episcopal Colleagues,* pp. 167–68, who takes a different view as to the meaning of "colic"; see notes to chapter 12. Roger of Howden's account, which creates the impression that Becket was to be sentenced to life imprisonment, is from RH, I, pp. 224–29. A short note by Ralph of Diss can be found in RD, cols. 537–38. The best modern interpretation of the events and significance of the council is from Knowles, *Episcopal Colleagues,* pp. 66–90, 163–66. The plan of Northampton Castle is from ibid., pp. 169–70. My interpretation differs in some important details, as I tend to prefer the accounts of William fitz Stephen and Herbert of Bosham, who were eyewitnesses, to that of Alan of Tewkesbury, who was out of the country at the time. But generally I follow Knowles on the key points of chronology and argument. An invaluable reassessment of the legal significance of the council and of fitz Stephen's role is by A. J. Duggan, "Roman, Canon and Common Law in Twelfth-Century England: The Council of Northampton (1164) Re-Examined," *Historical Research* 83 (2010), pp. 379–408. See also Barlow, pp. 109–14; Duggan, pp. 61–83. The events at the priory of St. Andrew once Becket had left the castle and decided to flee into exile are from *MTB,* I, pp. 40–41; *MTB,* II, pp. 334–35, 398–99; *MTB,* III, pp. 68–70, 312–13; *MTB,* IV, pp. 52–54; Guernes, pp. 70–71; Staunton, pp. 116–19; Greenaway, pp. 89–91. Henry's retort after Becket's departure is from *MTB,* IV, p. 55.

20 | EXILE

The best accounts of Becket's experiences on his journey from Northampton to Saint-Omer and Sens are by William fitz Stephen and Herbert of Bosham: *MTB,* III, pp. 69–72, 312–15, 318–35; Staunton, pp. 120–28; Greenaway, pp. 92–95. Other information is from *MTB,* I, pp. 41–45; *MTB,* II, pp. 335–37, 399–402; *MTB,* IV, pp. 54–60; Guernes, pp. 71–84; *TSE,* I, pp. 229–71. The stages of Becket's progress and those of Henry's envoys are from Eyton, pp. 74–77. See also Barlow, pp. 115–21. The composition of the king's deputation to the pope is from Knowles, *Episcopal Colleagues,* pp. 92–101. Invaluable background on Alexander's situation is from Smalley, *Becket Conflict and the Schools,* pp. 138–59. Arnulf of Lisieux's advice to Becket is from *CTB,* I, pp. 183–201. The attitude of Louis VII as related to John of Salisbury is from *CTB,* I, pp. 172–73. Fitz Stephen's description of Becket's arrival at Sens is from *MTB,* III, p. 74. Apart from the Earl of Arundel's speech, which is too innocuous, the best versions of the rival speeches at the curia are those by Alan of Tewkesbury and Herbert of Bosham: *MTB,* II, pp. 336–45; *MTB,* III, pp. 335–57; Staunton, pp. 128–34; Greenaway, pp. 95–100. The earl's speech appears to have been better reported in the lost "life" by Robert of Cricklade, later incorporated into the "Thomas Saga Erkibyskups": *TSE*, I, pp. 283–85; RC, p. 390. The rough draft of Becket's address to the pope is from *CTB*, I, pp. 143–49. William of Canterbury's account of the conclave is from *MTB*, I, pp. 46–49. The account from the "Thomas Saga Erkibyskups" is from *TSE*, I, pp. 271–311. Becket's retrospective account of the pope's absolution of him for binding himself to the customs at Clarendon is from *CTB*, II, pp. 830–31. Other information on the conclave is from *MTB*, II, pp. 402–4; *MTB*, III, pp. 72–76; *MTB*, IV, pp. 60–65; Guernes, pp. 84–90. The description of Pontigny is from the author's visit in 2009 and from C. Wiéner, *Pontigny* (Saint-Léger-Vauban, 1994), pp. 3–6, 13–40. See also J. C. Robertson, *Becket, Archbishop of Canterbury* (London, 1859), pp. 161–80. The fullest descriptions of Becket's asceticism leading to illness are by Edward Grim and Herbert of Bosham: *MTB*, II, pp. 412–13; *MTB*, III, pp. 357–79; Staunton, pp. 136–38. See also *MTB*, I, p. 49; *MTB*, II, pp. 345–46, 404; *MTB*, III, pp. 76–77; *MTB*, IV, p. 65; *TSE*, I, pp. 311–19. A fine critical evaluation of these sources is by Barlow, pp. 124, 127–29, 134–35. Herbert of Bosham's green tunic and cloak are from *MTB*, III, pp. 99–100. The scope of Becket's studies in exile is from William fitz Stephen: *MTB*, III, p. 77. Becket's book collecting at Pontigny is from *MTB*, III, p. 77; C.F.R. de Hamel, "A Contemporary Miniature of Thomas Becket," in *Intellectual Life in the Middle Ages: Essays Presented to Margaret Gibson*, ed. L. M. Smith and B. Ward (London, 1992), pp. 179–84; de Hamel, *Glossed Books of the Bible*, pp. 42–44. John of Salisbury's advice is from *CTB*, I, pp. 172–73; *LJS*, II, p. 49. The manuscript of the *Great Gloss* is from Smalley, *Becket Conflict and the Schools*, pp. 82–83. Three of its four volumes are now TCC, MSS B.5.4, B.5.6, B.5.7. Becket's other glossed and illuminated books described in this chapter are TCC, MSS B.3.11, B.3.12, B.5.5. The deluxe copy of Gratian may be either J. Paul Getty Museum, MS Ludwig.XIV.2, or fragments of the broken copy in the Cleveland Museum of Art and the Municipal Library at Auxerre, as described by W. Cahn, "A Twelfth-Century Decretum Fragment from Pontigny," *Bulletin of the Cleveland Museum of Art* 62 (1975), pp. 47–59. The full inventory of Becket's books is from *ALCD*, pp. 82–85. See also Smalley, *Becket and the Schools*, pp. 135–37. The significance of the philosophy of St. Ambrose is from J. T. Muckle, "The *De Officiis Ministrorum* of Saint Ambrose," *Medieval Studies* 1 (1939), pp. 63–80.

21 | ATTACK AND COUNTERATTACK

Henry's attack on Becket's clerks and relatives and on the Canterbury lands is from *MTB*, I, pp. 55–56; *MTB*, III, pp. 75–76, 373–75; Staunton, p. 135; Greenaway, pp. 101–2. See also Barlow, pp. 125–27. The exile to Sicily of one of Becket's nephews is from *CTB*, I, pp. 736–37. William fitz Stephen's prayer is from

MTB, III, pp. 78–81. His meeting with Thomas at Fleury is from *MTB,* III, p. 59. Henry's plans and preoccupations at the beginning of 1165 based on information supplied to Becket, possibly by John of Canterbury, are from *CTB,* I, pp. 177–79. Arnulf of Lisieux's advice is from *CTB,* I, pp. 183–201. John of Salisbury's advice is from *CTB,* I, pp. 171–77. The diplomacy with Matilda, Henry's mother, is from *CTB,* I, pp. 155–73, 211–13, 227. Ernulf's role in arranging the conference at Pontoise is from *CTB,* I, pp. 203–5. Its failure is from Guernes, p. 139. Information on the movements of Henry and Eleanor and their courts in the first half of 1165 is from Eyton, pp. 77–80, 85–86. The negotiations with Frederick Barbarossa are from *MTB,* V, pp. 184–95; RM, pp. 762–64; RD, col. 539; Warren, *Henry II,* p. 493; Hutton, *Thomas Becket,* p. 126; Barlow, pp. 136–37. The charge of perjury against John of Oxford is from *LJS,* I, pp. 183–85; *CTB,* I, pp. 391, 563, 569, 595. Pope Alexander's return to Rome is from *CTB,* I, pp. 176 and n. 1, 205–7, 225–29; *LJS,* II, pp. 51–57; WN, pp. 468–69. The papal annulment of the sentence at Northampton is from *CTB,* I, p. 149. The pope's restraint on Thomas, with its deadline of Easter 1166, is from *CTB,* I, pp. 224–25. Henry's campaign in Wales is from Hosler, "Henry II's Military Campaigns in Wales, 1157 and 1165," pp. 53–72; Warren, *Henry II,* pp. 163–65. Henry's and Eleanor's movements in 1166 are from Eyton, pp. 88–99. The birth of Philip Augustus is from J. Bradbury, *The Capetians: Kings of France, 987–1328* (London, 2007), p. 167. The visit of King Louis with Henry at Angers is from RM, p. 764. The audience of Becket's clerks on May 1 is from *MTB,* III, pp. 98–101; *LJS,* II, pp. 21–23, 77, 85–87; Staunton, pp. 142–44. John of Salisbury's attitude toward Becket is from *LJS,* II, pp. 21–23, 49, 93–101; Duggan, "John of Salisbury and Thomas Becket," pp. 430–38; Barlow, pp. 130–31. Henry's council at Chinon, where he spoke angry words against those who would not help him to silence Becket, is from *LJS,* II, pp. 109–11. Pope Alexander's letter confirming the end of the Easter deadline is from *CTB,* I, pp. 271–73. His grant of a papal legacy is from *CTB,* I, pp. 279–81. Becket's calls to Henry to repent, sent to him shortly before the council at Chinon, are from *CTB,* I, pp. 267–71, 293–99. Becket's pilgrimage to Soissons is from *LJS,* II, pp. 111–13; Barlow, pp. 146–47. His message to Matilda delivered by Nicholas of Rouen is from *LJS,* II, pp. 65–67; *CTB,* I, pp. 343–47. I have followed the editors of *LJS,* II, pp. xxvii–viii, in dating this letter. Information on Vézelay is from the author's visit and from J.-B. Auberger and J. Gréal, *Vézelay* (Paris, 2007), pp. 1–40. The Whitsunday sermon and the Vézelay sentences are from *MTB,* III, pp. 391–92; *CTB,* I, pp. 309–17, 323–29; *LJS,* II, pp. 113–15; Staunton, pp. 144–45; Barlow, pp. 147–48; Duggan, pp. 101–23. Alexander's letter of confirmation is from *CTB,* I, p. 489; Barlow, p. 149. Becket's letter to Henry delivered by Gerard with its third and final call to repentance is from *CTB,* I, pp. 329–43. The political situation following the Vézelay sentences is from *LJS,* II, pp. 117, 147–49, 201–3, 225–29. The appeal of the English bishops is from *MTB,* I, pp. 56–58; *MTB,* V, pp. 403–8; *LJS,* II, pp. 123–27, 135–37, 153–65, 171–77; *CTB,* I, pp. 373–83; Staunton, pp. 146–47; Knowles, *Episcopal Colleagues,* pp. 96–97. John of Salisbury's comment on Robert of Melun is from *LJS,* II, p. 173. Henry's letter to Rainald of Dassel is from *MTB,* V, pp. 428–29; *CTB,* I, p. xliii and n. 56; Knowles, *Episcopal Colleagues,* pp. 130–31. His attack on the Cistercians is from *MTB,* II, pp. 413–14; *CTB,* I, pp. 317–19, 321–23; Staunton, p. 148.

22 | SEARCH FOR A SETTLEMENT

Henry's renewed intervention in Brittany is from Everard, *Brittany and the Angevins,* pp. 34–35, 43–44, 94. John of Canterbury's report of the interception of Becket's letter to the pope describing Henry as a wicked tyrant is from *CTB,* I, p. 581. His account of Henry's state of mind during the winter months of 1166–67 is from *CTB,* I, pp. 575–81. See also Knowles, *Episcopal Colleagues,* pp. 130–31. The torture of Becket's courier is from *CTB,* I, pp. 545, 551. The political situation is from *CTB,* I, pp. 555–63, 575–81, 587–95, 613–15, 623; *LJS,* II, pp. 231–355. Eleanor's movements are from Eyton, pp. 108–9. Her attitude toward Becket is from *CTB,* I, pp. 214–18. On the influence of Ralph de Faye, see also Vincent, "Patronage, Politics and Piety in the Charters of Eleanor of Aquitaine," p. 48. Pope Alexander's attempt at a soothing letter to Becket is from *CTB,* I, p. 573. The mission of William of Pavia and Otto of Brescia is from *CTB,* I, pp. 613–15, 619–21, 625–35, 639–733; *MTB,* III, pp. 408–15; Staunton, pp. 150–54; Greenaway, pp. 117–23; Duggan, pp. 125–42; Barlow, pp. 163–73. Becket's explosive note is from *CTB,* I, p. 625. The pun on San Pietro in Vincoli is from *CTB,* I, p. 627; *LJS,* II, pp. 423, 611. Alexander's directions to the mediators on his arrival at Benevento are from *MTB,* VI, pp. 232–33. Gilbert Foliot's exclamation is from *CTB,* I, p. 589. Becket's letter to the pope on Frederick's rout in Italy is from *CTB,* I, pp. 641–45. John of Salisbury's report of Henry's reception of the mediators at Argentan and the arrival of the delegation of bishops is from *CTB,* I, pp. 687–95. The European background in late 1167 and early 1168 is from *LJS,* II, pp. 553–83. Henry's attempted blackmail at the curia is from *LJS,* II, p. 561. His offers of bribes and subsidies are from *LJS,* II, p. 661; *CTB,* II, pp. 944–45. Becket's envoys to the curia are from *CTB,* I, pp. 729–33, 751–53. Alexander's juggling act is from *CTB,* I, pp. 755, 765–67; *MTB,* VI, pp. 388–89. Becket's reaction is from *CTB,* I, pp. 771–87. The commissioning of the papal arbitrators, overseen by Simon, prior of Mont-Dieu, and Bernard de la Coudre, prior of Le Bois, is from *MTB,* VI, pp. 394–96, 437–40; *CTB,* II, pp. 819–21; Duggan, pp. 146–49; Barlow, pp. 179–81. The political situation in late 1168 and early 1169 is from RM, pp. 770–72; *Chronicles,* IV, pp. 237–39; *LJS,* II, pp. 603–19, 625–35; Eyton, pp. 113–19; Warren, *Henry II,* pp. 107–10, 496–98. Becket's critique of Henry's tyranny sent to his envoy at the curia is from *CTB,* I, p. 591.

The meeting at Montmirail is from *CTB,* II, pp. 819–25; *LJS,* II, pp. 637–49; *MTB,* I, pp. 73–75; *MTB,* III, pp. 96–97, 418–28; *MTB,* IV, pp. 113–14; *MTB,* VI, pp. 488–90; Staunton, pp. 154–62; Greenaway, pp. 123–27. Herbert of Bosham identifies the location as "in a flat field": *MTB,* III, p. 427. Becket's letters to the pope and cardinals giving his version of events are from *CTB,* II, pp. 821–25. His conciliatory letter to Henry is from *CTB,* II, p. 827. The falling-out and reconciliation of the exiles with King Louis is from *LJS,* II, p. 643; *MTB,* II, pp. 349–51; *MTB,* III, pp. 438–40; Staunton, pp. 162–63. Becket's letters to his allies at the curia are from *CTB,* II, pp. 939–63. The quotation is from p. 959.

23 | THE CASE AGAINST BECKET

The critical analysis of Arnulf of Lisieux, sent in a letter to Becket dated February–March 1165, is from *CTB,* I, pp. 183–201. See also Smalley, *Becket Conflict and the Schools,* pp. 166–67. For Becket's comparison of Gilbert Foliot with Judas, see, for instance, *CTB,* II, pp. 923, 1155. John of Salisbury's attacks on Foliot as Achitophel are from *LJS,* II, pp. 129–33, 153–65, 245–49; *CTB,* I, pp. 457–69. Becket's appeal from Pontigny to Foliot's spiritual loyalty is from *CTB,* I, pp. 251–55. Foliot's reputation for eloquence as abbot of Gloucester is from Smalley, *Becket Conflict and the Schools,* pp. 168–69. Foliot's *pièce justificative* on behalf of the English bishops is from *CTB,* I, pp. 373–83. John of Salisbury's responses, sent to Bartholomew of Exeter and Becket himself, are from *LJS,* II, pp. 139–65. Becket's defense of his cause is from *CTB,* I, pp. 389–425. His letter of reproach to Foliot is from *CTB,* I, pp. 427–41. The text of *Multiplicem Nobis* is from *CTB,* I, pp. 499–537. Its eighteenth-century rediscovery is from Lyttelton, IV, pp. 125–33. Mme. Foreville's critique is from *L'Église et la Royauté,* pp. 244–47. The proof of the document's authenticity and Foliot's authorship is from Knowles, *Episcopal Colleagues,* pp. 122–27, 171–80. See also Smalley, *Becket Conflict and the Schools,* pp. 182–84.

24 | CAT AND MOUSE

John of Salisbury's account of the interview at Saint-Léger-en-Yvelines is from *LJS,* II, pp. 645–47. Becket's version of the same events is from *CTB,* II, pp. 829–35. Prior Simon's version is from *MTB,* VI, pp. 516–18. See also Duggan, pp. 153–54. The Clairvaux excommunications are from *MTB,* III, pp. 87–88; Staunton, p. 164; *CTB,* II, pp. 849–73, 913–21. Information on their enforcement is from *CTB,* II, pp. 901–9, 929–33; Knowles, *Episcopal Colleagues,* pp. 101–15; Duggan, pp. 155–58. Henry's fine levied on Adam of Charing is from *CTB,* II, p. 853, n. 6. Reports of the delivery of the letters of excommunication at St. Paul's Cathedral and Foliot's synod are from *CTB,* II, pp. 901–9; *MTB,* III, pp. 88–90; Staunton, pp. 164–66. Background on Foliot's claim of metropolitan status for the see of London is from Knowles, pp. 122–23; Makower, *Constitu-*

tional History . . . of the Church of England, pp. 272–74. Becket's letter to the pope seeking confirmation of the Clairvaux sentences is from *CTB,* II, pp. 865–69. The pope's letters announcing the appointment of Vivian of Orvieto and Gratian of Pisa and suspending Becket's disciplinary powers are from *CTB,* II, pp. 889–95, 909–11. Herbert of Bosham's assessment of Gratian is from *MTB,* III, p. 442. The meeting of the papal envoys with John of Salisbury is from *LJS,* II, p. 651. Information on their series of meetings with Henry and Becket is from *CTB,* II, pp. 979–87; *MTB,* III, pp. 441–44; Staunton, pp. 166–68; Duggan, pp. 162–72. Henry's letter to the Cistercians is from *MTB,* VII, pp. 90–92; *CTB,* I, p. lvi, n. 81. The second mission of Reginald fitz Jocelin and Ralph of Llandaff to the curia is from *MTB,* VII, pp. 82–88; Eyton, p. 129. Becket's letter to the pope is from *CTB,* II, pp. 991–93. His letter to his envoys at the curia is from *CTB,* II, pp. 993–95. His reimposition of the Clairvaux sentences is from *CTB,* II, pp. 997–1001. The royal ordinances are from M. D. Knowles, A. J. Duggan, and C.N.L. Brooke, "Henry II's Supplement to the Constitutions of Clarendon," *EHR* 87 (1972), pp. 757–71, where a critical edition and commentary are provided as an appendix, along with full references to sources. See also *MTB,* VII, pp. 147–51; RH, I, pp. 231–32; Duggan, pp. 174–75. Becket's reaction to the new ordinances is from *CTB,* II, p. 1025. The backlash against the ordinances is from Knowles, *Episcopal Colleagues,* pp. 131–35; Duggan, pp. 175–76. Becket's anguished letter to his ally at the curia (Cardinal Hubald of Ostia) is from *CTB,* II, pp. 939–51; the quotations are from pp. 941, 943. The "ax" remark from William fitz Stephen is from *MTB,* III, p. 102. Becket's conditions for the talks at Montmartre are from *CTB,* II, pp. 1030–43. Herbert of Bosham's account of the interview is from *MTB,* III, pp. 445–51; Staunton, pp. 168–72; Greenaway, pp. 129–30. See also Barlow, pp. 193–95; Duggan, pp. 176–78. Lord Lyttelton's judgment is from Lyttelton, IV, p. 265. Becket's reports are from *CTB,* II, pp. 1045–67. King Louis's and Count Theobald's opinions are from *CTB,* II, p. 1051. The haggling over reparations is from *CTB,* II, pp. 1057–59; *MTB,* VII, p. 206. Vivian's disillusionment with Henry's lies and duplicity is from *CTB,* II, pp. 1047–49, 1067–69. His own report to Pope Alexander is from *MTB,* III, pp. 167–69. Pope Alexander's commissions to his special legates are from *MTB,* VII, pp. 198–204. See also Duggan, pp. 179–80. Becket's advice to Bishop Bernard of Nevers is from *CTB,* II, pp. 1165–77.

25 | A TRIAL OF STRENGTH

Information on Becket's sentences of excommunication and interdict after the failure of the peace conference at Montmartre is from *CTB,* II, pp. 1091–1119. The rival missions to Pope Alexander at Benevento are from *LJS,* II, pp. 691–97; Duggan, pp. 178–81; Barlow, pp. 196–97. John of Salisbury's summary of Henry's intentions is from *LJS,* II, pp. 691–95. Information on the absolutions of

Gilbert Foliot and Jocelin of Salisbury is from *MTB,* VII, pp. 208–9, 273–76; *CTB,* II, pp. 1181–91; RD, cols. 551–52; Barlow, pp. 200–201. Becket's angry protests to Pope Alexander and Cardinal Albert de Morra are from *CTB,* II, pp. 1181–89. His copy of St. Cyprian's letters is from *ALCD,* p. 84. Cyprian's views on martyrdom and resistance are from letters 31 and 58 in *The Epistles of St. Cyprian, Bishop of Carthage and Martyr, with the Council of Carthage on the Baptism of Heretics,* ed. H. Carey (Oxford, 1844), pp. 68–74, 142–50. Henry's return to England and movements after his arrival at Portsmouth are from Eyton, pp. 135–40. Information on Prince Henry's coronation and the events surrounding it is from *MTB,* III, pp. 103–7; *MTB,* IV, pp. 66–67; Staunton, pp. 173–74; Greenaway, pp. 132–35; *CTB,* II, pp. 1247–57; Knowles, *Episcopal Colleagues,* pp. 136–37. The payment for the coronation robes for Princess Margaret and her ladies is from Eyton, p. 139. The papal and archiepiscopal decrees sent to Henry and the bishops in an attempt to prevent the ceremony going ahead are from *MTB,* VII, pp. 216–17, 256–57; *CTB,* II, pp. 1141–42, 1211–25, 1235–45. The role of "Idonea" is from *CTB,* II, pp. 1233–35. See also *LJS,* II, pp. 705–6; Barlow, p. 311, n. 14. John of Salisbury's information concerning the reception of the documents is from *LJS,* II, pp. 705–7. Alexander's fresh commission to the special legates authorizing interdicts on Henry's continental lands is from *MTB,* VII, pp. 210–12 (although sent in late April or early May before the coronation, it could not have arrived in Normandy until late June); Barlow, pp. 204–5. Becket's letters of interdict are from *CTB,* II, pp. 1235–45. Master Ernulf's criticism of the legates is from *CTB,* II, p. 1251. The negotiations preceding the peace of Fréteval are from Eyton, pp. 140–41. See also Duggan, pp. 182–83; Barlow, p. 208. Becket's original terms as presented to Bernard of Nevers, which he was forced to dilute, are from *CTB,* II, pp. 1165–77. The three independent descriptions of the proceedings at the peace conference are from *CTB,* II, pp. 1261–79; *MTB,* III, pp. 107–12; *MTB,* III, pp. 465–67; Staunton, pp. 174–77; Greenaway, pp. 136–37. See also Barlow, pp. 208–12; Duggan, pp. 179–88. The text of Pope Alexander's 1161 license allowing a bishop of Henry's choice to perform his son's coronation must be inferred from the license issued to Roger of Pont l'Évêque, revoked in 1166, from *MTB,* VI, pp. 206–7. See Heslin, "The Coronation of the Young King in 1170," pp. 165–78; Warren, *Henry II,* pp. 500–502. A letter purportedly securing a renewal of the archbishop of York's right to crown is not to be found in a Vatican manuscript and is generally agreed to be a forgery: *MTB,* VI, pp. 206–7. See also *MTB,* VII, pp. 226–28. Arnulf of Lisieux's intervention is from *CTB,* II, pp. 1275–77. Geoffrey Ridel's outburst is from Guernes, p. 154. See also *CTB,* II, p. 1275–77. Pope Alexander's letter establishing that Becket had informed him that Prince Henry had sworn an oath "to preserve the evil customs" at his coronation is from *CTB,* II, pp. 1291–95. See also Barlow, p. 207. Foreville suggests that it is reasonable to assume that the younger Henry swore an oath to respect the liberties of the church, *salvo honore regni mei,* the same proviso his father inserted into the Fréteval agreement, but she cites no supporting evidence: Foreville, *L'Église et la Royauté,* p. 314. Henry's illness and movements are from Eyton, pp. 143–46. The (slightly differing) versions of Henry's writ to enforce the Fréteval peace are from *CTB,* II, pp. 1259–61; *LJS,* II, pp. 710–11; *MTB,* VII, pp. 346–47; RD, cols. 552–53. Cardinal Albert's opinion of the peace settlement is from *MTB,* II, pp. 1340–41.

26 | RETURN TO CANTERBURY

William fitz Stephen's account of the meetings between Henry and Becket in the Loire Valley are from *MTB,* III, pp. 114–16; Staunton, pp. 179–80; Greenaway, pp. 139–41. Herbert of Bosham's version is from *MTB,* III, pp. 468–71. The omission of the kiss of peace from the mass at Montlouis (or possibly Amboise) is from *MTB,* III, p. 469. See also Duggan, pp. 188–89; Barlow, pp. 214–15, 312–13, where the dates and places are carefully collated. Henry's writ from Chinon is from *MTB,* III, p. 12; Eyton, pp. 148–49, where the full witness list is given. The reports from Becket's advance party to England are from *LJS,* II, pp. 715–19 (strictly, this is one of John of Salisbury's letters to his friend Peter of Celle, but a similar report must have been sent to Becket, since he had commissioned John to send him news); *CTB,* II, pp. 1303–9, perhaps written jointly by John and Herbert of Bosham. See also the report by William fitz Stephen from *MTB,* III, pp. 112–13; Staunton, pp. 177–78. Becket's own account based on the reports he received is from *CTB,* II, pp. 1345–49. The allegation of piracy is from *CTB,* II, p. 1309, n. 15; *MTB,* III, p. 124. Becket's letter to the pope urging moderation in the cause of peace is from *CTB,* II, pp. 1321–29. See also the excellent accounts by Duggan, pp. 192–93; Knowles, *Episcopal Colleagues,* pp. 136–37; Barlow, pp. 218–19. Pope Alexander's letters and decrees sent to Becket in September and October 1170, which reinstated his excommunications and reinforced his legatine and disciplinary powers, are from *CTB,* II, pp. 1291–95, 1301, 1309–17. Those addressed to William of Sens and Archbishop Rotrou are from *MTB,* VII, pp. 376–79. See also *MTB,* VII, pp. 383–84, where an interdict is threatened on Henry's continental lands. Becket's last letter to Henry is from *CTB,* II, pp. 1333–35. The scene at Rouen is from *MTB,* III, pp. 116–17; Staunton, pp. 180–81; Greenaway, pp. 140–41. The scene at Wissant is from *MTB,* I, pp. 86–87; *MTB,* III, pp. 117–18, 471–72; Staunton, p. 182. The intelligence of Milo, dean of Boulogne, is from *MTB,* I, pp. 86–87; Staunton, p. 182; *CTB,* II, p. 1349. Information on Becket's landing at Sandwich and triumphant reception at Canterbury is from *MTB,* III, pp. 127–28, 476–80; *TSE,* I, pp. 489–95; Staunton, pp. 182–85; Greenaway, pp. 142–45; *CTB,* II, pp. 1345–55; *LJS,* II, p. 721. The clash with the delinquent bishops is from *LJS,* II, pp. 721–23; *CTB,* II, pp. 1349–53; *MTB,* III, p. 480; Guernes (who supplies the figure of £10,000), pp. 173–74;

TSE, I, pp. 497–501; Staunton, pp. 184–85, 188; Knowles, *Episcopal Colleagues,* pp. 137–39. See also Duggan, pp. 198–200. The plot against Becket is from *CTB,* II, pp. 1353–55; *LJS,* II, p. 721. Becket's failed journey to visit the junior King Henry is from *LJS,* II, p. 723; *MTB,* III, pp. 121–24; Staunton, pp. 185–86; Greenaway, pp. 143–45. His and the junior king's movements are from Eyton, pp. 151–52. The mission of the abbot of St. Albans is from *MTB,* III, p. 124; Staunton, pp. 186–87. The incident involving Reginald of Cornwall is from *MTB,* I, pp. 114–15; Barlow, p. 231; Duggan, pp. 203–4. The predations of the de Brocs in Canterbury are from *MTB,* III, pp. 126–27; *TSE,* I, pp. 495–96, 509; Staunton, p. 187. Information on Becket's Christmas Day sermon and excommunications is from *MTB,* II, pp. 17–18; *MTB,* III, p. 130; Greenaway, pp. 146–47; RD, col. 555. The dispatch of Becket's favorite clerks is from *MTB,* III, pp. 485–86; Staunton, p. 194; Greenaway, p. 147. Becket's last letter to Bishop William of Norwich is from *CTB,* II, pp. 1360–61. The background of Bishop William is from Knowles, *Episcopal Colleagues,* pp. 61, 81, 108–9, 134. My reconstruction of the events in Normandy and of the charges leveled at the great council of barons and prelates is worked out from Guernes, pp. 174–78; *MTB,* I, pp. 121–23; *MTB,* II, pp. 428–29; *MTB,* III, pp. 127–30, 487–88; *TSE,* I, pp. 501–3, 512–15; Staunton, pp. 188–90, 191–92; Barlow, pp. 234–35; Duggan, pp. 205–7. For Henry's opinion of Becket as a highly dangerous enemy who had broken the peace and maligned him, see also *MTB,* VII, pp. 418–20. For the charges leveled by Arnulf of Lisieux, see *Letters of Arnulf of Lisieux,* ed. Barlow, pp. 104–12. Guernes's version of Henry's famous outburst is from Guernes, p. 175; Edward Grim's version is from *MTB,* II, p. 429; Gervase of Canterbury's version is from GC, col. 1414. The eighteenth-century renditions are from Lyttelton, IV, p. 353; T. Mortimer, *A New History of England from the Earliest Accounts of Britain to the Ratification of the Peace of Versailles* (2 vols., London, 1764–66), I, p. 268. Background on the four knights is from a brilliant reconstruction by Professor Nicholas Vincent, who clears up centuries of accumulated myth and confusion about their true identity and provides other invaluable information: "The Murderers of Thomas Becket," in *Bischofsmord in Mittelalter: Murder of Bishops,* ed. N. Fryde and D. Reitz (Göttingen, 2003), pp. 211–72. Information on the journey of the four knights and their arrival at Canterbury is from *MTB,* II, pp. 429–30; *MTB,* III, pp. 128–30, 131–32, 487–88; Guernes, pp. 178–81; Staunton, pp. 194–95; Greenaway, pp. 146, 148–49; Knowles, pp. 140–41. The reports of Edward Grim and Roger of Pontigny that the knights would have murdered Becket with the haft of his own cross at the very outset of the confrontation are from *MTB,* II, p. 431; *MTB,* IV, p. 71; Knowles, p. 142. Herbert of Bosham's report of the terror of the knights after the murder is from *MTB,* III, pp. 512–13.

27 | MURDER IN THE CATHEDRAL

Some ten accounts of Becket's murder exist (if the "Thomas Saga Erkibyskups" is counted as an independent source). I have done my best to produce a consolidated account, giving firm priority to those sources known to have been eyewitnesses. Five accounts are by authorities present in the cathedral during the murder: Edward Grim's is from *MTB,* II, pp. 430–39; *EHD,* pp. 812–20; Staunton, pp. 195–203. William fitz Stephen's is from *MTB,* III, pp. 132–47; Greenaway, pp. 149–60. John of Salisbury's is from *LJS,* II, pp. 725–39 (earliest version); *MTB,* II, pp. 316–21 (later versions). William of Canterbury's is from *MTB,* I, pp. 128–36. Benedict of Peterborough's is from *MTB,* II, pp. 1–16; Staunton, pp. 203–5. Of the most valuable supplementary accounts, Herbert of Bosham's is from *MTB,* III, pp. 488–514; Roger of Pontigny's is from *MTB,* IV, pp. 70–78; Gervase of Canterbury's is from GC, cols. 1414–17; Guernes of Pont-Sainte-Maxence's is from Guernes, pp. 181–95; and the account from the "Thomas Saga Erkibyskups," possibly using material from the lost "life" of Thomas by Robert of Cricklade, is from *TSE,* I, pp. 523–49. An invaluable collation and analysis of the different accounts, showing most of the minor inconsistencies and pinpointing a few serious discrepancies, is E. A. Abbott, *St. Thomas of Canterbury: His Death and Miracles* (2 vols., London, 1898), I, pp. 27–174, still a standard work. See also Duggan, pp. 209–14; Barlow, pp. 240–48; Knowles, pp. 140–47; Vincent, "Murderers of Thomas Becket," pp. 244–65. My account of the sequel to the murder and Becket's burial is based on the three most authoritative eyewitness accounts: John of Salisbury's is from *LJS,* II, pp. 735–37. Benedict of Peterborough's is from *MTB,* II, pp. 14–19; Staunton, pp. 203–5; *EHD,* pp. 820–21. William fitz Stephen's is from *MTB,* III, pp. 144–49; Greenaway, pp. 157–60. For much further debate and some speculation, see also Abbott, *St. Thomas of Canterbury,* I, pp. 175–91; Duggan, pp. 214–23; Barlow, pp. 248–50; Knowles, pp. 147–49. The earliest miracles are from *MTB,* III, pp. 149–52; Staunton, pp. 205–6; *LJS,* II, p. 737. Further information on Becket's interment is from W. Urry, "Some Notes on the Two Resting Places of St. Thomas Becket at Canterbury," in *Thomas Becket: Actes du Colloque International de Sédières, 19–24 Août 1973,* ed. R. Foreville (Paris, 1975), pp. 196–97.

28 | AFTERMATH

John of Salisbury's newsletter is from *LJS,* II, pp. 725–39. Roger of Pont l'Évêque's letter to his suffragans is from *LJS,* II, pp. 739–43. John's counterattack is from *LJS,* II, pp. 743–49. The letter of Arnulf of Lisieux to the pope is from *Letters of Arnulf of Lisieux,* ed. Barlow, pp. 122–23; *EHD,* pp. 821–23; Greenaway, p. 161. Henry's movements are from Eyton, pp. 150–57. His barefaced letter to the pope is from *MTB,* VII, p. 440. For this letter and the maneuvers surrounding it, see also A. Duggan, "Diplomacy, Status, and Conscience:

Henry II's Penance for Becket's Murder," in *Forschungen zur Reichs-, Papst- und Landesgeschichte: Peter Herde zum 65. Geburtstag von Freunden, Schülern und Kollegen dargebracht,* ed. K. Borchardt and E. Bünz (2 vols., Stuttgart, 1998), I, pp. 265–69. A report from Richard of Ilchester on the reception of Henry's envoys at the curia is from *MTB,* VII, pp. 475–78; *EHD,* pp. 823–26. The letter of William of Sens to the pope is from *MTB,* VII, pp. 429–33. See also Greenaway, p. 162. Information on the mission of Cardinals Albert and Theodwin and the reconciliation at Avranches is from *LJS,* II, pp. 752–55; *MTB,* IV, pp. 173–74; *MTB,* VII, pp. 513–23; RH, II, pp. 35–39; *EHD,* pp. 825–27; Staunton, pp. 216–17; Greenaway, pp. 162–63; A. Duggan, "*Ne in Dubium:* The Official Record of Henry II's Reconciliation at Avranches, 21 May 1172," *EHR* 115 (2000), pp. 643–58; Duggan, "Diplomacy, Status, and Conscience," pp. 272–78; A. Duggan, "Henry II, the English Church and the Papacy, 1154–76," in *Henry II,* pp. 175–77; Foreville, *L'Église et la Royauté,* pp. 330–61; Barlow, pp. 260–61. Henry's campaign in Ireland is from Warren, *Henry II,* pp. 193–201; Eyton, pp. 163–67. The impact of the settlement at Avranches is from Z. N. Brooke, "The Effect of Becket's Murder on Papal Authority in England," *Cambridge Historical Journal* 2 (1928), pp. 213–28; M. G. Cheney, "The Compromise of Avranches and the Spread of Canon Law in England," *EHR* 56 (1941), pp. 177–97; Duggan, pp. 220–21. Herbert of Bosham's complaint that some of the "obnoxious customs" were still observed is from *MTB,* III, p. 546. Information on the amnesty and alms for Becket's relatives is from Barlow, p. 262; Duggan, "Diplomacy, Status, and Conscience," p. 281. Bishop Hamo's murder is from Everard, *Brittany and the Angevins,* pp. 57–58, 69; Vincent, "Murderers of Thomas Becket," p. 247. Robert of Torigni's misleading entry for 1170 is from *Chronicles,* IV, p. 249. Ralph of Diss also throws up a smoke screen, reporting Becket's murder but ingeniously muffling its effects by coupling it to other near-contemporary assassinations. One was Hamo's. The next was that of Hugh de Cervello, archbishop of Tarragona, a short-lived crusader principality in Muslim Spain, who would be brutally stabbed in April 1173 for allegedly insulting a commoner. The third was the revenge killing of Raymond Trencavel, not a priest but the lord of Béziers and one of Henry's more dependable allies in his Toulouse campaign of 1159. While standing before the high altar in the town's cathedral in October 1167, attempting to do justice to a townsman, he was bloodily stabbed in a short-lived populist revolt. See RD, cols. 555–57; OV, IV, p. 117; WN, pp. 457–59; Vincent, "Murderers of Thomas Becket," p. 247. The miracles at Becket's tomb are from *MTB,* I, pp. 155–87; *MTB,* II, pp. 37–66; Staunton, pp. 207–10; Abbott, *St. Thomas of Canterbury,* I, pp. 249–301; Barlow, pp. 264–69. Information on the tomb monument in the crypt is from Urry, "Some Notes on the Two Resting Places of St. Thomas Becket at Canterbury," pp. 196–99.

The younger Henry's visit to Canterbury is from Duggan, "Diplomacy, Status, and Conscience," p. 282. The younger Henry's discontent is from T. M. Jones, "The Generation Gap of 1173–74: The War Between the Two Henries," *Albion* 5 (1973), pp. 24–40. Background on the revolt and civil war is from Norgate, *England Under the Angevin Kings,* II, pp. 120–68; Warren, *Henry II,* pp. 117–49. The elder Henry's movements are from Eyton, pp. 172–87. His second penance at Canterbury is from GC, cols. 1427–28; Guernes, pp. 209–17; WN, pp. 493–95; *MTB,* II, pp. 445–48; Staunton, pp. 217–19; Duggan, "Diplomacy, Status, and Conscience," pp. 278–84. Information on the last days of the four knights is from Vincent, "Murderers of Thomas Becket," pp. 248–65. See also *MTB,* III, pp. 535–38; *MTB,* IV, pp. 161–64; Staunton, pp. 213–15. The quotation from Romuald of Salerno's *Annals* is from *Monumenta Germaniae Historica Scriptores,* XIX, ed. W. Arndt (Hanover, 1866), p. 439, l. 13. The knights' epitaph recorded by Roger of Howden is from *Chronicles,* II, p. 17.

29 | MARTYR

The disruption of the four knights' inheritances is from Vincent, "Murderers of Thomas Becket," pp. 237, 259–62. Henry's deal to defer his departure on crusade is from Duggan, "Diplomacy, Status, and Conscience," pp. 285–87. His monastic endowments at Eleanor's expense are from Vincent, "Patronage, Politics and Piety in the Charters of Eleanor of Aquitaine," p. 26. His cash hoard in the East is from H. E. Mayer, "Henry II of England and the Holy Land," *EHR* 97 (1982), pp. 721–39. Becket's critique of Henry's methods is from *CTB,* II, pp. 1166–67; John of Salisbury's is from *LJS,* II, pp. 32–33. The exchange over the ancestral customs at Montmirail is from *LJS,* II, pp. 639–47. See also Smalley, *Becket Conflict and the Schools,* pp. 160–63. Herbert of Bosham's report of Henry's attempted defense of the ancestral customs is from *MTB,* III, pp. 266–67. Henry's visits to Becket's shrine at Canterbury are cataloged by Duggan, "Diplomacy, Status, and Conscience," pp. 283–84. Information on royal burials and pilgrimages is from Urry, "Some Notes on the Two Resting Places of St. Thomas Becket at Canterbury," p. 207; M. Evans, *Death of Kings: Royal Deaths in Medieval England* (London, 2003), p. 27; H. Schnitker, "Margaret of York on Pilgrimage: The Exercise of Devotion and the Religious Traditions of the House of York," in *Reputation and Representation in Fifteenth-Century Europe,* ed. D. Biggs, S. D. Michalove, and A. C. Reeves (Leiden, 2004), pp. 117–19; *Calendar of State Papers and Manuscripts Relating to English Affairs, Existing in the Archives and Collections of Venice and in Other Libraries of Northern Italy* (38 vols., London, 1864–1947), III, pp. 14–16; *Letters and Papers, Foreign and Domestic, of the Reign of Henry VIII,* ed. J. S. Brewer, J. Gairdner, and R. H. Brodie (21 vols. in 32 parts and *Addenda,* London, 1862–1932), III, p. 1541. The building history and appearance of the new shrine at Canterbury is from M. F. Hearn, "Canterbury Cathedral and the Cult of Becket," *Art Bulletin* 76 (1994), pp. 19–52; S. Blick, "Reconstructing the Shrine of St. Thomas Becket, Canterbury Cathedral," in *Art and Architecture of Late Medieval Pilgrimage in Northern Europe and the British Isles,* ed. S. Blick and R. Tekippe (2 vols., Leiden, 2005), I, pp. 405–41; Urry, "Some Notes on the Two Resting Places of St. Thomas Becket at Canterbury," pp. 197–207. See also R. Willis, *The Architectural History of Canterbury Cathedral* (London, 1845), pp. 97–113. Erasmus's description is from *Pilgrimages to Saint Mary of Walsingham and Saint Thomas of Canterbury,* ed. J. G. Nichols (London, 1849), pp. 55–56. The "Book of Miracles" is from *MTB,* I, pp. 137–546. The Becket legend from the *Golden Legend* is from *Legenda Aurea Sanctorum,* ed. W. Caxton (London, 1483), fos. cv–viii, ccxii–xiii. Peter of Celle's letter to John of Salisbury is from *LPC,* pp. 669–71. Arnulf of Lisieux's letter to the pope is from *Letters of Arnulf of Lisieux,* ed. Barlow, pp. 110–12. Becket's appeal to St. Alphege is from *MTB,* III, p. 141; *MTB,* IV, p. 77. A rare critic of the Becket cult was Master Roger the Norman, who argued that Thomas's "obstinacy" brought about his death: Staunton, p. 238; Smalley, *Becket Conflict and the Schools,* pp. 201–2. Anselm's opinion of St. Alphege is from *English Lawsuits,* ed. van Caenegem, pp. 440–41. For similar views by Becket's biographers, see *MTB,* II, pp. 14, 301–2, 323; Smalley, *Becket Conflict and the Schools,* p. 194. The speeches of the fourth tempter and Richard Brito from T. S. Eliot's "pageant play" are from *Murder in the Cathedral* (London, 1935), pp. 37–39, 81–82. Pope Paul III's critique of Becket is from *Letters and Papers,* ed. Brewer, Gairdner, and Brodie, VIII, p. 437. Peter of Celle's letter to Bartholomew of Exeter is from *LPC,* p. 435. The spread of Becket's cult across Europe is from K. B. Slocum, *Liturgies in Honor of Thomas Becket* (Toronto, 2004), pp. 98–126. Henry VIII's attack on the shrine is from *Pilgrimages to Saint Mary of Walsingham and Saint Thomas of Canterbury,* ed. Nichols, p. 167; *Concilia Magnae Britanniae et Hiberniae,* ed. D. Wilkins (4 vols., London, 1737), III, pp. 835–36; *A Chronicle of England During the Reigns of the Tudors, from* A.D. *1485 to 1559,* ed. W. D. Hamilton, Camden Society, new ser., 11 (2 vols., London, 1875–77), I, pp. 86–87; Willis, *Architectural History,* p. 100. The burning of Becket's bones has been denied by Henry's supporters and Protestant propagandists for some 450 years, but in 2007 Professor T. F. Mayer, using newly discovered documents in the Vatican and the Mantuan State Archives, showed that the evidence for it is overwhelming. See his "Becket's Bones Burnt! Cardinal Pole and the Invention and Dissemination of an Atrocity," in *Martyrs and Martyrdom in England, c. 1400–1700,* ed. T. S. Freeman and T. F. Mayer (Woodbridge, U.K., 2007), pp. 126–43. See also A. J. Mason, *What Became of the Bones of St. Thomas?* (Cambridge, 1920); J. Butler, *The Quest for Becket's Bones: The Mystery of the Relics of St. Thomas of Canterbury* (London,

1995). For the origins of the Tudor attack on Becket, see *Letters and Papers,* ed. Brewer, Gairdner, and Brodie, VIII, pp. 236–37. Henry VIII's proclamation against Becket is from *Tudor Royal Proclamations,* ed. P. L. Hughes and J. F. Larkin (3 vols., London, 1964–69), I, pp. 275–76. Professor Mayr-Harting's assessment of Becket is from "A Vital Relic of Our Past," *The Times,* June 29, 1996.

ILLUSTRATION CREDITS

The Bridgeman Art Library

Matilda, only legitimate daughter of King Henry I, seated and holding a charter, from the Golden Book of St. Albans (c. 1380) in Cotton MS, Nero D. VII, fo. 7, British Library / The Bridgeman Art Library.

Archbishop Theobald crowns Henry II, from "Flores Historiarum," by Matthew Paris (thirteenth century) in MS 6712 (A.6.89), fo. 135ᵛ, © Chetham's Library, Manchester / The Bridgeman Art Library.

Becket pronounces the Vézelay excommunications (left) and addresses Henry II and Louis VII at their peace conference at Montmirail (right), from the Becket Leaves (c. 1220–40), photo British Library / The Bridgeman Art Library.

The younger Henry is crowned and anointed by Roger of Pont l'Évêque, assisted by Gilbert Foliot and Jocelin of Salisbury (left), and the elder Henry serves his son at the coronation banquet (right), from the Becket Leaves (c. 1220–40), photo British Library / The Bridgeman Art Library.

While making ready to sail home to England, Milo, dean of Boulogne, warns Becket that the coasts are being closely watched, from the Becket Leaves (c. 1220–40), photo British Library / The Bridgeman Art Library.

The oldest and most authentic image of Becket's murder, prefacing a copy of the text of John of Salisbury's letter of early 1171 describing it, from Cotton MS, Claudius B. II, fo. 341, British Library / The Bridgeman Art Library.

Cambridge University Library

A plan of the priory of Christ Church, Canterbury, showing the buildings as they existed before the fire of 1174, from *Vetusta Monumenta,* vol. 2 (London, 1754), plate 15, shelfmark T474.bb.6.2, with kind permission of the Syndics of Cambridge University Library.

A clumsy seventeenth-century attempt to depict Becket's shrine, from a drawing reproduced in *Monasticon Anglicanum,* vol. 1 (London, 1718), plate facing p. 8, shelfmark S100.a.71.1, with kind permission of the Syndics of Cambridge University Library.

Clare College, Cambridge

A queen greets her son as he comes to fight his brother (early fourteenth century), from MS Kk.5.3., fo. 36, with kind permission of the Master, Fellows, and Scholars of Clare College.

A king enthroned with his legs crossed, probably Stephen (early fourteenth century), from MS Kk.5.3., fo. 24, with kind permission of the Master, Fellows, and Scholars of Clare College.

Fitzwilliam Museum, Cambridge

A cardinal presiding over a busy church court (fourteenth century), from MS 331^{r} (detail).

Parker Library, Corpus Christi College, Cambridge

The sinking of the *White Ship* (thirteenth century), from MS 26, fo. 111^{v}, with kind permission of the Master and Fellows of Corpus Christi College.

Presentation copy of John of Salisbury's *Policraticus* to Thomas Becket (twelfth century), from MS 46, fo. 2^{v}, with kind permission of the Master and Fellows of Corpus Christi College.

The murder of Thomas Becket showing Edward Grim attempting to deflect the knights' blows (thirteenth century), from MS 26, fo.132^{r}, with kind permission of the Master and Fellows of Corpus Christi College.

Private Collection

Henry II, an eighteenth-century engraving, with a panel showing Becket's murder below.

Pope Adrian IV, from an eighteenth-century engraving.

The murder of Thomas Becket, from an engraving made at Venice c. 1660.

Henry II's second penance at Canterbury, from a nineteenth-century engraving.

Yale University, Beinecke Rare Book and Manuscript Library

Medieval scholars reading a book (twelfth century), from MS Marston 67, fo. 65.

Falcons sitting on a perch in a niche (fifteenth century), from MS 446, fo. 1.

Other Illustrations

Pevensey Castle, Sussex, photograph © 2012, John Guy.

Auxerre Cathedral exterior, photograph © 2012, John Guy.

Thomas Becket, a late-twelfth-century stone relief set into the wall of the ambulatory at Sens Cathedral, photograph © 2012, John Guy.

The monks' cloister at Canterbury Cathedral, photograph © 2012, John Guy.

Orford Castle, photograph © 2012, John Guy.

The ruins of Battle Abbey, believed to be the refectory, photograph © 2012, John Guy.

Thomas Becket, a modern panel made from fragments of thirteenth-century stained glass, Canterbury Cathedral, photograph © 2012, John Guy.

Canterbury Cathedral exterior, photograph © 2012, John Guy.

The nave at Sens Cathedral, photograph © 2012, John Guy.

The nave at Vézelay Abbey, photograph © 2012, John Guy.

Pontigny Abbey exterior, photograph © 2012, John Guy.

The nave at Pontigny Abbey, photograph © 2012, John Guy.

Becket with Henry II and Louis VII at the peace conference at Montmirail, from a stained-glass panel at Sens Cathedral, photograph © 2012, John Guy.

The site of Becket's murder in the northwest transept of Canterbury Cathedral, photograph © 2012, John Guy.

The Norman crypt at Canterbury Cathedral where Becket was first interred, photograph © 2012, John Guy.

Scenes from the life of Thomas Becket from a stained-glass window at Sens Cathedral, photograph © 2012, John Guy.

Miracles of healing at Becket's shrine, from a stained-glass panel at Canterbury Cathedral, photograph © 2012, John Guy.

The shrine of St. Alban, from St. Albans Cathedral, photograph © 2012, John Guy.

INDEX

The use of surnames was uncommon in the Middle Ages, so in line with convention, persons alive before the year 1600 are indexed under their first name. Relationships in brackets refer to Thomas Becket unless otherwise indicated.

ABOUT THE AUTHOR

JOHN GUY is a Fellow at Clare College, University of Cambridge. He was formerly provost and professor of modern history at the University of St. Andrews in Scotland and has been a visiting professor at the Johns Hopkins University. He has written several books, consults for the BBC, and has hosted several television documentaries. He lives in London and is married to the historian Julia Fox. His biography of Mary Queen of Scots was a finalist for the National Book Critics Circle Award.

John Guy's websites are:
www.johnguy.co.uk
www.tudors.org